CHARLOTTE LYDIA RILEY

Charlotte Lydia Riley is a historian of twentieth-century Britain at the University of Southampton, specialising in questions about empire, politics, culture and identity. Her writing has appeared in a wide range of publications including the *Guardian*, *New Statesman*, *Prospect* and *History Today*. She also co-hosts the podcast *Tomorrow Never Knows* in which she and Emma Lundin discuss feminism, pop culture, politics and history. She tweets @lottelydia.

T0333031

CHARLOTTE LYDIA RILEY

Imperial Island

A History of Empire in Modern Britain

VINTAGE

1 3 5 7 9 10 8 6 4 2

Vintage is part of the Penguin Random House group of companies
whose addresses can be found at global.penguinrandomhouse.com

First published in Vintage in 2024
First published in hardback by The Bodley Head in 2023

penguin.co.uk/vintage

Printed and bound in Great Britain by Clays Ltd, Elcograf S.p.A.

The authorised representative in the EEA is Penguin Random House Ireland,
Morrison Chambers, 32 Nassau Street, Dublin D02 YH68

A CIP catalogue record for this book is available from the British Library

ISBN 9781529923803

Penguin Random House is committed to a sustainable future
for our business, our readers and our planet. This book is made
from Forest Stewardship Council® certified paper.

For Raphael

Contents

Contents

Imperial Island

Imperial Island

Introduction

Empire's Shadows

A man with a trim moustache and neat, side-parted hair, wearing a smart suit with a waistcoat and shiny striped tie, sits and smiles broadly at the camera. He is surrounded by a busy group, a few adults but mostly children, who range in age from babies and toddlers to perhaps ten years old. The children are wearing party dresses, little suit jackets, long socks and fancy hats. Their faces have been scrubbed clean, their hair pushed into neat partings and pigtails. Some of the children have solemn expressions, some mischievous, not all of them are looking at the photographer. Almost none of the people in the picture are white.

The man at the centre of the picture is Kamal Chunchie, and the children are his guests at the Coloured Men's Institute in Canning Town. Born in Ceylon (Sri Lanka) in 1886, Kamal had moved to London at the end of the First World War, arriving at the nearby Royal Docks, like many soldiers and sailors from the colonies, having served in the British Army. His ship had come from Malta, where he had been sent for convalescence after a bad injury and where he had converted to Christianity. He arrived in an area that in the early nineteenth century had been mostly peaceful fields but which today is the borough of Newham, a busy urban space containing some of the most overcrowded housing in the UK. This change dates back to the 1850s, when, in response to an increasingly chaotic trade environment on the Thames, first the Victoria and then the Albert Dock was constructed and opened. Slowly this area had become London's main docks. Once it was connected to the railways, via Stratford, and the arterial Barking Road, constructed in 1894, it became the heart of imperial trade. Here, warehouses and granaries were built to house the produce being brought into the country, while homes were built in Canning Town, Woolwich, Silvertown and the surrounding areas for the workers who handled this precious imperial cargo.

Kamal was not the only former soldier to settle in the area when he did. In the decade after the war, the houses around Crown Street, Catherine Street, Cundy Street and Victoria Docks Road, where couples and families lived and loved across the colour line, became known as 'Draughtboard Alley', because the community was so unusually integrated. Kamal himself married a local white girl, Mabel Williams Tappen, with whom he had a daughter, and became a Methodist minister. Kamal and Mabel worked together to found the docklands' first Black Wesleyan Methodist Church, and also the Coloured Men's Institute, which was based on Tidal Basin Road in Victoria Docks, and provided religious and social welfare support to sailors and local residents. This was a popular resource among the local community, although the Universal Negro Improvement Association East End Branch was suspicious of Chunchie's religious tone, which they saw as patronising, and his attempts to (they believed) foster segregation by catering to Black and Asian communities separately to white residents of the East End.

The area continued to thrive economically, attracting workers to the manufacturing, shipping and pharmaceutical industries; in 1921, the final dock, George V, was built, and the area became known as the Royal Docks. By 1930, Newham, and specifically Canning Town, had the largest Black population in London. This was not always a happy story of interracial harmony, however.[1] The economic difficulties that the area experienced during the First World War and in the depression of the late 1920s and 30s often led to racism against the Black and Asian workers who were targeted by groups like the British Union of Fascists for stealing 'British' jobs. Local people of colour had to work hard to support themselves and one another.

In 1930, the building in which the Coloured Men's Institute was housed was demolished as part of West Ham's municipal road-widening scheme, and Kamal and his wife moved their work into a local Methodist church on Victoria Dock Road. Here, they fed breakfast to hungry children attending Sunday school, provided clothing and shoes to those who needed them, and organised excursions to the seaside, an annual Christmas meal and a new year's gift-giving party for needy families. Kamal, a charismatic preacher who spoke passionately against racism, worked to bring support to the local transient population of imperial seamen moving through the docks, as well as the community of people of colour in the docklands, many of whom were part of mixed-race families, as well as students from across the colonies who were studying in the metropole.

Kamal Chunchie had a vibrant associational and political life beyond the church. He travelled across Britain speaking about the scourge of racism to Methodist congregations. He was the vice president of the League of Coloured Peoples from 1935 to 1937, working for this pioneering and radical anti-racist organisation with its founder Dr Harold Moody. In 1931, the Royal Empire Society became one of the first royal societies to admit Black and Asian members, and Kamal duly joined; the organisation was the site of many famous speeches by anti-imperialist actors from Britain and around the empire, and Kamal would visit to play bridge and snooker and to network with potential supporters of his work. During the Second World War, he was an auxiliary firefighter, protecting the capital and its population. He played cricket for the Gentlemen of Essex and was invited to the 1948 Olympics and the Queen's coronation in June 1953. But at the end of that month, he suffered a heart attack, and on 3 July 1953 Kamal Chunchie died at the age of sixty-seven. Without Kamal's passionate leadership and with few material resources, his wife and daughter were unable to keep the work of the Coloured Men's Institute going and it folded that same year.[2]

Kamal's life and work had been intricately, politically and spiritually bound up with Newham's dockland community. But his was also a life shaped profoundly by empire, not least by its cultures of migration and racism, as were the lives of so many of his neighbours. He had come to Britain through his experience in the army, travelling by boat from Ceylon, to Singapore, to Europe – France, Salonika and Malta – before arriving in London. He had settled in Canning Town because it offered the possibility of a multi-racial, multicultural metropole. His experiences there also starkly demonstrated the poverty and racism faced by people of colour living at the heart of the empire. His work began at the highpoint of British imperial expansion – the interwar years, when empire was at its greatest territorial extent – and ended, in the year of Elizabeth II's coronation, when the imperial project was looking altogether less secure: half a decade after Indian independence, three years before the Suez Crisis, four before Ghana would become the first British African colony to gain its freedom.

The lifespan of the docks in Newham echoed British imperial history too. Like the empire, the docks were busiest in the interwar period. Key imperial industries, such as sugar, were based in the borough, with Tate & Lyle opening sites in Plaistow Wharf and Canning Town. Other industrial employers based themselves in the borough close to the docks and the supply lines bringing raw materials from across the empire. But this reliance on imperial trade, which had helped make Newham profitable for industry and a reliable source of income for a diverse workforce, meant that the docks were hit hard by the decline of empire.

This in turn had a critical effect on Newham as a community. Initially, decolonisation saw Newham – which was formed in 1965 by the merger of West and East Ham – build a thriving multicultural population. Local employers, such as Ford, based in neighbouring Dagenham, started to employ more workers of Caribbean origin, as they expanded production to meet a new post-war demand for motor cars. Asian families who had initially moved to the north of England and the West Midlands to work in the garment trade, or who might have settled first in Tower Hamlets, started to relocate to Newham where there were increasingly forming Gujarati, Punjabi and Kashmiri communities, who had been displaced by Partition. These were later supplemented in the 1970s by Asian families from Kenya and Uganda, and by Tamils fleeing civil war in Sri Lanka.[3]

This region of London had been poor for a long time – in 1905, West Ham had been the first borough to bring in the Unemployed Workmen Act. Poor housing conditions had been exacerbated by the Second World War, in which the borough lost a quarter of its housing stock through bombing. Although the local authorities responded by building new estates, like the Keir Hardie estate that sprawls from Canning Town to Custom House, and hastily erecting tower blocks, such as the infamous Ronan Point, this could not fully address the housing shortages in the area. By 1967, a Ministry of Housing report named Newham as the borough with the second-highest number of slums in the city.[4]

This experience of poor housing – which in some ways bucked the trend of post-war redevelopment and affluence – went hand in hand with worsening labour conditions. As much of the empire gradually and then quickly achieved independence, the jobs and security that had been afforded by imperial trade dried up. The London docks were gradually wound down from the late 1960s; from the 1950s to the 1980s, almost every one of the 30,000 people employed in the industry lost their job.[5] Inevitably, people began looking elsewhere for homes and work. Between 1951 and 1981 the population of the borough dropped by almost 85,000.[6] Meanwhile, those who stayed lived in increasingly difficult circumstances. People of colour in Newham often found themselves the targets of far-right violence, instigated by activists who encouraged the white population to blame immigration and immigrants from the former empire for the absence of jobs, long housing waiting lists, low wages and the general local sense of stagnation and decline.

By the 1970s and 80s, Newham had become infamous for this violence. In the Newham South by-election in May 1974, the National Front (NF) candidate won 11.5 per cent of the vote, pushing the Conservatives into fourth place. That same year the NF had set up an office in Canning Town to drum up anti-immigrant feeling through the guise of providing housing advice to white residents. In

1978 it supported striking (white) workers at the Tate & Lyle factory. Through its increasing activity in the borough, the NF cast the problems of Newham at the feet of its immigrant community; it was claimed by the NF they sold more newspapers outside the Boleyn stadium, West Ham's home ground, on match days than outside any other football club. By 1987, a piece in the *London Review of Books* stated that 'Newham is like a macabre laboratory for studying the hideous cruelties which whites are capable of inflicting on people of a different colour'.[7]

This violence and the Newham community's response to it are detailed later in this book. But even this brief description of the rise and fall of the borough shows how empire and imperialism, and the experience of decolonisation, shaped British politics and society, and British people's lives, on a large and small scale. There is no way of telling this history of this little corner of London, without talking about imperialism. And the same is true of Newham today.

As I write – sitting at a desk in Newham – this borough is one of the most diverse places in the United Kingdom: over a hundred different languages are spoken in the community. The most recent census reflects this diversity. Almost 16 per cent of the borough is Bangladeshi, almost 15 per cent white British, 14 per cent white 'other', 11 per cent Indian, 11 per cent African, 9 per cent Pakistani, with other groups of migrants recording themselves as Caribbean, Chinese, Arab, other Asian, other Black, 'other'.[8] But despite this shift, it is not becoming less British. Even as the 'white British' share of the population becomes comparatively smaller, the overall group of people who identify themselves as either British or English has grown.[9]

There are lots of factors that determine how you feel about your own national identity, and where you feel that you belong. Some of your feelings might be shaped by your legal rights to citizenship, or your practical conditions of residency. Some feelings might be tied up in your family, whether they are close or far away, and your relationship to the community in which you live. Sometimes your feelings might be determined by the politics of identity, and whether you feel represented, included or welcomed. And some of those feelings might be shaped by history, by your connections to people and places in the past.

Newham is a dense forest of family trees that are all rooted in different parts of London's past and Britain's history. The people who live in this borough are all, right now, Londoners. Some of them have been Londoners for generations; some of them belong to families who have lived in this same borough, on their very street, in their actual house for generations. Some of them became Londoners themselves when they chose to come to the city to live, work and stay (Newham Council's motto). But either way, the people here have family histories that are part of a bigger picture. And most of those family histories, like Kamal's, intersect with the British empire in some way. The famous axiom of the British imperial migrant in the metropole – we are here because you were there – applies to so many people in Newham, whether their families are rooted in the motherland or in the colonies on the periphery. Even those whose families don't have direct connections to the British empire – the communities from Eastern Europe, for example, who often came to Britain after the expansion of the EU – live lives knitted out of imperial legacies: from the border regime that enabled their migration, to the curricula in the schools where their children study, and the languages spoken and religions practised by their neighbours and friends.

There is no sense in trying to understand how and why Newham looks like it does today without examining how the empire and its ending fundamentally changed the lives of British people, not least in the way that it ensnared communities around the globe, creating new identities of Britishness in the periphery which slowly but surely made their way back to the metropole. For many British people, empire was – and for a significant proportion, still is – something that happened in Victorian times, in an age of gin and tonics on the veranda, tiny blond children waving Union Jacks, and men with pith helmets and enormous moustaches charging around the globe planting flags for Britannia. The story of Newham shows us that empire's legacy is soaked into our landscapes and built into our cities. It is in our national DNA.

Modern Britain as a whole is in so many senses the product of British imperialism. The controversies about whether British museums should repatriate their plundered imperial treasures, the arguments about whether cities like Bristol or Liverpool should apologise for their slave-trading pasts, the constant furious debates about how much imperial history is taught in schools and what stories we should tell our children about our national past, from the food we eat and the books we read to the way our entire nation looks, both its geography and its people: all of these are the living legacy of British imperial rule and decline.

When writing a book like this, it can be tempting to claim that the real story of empire has yet to be uncovered – that it is a secret history, with stories that have never been heard before (until now!). But there are no secret histories and there are very few forgotten histories: history leaves its mark on people and places and there is always someone, somewhere, who knows where the bodies are buried. There are instead histories that have been ignored; voices that have been silenced. The histories that we choose to remember as a nation tell us a lot about who we want to be – and who we pretend to be – today. But if we are ever going to understand what it actually means to be British, the *full* story of Britain and the empire in the latter half of the twentieth century needs to be told.

The history of British imperialism is not a happy one. The rise of a small nation to global power is a story of plunder, exploitation, oppression and violence. Britain was able to bring about an end to the slave trade because Britain was one of the biggest and most efficient slaver nations, buying and selling millions of African men, women and children. The colonies were not a big happy family: the British empire was built on a world view underpinned by a racist hierarchy, ruled over with economic, military and structural violence, and resisted desperately by many colonial communities.

Today, even its apologists are starting to acknowledge that Britain's imperial past is dark and murky. But its post-imperial past – the story of what happened after empire 'ended' – is often simply ignored.

Part of the reason is obvious. In the hundred years between 1815 and 1914, Britain conquered much of the world; the empire expanded by 10 million square miles, ensnaring around 400 million people within imperial boundaries. Given the rapid and unprecedented growth, the twentieth century could seem like an afterthought, and the second half of the twentieth century even more so.

In fact, British imperialism is a very modern story. The British empire reached its greatest territorial extent in the interwar period. The Second World War saw Britain demand enormous sacrifices of its colonial populations, who contributed money, resources and their own lives to the Allied war effort. The mass migrations to Britain from the end of the Second World War onwards brought imperial subjects to the 'motherland' and changed what it meant to be British. And decolonisation did not end the empire in a single stroke, but was an ongoing process that gradually reshaped the relationship between Britain and its former colonies. The twentieth century saw the empire tested, reshaped, dissolved – but the echoes of imperialism survived, in debates about multiculturalism, overseas aid and the EU referendum, and the scandal of the Windrush generation being denied their rightful citizenship.

Nor did decolonisation end the economic and political difficulties experienced by former colonies as a result of British imperial rule, political interference by the British and other foreign powers, and the structural inequalities faced by countries across the Global South. Those former colonies know that decolonisation was not an event, but a reckoning, one that has perhaps not yet finished. Only Britain is in denial about this.

There have been many histories written and stories told about British imperialism – from *Boys' Own* adventures set in tropical jungles and arid deserts, to academic texts exploring British imperial policy around the world. Imperialism has been spun as a tale of expansion and adventure, with tales of intrepid Brits travelling across land and sea, discovering rare plants or building railways. Many of the canonical images of the pink-on-the-map empire hail from the late nineteenth and early twentieth centuries: they help us to imagine the empire as something relegated firmly to the past, which happened somewhere foreign to Britain, 'over there'. Until recently, this has stopped us from interrogating how the British empire influenced, enriched and disrupted British politics, society and culture at home, and how it continued to do so well into the twentieth century. But today many British people are doing the work to uncover these stories, by campaigning for the national curriculum to be widened to include empire and migration histories, demanding that museums better acknowledge the provenance of their imperial collections, or pulling down statues and throwing them into harbours. There is a need, but also a growing appetite, for more nuanced and critical histories of Britain's imperial identity.

This book seeks to help write this history, and in doing so to set out why people in Britain today should care about their nation's imperial past and its unexpected echoes through their contemporary culture. It explores a period of just over eighty years, from the Second World War to today, to show how Britain went from having a global role at the heart of empire and Europe to being an island nation, divorced from Europe and struggling to confront its imperial past.

It is mostly chronological, beginning with Britain's and Britons' experience of the Home Front. It then traces how the Attlee government attempted to rebuild Britain in the peace that followed, and what this meant for the British empire and British imperial subjects. I hope to show that the 1950s, often dismissed as a little grey and boring, might actually hold the key to unlocking our post-war identity. The book examines in some depth the process of decolonisation through that decade and the next, and goes on to explore migration, racism and British culture across the 1960s and 70s. Three key events – the Falklands War, the Live Aid concert and the end of apartheid in South Africa – provide a lens with which to understand developments in the 1980s and early 1990s. At the end of the 1990s it explores the moment of 'Cool Britannia', when Britain tried to shift its identity on the world stage. Finally, I look at how imperialism continues to shape society, politics and culture in the nation today, from the Windrush Scandal and the Colston Must Fall campaign, to the recent 'culture wars' that represent a clash of different understandings of British imperial legacies.

The 2016 referendum on British membership of the EU exposed the gulf between these different attitudes to Britain, and the way that its history underwrites its identity today. For many Leavers, quitting the EU was about taking back control of British politics and British culture. To reassure the nation that this was possible, those leading the campaign often invoked the Second World War, specifically that moment when – after the fall of France, before the United States had entered the conflict, before the Russians had declared war on Germany – Britain stood alone. Plucky little Britain, standing up to fascism on the continent, and going on to save the day: it is a powerful historical image, and one immortalised in a David Low cartoon from June 1940. In it, one soldier bravely shakes his fist at the roiling sky and says, 'Very well, alone', as he faces his fate at the hands of Hitler's forces.[10] But Britain never stood alone. The next month, *Punch* published a cartoon by Cyril Fougasse. It shows two soldiers reclining on a grassy knoll, looking out across the Channel to France. The first soldier remarks, 'So our poor old Empire is alone in the world.' The second counters, 'Aye, we are – the whole five hundred million of us.'[11]

Even during wartime, the British people did not buy into the rhetoric of plucky little Britain as an isolated figure fighting the Nazis. Rather, they understood themselves to sit at the heart of a vast empire, which stretched from Aden to Zanzibar. In fact, it was during the war that many of them encountered it directly for the first time – either by travelling out to fight in Africa and Asia, or because imperial subjects had travelled to the metropole as part of this great war effort. And in the years following the war, from all over the world, people kept coming 'home' to a country that was often ambivalent or outright hostile towards them.

This book traces these journeys. It tells the stories of white settlers who had moved to Kenya and Rhodesia in the 1920s and 30s and who returned in the 1960s with their children to a home they had never known. It describes the experiences of the colonial subjects who moved at first freely, and then with increasing difficulty, from their homes in the empire to a Britain that could be profoundly unwelcoming. It follows the soldiers, sailors, traders, missionaries, charity workers, nurses, doctors, students and teachers who moved from metropole to colonies and back again, and the imperial pathways that shaped their lives.

Traditional narratives of empire have tended to focus mostly on leaders: the generals who sent armies into battle, rather than the soldiers who are buried in unmarked graves; the politicians who sat in rooms talking about their manifestos and their mandates, rather than those who did or didn't vote for them (let alone those were not allowed to vote); the Queen, waving down from her balcony, rather than the crowd of subjects enthusiastically waving back or those half watching on their televisions while they ironed their shirts or fed their kids. But national history is not – or should not be – about individual leaders, who are single strands in the broad fabric of a nation's lived experience. E. P. Thompson, the eminent New Left historian, wrote in *The Making of the English Working Class* of rescuing the people of the past from 'the enormous condescension of posterity'.[12] This book seeks to dignify unpowerful, unfamous people's lives with the idea that they mattered, and furthermore that they still matter; a meaningful national history should not be a retelling of tales about the powerful and their victories, but the recovery of voices from the past who might otherwise be forgotten.

In other words, you might say that this book focuses on the stories of 'ordinary' people. (Historians love to put quotation marks around words like 'ordinary', as if we are holding them delicately, and perhaps with slight distaste.) But the 'ordinary' person is a tricky figure: who is ordinary, really? Who would want to be so identified? The twentieth century and, perhaps even more so, the twenty-first might be characterised as an extended moment of ordinary people trying to become extraordinary: the decline of deference and the rise of celebrity and (later) reality TV and social media have all given people the tools to break free from their ordinary boxes. The rise in living standards of the immediate post-war moment meant that 'ordinary' people could demand better conditions for themselves and their families; the attacks on the welfare state and the labour movement under Thatcherism and beyond meant that the quiet dignity afforded the 'ordinary' worker was now largely illusory. To be 'only' ordinary in twenty-first-century Britain is not something to which most people aspire.

And yet, historians have become increasingly interested in the 'ordinary' people of the past. If the Great Man approach to history was about kings and prime ministers, and ascribing historical events to their actions, decisions and mistakes, the social history movement from the 1960s onwards was concerned with capturing the experiences of the ruled over those of the rulers. Social history recovered the stories of the working-class masses. Women's history in Britain followed this path and while it focused on the extraordinary lives of pioneering women, it also sought to capture the lived experience of women at every level of society. The rise in Black British history and that of other minority ethnic groups has seen the spotlight turned not only on the leaders of movements but also on those whose quiet individual lives made up the full story of people of colour in modern Britain. These approaches to history weave a rich tapestry; ordinary people are the threads within it.

But we also have to be careful with ordinary people. Historians put quotation marks around 'ordinary' because it has no clear definition, no agreed meaning, and so to put someone in this category is a political act as much as a historical one. 'Ordinary' can be a scathing critique or a mark of approval. On the one hand, to characterise someone as ordinary is akin to dismissing them as boring, suggesting that they have no significant, distinguishing identity of their own. On the other hand, the label can be used to exclude those who are *not* ordinary as unusual, or weird, or even abnormal. When Enoch Powell made his Rivers of Blood speech in 1968, he referred to one of his constituents as a 'quite ordinary man'. This sounds, on the face of it, to be a neutral description. In fact Powell was doing something careful and political. He was pitting the concerns of a 'quite ordinary man' against those of the immigrant, specifically the immigrant from the Commonwealth, and even more specifically the immigrant person of colour. He never names the man as white, but he does not have to. Powell's audience understood what he meant when he referred to someone as ordinary; what's more, Powell knew that his audience's imagining of a 'quite ordinary man' could only ever produce a picture of a white man. And we know from the speech itself that the man is white because Powell uses 'his' concerns to ventriloquise a deep and abiding anti-immigration sentiment. The point of Powell's construction of 'quite ordinary men' as necessarily white, and the reason it was a political act, is that it is designed not to describe but to divide. By including some, he deliberately excludes others.

This was a trick with long roots in British imperialism, which was fundamentally invested in defining some people as ordinary and some people as abnormal and delineating aggressively between them. People who fell outside the acceptable boundaries of what it meant to be British in the empire were punished, exploited, oppressed or excluded; this holds true in sexuality, religion, class and, above all, in race. British identity, built on imperial narratives, privileges the white Briton as 'ordinary' despite the fact that Black British people have existed for longer than the empire did. This book tries to explore more carefully who might be 'ordinary', and how their lives intersected with empire in the period from the Second World War to the present day. In doing so, I hope to demonstrate that imperialism is not something that happened 'over there' and to other people but is part of all of our national heritage and is woven into our contemporary politics and culture.

Home and Away in the Second World War

In 1937, the organisation Mass Observation was established by an anthropologist, a film-maker and a *Daily Mirror* journalist, who ended up creating a revolutionary social research platform that would ask fundamental questions about Britain and the British. The independent organisation was intended as an 'anthropology of ourselves': an attempt to explore the thoughts, beliefs and feelings of the 'ordinary' British people about key events and their own daily lives, through the use of questionnaires ('directives') and unstructured diaries produced by volunteers.[1] Its timing was fortuitous: throughout the Second World War, Mass Observation collected a vast quantity of material that examined the British people's attitude to the conflict. In one month in 1940, it produced reports on topics as diverse as the present condition of poetry, the prevalence of antisemitism in the East End of London, and public opinion on the Finnish–Russian peace agreement. In 1942, with great swathes of Europe under German occupation and bitter fighting under way in North Africa and on the Eastern Front, Mass Observation chose to survey the British people to discover their 'feelings about the British Empire'.

The 1942 questionnaire did not just address the empire. Respondents were asked to provide a 'detailed account' of everything that they did on Wednesday 25 February, as well as answering questions on the food situation (and particularly women's attitude to food) in their local areas; what they understood by the term 'prejudice' and who they thought might be 'prejudiced' and why; whether the war had affected the type of music that they liked to listen to; and the funniest joke they had ever heard (and, if they could explain, why they found it funny) as well as another six 'particularly good' jokes or anecdotes. The empire question was number 4, of 6: 'What are your present feelings about the British Empire? Have they changed since war began?'[2]

The questionnaire was sent to 1,300 'observers', and their answers were duly compiled by the Mass Observation researchers. It was decided, however, that statistical analysis of question 4 was impossible: feelings about the British empire were 'ambiguous and complicated'.[3] Understandably many people felt a duty to be loyal to Britain at this precarious moment, but there was also some expression of shame about the way that its colonies had been acquired. One person crowed that the British 'tolerance of exploitation' was 'coming home to roost'; another proclaimed bluntly that 'the sooner we "lose" [the colonies] the better'. Another confessed that they had always felt discomfort with the tropes – 'the "far flung flag", Kipling, the pukka sahib' – of imperialism, disliked the practice of sending missionaries overseas, and were upset by the notion that 'the coloured peoples have so often been exploited'. Others objected to imperialism mostly on the idea that it was now 'out of date', reminding them more of the German Reich than of the Victorian heyday of imperial conquest: 'Am I proud of the British Empire? Well, I was always taught to be at school, and suppose it has been a great achievement, but somehow I think its day is over.'

Where people were positive about the empire, their feelings were shaped mostly by the contribution that the colonies and dominions were making towards the war effort: 'a number of people express surprise that the enthusiasm and solidarity of the Empire with this country has proved as great as it has'. The only unqualified positive response was from an interviewee whose cousin lived in Rhodesia and frequently sent letters full of 'glowing admiration for what the motherland is doing'. The report summarised these responses as expressing two contradictory desires: on one hand, 'a half-repressed desire to see the Empire go', combined with 'a desire, on the other hand, not to see the Empire go, not to have suspicions confirmed'.

During the Second World War, the empire was arguably more mobilised, more centralised and more British than ever before. Its war effort was sustained and powered by its colonial populations and imperial resources. Soldiers from across Africa, the Caribbean, Asia and Australasia fought against the Axis forces. But Britain's demands on the colonies during wartime heightened demands for independence once the war was over. Campaigns for freedom from colonial exploitation took on a new urgency and vigour in the context of the recent fight against fascism, the new language of 'human rights' at the end of the war empowering many independence movements around the globe. And the war left the metropole shaken too: it destroyed its economy, it ravaged its towns and cities, and it killed tens of thousands of civilians and soldiers. In many ways, the Second World War brought Britons into direct contact with empire as never before. But it also made Britain's imperial identity more precarious than ever.

The British people had not gone into the Second World War gung-ho. Only twenty years after the end of the First World War, the communal memory of that conflict was still raw, and the death toll still visible in villages and towns across Britain, inscribed on the local memorials erected with the names of sons, brothers and fiancés. Indeed, the whole empire had contributed to the First World War, with troops from India, the Caribbean, Africa and Australasia fighting for the British cause. Many too had come to the metropole as part of this conflict – for example, the Indian soldiers injured on the Western Front who had been treated in a hospital hastily assembled in the Brighton Pavilion – or had fought in campaigns, such as the Australian and New Zealand (ANZAC) troops slaughtered in Gallipoli, that had been followed with concern by British newspaper readers at home.

And yet the imperial contribution to the First World War had been pushed out of many British people's minds once the war had ended. People worked in committees to erect local memorials to their own sons and brothers, not to the missing and killed from around the empire. Although the abstract symbolism of Edwyn Lutyens' Cenotaph memorialised all the fallen in its inscription to 'The Glorious Dead', the inclusion of imperial soldiers was not explicit. (Nonetheless, replicas of, or homages to, the Cenotaph were subsequently erected in many sites around the empire, including Hong Kong, Bermuda, Auckland and Toronto.)

The First World War was grieved in a national British context – the minute's silence, the annual ceremony of Armistice Day, the laying of wreaths by local dignitaries – as well as a personal one, but the imperial dimension was elusive. The British turned inwards during the interwar period, away from the horror of the trenches and industrialised killing. British men returned from the Front to the aspirational suburban semi, and quietly dug their gardens, read detective fiction and listened to the wireless; their wives largely drifted back into the home from their brief experiences of the factory floor or the auxiliary forces. People grieved their losses quietly and domestically. In this context, a new world war was not a chance for Britain to flex its imperial might or prove its global leadership, but a threat to a quiet peace that had been bitterly fought for and seemingly won.

In the mid-1930s this anxiety about war fuelled support for the League of Nations Union (LNU), an organisation made up of ordinary men and women who were dedicated to peace through international cooperation as enabled by the League of Nations. In 1935 the LNU ran a 'Peace Ballot', taken door to door by half a million volunteers who hoped to prove that the British people supported the maintenance of peace through collective security. These volunteers were armed with a leaflet, to share on the doorstep, and a booklet, to be kept to themselves, that pre-empted many of the objections people might have to the LNU. The purpose of the ballot was not just to take the national temperature, but also to actively persuade voters that collective security, disarmament and international cooperation were the paths that they favoured in diplomacy.

In the canvasser's secret booklet, one anticipated objection to the LNU was that 'The British Empire Must Be Able to Defend Itself'.

Volunteers were equipped to counter this with several arguments: the power and strength of the British empire was not what it used to be in the nineteenth century, so collective security was necessary to protect imperial interests; making ad hoc alliances outside the League of Nations would lead to an entangled world such as that which led to the First World War; and finally, and most compellingly, that the empire was itself a vulnerable entity. What, the authors of the pamphlet asked, should Britain do 'if Germany attacked the British Isles from the air while Italy closed the Mediterranean route by air-power and occupied the Nile Valley by land power (from bases in Libya and Abyssinia) and Japan simultaneously attacked Hong-kong, Malaya, New Zealand and Australia by sea?'[4] Their answer, of course, was to rely on the collective measures of the League of Nations. These hypotheticals show that the empire at this time was not always seen as a source of strength by the British people but as a liability, a source of vulnerability; it was precisely this anxiety that the League of Nations Union doorstep volunteers hoped to capitalise on for their pacifist cause. In the end, the results of the ballot seemed to show a public that was idealistic in its support for international disarmament, that agreed collective security was important, but which hesitantly supported military measures to maintain security if other approaches failed.

As war became more likely, people in Britain and across the empire listened to the radio anxiously, kept one eye on the newspapers, and were not always reassured by what they found. In 1938, however, the prime minister, Neville Chamberlain, returned from Munich with his famous piece of paper in his hand: an agreement between Britain, Germany, Italy and France to accede to Germany's illegal annexation of the Sudetenland in return for peace. The outpouring of relief was immense. For two hours before his plane landed at Heston Aerodrome, 'the narrow roads leading to the airport were made almost impassable with traffic' as people tried to get as close as possible to the returning hero; 120 schoolboys from Eton, 'on their own initiative', lined the road leading from the airport buildings to the gate and cheered the prime minister as he returned.[5]

Chamberlain went straight to Buckingham Palace, where he waved from the balcony with his wife, and the King and Queen, to a crowd that had stood waiting for several hours, sheltering under newspapers through heavy rain and rewarded with a rainbow over St James's Park. The sense of stepping back from the brink is palpable in news reports from the time: one woman, as she watched the prime minister speak, heralded him as 'the man who gave me back my son'.[6] This relief was felt around the empire: in Australia, the *Argus* and the *Age*, two prominent newspapers, published letters praising Chamberlain's achievements and attributing his success to the prayers of people around the Commonwealth. Two Australian firms organised their workers to send telegrams of congratulations to the British prime minister, and an Australian journalist recorded that on the Sydney to Melbourne train, passengers found out about Munich and broke into relieved chatter with the strangers sitting around them.[7]

Empire was an important element, in fact, in the negotiations that had been stilled but not ended by the Munich Agreement. The newspapers reported anxiously that Hitler, having secured access to the Sudetenland, now turned his attention to the former German African colonies, particularly Tanganyika (Tanzania); in 1938 a British protectorate, this colony, along with German South-West Africa (Namibia) had been confiscated from Germany in the settlement at the end of the First World War. The *Manchester Guardian* carried a report from Dar-es-Salaam that recounted the anxieties of the British colonial officials in Tanganyika about the potential for British capitulation in the face of German aggression, and the 'considerable consternation' among the wider community.[8] The *Telegraph* in February had published a letter from the Committee of the British Union of Tanganyika expressing concern that a German takeover of the colony would be 'even more disastrous to British settlers than the natives', a 'loyal and patriotic body of men', and proposing that the colony be merged with Kenya to further shore up the position of the white community there.[9] By October, the *Manchester Guardian* was reporting an apparently spontaneous demonstration among the Tanganyikan people in support of continued British rule: 'a procession composed of many tribes marched along the main streets of the town led by an amateur brass band', under Union Jacks and 'vernacular' banners expressing their desire to remain part of the British empire. The reporter was keen to point out both that the procession had been 'perfectly orderly' and that it had been organised 'by the natives themselves', perhaps to emphasise that German occupation of the colony would have dire consequences for the Black African community and to justify support for British colonialism from a left-wing newspaper for rather different reasons than those of the brigadier generals writing to the *Telegraph*.[10]

A number of organisations worked to educate British people about this concern. British Youth Peace Assembly (BYPA), in collaboration with the Student Christian Movement Press, produced a pamphlet, 'Youth and the Colonies', which sought to inform young people about this ongoing colonial controversy. Sold for threepence, it argued that its readers had a duty to consider questions such as 'Where are the colonies? What is their importance in world trade? Why does Hitler demand them and what are we to reply? Is Germany fit to rule colonies? Is Britain?' The pamphlet began with a detailed exploration of what the empire actually was, where the colonies were and how the system was administered, an approach demonstrating both an assumed lack of knowledge about the empire among its young readership, but also a desire to learn. The pamphlet is unsurprisingly critical of Hitler's plans for the colonies and the Nazi ideology surrounding colonial – 'so-called backward' – people, and argues that the racial science of Nazism means that submitting the colonies to German rule would be irresponsible and immoral: 'this racial theory, which is by no means new in Germany, allows for the exploitation of coloured peoples'. But there is significant critique of the British empire too: Kenya is cited as an example of British colonial policy having 'a profound and disturbing effect on African life', and the colonial administrators are attacked for their pursuit of policies such as 'hut tax' (a tax by household, payable in cash, which often pushed African children into the labour market and which led to widespread local resistance to British imperialism in the colonies where it was imposed).[11] The BYPA had a dedicated colonial committee, which focused on educating young people about the colonial world and fostering closer connections between students throughout the empire; before the outbreak of war, they had intended to hold a series of conferences in the spring of 1940. Their nuanced critique of British imperialism, even in defence of the British empire against German aggression, shows that many ordinary people in Britain did engage with these issues with a great deal of care and thought.

However, not everyone was willing to risk war for the sake of colonial peoples far away, and many British people neither thought nor cared about the experience of southern African colonies that they barely knew existed. The British government were certainly far more concerned about Tanganyika than Namibia, as the former was in an important strategic position and could be used to interfere with British African communications and to establish hostile submarine and air bases; however, Chamberlain was recorded in discussion with the French deputy prime minister as saying that he believed the British people would 'not reject' a colonial sacrifice to keep peace in Europe, and that the government could potentially find an 'equivalent . . . sacrifice' to placate Hitler.[12]

It seems that his reading of ordinary British people was, in this case, correct: many were indeed willing to cut British losses in Africa to keep the peace in Europe. One woman from Essex, Miss Akhurst, wrote to her local MP (who happened to be Winston Churchill) on behalf of herself and her sister, anxiously suggesting that Britain should offer 'some national or imperial interests' to Germany. Her assumption, in fact, was that Hitler's invasion of Czechoslovakia was motivated by the German people's 'hunger for a comfortable place in the world', which would surely be provided by African colonies.[13] Jettisoning part of the empire obviously seemed a small price to pay to avoid conflict for both the British and the Czech people. In the end, Tanganyika and Namibia were never ceded. Germany and Britain were at war before any agreement over the colonies could be reached. But this debate demonstrates that war with Germany had an imperial dimension that preyed on people's minds alongside the concerns about bombing campaigns and conscription.

Despite the understandable reluctance to fight another war, appeasement was a controversial strategy, cast as either desperate yielding to a dictator or a wily move that enabled Britain to rearm and prepare for fighting. Many people in Britain felt a deep sense of shame when Chamberlain signed the 1938 agreement, as if they had been implicated in the sacrifice of Czechoslovakia for the greater good of Europe. The writer and political activist Mary Agnes Hamilton recorded in her diary that she was 'ashamed to be a British subject', scribbling that 'peace without honour – better than war – but surely needlessly dishonourable'.[14] In Auckland, New Zealand, the local Communist Party protested against the agreement, marching with banners proclaiming 'Hitler thanked Chamberlain: why should you?' before they were halted by police.[15]

Even for those who did not overtly protest the Munich Agreement, there was a sense that it was simply buying time not peace. In the beautiful bright summer of 1939, British people recorded their anxieties at the seemingly inevitable march to another conflict. In August, Mrs E. Taunton of Leyton in east London noted sandbags appearing around her workplace, her neighbour building an air-raid shelter and hoping that Hitler 'wouldn't have the heart' to bomb her geraniums, and the 'undercurrent of edginess' that pervaded it all.[16] Empire was present, too, in this anxiety: she recorded that her brother, an army reservist, was grateful that he had not been sent to Egypt like many of his friends.

In September 1939, Loleta Jemmott was a six-year-old living in Barbados, where she had been born. Like many others, her memory of the moment that war broke out was marked by sounds. 'I can remember the church bells ringing out and people crying out and that was the announcement that the war had started.'[17] This soundscape united the experiences of people across the empire and across Britain, where church bells were rung in many village communities to mark Chamberlain's declaration; the BBC ended the prime minister's speech by playing a short clip of church bells, before broadcasting a series of public service messages.

Other people around the empire experienced the declaration in more unusual circumstances. Mercedes Mackay lived in Tanganyika where her husband Robert, a mining geologist, was stationed in the Mines Department in Dar-es-Salaam, before being transferred to Nigeria in 1941. Mercedes was a journalist with the *East African Standard* and later worked in radio broadcasting in Jos. Her memories of the declaration of war were captured as part of the BBC oral history radio series *Tales from the Dark Continent*.

> We were playing a cricket match in which all the men dressed as women and all the women as men. There were some absurd costumes and some very peculiar cricket was played . . . we were all laughing so much that we could hardly speak when suddenly a car appeared and a man got out and said, 'Come quickly to the club, the Prime Minister is about to speak.' So we beetled off in our cars round to the club and we all stood round in our ridiculous costumes and they turned on the wireless and there was that fatal announcement. And I remember looking across at the Inspector of the Public Works Department, who had dressed himself up in a long, black flowing dress with a red wig as a madam of a brothel, and he was standing there with tears pouring down his face . . . It was one of the most tragic-comic situations that I can ever remember.[18]

Britain's entrance into the Second World War had dragged the colonies into the conflict too; colonial governments, who were in any case almost entirely made up of white British officials, did not have an independent foreign policy. The position for the dominions was a little more complex. The Statute of Westminster, passed in 1931, had given legal independence to Australia, New Zealand, Canada, Newfoundland, South Africa and the Irish Free State; this had formalised the arrangement drafted by Arthur Balfour in 1926, defining these 'dominions' as 'autonomous Communities within the British Empire, equal in status, in no way subordinate one to another in any aspect of their domestic or external affairs'.[19]

In the First World War, troops from these nations had been drawn into conflict because they were bound, by imperial structures, to fight any war in which Britain was engaged, and forces from Australia, Canada and New Zealand had fought in key European battlefields such as Gallipoli and Vimy Ridge; Indian soldiers, too, had been part of the British imperial forces on the Western Front; African soldiers had been deployed against German troops across the African continent, and Caribbean men had been a vital part of the imperial Labour Corps, although they had not been allowed to take up arms alongside white soldiers. The Second World War pulled in troops from the colonies – in India, the Far East, Africa and the Caribbean, as well as migrants from these communities living and working in Britain when war broke out – but the newly independent governments of the dominions were no longer required to go to war alongside the British. Despite this independence, though, all of the dominions (except, importantly, Ireland) joined the British empire in the war against the Axis powers. When it came down to it, for many of the people living in these territories, the ties that bound Britain to its dominions had not changed, even if the law had. The Canadian writer Stephen Leacock explained in an essay in the summer of 1939 that if any Canadian were asked if their government had to follow England [*sic*] into war, 'he'd answer at once, "Oh, no." If you then said, "*Would* you go to war if England does?" he'd answer, "Oh, yes." And if you asked, "Why?" he would say, reflectively, "Well, you see, we'd *have* to." '[20]

Despite their formal independence from Britain, in other words, many white settlers living in the dominions still felt culturally and emotionally bound to their motherland, and so the choice to go to war to support the British government was really no choice at all.

The Second World War is so ingrained in the British psyche in part because of the Home Front: the idea that domestic civilians were not merely living through wartime but actively contributing to a 'war effort' on a 'front' that was not a line on a map in Europe or the Far East but in their classroom, kitchen or workplace. A number of previously mundane, quotidian actions became recast as a way for citizens to Do Their Bit, regardless of whether they had been formally conscripted. Food, clothing and petrol were rationed; citizens were encouraged to 'make do and mend' and 'dig for victory'; the blackout, the air-raid siren, the carrying of gas masks and the evacuation of their children, all represented practical contributions to the war effort and to personal and community safety, but also demonstrated the extent to which the civilian population was caught up in the demands of a war economy and society.

The same was true all around the empire. New Zealand, for example, introduced rationing during the war as they exported the vast majority of their meat and dairy supplies to support American soldiers in the Pacific and British consumers suffering from food shortages in the UK.[21] The empire in the Second World War was sold to the British people as a supplier of food that might help them to win the war, such as in the propaganda film *Food from the Empire*, where a typical 'shopping basket of the British housewife' was unpacked to show items like butter and cheese from New Zealand, lamb and wheat from Australia, vegetable oil from the Gold Coast and tea from Ceylon. Imperial subjects are depicted as eager to help the British people, and 'anxious to send every ounce they can to the United Kingdom for they know that upon the ability of Great Britain to hold out depends their own freedom'.[22]

As the wartime generation ages and dies, it is perhaps not surprising that it is the experiences of children and young adults that remain most vivid in our collective memory. Evacuation and conscription, which divided families, separating children from parents at a moment of terrifying danger, were inherently emotional experiences that have left a deep scratch on the British national psyche. Both were fundamental parts of the Home Front experience. Both also had an important imperial dimension.

Plans for evacuation had been drawn up in the late 1930s, and had initially been implemented in 1938. The government largely focused on domestic evacuation procedures, splitting the country into three zones (evacuation, neutral and reception) and arranging for the mass movement of children, babes-in-arms and their mothers, and the elderly and infirm from the first zone to the third. Evacuation was trialled in September 1938, in anticipation of the possible failure of the Munich Agreement; this meant that in 1939, the authorities were reasonably well prepared, and evacuation of children actually began a couple of days before war was formally declared.

Evacuation was a difficult and complex process, which both created and uncovered a great number of social and cultural problems: there was little official vetting of potential reception families, leading sometimes to neglect and abuse; children were often deeply unhappy to be away from their parents; and where mothers were evacuated with their babies there was a great deal of friction between families newly billeted together. One Mass Observation report from November 1939 detailed the enormous problems faced by host families dealing with traumatised and often extremely deprived children – they were often 'verminous', had poor eating habits, a lack of sufficient clothing, and problems with toilet training – concluding that 'we haven't intended to stress the more depressing side of the business, but in fact most of the material seems to be like that'.[23] Children from urban centres often found it hard to adjust to rural life, and there was a significant amount of class-inflected prejudice about the behaviour of 'inner city children' who were chastised for many things, such as having head lice, that would seem to be beyond their control. The *Our Towns* report of 1943 gently pointed out that many of these issues were due to poverty, not bad parenting or poor discipline, and many foster families did realise this and reacted accordingly; others were galvanised by their exposure to urban poverty to call more vocally for post-war reforms in health and welfare.[24]

Many children, of course, did have fond memories of their time in the countryside; others did not. Children of colour often suffered especially through being removed from peer groups and community support and taken to rural areas with overwhelmingly white inhabitants. The League of Coloured Peoples (LCP), formed in 1931 by the Jamaican doctor and activist Harold Moody, had grown into a campaign group that fought for the rights of people of colour in

Britain and around the world, with the Jamaican feminist poet and journalist Una Marson, the Kenyan politician (and that country's first independent leader) Jomo Kenyatta, and the Trinidadian Marxist historian C. L. R. James among its members. In the 1930s, the LCP had mostly been focused on the rights of people of colour as workers, setting up branches in sectors as diverse as shipping and medicine. But when the war began, one of the LCP's main campaigns instead became the fight for the right of children of colour from British cities to be evacuated with their peers. It was hard to find families in rural areas who would accept non-white children, and many of those who were placed had ambiguous – at best – experiences. Paul Stephenson, whose estranged father was West African and whose mother had both African and white British heritage, was evacuated as a child from Rochford in Essex to a care home in a village in the Essex countryside with seven white children. Although he enjoyed a bucolic childhood exploring the countryside, he also had to contend with casual racism, including a schoolteacher who cut locks of his hair 'for good luck'.[25]

Evacuation was not only a domestic process – it had an imperial dimension too. Many British people felt that the empire provided an ideal sanctuary for their most vulnerable, away from a theatre of war which was still largely being imagined as taking place in Western Europe. The British government was initially encouraging of this process, through a scheme called the Children's Overseas Reception Board (CORB), but quickly became overwhelmed by the number of applicants and increasingly concerned about the threat of U-boat attacks on the long journeys abroad and the toll that this could take on British morale. Despite the huge number of applications for overseas evacuation, in total only around 2,600 children were sent to the dominions by the government through the CORB. This included 1,500 sent to Canada, placed as 'British Guest Children'.[26] Many of these children had extremely positive experiences, despite the distance from their family and the perilous journey, and in contrast to the domestic evacuation scheme, there was ongoing monitoring of their circumstances, their health and their situation.

Three children from Middlesbrough were sent to stay with Mr Kelly, the editor of the *Halifax Herald*, and apparently had a lovely time; the children each put on ten pounds in weight, developed Canadian accents, and had little desire to leave their new home, which was luxurious and comfortable despite, as the British high commissioner in Canada wrote to the director general of the CORB, the 'extreme lack of taste', which he believed to be universal in Canadian interior design.[27]

Many more children were sent by well-off families with imperial connections; over 5,000 children were evacuated privately to Canada alone. On 4 July 1940, the *Duchess of Atholl* set sail across the Atlantic: on board were one hundred girls and eight female teachers from St Hilda's, a convent school in Whitby; thirty girls and three teachers from Sherborne School for Girls who were headed to Branksome Hall School in Toronto; forty-eight girls from Roedean who were bound for Edgehill School in Nova Scotia; and five teachers and twenty-eight children of Byron House School, in Highgate in north London, travelling to Ottawa. The Byron House pupils, some of whom were only three or four years old, stayed in Canada between 1940 and 1944, housed in a variety of large private houses. Similarly, twenty boys from Belmont School in Hassocks, Sussex, were evacuated to Nassau, in the Bahamas, for the duration of the war. An amateur film produced for concerned parents shows the boys arriving at the docks, walking about the school grounds in their uniforms, and taking part in music, religious worship and sports, before being visited by the Duke and Duchess of Windsor.[28]

These evacuations were seen as providing an informal ambassadorial connection between Britain and the colonies, with school groups being used to build a sense of wartime solidarity between the metropole and their colonial populations. However, some private schools refused to send children to the dominions, despite parental enthusiasm, because they worried about the effect of exposure to colonial life. The boys of Sherborne School remained in Britain for the duration of the war, subject to rationing and air raids, because, as one housemaster explained to a concerned father, relocating the school to the empire 'could not hope to reproduce the character or the training' of the existing, historic establishment set in the British countryside.[29]

Conscription had started in Britain in spring 1939 for men aged between twenty and twenty-two, with around a quarter of a million registering for service. Initially, however, there was a colour bar in place which limited conscription to those of white British heritage. When war broke out, Harold Moody's son, Arundel (more commonly known as Joe), went to Whitehall for an interview to be commissioned as an officer and was dismayed to find he was not eligible because of the colour of his skin. The LCP immediately began a campaign and in October 1939 the Colonial Office declared that 'British subjects from the colonies . . . including those who are not of European descent' were now eligible for emergency commission during wartime.[30] Joe tested this policy and joined the army as an officer cadet, only the second Black officer to be commissioned in the British Army; he eventually rose to the rank of major in 1945, serving across Europe and in the British African territories.

The women's forces had also started to mobilise in advance of the official declaration of war. The Auxiliary Territorial Service (ATS), the women's branch of the army, was formed in September 1938 as the equivalent had been disbanded at the end of the First World War, as had the Women's Royal Naval Service (WRNS), which was re-formed in April 1939; the Women's Land Army was established in June 1939. These services were voluntary, recruiting from a wide range of women across the country, until limited female conscription was introduced in December 1941. At this stage those women who were conscripted could choose between going into industry, agriculture, nursing, or the various armed services – as well as the First Aid Nursing Yeomanry (FANY), which included among its ranks the Special Operations Executive for female spies, mostly drawn from France and Britain, but also including Nancy Wake from New Zealand, Phyllis Latour from South Africa and Noor Inayat-Khan, who was of Indian Muslim heritage.

Amelia King, a third-generation migrant from the Caribbean who was born in Stepney, had hoped to join the Land Army; she applied to the Essex County Branch in 1943 but was rejected because of her race. Her MP, Walter Edwards, raised the issue in the House of Commons and the refusal was defended by the minister of agriculture, who said that there had been efforts to find employment and a billet for the twenty-six-year-old but that 'when it became apparent that this was likely to prove extremely difficult, she was advised to volunteer for other war work where her services could be more speedily utilised'. Other MPs weighed in, forcing the minister to deny that he endorsed a colour bar.[31] Despite the lack of action by the government, the case became a cause célèbre, and Amelia was soon offered work by a Mr Roberts on his farm in Wickham, near Portsmouth.[32]

The War Office had initially simply refused to allow women of colour from around the empire to join the voluntary services, arguing that they would be unable to adapt to the British climate or social conditions. The Colonial Office disagreed, and kept up the pressure on the rest of the British government for a recruitment policy that would allow women from the empire, specifically the Caribbean, to make a contribution to the war effort, as a method of improving relations between the metropole and the West Indies. Eventually, in 1943, the War Office changed their policy and specifically allowed the recruitment of West Indian women in the ATS, which was the largest, but least glamorous, of the women's auxiliary services. By 1944, there were enough West Indian members of the ATS in Britain that the Colonial Office held a number of tea parties to celebrate their contribution to the war effort. One press photograph features a group of young Black women, dressed in their ATS uniforms, being served tea at Dover House, the Colonial Office HQ in London, while another, taken by the Ministry of Information photo division (and thus produced as a piece of government propaganda), shows a different group relaxing on the grass under a tree, enjoying tea and sandwiches being served by white women from the Women's Voluntary Service.[33] By June 1945, about

200,000 women from across the British empire had joined the ATS, from the dominions, the West Indies and India.

To begin with, much of the imperial contribution to war was centralised through the British metropole. The RAF 145 Squadron, which was one of the most successful against Axis planes in the Battle of Britain, consisted of pilots from the United States, Britain, New Zealand, Argentina, Trinidad, Canada, South Africa, Australia and Poland: a mishmash of imperial forces with others who wanted to fight against Hitler but whose nations either were not yet in the war or had already been defeated. A photograph from October 1940 shows some of the first twenty-six Indian pilots arriving in Britain, being greeted at a train station by Sir Louis Leisler Greig from the Air Ministry, in their smart uniforms and warm overcoats, clutching pith helmets.[34] Among them is Mahinder Singh Pujji, one of the first Sikh pilots to volunteer to fly with the RAF, who would be awarded the Distinguished Flying Cross for his missions in Europe, North Africa and Burma (Myanmar). Pujji's experience of visiting Britain for training, and flying alongside British aircrews, was generally positive – he was, for example, allowed to modify his flying uniform so that he could continue to wear his turban – but he was frustrated after the war that his contribution, and the contribution of his fellow Indian pilots, was largely forgotten, with no attempt to include him in the commemorations around the seventieth anniversary of VE Day.[35] After his death in Gravesend in 2010, the town commissioned the sculptor Douglas Jennings to produce a statue of Pujji, which stands now as a memorial to 'those from around the world who served alongside Britain in all conflicts 1914–2014'.

Many young men from around the empire were also pulled into military service through their own colonial and dominion forces. Some were eager to sign up, and some were repelled by the summons to fight for King and Country, asking whose country was really at stake. (Even Mahinder Singh Pujji's memoir, published in 2010, was titled *For King and Another Country*.) But there was a significant contribution to the war effort from colonial subjects and citizens. The 28 Māori Battalion was formed at the urging of the Māori politician Sir Apirana Ngata and other Māori MPs at the beginning of the war. The battalion was brought to Gourock, a small town near Glasgow, in June 1940 after a 17,000-mile journey by boat, where they were greeted by reporters and the BBC recording unit; they then had a twenty-hour train journey down to a training camp in Ewshot, Hampshire, speeding through the unfamiliar English countryside. The men spent their days training, with leave spent either visiting London ('Just like Wellington, only bigger'), or in the local town of Farnham, once taking part in – and winning – a competition at the Farnham Swimming Baths; they also travelled to Wales to stage a rematch of the 1905 Wales v. All Blacks match. The battalion was used in the autumn of 1940 to mount a defence in Kent against possible invasion from Europe, and spent a bitterly cold white Christmas in England, before being sent eventually to Egypt to join the rest of the New Zealand troops.[36]

The dominions had more control over their contribution to the war than the colonies, which were expected to provide what they were asked for by the metropole. For much of the war, the War Office was resistant to the idea of a Caribbean regiment because of deep-seated racist assumptions about the work ethic and commitment of Caribbean men to the war effort. However, Black men were able to join other regiments – the army, and later the RAF, opened recruitment to Black servicemen to cope with heavy losses at the beginning of the war. Many made their way to Britain to enlist and fight, including Cy Grant, who became a flight lieutenant navigator after being recruited as aircrew and travelling to Britain for training, where he was appointed one of the few Black officers in the RAF. On his third operation, Cy was shot down over the Netherlands and was imprisoned for two years in Stalag Luft III, the camp that would become famous as the setting of the *Great Escape*. After the war, Cy trained as a lawyer but, unable to find work, became a successful calypso singer and distinguished actor, one of the first Black figures to appear regularly on British television screens.[37] Grant was one of 10,000 Caribbean men who contributed to the British war effort in this way. Eventually the War Office relented, and after discussions with the Colonial Office, the Caribbean Regiment was formed in April 1944, with 1,200 volunteers.

Beyond the battlefield, imperial citizens contributed to the war effort in a multiplicity of ways. They were not just soldiers or pilots, but also sailors, engineers, medical teams and infrastructure workers, often travelling across the empire to fight against fascism in Europe, facing racism and discrimination from the British even as they were risking their lives for Britain. In 1941, Scotland was confronted with a workforce crisis in the timber industry, which was needed for wartime construction. British Honduras (Belize) was one of the main colonial suppliers of timber, and so had a skilled workforce available in the imperial Forestry Unit: five hundred volunteers were sent to Scotland in 1941, and four hundred more followed the next year. The men were billeted in camps in East Lothian, the Scottish Borders, Sutherland and the western Highlands, in extremely poor conditions, and suffered through the bitter Scottish cold and the prejudices of the local landowners and military hierarchies. Many of the men returned to Honduras in 1943 when the unit was disbanded, but some remained in Scotland and built new lives in the metropole. Sam Martinez married a local woman, Mary Jane Gray, with whom he had six children, and stayed in Scotland until his death at 106; he was active in a number of local community organisations and a passionate Hibs fan, initially because Hibs shared a kit with his childhood team.[38]

It was not only those within the metropole who experienced the empire in new ways during wartime. The conflict meant that men and women travelled from Britain around the empire, too, as soldiers, pilots, engineers and medical staff. Jack Connor was born in Rutherglen in Scotland and served in the 17th Indian Division in the Second World War, fighting in India and later in Burma. Writing home from India in 1942 to his sister Cathie, he described his first vision of the colony, 'gazing at sights I had only read about, The Gateway of India. There was the Tajmahal Hotel and Green's Hotel, official residences of the "Bombay whites". What an artificial front to this India, Britain's gem of the East and Asia's poorest country.'[39] The glamorous sights that Connor had read about evidently jarred with his experience of Indian poverty; as British people became eye-witnesses to empire, sometimes they rejected the imperial fairy tales celebrated in the metropole.

Mussolini had taken the opportunity of the Second World War to try to bolster Italy's overseas empire in Africa after the unsuccessful campaign in Abyssinia (Ethiopia); when Italian forces were pushed back by British forces in neighbouring colonies, Germany sent the Afrikakorps under the command of Rommel to support their fascist ally. Spike Milligan, who had been born in India to an Irish father and British mother and had lived in India and Burma before coming to England with his family, was one of the 36,000 British forces who fought in this campaign. His war memoirs, especially the second volume, *Rommel? Gunner Who?*, detail the experience of fighting in the desert, the heat and the dust and the unrelenting grind of putting up camp and tearing it down again. The books, which provide a lyrical account of his struggles with depression and his nervous breakdown, also help to illustrate the soldiers' attitudes to their African imperial surroundings and the colonial subjects who occupied them. For Milligan, North Africa meant privation, danger and boredom, but it was also a wonderland that brought to mind childhood encounters with the exotic empire in books and films. 'This vision, the name of Sheba, the sun, the crystal white and silver shimmer of the salt lagoon made boyhood readings of Rider Haggard come alive.'[40] The writer Roald Dahl also fought in Africa during the war, stationed on an air base in Dar-es-Salaam, having moved to the colony in 1938 to work for the oil company Shell. In his memoir of the period, *Going Solo*, Dahl recalls encounters with African wildlife and dramatic scenes of bravery and excitement as his squadron fly their planes across the desert. Again, Africa is primarily a landscape for exotic adventure.

In December 1941, the Japanese attacked the British colonies of Malaya (Malaysia), Burma and Hong Kong. In February 1942, having been victorious in these places, they moved on to Singapore, which was of critical strategic importance to the British, but which despite its reputation as 'Fortress Singapore' was poorly defended, and had been identified as such in frank British documents that had been intercepted by Germany and passed to the Japanese. There had been some anticipation of a Japanese invasion, and the existing significant imperial forces in these regions had been bolstered by troops sent from the metropole; a photograph from October 1941 held in the Imperial War Museum shows a pile of cheerful white British soldiers, sitting on top of their kitbags on board a troop ship, grinning and flicking V-signs at the camera.[41]

In early January 1942, around 2,800 men, women and children from across Hong Kong were imprisoned in the Stanley internment camp. One of these was Hilda Selwyn-Clarke, a socialist activist who had been nicknamed 'Red Hilda' because of both her hair colour and her supposed sympathies with the Chinese Communist Party; Hilda had arrived in Hong Kong in 1938 with her husband, Dr Selwyn Selwyn-Clarke, the new director of medical services for the colony. Hilda, alongside her husband, worked to try to address the problems of poverty, refugees (who arrived in great numbers fleeing the Japanese invasion of China), maternal and child health, and the provision of birth control.[42] Her socialist and anti-imperialist politics meant that she often actively went against the goals of the colonial administration, including refusing to leave Hong Kong in the general British evacuation of women and children, and so she was interned in Stanley for the remainder of the war. There was great concern in Britain about the prospects of the Stanley prisoners: one letter to the *Manchester Guardian* from a woman named Rose Hunt in Cambridge urged the editor to do what he could in trying to organise the repatriation of 'any civilian prisoners still surviving', and worrying that British citizens with family and friends imprisoned there were 'left for many months without news' or letters from Hong Kong.[43]

Many people within the British empire thus found that wartime was a moment of widened horizons: they travelled to or from

Britain for the first time, and their experience of conflict brought them into contact with allies and enemies from around the globe. But even those who spent the war at home had their worlds expanded. Throughout the conflict, most British people understood their own role in the fight within a much broader, imperial struggle.

In political speeches, on propaganda posters and in newspaper reports, the Conservative government of Winston Churchill and the monarch repeatedly underlined the contribution of the empire to Britain's war and the shared honour that was therefore its due. British values were explicitly presented as an alternative to fascist dictatorship for which British people, and their colonial subjects, were expected to make such great sacrifices. On Empire Day in 1940, the King made a speech that was broadcast by the BBC to the nation – and for which cinema programming was temporarily halted – as well as around the colonies. In it, he conceded that 'there is a word that our enemies use against us – Imperialism. By it they mean the spirit of domination, the lust of Conquest', but argued that instead 'Our one object has always been peace – peace in which our institutions may be developed, the condition of our peoples improved.'[44] In this way, British imperialism was cast not as a dominating, violent or illiberal force, but as its opposite, a virtuous resource in the fight against fascism.

In 1943, looking back at one of the bleakest moments of the war, Churchill framed the imperial contribution to the British war effort as one of sacrifice and fraternal honour: 'Three years ago . . . we stood alone . . . Then, surely, was the moment for the Empire to break up, for each of its widely dispersed communities to seek safety on the winning side, for those who thought themselves oppressed to throw off their yoke . . . but what happened? It was proved that the bonds which unite us, though supple and elastic, are stronger than the tensest steel.'[45] The idea that colonies could have simply chosen to join another empire rather than fight for Britain seems ludicrous, although there was certainly concern in the metropole that South Africa, for example, could be lured onto the Axis side.

(Indeed, there was a strong sympathy for Nazi Germany among the Afrikaner population during the 1930s and throughout the war, not just at a political level among figures like D. F. Malan – later the prime minister who oversaw apartheid – but also at a grassroots level, as seen in the arson attacks on the Jewish shops and businesses in the town of Oudtshoorn in 1940.)[46] But, of course, Churchill's speech was not a statement of facts about paths not taken, it was a piece of propaganda aimed at bolstering Britain's imperial identity in the post-war world and was reprinted in a booklet, 'What the Empire Has Done: Facts and Figures', for precisely that purpose.

Much of this work was done through the Ministry of Information (MOI), the propaganda department set up at the start of the war, which employed writers and broadcasters to create a unified message of British wartime values and to control the narrative around British war efforts. George Orwell, in his role at the BBC during the war, broadcast talks to India that had been approved by the MOI, while his wife was employed in its censorship department; he later used the ministry, and its Senate House headquarters, as the inspiration for the Ministry of Truth in *Nineteen Eighty-Four*.

One of the MOI's most famous creations, produced in August 1941, was the 'Together' poster, which showed seven members of the imperial armed forces – soldiers from West Africa, Britain (in a pith helmet), India, Australia and New Zealand, a Canadian airman, and a sailor in the Royal Navy – marching together under a fluttering Union Jack. Unsurprisingly, perhaps, the Indian and West African soldiers are pushed to the back of the poster, but the emphasis on joint contributions to the war effort and the creation of a shared Empire/Commonwealth identity under wartime was an important part of the government's attempt to build morale.

Another poster took the form of a map of the 'British Commonwealth of Nations'. This presented the empire not only geographically but also politically and economically. A key indicated the form of government deployed in each territory – India, for example, enjoyed 'almost complete self-government in provincial affairs' – and a table at the bottom showed the principal products of the various territories. With the exception of coal, the United Kingdom's were almost entirely finished consumer goods and industrial products: 'Textiles; Machinery; Iron and steel; Vehicles; Chemicals, drugs and dyes; Clothing; Electrical goods; Pottery and glass; Paper and cardboard; Furniture'. From West Africa, by contrast, there came exotic raw materials: 'Cocoa; Gold; Palm oil and kernels; Groundnuts; Tin; Manganese; Diamonds; Hides and skins; Iron ore; Kola; Timber: mahogany, walnut and ebony; Cotton'.[47] Yet another government poster had 'Your Planes and Your Work Defend Your Empire!' emblazoned in red across part of a front page from the *Star* newspaper which read 'HURRICANES FIGHT AT SINGAPORE: We Attack On The West'.[48] (Despite this, Singapore would fall to the Japanese forces at the end of the year.)

'Playing their Part', a booklet of photography decorated on the front cover with a waving Union flag, was produced by the MOI to illustrate to the British people the many and varied wartime contributions of colonial populations. A number of individuals are singled out for heroism and courage, such as Corporal Sefanaia Sukanaivalu, the first Fijian to be awarded the Victoria Cross for giving his life for his fellow comrades. A series of portraits by Honor Earle includes Flying Officer Dick Fairweather from British Honduras, Ordinary Seaman P. E. Biggs from the Falkland Islands, and Hezekiah Danial Gibbs, a Second Radio Officer from Gambia. There are also pictures showing colonial forces in skilled roles, such as members of the East African Pioneers making mechanical adjustments to a Bren-gun carrier's engine, and a section entitled 'Women Work for Victory' that showed nurses, munitions workers and electrical and mechanical engineers.[49] As well as justifying British imperialism by celebrating the role of imperial subjects in the fight against fascism, pamphlets like this also served to tether the British to their imperial identity and reassure them that might as well as right was on their side: as Fougasse's reclining soldier had it, all 800 million members of the imperial family were fighting together to defeat Hitler and Hirohito.

Children and young people were also on the receiving end not just of government propaganda about imperialism but through organisations such as the Boy Scouts and their schools and youth groups. The Empire Youth Movement had been established in 1937 by Major Frederick Ney, an eccentric Canadian and staunch imperialist, who had inaugurated the movement with an 800-strong rally he had organised in the Royal Albert Hall to mark the coronation of George VI. The Empire Youth Movement (renamed the Commonwealth Youth Movement in 1957 and still active into the 1960s) sought to build ideas of fraternal citizenship among young people around the empire, to strengthen the ties they felt to British imperialism, and to act as a bulwark against totalitarianism and communism. There seems to have been some official concern about the name of the organisation, with 'Empire', 'Youth' and 'Movement' all apparently controversial terms in the late 1930s. Ney wrote an enthusiastic, didactic pamphlet justifying the name, and his plans for the organisation: he wanted to 'inculcate a greater sense of personal responsibility' for the empire's future among young people while also building bonds of friendship between young people across the colonies and dominions.[50]

In the war, the movement took on another level of patriotic fervour. The Empire Youth Sundays became a particular focal point, and brought together young people, supposedly from across the empire – but mostly white communities from the dominions – and the United Kingdom. Empire Sunday also became a way to combine imperial pride with a show of civic wartime capability. One piece of amateur film from Nottingham in 1944 shows members of the Air Training Corps, both male and female, marching past a group of local dignitaries on Empire Youth Sunday before presenting their flags to be blessed by a vicar; captions remind the viewer that the cadet forces are 'the royal road to the Royal Air Force'.[51] This echoed events around the country, from Wigtownshire to Penzance, with young people participating in pageants, plays and other forms of communal imperial celebration.

Newspapers, novels, radio programmes, Christmas cards,

children's annuals: all tell a story about an imperial conflict. The top UK box-office attraction of 1942 was the film *Mrs Miniver*, which told the domestic story of a middle-class family in a small, white, rural community during the war, depicting their hope and grief and fear. World events intrude with the arrival of a German soldier and when the daughter is killed by stray machine-gun fire from a dog-fight between a Luftwaffe and RAF plane. Exceptionally, empire and the imperial people are entirely absent from the film. But *Mrs Miniver*, as popular as it was with British audiences, was actually an American film. Its depiction of steadfast British patriotism was intended to inspire American audiences to support the war effort; the idea of the British 'clinging to an empire from which Americans had mercifully escaped in 1776' would not have inspired much fellow-feeling or solidarity.[52]

Many fiction and non-fiction books published during the war tried to explore the future of imperialism in a world where – it was hoped – the British, the Allied forces and democracy would triumph. Some of these, such as the florid poetry of Cumberland Clark, were patriotic works that imagined British colonialism thriving in a new world.[53] Others were more circumspect about the empire's future. The Left Book Club, founded in 1936 as a subscription service by Victor Gollancz, published leading socialist luminaries such as Beatrice and Sydney Webb, G. D. H. Cole, and George Orwell, whose *Road to Wigan Pier* was originally published by the club. Its other offerings included Leonard Barnes's *Empire or Democracy* (1939), which explored 'the forcible subjecting to British rule of India, Ceylon, tropical Africa, the West Indies, and the rest of the so-called dependencies and mandated territories',[54] and John Burger's *The Black Man's Burden* (1943), which sought to explain how capitalism heightened the exploitation of the Black population in South Africa. Similarly, the Penguin Specials series published numerous titles concerned with empire during the war: Hugh J. Schonfield's *The Suez Canal* (1939), K. S. Shelvankar's *The Problem of India* (1940), W. K. Hancock's *Argument of Empire* (1943) and *Soviet Light on the Colonies* (1944) by Leonard Barnes (again). The British left-wing intelligentsia saw in imperial politics the opportunity to develop arguments and ideas about their own political future.

In a wartime nation that was concerned, more than anything, with how to repel outsiders, the question of who belonged on the inside became fraught. The official line was that Britain and its empire had never had a colour bar – that racial discrimination might unfortunately exist but it was not built into the system. This was a fiction. Throughout the 1930s, the LCP worked tirelessly to show how people of colour found themselves discriminated against in the workplace, in housing and in public spaces. During the war, the LCP also fought to highlight other civil rights issues, such as the persecution of Jews in Germany, and offered financial assistance to migrant families in Britain struggling to support themselves. But they maintained their focus as a campaign group dedicated to exposing the structural racism of British society and helping to advocate for those who found themselves its target. In 1944, the LCP held a conference and drew up a Charter for Coloured Peoples, which explicitly connected the experience of people of colour in Britain with those living around the empire: the Charter simultaneously called for an end to colonial exploitation overseas, with clear plans for economic development and independence for the colonies, and an end to racist discrimination and the colour bar at home.[55]

The polite fiction that Britain was a non-racist state was tested further after 1942 when the Americans entered the war and GI troops were stationed in Britain. The arrival of Black GIs forced British people to confront the realities of racism in new ways. Many were horrified at America's racial segregation, and there are many heart-warming tales of African American soldiers being welcomed into British shops, restaurants and homes (and, in the case of some people, their hearts). Anthony Burgess, who at that time worked as a lecturer at a teacher training college in Lancashire, recalled later that when the US military authorities had demanded that the local pubs impose a colour bar, one landlord had responded with a sign that said 'Out of Bounds to White Soldiers'.[56] Many Black GIs remembered their time in Britain fondly. Arthur Guest, serving in Britain in this time, described the relatively equal treatment he received by British people as a 'spark of light' compared to the segregation of the US.[57]

But as the LCP had already highlighted, people of colour in Britain did face significant prejudice. Some business owners preferred the promise of white American soldiers over potential Black customers and were happy to maintain an informal policy of segregation to ensure white custom. A white British soldier wrote to the *New Statesman*, indignant that 'part of a well-known restaurant' in one English port city was barred to African American troops by management, although the employees themselves felt uncomfortable with this restriction.[58] In the village of Worle, Weston-super-Mare, the vicar's wife prepared a six-point plan for white women to avoid fraternising with Black GIs, including not only a ban on inviting them into their homes, but also instructions to cross the pavement to avoid walking alongside Black men and leaving their place in a queue if a Black man entered the shop. This list made its way both to the Ministry of Information and the media; the *Sunday Pictorial* carried a scathing story about it in May 1942 with the headline 'Vicar's Wife Insults Our Allies', quoting one woman as saying 'I was disgusted, and so were most of the women there. We have no intention of agreeing to her decree.'[59] It was not always civilian authorities enacting this ban; in Birmingham, an African American member of the US Women's Army Auxiliary Corps had been welcomed into the town's Turkish baths, only for the US Army authorities to impose a ban on women of colour in her unit using these facilities, which the council felt unable to overturn.[60]

The British government was unwilling to be implicated in segregation policies, not least because of the number of people of colour from the Commonwealth among the British forces; Herbert Morrison, Labour MP and Home Secretary, would not allow British police to be used to uphold segregation for US troops, and there was a great deal of concern that the colonies might hear of 'colour bar' policies in the metropole and that this would undermine the war effort. But it is a myth that Churchill refused the Americans' request that Black soldiers be kept separate from white soldiers and civilians. British government policy was in fact that the Americans must be allowed to practise segregation on British soil, including mandating which British businesses could be visited by Black or white GIs; the Cabinet agreed that it was 'desirable that the people of this country should avoid becoming too friendly with coloured American troops' in order to avoid political problems among Allies.[61] And in reality, these policies were even allowed to affect British and colonial citizens. Learie Constantine, the celebrated West Indian cricketer who worked during the war for the Ministry of Labour and National Service advocating for the welfare of West Indians working in British factories, successfully sued the Imperial London Hotel management for refusing to let him and his family take up their booked rooms when he had travelled to London in 1943 to play a charity cricket match at Lord's.

At the end of the war, the LCP conducted a survey and found that around 550 babies had been born to white British mothers and Black GIs.[62] These women and their children often faced significant oppression from their communities and the state, both because of racism and because of prejudice against single mothers. Many were pressured to give their babies up, and their children often then struggled with racism in the care system; Jimmy Rogers, who grew up as the only Black child in a Newcastle children's home in the 1940s, described the experience as one only of 'survival'.[63] Learie Constantine was motivated by the plight of these children to try to build a home specifically to look after them, and for a time donated the profits of his cricket matches to the LCP for this purpose; Harold Moody himself met with British government officials to try to help these children overcome 'the double disability of colour and illegitimacy' in a British society that was far from progressive on questions of sex and race.[64] But the LCP was still trying to help these children years after the war had ended, to the extent that in 1951 it pursued the possibility of registering itself as an adoption agency; the existing services were insufficient, with one children's officer admitting that there was clearly a colour bar in the care system and that even white families who were willing to adopt Black children did so 'as a child would choose a quaint and unusual toy'.[65] That year LCP's newsletter carried a review of a play written by Hurford James, which presented an English farming family coming to terms with their daughter giving birth to a Black baby after a drunken tryst.[66] It was called *The Coloured Brat*.

In July 1945, when the war in Europe was over but before Allied victory in Japan, the people of Britain were asked to elect a new government. British soldiers were still stationed across the globe; in fact, those in the Far East were still fighting. The 2nd Battalion Durham Light Infantry broke from their ordinary wartime duties to hold a 'victory parade' for a war in Europe that was over while theirs in Rangoon was still very much alive. The parade took place in a monsoon and the soldier writing in the battalion's magazine recounted the men marching 'shivering, half-blinded by the rain, our boots full of water' past Louis Mountbatten and a local audience who were, at least, broadly appreciative.[67]

News footage from the time shows British soldiers across the empire engaging with the election. 'The men of South East Asia Command got their ration of electioneering like the rest of us,' begins one Pathé film from the end of July, as a shirtless army speaker in Burma is shown gesticulating wildly to a crowd of seated soldiers who eventually throw a bucket of water in his face. An army postman waylays soldiers as they lounge in doorways of huts, sleep in tents or peg washing on a line to dry, and hands them their voting forms which had been sent out to the forces by airmail. Soldiers vote in hastily assembled 'jungle polling booths', cloth tents that were 'more primitive' than those at home but 'secret nonetheless': a striking emphasis on British democratic processes surviving not just the war, but also the empire. One sergeant is shown casting his ballot – again shirtless – with an 'adviser', a monkey sitting on his shoulder;[68] the election is presented as an important, but relaxed and humorous, affair.

Some of those in the armed forces would not have quite agreed with this presentation. One twenty-two-year-old instrument repairer stationed with the air force in West Africa documented how the election had unfolded among his fellow airmen.[69] There had been a mock election scheduled as entertainment, which had hastily been cancelled and replaced with a quiz; the rumour was that one airman had insisted on 'standing' as a Communist candidate. The writer recorded many political arguments among the men in the Navy, Army and Air Force Institutes, 'tongues loosened' by the beer on sale. The air-force station included people from many different backgrounds – a Scottish miner who was a staunch socialist, a service policeman who had intended to vote Labour until his wife informed him that their candidate was Jewish, at which point he felt forced to switch his vote to the local Tory, a young MP who argued that socialism equated with 'mob rule'. Here the empire was a microcosm for political debates taking place at home.

The vote took three weeks to count, partly because many of the armed forces were spread around the globe. In the end it was a Labour landslide; despite some lingering affection for Churchill in many quarters, soldiers stationed around the empire and across Europe, as well as their families at home, voted for a new beginning. Mass Observation reported that the electorate was 'astonished and taken aback' by the news. Indeed, some Conservatives characterised it as akin to a Bolshevik victory, which would lead to violent revolution or the collapse of the economy; one ex-bank manager described it as a 'worse catastrophe than if we had lost the war'. Of course, some people felt that the promise of revolution was a good thing: one woman from Sevenoaks recorded that she had 'a sense of renewed hope for the future' and for a government that would pursue a socialist planned economy and a more progressive approach overseas.[70] After six years of war, many people had a somewhat more equivocal reaction; Edie Rutherford, a Mass Observation diarist, wrote simply that it was 'nice to have a Prime Minister whose wife does some housework and her own shopping'.[71]

At the end of the war, there was a great movement of armed

forces around the globe as armies demobilised and prisoner-of-war (POW) camps were emptied. British soldiers returned home, often from their first experience of being abroad. Many of these men had seen something of the empire: in North Africa, in Burma, Singapore or Malaya, or in Gibraltar or Malta. Colonial servicemen, many of whom had also been prisoners of war, were also gradually dispersed back to their home countries. Among them were the African troops captured by Axis forces at Tobruk and who had been POWs in Germany. These men had been treated extremely badly during their imprisonment, and before being returned to their homes in the colonies, they were flown to new camps in Britain to help them recover. As part of this rehabilitation, the men were taken on day trips to Arundel and Windsor, 'some of the great cathedral cities' and London landmarks like the Houses of Parliament and Westminster Abbey. The visits were intended to reaffirm and strengthen their colonial ties and thus ease these men back into a version of normality in which the empire was a beneficent force.[72]

Empire had indeed been central to the British war effort and, for the British masses, the war had brought empire into focus as never before, not only in debates about appeasement or propaganda about wartime spirit, but first-hand: as children evacuated to Canada or as soldiers fighting in North Africa and the Far East, as Jamaican women manning anti-aircraft guns or Honduran foresters working in the Scottish Highlands. The British found themselves confronted with different races but also with racism, with affirmations of nationality and challenges to identity, with the reality of the discrimination faced by people of colour in a conflict that was supposedly being fought to defend values of tolerance and humanitarianism. From London to Lagos, attitudes to empire had shifted. After six years of frightening conflict, people all around the empire attempted to return to normality in a world now completely changed and uncertain. Even for civilians who had spent the entire war at home, 1945 seemed to augur an unsettling and unpredictable future.

2

The People's Peace:
the Attlee Government, 1945–51

On 8 June 1946, a year after fighting in Europe had ended, Britain marked the recent memory of victory in the Second World War. In London, this day of celebrations consisted of a military parade of British, empire, Commonwealth and Allied forces, followed by a spectacular evening fireworks display in front of the Houses of Parliament, only somewhat marred by the heavy rain. There were events for children organised in London's parks throughout the day and every British schoolchild was sent a postcard with a message from the King, a list of major battles and a space to record 'My Family's War Record'.[1] Around the country, there were smaller local events, although many people chose to avoid the rather gloomy early summer (1946 saw some of the worst weather in living memory) and to stay at home and listen to the events on the radio, or if they were very lucky to watch them on television: the BBC restarted its television services after the war by broadcasting a two-hour report from the celebrations.

Colonial troops made up a significant part of these victory day events. Men and women from every country of the empire arrived on troop ships into Liverpool and Portsmouth and were accommodated in camps in Hyde Park, Regent's Park and Kensington Gardens. They were caught on film being visited by the colonial secretary and undersecretary, before a select group were taken for tea at the Colonial Office where they also met the prime minister, Clement Attlee. Other social events included a tour of London to see sights like the Victoria Memorial, Buckingham Palace and Big Ben, a day at the Epsom Derby, and a trip to Edinburgh, where the band of the King's African Rifles played music to a local crowd that included African students studying locally at the university. The actual parade saw the troops marching through London, arranged country by country, passing and saluting the royal family, Attlee and Churchill, as well as Mackenzie King of Canada and General Jan Smuts of South Africa. First came representatives of each British regiment, then most of the Allied nations, then the dominions and finally the long list of colonial territories. These began with the African troops, to celebrate their fighting record, with Malta – who had been awarded the George Cross as a nation to 'bear witness to the heroism and devotion of its people' in resisting sieges by Italy and Germany between 1940 and 1942 – in place of honour bringing up the rear.[2]

The crowds cheering in London, and those listening to and viewing the live broadcasts, could not help but be struck by the sheer number of different dominions and colonies represented by the men and women marching past the saluting base. *The Times* reported approvingly on this diversity, which it saw as indicative of the richness and beneficence of the empire: the troops, it argued, illustrated the 'many stages of civilization and independence, years of training, education and example' that existed under British colonial rule.[3] In staging such an event and including the imperial forces so prominently, the British government was seeking not only to celebrate the imperial contribution to the war effort, but also to cement the idea that the empire had been bound together by its wartime experience and to affirm its strength and continuity.

The election of the Attlee government is often cast as a moment of profound change in British political and social history. This Labour government is remembered for implementing the social reforms that had been proposed during the war by reformers such as William Beveridge, who wanted to eradicate the 'five giants' of want, ignorance, squalor, disease and idleness in the post-war peace. Most famously, this led to the creation of a National Health Service, credited primarily to the fiery Welsh health minister Aneurin Bevan, and which has been celebrated ever since as a particularly potent symbol of the benevolent British state. These totemic institutional changes tend to overshadow the imperial dimension of Attlee's time in power – even despite the fact that he presided over the end of empire in the Indian subcontinent. And yet the later 1940s was a period in which Britain was profoundly, innately bound up with imperial culture and politics: in its foreign policy, in its attitude to immigration and racism, and in the ways that it thought and spoke about and celebrated its own identity.

Perhaps one reason that empire is sometimes left out of this story is the assumption that the Labour Party were less invested in imperialism than their Conservative counterparts. A cartoon in the *Daily Mail* from 1948 shows two men, a Colonel Blimp-ish figure and a tweedy lefty man, deep in conversation. The former is interrogating the latter, either indignantly or indulgently asking, 'And what do you confounded socialists intend to use in place of "British Empire" – "Commonwealth Co-operative Society"?'[4] For many Conservatives, the election of the Labour Party was indeed a terrifying omen for the future of British imperial power. And it was true that many left-wing political activists in the early half of the twentieth century had been critical of the Boer War, imperial expansion and the labour conditions which supported imperial trade. Labour's platform of social and economic reform – the implementation of the welfare state, their proposals for nationalisation of key industries – combined with their reputation for anti-imperialism, led many social conservatives to worry for the future of the nation. Another cartoon, published in the *Evening News* in 1949, shows two elderly men at a gentlemen's club, with one saying to the other, 'Terrifying days, Caversham: Attlee in charge of the British Empire and babes-in-arms playing for England.'[5] Brian Close had recently been selected to play a test match against New Zealand at the tender age of eighteen; old England was slipping away.

The elderly men at Britain's gentlemen's clubs need not have been quite so concerned. Ultimately, Attlee's government would not oversee the end of British imperialism. It is plausible that the Second World War precipitated some imperial unrest – and the notion that colonial populations that had fought for Europe's freedom then turned their attention to their own, or alternatively were rewarded for their loyalty with independence granted by a generous and benevolent Britain, does make sense on paper. But the story did not unfold quite that easily. In fact, although the war definitely sped up decolonisation in some areas of the empire, such as India, other areas, such as the African colonies and the Caribbean, actually came more directly under British control. In other words, the British people did not experience this period exclusively as one of imperial decline; on the contrary, for some it led to increased exposure to empire and imperial peoples. And for many within the empire, they became much more intimately familiar with their imperial 'motherland'.

For many British people in the 1940s, not least the British government, the empire remained part of a reassuring continuum. The government had little sense that decolonisation was imminent, predicting only that some African colonies might attain self-government – not even independence – by the end of the century. Despite the rise of independence movements in many areas of the empire, British colonial policy operated as if the continued integrity of the empire was a given, at least for the foreseeable future.

In fact, while decolonisation swept through British Asia in the late 1940s, the West Indies and British Africa and other colonies dotted across the world not only remained firmly under the control of the metropole, but they also witnessed the implementation of various development schemes. In this sense, the Attlee government embraced imperialism in these regions. The East African Groundnut Scheme, a programme for growing peanuts in Tanganyika to provide fats and oils for the domestic consumer, was the headline project, but there were a large number of programmes that focused on 'developing' imperial economies through agricultural, industrial and infrastructural resources. Thanks to the influence of Colonial Secretary Arthur Creech Jones and his long-standing work with the Fabian Colonial Bureau, these projects also included some spending to improve health care and education among colonial populations;

the influence of the Labour government can be seen in the fact that they also promoted the expansion of trade unionism among imperial workforces.

British people followed the development schemes in the news and waited to see the fruits of the programmes in their rationing-deprived local shops. Many even lobbied their MPs in favour of them. In a House of Commons debate on overseas development, the MP Jean Mann used her time to praise the effect of the bill 'on the home and on the housewife', and spoke about women's frustration with being unable to use ingredients in sufficient quantities: 'one does get exasperated to read cookery recipes every week telling one just to "dot with margarine" when one knows that the whole week's ration is only a dot of margarine', she said ruefully.[6] The housewife was an important figure in the Groundnut Scheme – when the organisation Mass Observation polled the British people about their knowledge of the programme, they asked them specifically if they knew how the scheme 'would help the British housewife'.[7] A cartoon by the famous illustrator 'Giles' published in the *Daily Express* shows two colonial administrators sitting under a tree while colonial workers toil around them. One reports to the other that he has a letter from a lady in Cheltenham, who 'says in view of the fact that we're spending £25,000,000 of her taxes, can we let her have a few nuts for her cake'.[8] On second glance, the administrators are not surrounded by workers at all, but monkeys: the intention is no doubt to mock Labour's development schemes, but also the very idea that Africans are as capable as Europeans (or indeed any other human beings) and could be relied on as such.

The development schemes were sometimes successful – particularly when they were focused on responding to the needs of colonial populations on the ground and provided much needed social welfare resources such as primary schools and medical clinics – but were more famous for their failures, which abounded. The Groundnut Scheme in particular became a synonym for disastrous projects and was used to berate the Labour government for its commitment to socialist centralised planning. A book by the

British-Australian journalist Alan Wood, who had worked on the scheme, described it as 'a tragedy, with many elements of a tragi-comedy', a story of 'failure, frustration, heartbreak, bad luck and bad blunders'.[9] It was rumoured that the British government had tried to ban publication of the book, rumours which were not dispelled by the minister for food refusing to either confirm or deny the suggestion in Parliament.[10] The Groundnut Scheme became so infamous that it was mocked in 1950 in the Dan Dare comic strip that appeared in the children's magazine *The Eagle*. The cartoon is set forty-five years into an imagined future, and in this fictional 1995 a headline on a mock-up newspaper proudly proclaims 'Success in East Africa – Peanut Arrives in London' as a future Ministry of Food celebrates the harvest of one 'whole, unblemished peanut'.[11] Children perhaps would not have got the joke, but their parents would presumably have chuckled or rolled their eyes.

This work to make imperialism – or rather, what remained of it – more profitable was partly necessitated by the changes to the British empire wrought by the Attlee government. Britain lost a major producer of cooking fats and oils, alongside many other goods and products, with the independence of the Indian subcontinent. For many British people, this was a momentous psychological and emotional moment. The British Raj, with its dazzling lifestyle, adventure and glamour, was considered the jewel in Britain's imperial crown.

India's independence had been long in the making, but the war was undoubtedly a catalyst for its arrival. In 1942, Stafford Cripps, the Labour Party statesman, had travelled to India to try to whip up support for the war effort; as a quid pro quo, he was willing to offer elections and full dominion status after the war was won. Pathé news footage shows him strolling, smiling and holding his pipe, to meet with various Indian representatives on what the news announcer calls 'the most delicate mission in the history of the British Commonwealth'.[12] Cripps stands next to Jawaharlal Nehru – who would become India's first prime minister after independence – clutching a document file, and sits with Mahatma

Gandhi 'clad in his loincloth and shawl'.[13] The Cripps mission ultimately failed because the proposals had been satisfactory neither to the nationalist leaders representing the Hindu or Muslim populations in India who wanted full independence – Gandhi famously dismissed the promise of future dominion status for India as 'a post-dated cheque drawn on a failing bank' – nor to Winston Churchill, who was unwilling to oversee even this level of independence.

Indian forces continued to contribute to the war effort, with the notable exception of those radicals led by Subhas Chandra Bose, who preferred to ally with Nazi Germany against the imperialist British. But the idea that Britain would withdraw after the war was over had irrevocably taken hold. The Indian National Congress (INC), led by Nehru, moved to embrace the 'Quit India' movement after Gandhi gave a speech on 8 August 1942 calling for the 'orderly withdrawal' of the British. In response, the British government imprisoned most of the INC leadership and violently suppressed the strikes and demonstrations in support of independence that sprang up across the country. More than 100,000 people were arrested.

There was some support for the Quit India campaign in Britain – a rally was held at Conway Hall in London, for example – but there was also a great deal of resentment and criticism of the Indian independence movement for what was perceived as their lack of support for the war effort: one fifty-year-old man, interviewed for Mass Observation, described Gandhi as 'a double-crossing little bastard', and among those surveyed his arrest was found to be 'very popular', although one woman said she thought Gandhi might have become embittered towards the British because of the 'colour prejudice' he had doubtless encountered during his time in England.[14]

The British had initially wanted to create a single independent Indian state, both as a sentimental testament to their own legacy and as a formidable force in imperial defence in the region, but were forced to agree to partition after Jinnah, the leader of the Muslim League, refused to accept plans that would have seen Muslims remain a minority population in a newly independent nation. In

July 1946 Jinnah declared a 'Day of Action' on 16 August in support of a separate Muslim state. One British businessman who was in Calcutta during this event described for readers of the *Manchester Guardian* the 'fire, cruelty and murder' that he had witnessed during the riots in the city, which he believed were 'a vivid warning to India of the dangers which may arise from the politics of communalism'.[15] The British colonial administration agreed that partition was the only way forward and, together with the Muslim League and the Indian National Congress, drew up plans for independence along these lines. This policy would lead to the deaths of somewhere between 200,000 and 2 million people.

A film produced by British Pathé, *India Takes Over*, examined Indian independence for British audiences, showing the formal commemorative events in London interspersed with footage of Indian crowds and cities. The voice-over pronounced seriously that 'an era has ended, a new epoch begins', as a subcontinent 'larger than Europe' became two new nations.[16] The various men at the head of the new Pakistani and Indian governments were introduced, last among them Gandhi, 'the 78-year-old mystic' who stands 'inscrutable and aloof'. According to the film, the British 'gave India law and order, they built roads and railways, they irrigated the land'. It then warns its audience about the ongoing communal violence and the extent of poverty and starvation in India, but there is no hint that British imperial rule might have been in any way responsible for these things as well. The film ends by saying that Britain has 'fulfilled her mission' (how, if 7 million people a year die of famine?) and that it is now up to India (and Pakistan) to 'make her destiny'.

Many people in Britain accepted the necessity of Indian independence and were sympathetic to figures like Gandhi. The left-leaning *Manchester Guardian* and the *Observer* saw independence as a victory for progressive ideals, with the *Guardian* stating that the British had 'neither the desire nor ability to rule a people which had recovered the will to rule itself'.[17] But both papers, and their readers, also celebrated Indian independence as a victory for Britain and British values: 'Once more the strength and flexibility of the British

Constitution and British Commonwealth have been proved.'[18] In fact, British people could celebrate Indian independence while still holding profoundly imperialist attitudes to the rest of the empire; many contrasted the supposedly 'mature' Indian political class, for example, with the rest of the colonies which were judged to be as yet unprepared for self-government. And yet many Anglo-Indians, white British people who had lived or worked in India and had strong emotional ties to the subcontinent, were horrified by independence. A Mr Clifton H. Stephenson, of Bangalore, wrote to the independent MP John Anderson to decry British withdrawal as a 'shameful and disgraceful act of the blackest treachery and cowardice'.[19]

Independence and partition had led to the uprooting and migration of millions across the distant land of the Indian subcontinent. The following year, a change in British immigration law brought questions of empire home to the inhabitants of the United Kingdom, not as abstract concepts but in the bodies and lives of those imperial subjects who sought to make the metropole their home too. The British Nationality Act, which came into force on 1 January 1949, granted citizenship 'of the United Kingdom and Colonies' to anyone who had been born in Britain or a British colony. The act applied retrospectively and thus, in one fell swoop, almost every inhabitant of the British empire (or the former British empire, in the case of India, Pakistan and Sri Lanka) was formally granted the right to live and work in the United Kingdom with no further paperwork required. This effectively reaffirmed, codified and clarified existing rights within the empire, rather than fundamentally introducing any new rights. The act was passed in response to the Canadian government establishing its own citizenship in 1946 and amid concerns that other dominions would follow suit, and was intended to maintain a sense of unity among the empire and new Commonwealth.

One clause of the British Nationality Act also granted British women the right to retain their citizenship on marriage to a non-British person; prior to this, they were effectively stripped of their British citizenship and forced to take their husband's. This change in the law meant that when Peggy Cripps, daughter of Sir Stafford, married Joe Appiah, an activist for Ghanaian independence, she remained British. The two met at a student dance in 1951 – Peggy was working as a secretary for the organisation Racial Unity while Joe, who had sailed to Britain in 1943 to study law, was the president of the West African Students Union, established in 1925 to advocate for the welfare of West African students in London and for progress in their colonies of origin. The couple married in 1953, moving to Ghana the following year where they raised their four children; they remained a subject of fascination for newspapers such as the *Daily Mail*, with their family life often being narrated in the society pages. One story, reporting on Peggy's return to England in 1957 for an extended trip, quoted her saying that she had 'not a single' regret about her 'mixed marriage' in which she and her husband were 'very, very happy'; the *Mail* reporter commented approvingly on her two 'charming' and 'advanced' children with their 'light *café-au-lait*' skin, their 'soft, brown-black hair' and their 'European' features.[20]

The British Nationality Act was an important milestone in British and imperial identity. But as the stories of people like Joe Appiah demonstrate, the Act did not create migration from the empire to the metropole. In fact, it was mostly the context of the end of the war that saw migration increase, rather than the passing of the Act itself. The most famous group of immigrants in this period are undoubtedly the passengers on board the *Empire Windrush*, which arrived at Tilbury Docks in Essex from Jamaica in June 1948, a month before the British Nationality Act received its royal assent. The ship had initially been a German passenger liner, the *Monte Rosa*, and was used during the war as a troop ship. At the end of the fighting, the ship was claimed by the British government as spoils of war, was renamed *Empire Windrush*, and was operated by the New Zealand Shipping Company, for the British government, on the Southampton–Gibraltar–Suez–Aden–Colombo–Singapore–Hong Kong line; a route that connected a major British imperial port with a European empire outpost, a major piece of imperial infrastructure, British interests in the Middle East and British trading posts in its Eastern empire. A more imperial shipping line is hard to picture.

But the ship's most famous journey did not follow this route. Instead, in 1948, it was used to expatriate the last remaining Caribbean servicemen from Britain back to their home islands.[21] For its return to the metropole, it exchanged them for 1,027 people, most of them giving a Caribbean country as their last place of residence. Among the passengers, 292 were female, and 45 were aged thirteen or under, children travelling with family members. The youngest passenger, Richard Carton, was just five months old; the oldest, Gertrude Whitelaw, was eighty. As well as those coming from the Caribbean and Bermuda, there was a group of Polish refugees who had been living in Mexico and had been granted British citizenship, along with various British citizens returning home after work, travel or military service, including the author Nancy Cunard. Some of the men on board the *Windrush* had in fact served in Britain during the war and were returning to a country they already knew. After Kingston, the ship docked at Trinidad, Bermuda and Tampico before sailing for England. Local Caribbean papers had advertised the vacant berths on the ship at £28 per person.

The original landing cards from the *Empire Windrush* were destroyed by the Home Office in 2010. But the passenger list remains and has allowed researchers to reconstruct the cards and show all the individual stories of people who arrived in Essex in June 1948.[22] So there were Stella and Joseph Dugdale, a married couple aged thirty-one and twenty-nine, she a domestic servant and he a planter, who boarded in Trinidad; Diana and Phyllis Cort, aged twenty and twenty-nine, presumably sisters, who boarded in Bermuda and were both working as actresses; Emilia Le Wars, a thirty-year-old secretary, who got on the ship in Kingston with her two-year-old daughter Rosemary. Winston Levy and his brother also boarded the ship in Kingston; Winston bought a postcard showing the *Empire*

Windrush in all its glory and carefully recorded the length and width of the ship on the back, along with the time and date that they set sail. These postcards seem to have been popular souvenirs, and so there are copies today in many second-hand bookshops as well as family collections – such as that of the author Andrea Levy, who was Winston's daughter and who shared her father's postcard with the British Library for their Windrush exhibition in 2018.

The *Empire Windrush* was received in Britain to great fanfare. The famous front page of the London newspaper the *Evening Standard* proclaimed 'Welcome Home!' above a picture of the arriving ship, taken using the paper's own plane, the deck thronged with people (although it should be noted that the main headline of the day was 'Meat: Last Reserves', reflecting domestic concerns about food shortages and the continued privations of rationing). The *Daily Worker* was among many newspapers covering the event. One article drew attention to the number of Jamaicans on board, focusing on the 'five hundred pairs of willing hands [that] grasped the rails of the Empire Windrush' as it came in to land at Tilbury; its point was that these people were in Britain to work, and their emigration was blamed on unemployment and low wages in the Caribbean.[23]

The *Guardian*'s reporter found it 'curiously touching' to see the new arrivals – wrongly presented as being entirely from Jamaica and Trinidad – whom he described as a sea of 'dark, pensive faces'. His piece split the men into three groups: 204 had friends and jobs already to go to and were sent on their way with a ten-shilling travel loan; 52 had fought in the war and wanted to rejoin the army, and were connected with recruiting officers; and 236 were 'friendless and jobless', and were sent to London to await placement. The journalist speculated about whether these men thought of England as a 'golden land in a golden age', but dismissed such beliefs, if they existed, as a 'quaint amalgam of American optimism and African innocence'.[24]

John Smythe, a Sierra Leonean man working in the Colonial Office Welfare Department who had been on the crossing himself, had told the passengers that he could not 'honestly paint' a 'very rosy picture' of life in Britain, and that they would need to work hard, in any job that they were offered, and try to 'win the respect' of the British people they met.[25] Ivor Cummings, a civil servant with ancestry from Sierra Leone who had become the first Black official working in the Colonial Office during the war, greeted the arrivals in the port; he likewise told those who arrived with no particular plans for accommodation or employment that they would probably encounter 'many difficulties'.[26] The *Windrush* passengers from the West Indies had as much right to be in Britain as the citizens who had been born there. Given that the country was currently hosting workers from across Europe, such as the Poles who had been displaced and could not return to their home country, it is hard to read this resistance to the presence of the Caribbean workers as anything other than racism. As one man asked, 'Surely, then, there is nothing against us coming, for we are British subjects. If there is, is it because we are coloured?'

Two weeks later, the *Daily Worker* journalist Peter Fryer – later a prominent historian of Black British culture – wrote a follow-up story, headlined 'The Men from Jamaica are Settling Down', focusing on the 236 'friendless and jobless' arrivals who had been sent to south London to be found employment. Despite the fact that they comprised a minority even of the West Indians on board the ship, this particular group of immigrants were evidently considered the most interesting to readers. Their experiences over their first few days in Clapham, where they had been living in a deep-level shelter at Clapham South Tube station, first constructed for Londoners to use during the Blitz, were examined mostly through the lens of work. Fryer reported happily that of the 240 [*sic*] who had asked the Colonial Office to find them employment, only thirty were still without jobs, while the rest were working as welders, farm labourers, electricians, railwaymen, plumbers or in clerical positions.[27] He also considered to what extent the challenges these men faced were made worse by racism. A white British man from the Ministry of Labour was quoted, saying he had 'travelled about the world too much' to hold with a colour bar; Fryer contrasted this with the report of one of the men, Mr Festus J. Fairweather, that 'a cafe proprietor here, a landlady there' might have expressed 'colour prejudice'. Fryer also described how two men who had reserved rooms by phone had been told on arrival that there had been a mistake and the lodgings were full. Generally speaking, the men of *Windrush* were presented as content: Fairweather had 'had a few difficulties', he admitted, but he and his friends would 'hold on until we settle'. It seems that Fairweather's 'broad smile' did a lot to reassure Fryer that this was an expression of optimism rather than a grim assessment of the resilience needed in the face of hardship and prejudice.

The arrival of the *Empire Windrush* has since become an iconic event in the history of post-war British migration. As early as 1953, the sociologist Michael Banton described the ship as emblematic of a wave of 'recent migration', which had apparently brought 492 people, 'mostly Jamaicans', to Britain from the West Indies.[28] On the fiftieth anniversary of the ship docking at Tilbury, the historian Stuart Hall described its 'human cargo' (an unmistakable reference to the forced migration of entrapped and enslaved Africans in a previous era) as being 'Britain's first post-war Caribbean migrants'.[29] For many Black British people, *Windrush* has become significant as a moment when their presence was finally felt and acknowledged in the metropole. More broadly, its arrival has come to be seen as a watershed denoting the beginning of a new multiculturalism.

In fact, most of the passengers on the *Empire Windrush* were not men from the West Indies, nor was it even the first ship to arrive in Britain after the war carrying migrants from the Caribbean. Two ships, the *Almanzora* and the *Ormonde*, had arrived in Britain in 1947 carrying smaller numbers of migrants from the region, docking in Southampton and Liverpool respectively. Their arrivals went largely unnoticed at the time, and have been largely uncelebrated since.[30] People like Allan Wilmot, who arrived from Jamaica on the *Almanzora* on a freezing December day and worked washing dishes in a Lyons Corner House before achieving musical success as part of the Southlanders, are instead remembered as part of the 'Windrush

Generation'.[31] In this way, *Windrush* has come to represent the post-war Black migrant experience, and to some extent migration more generally. In 1998, on the fiftieth anniversary of the ship's arrival at Tilbury, the public space in Brixton known first as the Brixton Oval and then the Tate Gardens was renamed 'Windrush Square'; it is now the site of both the Black Cultural Archives and the African and Caribbean War Memorial, erected in 2017 to commemorate the contribution made by people from these regions in the First and Second World War (itself a testament to the presence of Black migrants to Britain pre-*Windrush*).

What all of this iconography and memorialisation can obscure are the hundreds of individual stories of migration. Sam King first came to Britain during the war to work as an aircraft fitter for the RAF at a base in Folkestone. He came back on the *Empire Windrush* aged twenty-two as a carpenter, looking for work. Sam was 'glad when his foot touched England' for the second time and settled into life in Britain quickly; he sent for his two brothers a couple of years after he arrived and they became only the second Black family to buy a house in Camberwell. He rejoined the RAF, then worked for Royal Mail, while becoming gradually more active in London politics and community organising. In the early 1980s he was elected the Mayor of Southwark, at the time the only Black mayor in London. Looking back at his life in an oral history interview for the Imperial War Museum, Sam said that, fundamentally, the 'establishment did not want us here' and that the British still did not realise they had lost the empire, but he was, overall, 'proud to be British'; migration to the metropole had given his children and especially his grandchildren far more opportunities than if he had stayed in Jamaica.[32]

And, of course, the West Indies were not the only colonies sending people of colour to the 'motherland' to build new lives. Gilli Salvat was one of many people who came to Britain with their families from India and Pakistan in the aftermath of the bloody violence of partition. She remembered standing at the rail of the boat and watching India 'getting smaller and smaller' as they sailed towards her new home. Her family docked at Tilbury, too, on a grey and drizzly day in 1948, and were quickly housed in an 'immigrant camp' in the basement of a church near Selfridges. Here, she slept on an iron camp bed and was policed by white British 'warders' who separated families, keeping men in one space, women and children in another. People were so unused to seeing Indian families that they would stop on Oxford Street to stare and point.[33]

There are countless personal testimonies like this, of migrants who came from Asia, Africa and the Caribbean to Britain in the years after the war, and many of them are positive: they recount lives well lived, communities established, the pursuit of love and families and the putting down of roots. But for others, this process was difficult and jarring. Britain had been a multiracial nation for a long time, with African, Asian and Caribbean people living in small communities around the country since the nineteenth century, particularly in London. But in the 1940s, 50s and 60s, Britain became truly multicultural as never before. While many white British people embraced these changes, many others reacted with anxiety, fear and even violence.

On the day that the *Empire Windrush* docked at Tilbury, eleven Labour MPs wrote to the prime minister to express their concern at a possible influx of new West Indian migrants to Britain. Attlee pointed out that 'British subjects, whether of Dominion or Colonial origin (and of whatever race or colour), should be freely admissible to the United Kingdom', that limiting this migration would lead to an outcry in the colonies, especially when the metropole clearly needed a workforce, and that it would be 'a great mistake to regard these people as undesirable or unemployables'. Besides, he reassured them, he did not predict any further 'large influx' of migrants from the region in the future.[34]

Nonetheless, the Attlee government evidently shared some of these eleven MPs' concerns because it commissioned researchers to track and monitor colonial immigrant communities. One report, produced for the Labour Party's committee on imperial questions by the anthropologist Kenneth Little, examined the experience of people of colour in Britain in 1948. Little, a white man, had written his PhD thesis, at LSE, on the community of people of colour living in Cardiff in the 1940s.[35] Little's memorandum for the Colonial Office on 'the colour problem in Britain and its treatment' bluntly stated that 'generally speaking, the darker his or her complexion, the more likely the individual stated is to face difficulties.', and highlighted that, for example, 'it is generally much more difficult for a person of colour to obtain lodgings or accommodation in a boarding, lodging house or hotel than a white person', and that they could also be effectively barred from dance halls, cafes, restaurants and pubs.[36]

This was corroborated by a report produced by Derek Bamuta, a social work student from Uganda who was staying in the East End and volunteering at the Bethnal Green Family Welfare Association as part of his training. Bamuta detailed the living conditions of three groups of colonial migrant men – Indians, West Indians and Africans – who mostly came to live in Stepney via employment on the ships and docks of the East End. He explored their social lives, which revolved around cafes and the cinema, as well as pubs and dance halls, and their living conditions, which were extremely poor, with the African community in particular mostly living in bombed-out housing. His report also detailed the risk to these men from white men looking for male sexual partners, and from 'promiscuous' white women, many of whom, he believed, travelled from Cardiff, Liverpool, Manchester and Newcastle with the express intention of preying on these communities for money and sex (though he conceded that there were also a number of happy partnerships between white women and men of colour). Like Little, the main problem he identified was a tacit, informal but unquestionably real colour bar, which he argued was largely caused by the violent reactions of white men to relationships between white women and men of colour, as well as from the very poor social and welfare services available to these men, which prevented them from integrating into British society and pushed them into unhealthy habits.[37]

Bamuta's report was forwarded to the government by a magistrate who had been convinced by its findings, ultimately reaching the desk of the prime minister, who then passed it to the Colonial

Office.[38] Arthur Creech Jones, the Colonial Secretary, wrote back to confirm that the report seemed accurate and that it also reflected conditions in cities such as Liverpool and Cardiff. However, he was fundamentally opposed to setting up any formal social welfare support for these communities, preferring to rely on voluntary services, not because he felt that the voluntary services would necessarily do a better job but because 'if special efforts are to be made on behalf of colonial people . . . more stowaways may be encouraged to come here from the West Indies and West Africa'. This would be a problem, apparently, because 'experience shows that many of these people are virtually unemployable in this country and are the source of a good deal of racial friction'. This position seems to clash with the conclusions of Bamuta's report, which showed that most of these men were in work – although it was often badly paid and precarious – as well as showing very little concern for the fact that these migrants had the right to live and work in the metropole, as Bamuta had pointed out, and that their welfare was in fact the concern of the British government. The fact that these questions on migration were of particular interest to committees on imperial questions and the Colonial Office also shows the extent to which these communities were still perceived as a colonial, not domestic, problem.

The Home Office, too, was cautiously monitoring the new colonial immigrant population, watching uneasily for any sign of law-breaking and in particular crimes connected to sex and drugs. The Home Office Drug Branch in November 1948 produced a short memo on the import of 'Indian Hemp' (cannabis) to the United Kingdom, in which they concluded with relief that it was only 'Negroes, Indians and Arabs' who indulged in the drug and that it had not yet spread to white men or women.[39] This was building on an earlier report which explained that more cannabis was being seized at British ports partly because the customs officers had undergone special training: 'until these officers were shown samples of the various Dangerous Drugs, including Indian Hemp in its various forms, many of them were unaware of the nature of these innocent-looking "dried herbs" ... this loophole is now closed'. The report, and the police and customs officials, explicitly connected the presence of the drug with the arrival of Indian and West Indian seamen on boats from African ports. In two cases, white British men 'of a "Bohemian" character' had also been involved in the arrival of the contraband but the authorities decided that 'the two cases involving white men can be discounted' as 'they were of a type that dabbles with the fringes of exotic vice and had the misfortune to be caught out'.[40]

These panics about drugs and sex, connected with wider concerns about competition for jobs and housing, were a constant theme of anti-immigration racism among British people in the 1940s and 50s. Sometimes this sentiment exploded into violence. Docks had long been sites of moral and social anxiety because of their multicultural communities, their association with physical masculinity and their role as entry point to the country for potentially undesirable elements. In 1919, widespread violence aimed mostly at so-called 'coloured seamen' had seriously disrupted dockside areas in Cardiff, Glasgow, South Shields, Hull, Newport, London and Liverpool, with white rioters terrorising the Black and Asian communities in these cities, blaming them for the high level of unemployment after the Great War. Two decades later, there were around 8,000 people of colour living in Liverpool, many employed to work on the ships or on shore; this was one of the largest and oldest Black communities in the country. Rather than supporting these workers, the local branch of the National Union of Seamen tried to implement a colour bar to ensure that white dockers were given jobs instead of their Black neighbours; there was an enormous amount of hostility to the Black workforce, both because of the very high levels of unemployment generally in the city, but also because the Black community were often assumed to be 'stowaways' who had arrived in the country illegally but who were, after a short stay in prison, allowed to remain in the country to live and work.

On the evening 31 July 1948, at around 10 p.m., a crowd of roughly three hundred white people gathered outside an Indian cafe known for hosting Black men and their white female partners. When some- body threw a stone through the window, Michael Lasese, a ship's fireman described later by the *Daily Mirror* as 'a West African of huge build' and in other racialised terms, was prompted to leave the cafe and confront the mob.[41] When the police arrived, they restrained Lasese, who still managed to stab two of the rioters as the police removed him from the crowd. The next night, white rioters massed around a Black seamen's hostel, Colsea House; again, police responded by arresting Black residents from the hostel rather than making any particular effort to disperse the mob.[42] On the third and final night, the rioters targeted a social club, Wilkie's, in which a number of Black patrons had barricaded themselves. In their reporting, the newspa- pers chose to emphasise Black rather than white violence, breathlessly recounting that the Black men were armed with 'bottles, stones, swords, daggers, iron coshes and axes';[43] despite the apparent pres- ence of this alarming arsenal, the real violence occurred when the police arrived, dispersed the white mob, and broke into the club to have running battles with those inside. Overall, fifty-one people were arrested, forty-three of whom were Black; Michael Lasese, who was frequently described as the instigator of the riots even though he had clearly been acting defensively once the white mob had already assembled, was sentenced to fifteen months in prison.[44]

The relationship between the Black community in Liverpool and the police had irretrievably broken down. Black residents were moved to form the Colonial Defence Committee. Initially it raised money, with the support of the League of Coloured People and the Pan-African Federation, to pay for the defence of those arrested in the riots. Later it became an important rallying point for racial just- ice in the city.[45] The name of the committee spoke volumes: the Black community of Liverpool saw their treatment in the metro- pole as analogous to, if not a continuation of, the treatment they and their ancestors had been subjected to in the colonies from which they had migrated.

★

For some British people, empire was much easier to forget. A Mass Observation questionnaire conducted in 1948 on behalf of the Colonial Office seems on the surface to show a real lack of engagement with imperial matters among the populace. Only 25 per cent knew the difference between a colony and a dominion; almost a quarter of those surveyed believed the population of the colonies to be mostly white; only 49 per cent of those polled could name even a single British colony.[46] The *Daily Mail* reported with astonishment that among the places named by respondents as current British colonies were Wales, Scotland, Northern Ireland and even Lincolnshire.[47]

In truth this was a time of great change at home and in the empire so it is not entirely surprising that the British people found it difficult to keep up with the differences between a protectorate, a dominion and a colony. In recognition of the challenge, those analysing the survey introduced a new category, 'dubious answers', precisely because 'the exact status of countries like Palestine and Newfoundland is clear only to the expert in colonial affairs'. 'India' and 'Ceylon', which had until very recently been colonies, were allowed in this category – although so too was 'Africa', which seems like a rather different category error. In other respects, the survey found a reasonably good level of general knowledge about colonial affairs – 67 per cent of people, for example, had heard of the (doomed) Groundnut Scheme, 67 per cent 'knew' that colonial people had a lower standard of living than the British and 66 per cent 'knew' that the British were 'teaching native Colonial peoples to govern themselves'. In contrast, 3 per cent of people believed that America was still a British colony.[48]

More interesting perhaps than the knowledge (or lack of it) revealed by these questionnaires are the attitudes and opinions they solicited. Nineteen per cent of people thought that Britain had 'tended to be rather selfish in the past' towards the colonies, although a far greater number – 70 per cent – believed that regardless Britain was doing 'a better job' in 1948. Seventy-nine per cent of people believed that Britain would be worse off without the colonies; just over half felt in some way responsible for the governing of the colonies and their people. Strikingly, this feeling was weaker among those older than sixty, the group who had lived with the empire longest and who had been most present during its acquisition; perhaps this generation felt more disillusioned by events such as Indian independence, or perhaps empire was such an accepted fact of life that they gave very little thought to their own responsibility for maintaining it.

Despite the relatively nuanced responses to this questionnaire and the broad support expressed by the British people for Britain's colonial policy, the establishment felt the need to educate them on colonial affairs in this new post-war world. Between 21 June and 20 July 1949, a government-sponsored Colonial Exhibition was held at Oxford Street Hall in London. The festival was supposed to 'spread the spirit of co-operation and mutual understanding', while also providing entertainment and exotic spectacle. Visitors entered the hall through a mock-up of the 'temperature and oppressive greenery of a West African forest', and were able to see a 'modern African dwelling house', before being presented with a series of artefacts exploring the colonial lands and their peoples.[49] 'Colonial Month' was officially opened by the King, who visited the Colonial Exhibition and spoke of the 'splendid contribution' made by the Commonwealth to the British war effort, and welcomed visitors to Britain from the colonies 'who come here to study or for business or recreation'; he expressed his 'great pleasure' that the British would have the chance to learn more about their 'fellow-citizens' around the empire.[50] Boy Scouts from the across the colonies lined the halls as the royals perused the exhibits, and Queen Elizabeth, the King's wife, was presented with a bunch of flowers by an adorable four-and-a-half-year-old, Shahidah, whose family were from Malaya.[51]

The Colonial Exhibition was part of a 'colonial month' of activities offering people in Britain opportunities to engage with colonial culture and find out more about the empire's history and contemporary identity. Due to the limits of the British economy, Arthur Creech Jones explained to MPs that 'Museums, art galleries, missionary societies, and other institutions, including the Colonial Government offices in London, have been invited to stage on their own premises and at their own expense displays of Colonial interest.'[52] The Public Records Office museum displayed a series of government documents pertaining to imperial history, including a letter from David Livingstone reporting the 'discovery' of Lake Nyinyesi and an illustrated chart from one of the voyages made by Captain James Cook. The Victoria and Albert Museum put on an exhibition featuring eighteenth- and nineteenth-century colonial 'scenes and views'.[53] Visitors to London Zoo could see colonial animals specially 'featured', and the zoo was lucky to receive a gift of nine gentoo penguins from the government of the Falkland Islands at the beginning of the month; *The Times* reported that the birds appeared 'in excellent condition' and would be displayed in Three Island Pond.[54] Kew Gardens held a special display of plants and animals from the empire in its museum. The Boy Scouts and Girl Guides and various British missionary headquarters held exhibitions of colonial films, and the Royal United Services Institute displayed uniforms and other ephemera from colonial military forces.[55] The BBC radio programme *Art of the Colonies* described a variety of colonial artefacts held by museums and private collectors in Britain, such as those that had been rounded up and showcased by the Royal Anthropological Institute for 'Colonial Month'; unfortunately the art critic Wyndham Lewis had already judged the exhibition to have included 'very few things of artistic, as opposed to anthropological, interest'.[56]

He was not the only one to have reservations about the initiative. Mr H. Winston Greenwood wrote to the *Manchester Guardian* to object to its being too London-centric, despairing for 'the remaining three-quarters of the population of this country' who could not get to the capital to participate, 'as is usually the case in such matters'. In Stockport, the local savings committee decided to respond to the same perceived bias by mounting their own exhibition the next autumn to educate 'people in the provinces' about the 'ways of life and culture in the Commonwealth'.[57] In fact, there had been touring exhibitions sent around the country, although much of the effort in the provinces had been focused on encouraging shops to showcase colonial products among their wares.[58]

Milton Brown, a Nigerian man living in the United Kingdom, visited the exhibition at Oxford Street Hall and was so concerned by its contents that he wrote a piece for the *Daily Worker*, 'An African at the Colonial Exhibition', in order to dispel the falsehoods and inconsistencies he had encountered there. He objected most fundamentally to the title of the exhibition, 'Focus on Colonial Progress', a framing that impoverished colonial populations would not recognise as reflective of their experience of empire. He also felt that the spectacle of the 'jungle' entrance was exoticising and tawdry.[59] A writer for *Corona*, the magazine produced for colonial service employees, criticised these same aspects of the exhibition, particularly objecting to the depiction of a Masai warrior as 'crude and barbaric'.[60] However, the detractors were in the minority. Even the notably left-wing *Manchester Guardian* commended the 'Colonial Month' initiative as an 'excellent idea', given the 'gross ignorance' among the British population of colonial affairs and the 'manifold civilising tasks' that Britain was apparently undertaking around its empire.

About a quarter of a million people visited the Colonial Exhibition in its first month, a record for events held on the site, and it was decided to keep it running for longer.[61] However, it is undeniable that Colonial Month represented a far smaller enterprise than past imperial exhibitions, such as those held at Crystal Palace in 1851 and at the specially built Wembley Stadium in 1924. In 1951, on the centenary of that first imperial exhibition, the Labour government chose instead to hold a Festival of Britain, focusing on the 'autobiography' of the British, 'not of one city but of the whole nation'.[62] This was, distinctly, a domestic festival, with very little discussion of the empire-commonwealth or of colonial populations around the world, focusing instead on celebrating the arts, culture, science and industry of Britain at home.

As well as the central site on London's South Bank, where the Royal Festival Hall had been built and opened just before the festival started, there were arts events hosted in Aberdeen, Belfast,

Liverpool, St Davids, Dumfries, Brighton, Llangollen, Aldeburgh and Bath as well as many other communities across Britain. In London, there was the 'Dome of Discovery', which did cover the explorations of Francis Drake and Captain Cook but concentrated especially on scientific advancement, including 'electric power, radio and television, nuclear energy, plastics and synthetic drugs'. There was also a series of pavilions celebrating both 'the land' and 'the people' of the British Isles: among these, the 'Natural Scene' explored British wildlife, 'Country' examined how the British had shaped their landscape through agriculture, 'Power and Production' focused on 'the conquest of power' and the development of British industry, 'Homes and Gardens' showcased contemporary design in British domestic spaces, and 'The Lion and the Unicorn' explored 'the leading ideas, beliefs, traditions and eccentricities' of the British people; this last pavilion was curated by the author Laurie Lee and sought to convey the 'indefinable character' of the British through such characteristics as their sense of humour and their 'instinct for liberty'.[63]

And yet, despite its self-consciously domestic focus – and the reluctance of the Commonwealth, particularly the new governments of India, Pakistan and Sri Lanka, to participate in a festival so clearly focusing on *British* achievements and successes – empire still appeared in places. There was a focus on British prowess in science and technology that could not help but foreground empire; exhibitions that explored advances in tropical medicine, for example, or pictured the networks of telegraph cables that spanned the Commonwealth.[64] In addition, there was a 'Festival Ship', the *Campania*, which travelled around ports in the United Kingdom showcasing 'how closely our history, our achievement, and our destiny are linked with the sea', presenting this aspect of Britain's past through an unavoidably imperial lens.[65] The 1951 festival might have been intended to present British national identity, history and culture without the international context that had been so integral to previous festivals, but that, it turned out, was impossible for a nation still fundamentally construed and constructed through its empire.

3

Never Had It So Good? Britain in the 1950s

In 1956, the government produced and sold to the British public a glossy booklet that promised 'one hundred pictures to tell the story of 80,000,000 people'. Imperial peoples were captured in photographs and their lives and experiences presented for the interested domestic reader that was assumed to have little practical experience of the empire and its population. The pictures were wide-ranging, depicting people and places from across the different colonial territories, such as Cyprus, Malta and Gibraltar as well as those further afield. These included the 'remote tribesmen' of the 'pagan tribes' of Jos and their mud huts, workers on an ox-drawn cart on a sugar plantation in St Kitts, and Bajau horsemen in North Borneo in their ornate ceremonial clothing. Also included were the 'Hell's Gate' steel drum band playing at a bank holiday picnic in Antigua, the bustling commercial centre of Hong Kong, and a crowd of people – Black Africans on the left, white British settlers on the right – greeting the first train to arrive in Mityana on the newly extended Kenya–Uganda railway. Huge, modern oil refineries in Trinidad and a Black barrister in court on the Gold Coast were shown alongside a woman stooping to plant rice seedlings by hand in a paddy field in Malaya and a smiling leper in Zanzibar. Everywhere the old and the new were juxtaposed, and the 'new' was firmly associated with British colonial progress. British readers could flick through these pictures and feel pride in their nation's colonial adventures.

The booklet displayed the colonial people as part of a giant, sprawling imperial family, which were diverse in terms of language, skin colour – 'black, yellow, white or brown' – and the daily lives of their inhabitants. The colonies are shown as united mostly in their experience of exotic inferiority: 'nearly all are tropical, nearly all agricultural, nearly all struggling with a hostile environment, and nearly all poor – though the warmth of the sun eases the rigour of their poverty'.[1] Considering it was the British empire that might reasonably be felt responsible for this poverty, the booklet presents empire in a remarkably positive light, as 'a great and hopeful experiment in human organization'. The reason for this becomes apparent in its discussion of plans for decolonisation. While some colonies are 'very near' to independence, others are apparently too unprepared, too immature to be allowed to break away. Until 'their people are ready, when their leaders are skilled enough in the art of democratic government', Britain would be forced to continue their administration of these colonies. 'Great Britain can draw on social and political experience acquired in two thousand years of history. It would be a tragedy if a too hasty demand for independence should rob the Colonial Peoples of the benefits of that experience.'

Britain, in other words, was in the imperialism racket after the Second World War not for personal gain but from a sense of profound benevolent responsibility. The fact that the colonies themselves also had two thousand or more years of history on which to draw – the vast majority of which had been experienced free from British rule, benevolent or otherwise – does not seem to have occurred to the authors.

By the end of 1956, such pretences would be harder if not impossible to maintain. The year would be remembered not as one of imperial family connections but when the empire was shaken to its core by the bungling of the Suez Crisis.

Ever since, the 1950s have been 'written backwards' as a decade in which empire was imperilled, fragile, falling apart. And yet, for many British people, and for many around the empire, the 1950s did not feel like the end, but simply a reconfiguration. The question was: into what?

The 1950s were conservative in many ways, both politically – Winston Churchill was re-elected in 1951 and his party governed

Britain until 1964 – and culturally. The decade is often thought of as drab and dreary, still suffering rationing and shortages from the war, a holding period before the excitement of the 1960s. The journalist Katharine Whitehorn bemoaned the image as the 'damp patch' between 'battlefield' and 'fairground'. In fact, the decade was one of dramatic change for Britain, as women started to work more outside the home, more young people went to university, and the welfare state meant that standards of living improved for everybody: as Whitehorn pointed out, 'bar a few fogeys who bemoaned the loss of parlour maids and deference, we thought everything was getting better'.[2]

In the 1940s and 50s, British people did not have an overwhelming sense that imperialism was coming to an end: in fact, many of them chose this moment to start a new life in the empire. Migration in the first two decades of the twentieth century had mostly comprised single men going to East Africa to seek a fortune in coffee, gold or diamonds and escape the social strictures of British society (to the extent that the Colonial Office had to send out a 'sexual directive' in 1909 expressly forbidding white male British settlers from engaging in 'concubinage' with Black African women). In contrast to the migratory movements of the nineteenth century – military expeditions to India and South Africa, deportations to Australia and the Irish exodus to the United States – those of the early twentieth century reflected the fact that the British empire had become something of a playground for the wealthy and the dissolute.

This was somewhat tempered by the effects of the Depression in the 1930s, which badly affected the economies of Kenya and Rhodesia, tied as they were to the metropolitan banks, but even up until the brink of war there was a push to colonise the empire more fully to help to solve problems – particularly unemployment – in the metropole. In 1938, the Boy Scouts were urging their members to heed 'the call of the open country' rather than trying to make a living in the 'congested' United Kingdom; there was 'something so romantic', they said, in moving to 'the great prairie lands, lakes and forests of Canada [and] the vast unoccupied lands of Australia and

New Zealand'.³ Scouts who had made the move wrote glowing accounts of their experiences overseas to be read back home: their work on sheep stud farms and orchards, their weekends spent riding and hunting rabbits. One young man summarised his experience by saying, 'This open air life is the right life for me, and I am sorry that I did not come out here three years ago.'⁴

The war interrupted this sort of migration; if British people saw the empire between 1939 and 1945, it was likely to be with a gun in their hand. At the end of the war, however, as migrants started to come from the colonies to the metropole, there was a corresponding flow outwards of white British citizens. Even as decolonisation was getting under way, the British turned to the empire, still largely seen as wild and full of promise, to provide them with new opportunities.

The Colonial Development schemes described in the previous chapter had involved many white British people being sent out to the colonies as 'experts' in agriculture, industry or infrastructure. But there was also an increase in migration from people who were simply looking for a new life abroad; the empire and Commonwealth functioned as a sort of networked travel agency for adventurous Britons. India, of course, was independent by the 1950s, but there were a number of settler colonies, such as Kenya and the Rhodesias, as well as the 'white dominions', which all held a fascination for British émigrés. Half a million went to Canada in the twenty-five years after the Second World War, continuing the migrant flows of evacuees during wartime. British people also found new homes in Australasia, and in East and South Africa. There was such a trend, in fact, towards post-war migration, as the British fled the continued food rationing, housing shortages and bad winters of the late 1940s and 50s, that there were serious discussions among politicians about whether this migration was of greater benefit to the Commonwealth or detriment to the metropole.⁵ Winston Churchill made an emotive speech on the BBC Home Service in 1947 in which he encouraged would-be emigrants to 'stay here and fight it out' rather than abandoning their mother country in its time of need; privately he described those who sought new lives in the Commonwealth at the expense of the metropole as 'rats leaving a sinking ship'.[6]

These migrants from Britain to the empire were responding to powerful incentives. The Assisted Passage Scheme was established by the Australian government in 1945 to attract Britons. It cost £10 in administrative fees, hence the nickname 'Ten Pound Poms' for those who used it. The New Zealand government followed with an analogous programme two years later. In Australia, this was part of the 'White Australia' policy, which had its origins in the nineteenth century and sought to attract migrants from Britain and across Western Europe and the Mediterranean but, crucially, not from Asia, Africa or the Caribbean. In comparison to the far-off horrors of Gallipoli in 1915, the Pacific theatre of the Second World War had left Australian people feeling vulnerable at home, especially following the Japanese invasion of Papua New Guinea (itself a colony of Australia until 1975) and the air raids across northern Australia in which several hundred people, including civilians, had died. This sense of vulnerability led in the aftermath of the war to the idea that the nation needed to 'populate or perish'. For both Australia and New Zealand, white British people were extremely attractive migrants: they were part of the Commonwealth 'kith and kin', they spoke English, and there was a casual, racialised assumption of cultural affinity because of this.

The New Zealand government placed advertisements in British newspapers calling on 'all single men and women' to come to the dominion for a 'new way of life'. Men were encouraged to pursue careers in building, engineering, national development and farming; women could look forward to jobs as nurses, factory workers, secretaries or domestics. Both genders, as long as they were single and under thirty-six years old, could look forward to 'good jobs, good pay and good living'.[7] The 1953 tour of New Zealand by the Queen and Prince Philip also saw a 'substantial' rise in the number of enquiries to New Zealand House about the possibility of migrating to the dominion, according to Cliff Smith, the chief migration officer, who appeared on the BBC's *Radio Newsreel* to talk about this phenomenon and to drum up further interest.[8] The New Zealand authorities spent a substantial amount of money and resources trying to encourage migration from Britain, and many British people were attracted by the promise of 'wide open spaces' and a cleaner, healthier way of life, with little acknowledgement of existing indigenous populations. An Australian poster around the same time promised 'big opportunities with space to live'.[9] More than 75,000 British people had moved to New Zealand by 1975, when the assisted scheme ended.

Not all of this migration was undertaken willingly by consenting adults. As late as the mid-1950s, it was believed at an official level that the migration of unaccompanied, often orphaned, children from Britain to Australia could be beneficial to both countries; the Australian government had indicated in 1945 that they would be willing to absorb 50,000 unaccompanied child migrants from Britain to 'build up her population'.[10] As far as Australia was concerned, the younger the migrant, the more likely it was that they would adapt wholeheartedly to the Australian customs and climate: one British government report conceded that 'some State Governments consider that even children of thirteen are too old to adapt happily to the Australian education system and way of life'. From a British perspective, the sort of child who could be forced to migrate alone across the world was not necessarily the sort of child they wanted to keep at home. As the report baldly stated, emigrant children 'not only have not yet begun to contribute to the economy, but they have not completed their education . . . frequently come from broken homes and might, if they stayed in the United Kingdom, eventually become or continue to be a charge upon the rates'.[11]

In the 1950s, children's charities were also sending child migrants to Australia. Barnardo's had sent tens of thousands children to Canada from the 1880s, but stopped this practice at the start of the war and focused entirely on Australia from 1945; eight charities including Barnardo's were responsible for sending 3,170 children to Australia between 1947 and 1965, and children were also sent to New

Zealand and Southern Rhodesia, although in much smaller numbers. In November 1947, the *Ormonde* (which had brought Jamaican migrants to Liverpool in the spring of that year) docked at Freemantle with a cargo of over a thousand emigrants to Australia; among them were five groups of unaccompanied children, including the first contingent of Barnardo's children to leave Britain since the start of the war. The arrival was covered with excitement in the Australian press, not least because one teenage passenger, Raymond Willocks, had developed appendicitis on the voyage and had been treated by a fellow passenger, Dr Henderson, who had thus become 'one of the very few women to have operated for appendicitis at sea'. The smaller children, some of whom were as young as five years old, were destined for Catholic orphanages, while many of the teenage boys and girls were being sent to take up farming placements.[12] This was a standard pattern of migration, with many, such as the author and activist David Hill, being sent to Australia with the promise of education and a better life, but finding only hard agricultural labour on their arrival; some children with living parents in Britain were lied to by authorities on reaching Australia and told that they were orphans.[13] This practice continued, with the blessing of the British government, until 1970, despite the reports of multiple whistle-blowers exposing the poor conditions that these children often faced, including a lack of education and health care, and frequent instances of physical and sexual abuse.[14] Since December 2018, under an official British government payment scheme, former child migrants can claim £20,000 each, in recognition of the damage that this programme caused to their lives. Almost a hundred years after the end of transportation, Australia continued to be used to rid Britain of apparently troublesome elements.

Of course, many British people were understandably attracted by the chance to start a new life overseas, and the British were still in many ways considered the ideal migrant for the Commonwealth. In 1955, a twenty-one-year-old British woman called Barbara Wood was declared Australia's 'millionth migrant'. She and her fiancé, Dennis Porritt, were expecting a quiet move to Australia a month after their wedding, until an official from Australia House arrived in Redcar to tell Barbara of her good fortune. Her status as the 'millionth migrant' meant that a scarce rental home had already been reserved for the couple and Dennis had been found a job. Barbara, the *Daily Mirror* informed readers, was 5'10" in her heeled shoes, with vital statistics of 36-25-37; a picture of her on holiday, grinning in a swimsuit and pearls in front of Dennis in his swimming trunks, was used to illustrate the piece in which she gushed that she was 'so excited' by the news. The Australian official described Barbara in glowing terms as 'a natural Australian type' – which apparently meant 'tall, well-made, fair-haired and an outdoor girl'.[15] This quasi-eugenic description shows clearly the sort of British stock that Australia hoped to attract as part of its 'populate or perish' policy.

The migration drive continued into the 1960s. During that decade, the Australian government ran a television campaign in Britain with the slogan 'Australia brings out the best in you'.[16] The advert invited men to send off a coupon available in 'this week's local TV paper' to receive an information pack, which included pamphlets aimed at husbands (employment), wives (the 'women's angle') and parents (education). More than a million British people embraced the opportunities offered by the Assisted Passage Scheme between the end of the war and 1982 when it was ended. This included families such as the Gibbs, who boarded the ship *Fairsea* and travelled from Chorlton-cum-Hardy in Greater Manchester with their three small sons and young daughter in 1958; the boys spent their teenage years in Queensland, before Barry, Robin and Maurice returned to Britain in the late 1960s to find greater success in their career as the Bee Gees.

Australia and New Zealand were not the only focus of migration for white Britons in the 1950s. Canada, the Rhodesias and South Africa were all popular destinations, all for similar reasons: the perception of a new start, a healthy lifestyle, lots of clean fresh air, all again summarised by a colonial emphasis on wide, open (apparently unpeopled) spaces. (In 1948, a book written for the Left Book Club, which uncovered research from a report that had been commissioned and then buried by the South African government, pointed out that 'the latest handbooks for prospective immigrants from Britain' were clearly shaped by this sort of 'wishful thinking' – 'Only in passing do they refer to the existence of 9,000,000 non-whites on the map of South Africa, and although the brochures are liberally peppered with pictures showing industrial work, hardly hide nor hair of an African appears among them.')[17] In 1951 the Migration Council produced a pamphlet, 'Operation British Commonwealth', which urged British people to consider possible futures around the Commonwealth, contrasting 'spacious Canada' with 'congested London'. As well as providing opportunities for individual families, this migration was seen as strategically important in the context of the Cold War; the Migration Council believed that a 'large-scale, planned migration' was vital to protect the Commonwealth and to ensure that the British survived a potential Third World War by scattering themselves across the globe.[18]

The Migration Council might have been unusually paranoid, but the mid-1950s saw Britain's position in the world challenged in such a way that many British people did experience something of an existential panic. The Suez Canal had been constructed, largely using forced labour, in the middle of the nineteenth century after a French developer, Ferdinand de Lesseps, saw the potential benefits of providing a trade route from the Mediterranean to the Red Sea, allowing ships to travel from Europe to Asia without needing to navigate around the south of the African continent. Britain had originally been against the construction of the canal; Britain was the leading European imperial force in Asia at this time and believed that the French plans might undermine the status quo and thus diminish its imperial power. (The construction of the canal did indeed provide competition to the British shipping industry and contributed in Britain to the financial crisis known as the 'Panic of 1873'.) However, in 1875, the Khedive (leader) of Egypt, struggling economically, sold his 44 per cent share of the Suez Canal Company to the British government; by 1882, the British had invaded Egypt and effectively taken control of the country, although it was not formally a colony. The Suez Canal became seen as a vital part of imperial infrastructure, particularly at moments of crisis; a newsreel from the Second World War, 'The Flowing Tidal Wave of Supply', was set entirely in the Suez Canal and celebrated the port and the canal for their centrality to wartime supply chains.[19]

Despite this imperial dependence on the canal, Britain's relationship with Egypt was not straightforwardly colonial and its position in the region was always more tenuous than in other parts of the empire. In the 1936 Anglo-Egyptian Treaty made between the Egyptian monarchy and the British government, Britain had agreed to withdraw all troops from Egypt, except those needed to defend the Suez Canal. In 1952, a revolutionary movement led by General Gamal Abdel Nasser overthrew the Egyptian monarchy and installed General Naguib as its first president; in 1954, Nasser took power and became a key player in regional, pan-African and non-aligned movements. British newspapers followed closely; the *Telegraph* was concerned that British soldiers in the Canal Zone were increasingly being targeted and attacked in this new political context, arguing that 'the easiest Egyptian way of attracting the support of the mob' was 'inflaming it against Britain'.[20]

Ultimately, however, the British government had to deal with the Egyptian government as it was. In 1954, in negotiations with Nasser, Britain agreed to remove its remaining troops from the Suez region in a staggered departure, and this withdrawal was completed in June 1956. The next month, partly in response to the disappointment of British and French withdrawal from the Aswan Dam project, Nasser announced the nationalisation of the Suez Canal, which was owned by British and French shareholders. The British government was furious and colluded with the French and the Israelis to try to take the canal back; it was agreed that Israel would 'invade' Egypt, Britain and France would intervene to 'stop' the 'invasion', and they would retain the Suez Canal for its own safety, while Israel would be permitted to maintain control over Sinai.

One way that the Suez Crisis was embraced and amplified in

Britain was through the use of analogies comparing Nasser to fascist figures, and discounting any peace talk as 'appeasement'. The *Telegraph* described his government as 'Perónist'[21] and the uniforms of the revolution's youth movement as 'reminiscent of Hitler's Brownshirts'.[22] The *Daily Mail* labelled Nasser a 'new Hitler', in a piece in which the House of Commons was said to 'speak for Britain' in condemning his actions, the headline echoing the famous moment in the Second World War when Arthur Greenwood MP had been exhorted to 'speak for England' against appeasement of the Nazis.[23] Even the *Daily Herald*, the Labour paper, cried 'No More Adolf Hitlers!' from its front page.[24] These comparisons could occasionally be somewhat tenuous: the *Daily Mirror* described Nasser speaking to a crowd from a balcony 'such as Hitler and Mussolini favoured', conveniently ignoring that Churchill had also appeared, with the royal family, on a similar balcony to mark VE Day.[25] But the sense that Britain *had* to oppose Nasser, that to do otherwise would be cowardly to the point of immoral, was pervasive.

This feeling was heightened by the fact that Britain's prime minister at the time, Anthony Eden, had been in Chamberlain's cabinet in the 1930s and had resigned, along with Harold Macmillan, over the appeasement of Hitler and Mussolini; his reputation as a man who stood up to fascists helped to convince many that Britain's actions in Egypt were morally correct. The *Daily Mirror*, no friend to Conservative politicians, urged the prime minister to show that 'he has not changed his views' since his principled stand in 1938.[26] Only the *New Statesman*, *Tribune* and the *Economist* opposed military action from the start, the first two on socialist grounds that any intervention would be an illegitimate use of force, the last from a more pragmatic position which questioned what Britain would hope to achieve through an invasion.

The soldiers sent out to bolster British troops in August 1956 did not officially know where they were going; the men of the 16th Independent Airborne Brigade had been given their orders at three o'clock in the morning and had three days to get their vaccinations, paint their lorries 'desert brown' and daub 'Cyprus', their first stop, on their kitbags.[27] There were emotional goodbyes, such as that between Sergeant Stanley Wild and his wife Olive, captured by a *Picture Post* photographer, before he went to join his regiment of paratroopers to be shipped out to the Mediterranean.[28] At the same time, the civilians of the Suez Canal Company were being evacuated from Egypt back to the UK. Five hundred wives and children of men employed by the canal were the first to arrive at London Airport. Mrs Jean Kent and her five children were met by her mother and sister off the flight, and were also photographed for the *Picture Post*; Jean reported that Egypt was still 'all quiet'.[29]

Britain did not, in fact, initiate their 'police action' against Egyptian troops until October. By then, the context at home and overseas was very different. Despite initial support for British intervention to protect the Suez Canal, the British press and people had become less and less approving of military action. Some supported it because they saw Eden as taking hard decisions to protect British interests. Mrs A. Yates, from Llandudno, recorded her 'disgust' at a Cabinet minister, Sir Edward Boyle, who had resigned over Eden's hard-line policies, writing 'if their house was on fire, the first thing they would do would be to put it out, not wait until the fire brigade had a meeting, and that is what Sir Anthony Eden has done'.[30] But many newspapers had cooled on intervention even before British troops invaded, not least because the actual invasion was carried out under the pretence of the joint 'police action' with France to stop Israel from attacking Egypt. Research by Gallup showed that the British public saw through this: only 17 per cent of those surveyed thought British intervention was to 'keep the peace', compared with 31 per cent who believed it was to get control of Suez, and 7 per cent explicitly said they believed that the British motivation was to 'get revenge on Nasser'.[31] One representative poll conducted in September showed that only 37 per cent of the British public supported the idea of war, while 44 per cent felt that Britain should not invade Egypt.

There were mass protests across the country, including in Trafalgar Square, where in August thousands of protesters shouted 'Law, not war!' and held banners aloft proclaiming the same. They were met by

mounted police, who made numerous arrests, including of two protesters who were dressed as a camel pantomime-style and wearing a
sign that said 'The Tories Give Us The Hump: No War Over Suez'.[32]
These protests continued – on 12 September, thousands of people
from London, the Midlands, Yorkshire, Dundee and Aberdeen, many
of whom had travelled by specially organised coaches, queued outside St Stephen's Gate at the Houses of Parliament, in order that they
might pass through the lobby to ask their MPs to vote against war.[33]
Two women who had travelled down from Edinburgh on the train
reported that army reservists had wished them luck and success with
their protest. Three wounded ex-servicemen had themselves travelled down from Liverpool to tell their MP that they wanted to avoid
another conflict; Eric Cook, a paratrooper who had been wounded at
Arnhem, said that they had come because 'we've served in Colonial
countries and we know what their people are up against'. The workers at a Rolls-Royce factory had sent a delegation down to Parliament
to convey that the entire workforce was against a military action, as
had the National Union of Mineworkers.[34] Five thousand more
people marched through the centre of London chanting 'Down with
the Tories' and holding banners that said 'No war for Tory Profits'.[35]

Israel eventually invaded Suez on 29 October; days later, Britain
and France began bombing the region before landing their own
troops. On 31 October, the ITV programme *Free Speech* featured a
furious debate between its panellists, Robert Boothby (a Conservative MP), Michael Foot (future leader of the Labour Party) and the
historian A. J. P. Taylor, which nearly came to blows when Taylor
and Foot essentially accused Boothby of being a war criminal for
supporting the invasion. The next day, there was a fierce debate in
Parliament, sparked by a motion by Jim Griffiths, the deputy leader
of the Labour Party and a former minister for the colonies, in which
he condemned the military action not only because it was unjust
and unjustifiable, but also because 'for the people in the Commonwealth and the Colonies . . . this will be an attack by a powerful
white country on a weak country of coloured people'. Griffiths
recorded his astonishment that 'It is a Conservative Government, it

is the party which regarded the Empire almost as a branch of the Conservative Party, whose members talk about it as if it belonged to them – they are the Government who are breaking up the Commonwealth at this time.'[36]

Labour Party MPs furiously spoke out against the British military action, which the future Conservative foreign minister Rab Butler repeatedly refused to admit was a 'war' as opposed to a 'state of conflict'. Far from the earlier debates where Eden had been praised for his role in standing up to dictators, by this point the prime minister himself was being compared openly to Hitler in the chamber.[37]

The press echoed and escalated this criticism. The *Daily Worker* attacked Eden for what the paper saw as his warmongering in the Middle East, describing the British invasion of Egypt as 'an act of aggression as flagrant, as wanton, as inexcusable as any in the bloodstained history of Tory imperialism'.[38] The *Observer* and the *Manchester Guardian*, meanwhile, carried out a daring investigation to prove that Britain had colluded with France and Israel; the *Daily Worker* was also reporting by November that this was the view of the American State Department.[39] In the context of this increasing media hostility, the BBC came under attack from the government for its reporting of the crisis. At one point, *Radio Newsreel* broadcast a recording of a meeting at the Royal Albert Hall which included chants from a crowd that 'Eden must go'; this was later cited in the House of Commons by a Conservative MP, Peter Rawlinson, as evidence that the BBC was biased against the government.[40] It was a tension that would be played out again in the Falklands War, and again in the Blair years regarding the coverage of Britain's military interventions in the Middle East. On 4 November, there was a protest of 30,000 people in Trafalgar Square against the invasion, the largest peace protest in post-war Britain to date. The marchers were addressed by the Welsh MP Nye Bevan, who excoriated the government for following 'a policy of bankruptcy and despair, not a policy of civilisation' that had 'made us ashamed of the things of which formerly we were proud', and called upon Eden to 'Get out! Get out! Get out!'.[41]

It was American intervention – diplomatic, economic and military – which drove the British government to realise that withdrawal from Suez was inevitable, and they duly stood down British troops on 7 November, one week and two days after the invasion began. But the strength of public opinion – the crowd, for example, who after Bevan's speech had swarmed from Trafalgar Square to Downing Street, shouting 'Eden Must Go!', to try to literally pull the prime minister from his office – had undoubtedly spooked the government, as had its rapidly plummeting ratings in the opinion polls. Anthony Eden resigned in January 1957; the *Guardian* offered its commiserations for his 'tragically unrewarding' term in office, particularly given the 'fine reputation' in international politics that he had held before he became prime minister.[42]

The Suez Crisis was not the end of empire, but it was perhaps the real beginning of the end. There had always been an anti-colonial intellectual and political tradition in Britain, and this had continued after the Second World War, including a diverse group of people involved in the Movement for Colonial Freedom, the fringes of the Labour Party, and the campaign to end apartheid, as well as of course the diasporic colonial populations themselves; groups like the West African Students Union had long been a home for Black activists fighting for colonial independence. But 1956 was a moment when even those who had once been proud of British imperial power were forced to concede that the nation was no longer the dominant international force; the United States and the USSR between them had put paid to that idea once and for all when they came together, despite their Cold War, to condemn British actions at the UN, thus forcing its humiliating withdrawal. From that moment onwards, many former supporters of imperialism were tempted towards a 'Little England' approach, one that cast the colonies as a source of vulnerability and which resented the 'duty' towards colonial inhabitants that had once been the empire's driving force. Instead, they argued, Britain should gracefully withdraw to concentrate on reversing British decline at home.

*

Unfortunately for them, the empire was 'brought home' to the British in the 1950s like never before. Immigration from the 'new Commonwealth' – those countries with a majority non-white population – rose from around 3,000 in 1953 to over 40,000 in 1955 and almost 137,000 in 1961.[43] One of these thousands of migrants was Beryl Gilroy who came to Britain from British Guiana (Guyana) in 1952 to work as a teacher. She had qualified at teacher training college in 1943 in Georgetown, working for UNICEF before travelling to Britain, where she studied new approaches to child development and psychology at the University of London. She was a highly trained migrant, coming to Britain to pursue a job in a field with many vacancies, and initially had optimistic hopes that she would find suitable employment quickly. Her experience of being a student in the metropole was positive, but when she came to apply for jobs she hit a brick wall. 'As the months went by, my applications for a teaching post in an infants' school became "the matter". Time and again I was told that "the matter" was being considered. The fact was that, as a Guyanese, I simply could not get a teaching post.'[44]

Beryl's experience in Britain led her to realise that her imperial upbringing had left her in a sort of 'cultural no-man's-land'. She had sung 'I Vow to Thee My Country' on Empire Day (in the pouring rain – what could be more British!) as a child in Guiana, but despite being raised 'under a faraway flutter of the Union Jack', she found herself increasingly conscious of her exclusion from Britishness within the metropole.[45] She was forced to take a number of jobs outside education in order to make a living, and the variety of workplaces exposed her further to racism and discrimination shaped by British attitudes to the Caribbean. She eventually found work as an infant teacher, rising to become one of the first Black head teachers in London at a school with forty-four nationalities from all across the ex-empire and beyond. But even then she had to fight against the charge that this was simply because the Inner London Education Authority had, in the late 1960s, a rumoured policy called 'kindness to blacks'.[46]

Donald Hinds travelled to Britain from Jamaica in 1955 and worked on the buses in London while pursuing a writing career with the *West Indian Gazette*. In 1966, he published his ground-breaking memoir, *Journey to an Illusion: The West Indian in Britain*, which explored the grim realities of migrant lives in Britain. For the book, he interviewed other migrants from the West Indies, talking to schoolchildren about their experiences in the British education system, and working men about their ability to find jobs and housing. He wrote about estate agents and landlords and the ways they discriminated against people of colour, about British efforts to track and monitor 'race relations' through sociological studies and alarmist paperbacks, and about the West Indian organisations fighting back against racism and discrimination. The book is also interspersed with stories from his friends' lives and his own. One interviewee, Devon Herne, recounted his great feeling of dread upon arriving in London and seeing white porters unloading his bags from the boat train, and white men sweeping the streets and white women selling cigarettes in cheap shops. This was so concerning not only because it undid the 'myth of the mother country' that had been so central to imperial education in Jamaica, but because he realised that 'if a white man was sweeping the streets, then any job I asked for would mean a challenge to him'. And he also realised that he was not, as he had been taught, one of the 'mother country's children' but was instead 'one of her *black* children'; his place in the metropole would be determined accordingly.[47] Hundreds of thousands of others had their own particular stories of migration, all of them different and personal, but all of them shaped by the expectations and illusions of empire, all of them both tainted by racism and bolstered by community and solidarity.

In 1957, the Home Office was concerned enough about the possible effects of migration on the British metropole that they established a working party, 'to report on the social and economic problems arising from the growing influx into the United Kingdom of coloured workers from other Commonwealth countries'.[48] It had no remit to consider the advantages of such migration, nor the migration of white people to Britain, nor indeed of the experiences of migrants more generally – only those 'coloured' workers who were deemed to cause 'problems'. It set about its work by sending out a survey to forty-one police forces around Great Britain asking for details about their experience of migration and their impression of the local immigrant population. The questionnaires asked: what were the numbers of Commonwealth immigrants, how had they assimilated, how far did they represent a threat to public order, how often did they commit crime? They also enquired into living conditions: in which areas did these people reside, what sort of housing did they inhabit, and what state was it in? Although there was no explicit question about the prevalence of infectious diseases, many forces took it upon themselves to volunteer information about the presence of tuberculosis, for example, and venereal disease, both of which were official concerns of British border control. The government was certainly anxious about interracial sexual relationships: one topic that did feature in the Home Office questionnaire was 'miscegenation' and 'illegitimacy', despite the fact that mixed-race or extramarital relationships were not illegal and should not have been the concern of police forces.

To read these reports is to catch a glimpse of Commonwealth communities across Britain and how their lives were shaped by migration, as well as the different ways the various police forces understood what it meant to be a 'migrant'. Some reports describe communities where people of colour were evidently accepted and welcomed. Grimsby, for example, had 'not more than twenty-five' people of colour living in the town; four were doctors at the local hospital, one of whom had been in the country for a significant period of time and 'appears to be assimilated into the local society with mutual good will and respect'.[49] The report sent from Glasgow emphasised the extent to which the existing community welcomed migration: 'Glasgow people are very friendly towards the coloured people and go out of their way, as a rule, to help any obvious stranger.'[50] In Bolton, where the majority of immigrants were doctors, nurses and students at the city's Technical College, the police wrote that 'the presence of coloured people has not caused any problems, and there is no evidence of tension likely to lead to disturbances'; there had been some marriages between immigrants and local white residents, which seemed to be 'working out all right'.[51] In Essex, there were eighty-two student nurses, mostly from East and West Africa, who intended to return home once they were qualified, and the report claimed that 'in general there is a friendly attitude towards the coloured people from the natives of the district', although there was a limited degree of fraternisation between communities. It is clear, however, in Essex that the police were comfortable with these migrants mostly because they were explicitly temporary residents, and that they would prefer to keep the contact between Black and white citizens of Essex as limited as possible; the author wrote with some satisfaction that 'except for one instance', he had 'no knowledge of interbreeding having occurred'.[52]

Others were far less inclined to be positive. The author of the report from Reading insisted, despite a complete absence of evidence to corroborate his assertion, that 'I have every reason to believe that there has been an increase of the incidence of [venereal] disease in the Borough, and many girls have admitted that contact has been through coloured men'. The report from Derby claimed that large numbers of migrants were arriving into the country with gonorrhoea, and the author stated – again with no evidence provided – that he viewed with concern the idea that 'a great number of them believe in the fallacy that if they have intercourse with a white woman, particularly a virgin, they will be cured'. In South Shields, it was reported that the main problems caused by the Commonwealth migrant community were social, not criminal, including 'the large n[umber] of half caste children bred by them'.[53] Similarly, the Middlesbrough constabulary reported with disapproval that 'some young females from good class homes have formed associations with coloured men following meetings in dance halls' and that this had led, in some instances, to 'an increase of illegitimate births of half caste children'. In Middlesbrough, in fact, the police were going so far as to question young white women 'concerning their associations with coloured persons'; when the women denied that they were having sex with these men, they were subjected to a medical examination – despite the absence of any legal imperative or justification for doing so – and invariably found 'to be non virgo intacta'.[54] Most of the reports admitted, with some obvious reluctance, that the Commonwealth communities were generally law-abiding; perhaps that is why they covered these sexual relationships between consenting adults in such lurid detail.

By focusing its concerns about immigration entirely on migrants from the Commonwealth and in particular from the 'new Commonwealth', where the majority were people of colour, the Home Office defined immigration as a problem related directly to empire and to race, an approach that would shape the way Britain thought about the subject for decades thereafter. Its casual connection of 'coloured' Commonwealth migration and criminality, meanwhile, without any effort to explain *why* these people should be targeted by police forces in this way, also betrays the fundamental racism of its perspective and assumptions and the extent to which this racism was woven into the machinery of the British state. As seen in the police reaction to the racial violence in Liverpool in 1948, this could be an explosive combination.

In 1958, white racism and anger against West Indian communities boiled over into violence once more. On 29 August Majbritt Morrison, a white Swedish woman, and her husband Raymond, who was Jamaican, were arguing outside Latimer Road Tube station in west London. As people tried to intervene, a fight broke out between some white onlookers and some of Raymond's friends, who were Black. The following day, Majbritt was assaulted in the street by a group of young white men who threw milk bottles at her and shouted that she was a 'black man's trollop'. This was the spark that exploded the fragile race relations in the area. Later that night, more than three hundred white Teddy boys rampaged around the streets, attacking the houses of West Indian families. On the first night, five Black men were beaten unconscious; as the riots unfolded over the next week, houses and businesses were attacked and many people, especially local Black residents, were violently assaulted. One police officer who tried to intervene to stop a Black man being beaten with an iron bar remembered glass bottles raining down on them and blood running down his face. In the end, 108 people were charged with various crimes, of whom two-thirds were white; although the police officials tried to argue to the Home Secretary that the riots had not been racially motivated, the Old Bailey judge Lord Salmon handed out 'exemplary sentences' of four years each to nine white young men who had gone out 'hunting' for Black victims.[55]

The African Caribbean community reacted with frustration and anger directed at the Metropolitan Police, who had previously been unwilling to take their reports of violent racism seriously; the political group the Afro-West Indian Union released a statement blaming the government for the rise in racial tensions, asking the British labour movement to help try to smooth community relations, and requested that colonial governments should help to repatriate immigrants who 'through poverty, discrimination and the growing threat of unemployment' wished to return home.[56] This funding was not forthcoming, but the Trades Union Congress (TUC) did release a statement condemning the riots and calling for tolerance and understanding. Predictably, the TUC then received an onslaught of hate mail. In one letter an anonymous author stated there was no racial prejudice in Britain before laying into the 'n*****s living on dope and women and drawing the national assistance living in houses our own people should have'; the letter is particularly notable for the author's insistence that Commonwealth migrants had only fought for Britain in the Second World War 'for their own benefit and [because] the wages were good'.[57]

The *Universities & Left Review* – a publication associated with the 'new left' movement in Britain, which counted Stuart Hall and Raphael Samuel among its members – published material that showed how ingrained these racist attitudes were in the white community of Notting Hill. A group of fifteen-year-old schoolgirls had been asked by their teacher to write essays expressing their attitudes to the recent race riots and to the topic of immigration more generally. The magazine printed four extracts, the first of which opens: 'I honestly and truthfully hate the coloured people.' The girls repeat common tropes about the Commonwealth migrants, writing that 'they drug our girls and take them into brothels', get put at the top of the waiting list for council housing ahead of white families 'living in two rooms who have been on the housing list for years' despite not having 'been here five minutes', and that they were 'just to [*sic*] lazy and live on national assistance'. Parts of the essays are simply lists of insults: the immigrants 'smell like dog's muck, and eat like dogs to [*sic*]'. Only one girl expresses any compassion towards the Black community, but it is reserved for what she calls the 'better class', for example those who came to work as doctors or nurses. She alone concedes that it is not some inherent slovenly nature but the fact that they are 'looked down upon like animals' and discriminated against that explains why so many immigrants lived in poor, crowded housing conditions.[58] As Stuart Hall wrote in his commentary, printed alongside the extracts, the essays contained 'the unmistakable profile of Britain's colonial policy over the last century'; the girls were 'relaying second hand the catch words of colonial policy' based on the portrayal of Black people as 'primitive barbarian[s]'. Hall was concerned that so much of the violence in Notting Hill had been perpetrated by children and adolescents and was convinced that this was owing to the poverty and degradation of the area, the lack of employment prospects and poor-quality housing, and the development of an entire generation 'with nothing to hold on to'. As he concluded his essay, 'They are *our* children, and Notting Hill is London.'[59]

Diverse communities during this time were not all unhappy or fractious. Mixed-race friendships, relationships and marriages were found wherever people of colour lived. In South Shields, Toxteth, Tiger Bay and the East End of London, for decades men and women had met, romanced, married and raised children across the colour line. But nor were the 1958 riots an aberration in the history of British race relations. Notting Hill, in fact, continued to foster a significant number of far-right racist activists, inspired by leaders like Colin Jordan and Oswald Mosley (who stood as a parliamentary candidate in Kensington North in the 1959 election). A year after the riots, a thirty-two-year-old Antiguan man, Kelso Cochrane, was murdered as he walked home from Paddington General Hospital through Notting Hill. Footage from Kelso's funeral shows a community of hundreds of people, mostly Black, but including white faces as well, gathered outside the church as the cortège arrives and then following the coffin in procession towards the cemetery, as others line the streets. The film then cuts away to a poster advertising a speech by Mosley that had taken place the month before Kelso had been killed.[60] The three youths who stabbed him were never caught and there was significant community suspicion that the police had been complacent about or even complicit in the violence. Donald Hinds recorded that the murder of Cochrane had a profound effect on the West Indian community in West London, and on their relationship with the police: 'beneath the placid surface a cauldron bubbles with charges and denials'.[61]

And yet, despite this undeniably hostile environment, migration to Britain continued. In 1959, the BBC Caribbean Service produced a guide for would-be migrants to the United Kingdom; this pamphlet was created by people like David Muirhead, the chief community development officer for the West Indies High Commission, and Marjorie Nicholson, from the Commonwealth department of the TUC, but also Theo Campbell, owner of Theo's Record Store in Brixton (above which were the offices of Claudia Jones's *West Indian Gazette*, which Theo sold and sometimes wrote for), and the author Sam Selvon, who had come to London from Trinidad in 1950, working as a clerk to support his writing career. Selvon's pioneering novel, *The Lonely Londoners*, published in 1956, follows a loosely connected group of Caribbean migrants through the central character, the homesick and uncertain Moses Aloetta. Selvon's ambiguous attitude to London and the fate of the Black migrant in the metropole made him an unlikely contributor to an officially produced guide to migration, although perhaps this ambiguity was the point: after all, those coming to Britain from the Caribbean would need to be realistic about the feelings of loss and uncertainty as well as the racism and discrimination they were likely to experience. Perhaps, too, at this highpoint of migration from the West Indies to Britain, the British establishment had an ambiguous attitude towards immigration; perhaps they were unafraid of turning some people off the idea.

And so, *Going to Britain?*, despite its foreword by the prime minister of the West Indies and its introduction by the high commissioner, did not wholeheartedly encourage migration to the metropole.[62] There is talk of how cold the country is – 'colder than anything you have ever felt' – and how expensive warm winter clothes could be to purchase. There is plenty of practical advice about the journey over, about finding accommodation and work, getting access to doctors and registering children at school, the tone of which often implies that migrants should be prepared to find this experience difficult and time-consuming. In the advice on housing, it is noted that 'some landlords welcome coloured people, others turn them away'; it was not until the late 1960s that racial discrimination in housing became illegal, and even then it was extremely difficult for new migrants to take landlords to task for it. There is also guidance on social life – parties, cricket and church – suggesting that migrants can use cricket in particular as a way to forge relations with their white peers: learn about the county teams, but also keep up with the West Indies, be prepared for workplace discussions around England–West Indies tours. In fact, there is a whole section – written by Theo Campbell – on the etiquette of playing cricket as a West Indian either alongside or against white players.

The reader is told that they might encounter racism in the workplace, and there are examples of racist phrases, such as 'work like a Black', which the guide maintains are simply 'accepted expressions in England'. The advice given, in fact, is not to 'be over-sensitive and take offence'. In all situations, the migrant is urged to be polite and forbearing with the white British people that they encounter, and are reassured that much of the prejudice they experience will be due to ignorance. 'I knew a Barbadian who was asked, in all seriousness, if the people in his country lived in houses or if they lived in the jungles, and also, if he had ever worn clothes before he came to England.'

These sorts of questions are presented as deriving not from ingrained colonial racism, but from an imbalance of information: 'their knowledge of your country is much less than your knowledge of theirs'. It is a striking reversal: the white Briton is cast as innocently lacking in knowledge and experience, while the Caribbean migrant is in the position of power. And yet, even while it downplays the racism and discrimination they will face, the general tone of the guide is that the migrant's life will be hard: complicated, frustrating, often miserable.

In the annals of British imperial history, the 1950s have tended to be overlooked. It was a decade in which contradictions abounded. Migration to the empire continued, but decolonisation also gathered speed. The Suez Crisis seemed to show a nation exerting its imperial might, and then demonstrated the limitations of that power in the face of the 'special relationship' with the United States. For some British people, the empire was still a shining beacon of light in the world and a symbol of both the values that Britain had fought for in the war and its continued global power. For others, it was an anachronistic symbol of a world that should have been left behind, a political injustice that should be resisted, or simply an embarrassment.

Then, in 1957, the Gold Coast became the first European sub-Saharan African colony to liberate itself from colonial rule, formally becoming the independent state of Ghana on 6 March. Unlike the end of empire in India, which had been preceded by a long and well-documented independence campaign, the decolonisation of Ghana was a sudden shock for many British people. In conjunction with Suez the year before, it marked a profound shift in British imperial power since the end of the war. But they were not the only signs that the empire was starting to pull away from the metropole and that perhaps the centre could not hold.

4

Losing an Empire: Decolonisation, 1950s–60s

In November 1961, Queen Elizabeth, thirty-five years old and recently a mother for the third time, whiled away an evening dancing. Despite her pretty dress and pretty face, this might not have been front-page news for even the most devout monarchist, if her dancing partner had not been Kwame Nkrumah, Ghana's first post-colonial leader. A picture on the front page of the *Daily Mirror* showed the Queen being held by Nkrumah in a ballroom embrace, as they danced to 'the gay, hip-swinging high-life'.[1] (Margaret Thatcher was perhaps inspired by this picture when she took to the dance floor with Kenneth Kaunda, the Zambian president, in 1979 at a Commonwealth conference in Lusaka.) The dance between Elizabeth and Nkrumah was, the *Mirror* said, 'the final happy touch to a visit filled with happy touches'. Not everyone around the empire was impressed; a South African newspaper, *Die Oosterlig*, in a piece scathingly headlined 'Her Black Dancing Partners', said that any decent Afrikaner would be 'disgusted' to see a white woman – a Queen! – dancing with an African man, and further shamed Prince Philip, who had not objected but had 'waved with a happy laugh and danced the same dance with Mrs Nkrumah', who was Egyptian.[2] It was, the paper said, a relief that South Africa was no longer associated with a Commonwealth in which such behaviour was tolerated; the country had withdrawn from the organisation earlier that year, in order to better enact the policies of apartheid to which the Afrikaner government was becoming increasingly committed.

Most British newspapers – and their readers – seem to have had few such qualms. Pictures from the trip, which had been postponed to accommodate the Queen's pregnancy, were eagerly consumed by a British public enthusiastic about their young pretty monarch, her dashing husband and their royal colonial adventures. The couple were shown visiting markets, children's nurseries, the new Kwame Nkrumah University, horse races, boat races and many different receptions and galas. Again and again, they were shown surrounded by crowds of smiling, cheering Ghanaians: in one photograph, also apparently the 'happiest moment' of the tour, a Ghanaian woman had thrown a silk scarf down onto the ground in a 'Walter Raleigh tribute' and the smiling Queen walked over it as Nkrumah carefully held out a steadying hand.[3]

Princess Elizabeth had been on holiday in Kenya with Prince Philip when the news of her father's death had reached them in 1952, and a year after her coronation they had taken a seven-month tour of the empire and dominions, covering 40,000 miles across the West Indies, Africa, Asia and Australasia. In this way, from the very beginning, the Queen's reign was associated in the popular British imagination with imperial continuity, not only because of her formal role as head of the Commonwealth but also because of a more intangible sense of royal duty bound up with British and imperial pride, identity and values. In the mid-1960s, four-fifths of people surveyed agreed that 'the Royal Family helps keep the Commonwealth together', with one respondent saying, when questioned about republicanism, that 'if we had a President instead, the Commonwealth would probably fall to pieces'.[4]

But when the Queen danced with the Black leader of a newly independent African nation and British people read about high-life music over their morning cup of tea, it marked a particular watershed in British colonial history. In this 'happiest moment', fourteen years after the independence of India, decolonisation of the wider British empire was not only inevitable but something that had already begun. These pictures may have been an attempt to soften that reality, but any understanding of decolonisation as a happy event would not hold for the remainder of the decade; it was in this period that the majority of British people finally came to realise just how unpopular colonial rule had been.

*

For a moment, the independence of the Indian subcontinent had tricked the British into believing they had stemmed the tide of decolonisation: perhaps sacrificing the subcontinent meant that the rest of the empire could still be sustained. The Suez Crisis had destroyed this illusion. In the 1950s and 60s, Britain was forced to deal with the realities of diminishing British power overseas. Meanwhile, independence movements – often supported by groups of colonial migrants in the metropole, such as students studying at Oxford, Cambridge, LSE and UCL, and the members of the Movement for Colonial Freedom – pushed for decolonisation all around the empire. Kwame Nkrumah had himself studied at LSE and UCL, where he had been spied on by both MI5 and the US State Department. Where he and Ghana led, other African leaders and nations soon followed.

As the British people saw their empire around the world crumbling they reacted variously: with relief that the oppression of colonial peoples was ending, with anxiety about Britain's place in the world, or with satisfaction that Britain was no longer wasting time and money on maintaining out-of-date colonial connections.

Harold Macmillan visited British Africa for six weeks at the beginning of 1960, travelling to Ghana, Nigeria, Rhodesia and Nyasaland and finishing in South Africa. It was in the South African parliament that he gave the second iteration of his famous 'Winds of Change' speech; he had used the same phrase at a state banquet in Accra several weeks earlier without any press attention. But Macmillan knew that inclusion of the phrase in his speech in Cape Town would be especially controversial, so much so that he apparently vomited profusely from nerves before delivering it.[5]

In the speech, Macmillan described his trip across Africa – the first by a serving British prime minister – and spoke admiringly of the landscapes and people that he had seen across the continent and in South Africa itself. But as well as these platitudes, he set out a clear political position on both the decolonisation of the African continent and on the internal politics of South Africa itself. On the former, Macmillan stated that the British government would do for Nigeria and other African countries what they had previously done for 'India,

Pakistan, Ceylon, Malaya and Ghana': that is, they would grant them independence as 'the only way to establish the future of the Commonwealth'. In this context, he pronounced that although Britain had always sought to support South Africa as a Commonwealth member, there were 'aspects' of South African politics (namely apartheid, although this was not explicit) that made it 'impossible' for Britain to support the government. Macmillan approvingly quoted Selwyn Lloyd, the Foreign Secretary, who had claimed at a UN meeting the previous autumn that the British 'reject the idea of any inherent superiority of one race over another' and were committed to a 'non-racial' future for the Commonwealth. As such, the prime minister argued that apartheid went against Britain's 'deep convictions'. It certainly went against Britain's self-image and foundational imperial myths. Macmillan made a special effort to 'deprecate the attempts which are being made in Britain today to organise a consumer boycott of South African goods', and he had no desire to be associated with the anti-apartheid activism of the British left at home.[6] But this was not enough to placate his critics.

The speech was controversial in the empire and at home. Macmillan's condemnation of apartheid led Prime Minister Verwoerd to respond with a defence of South African colonial settlement and 'the white man who has made all this possible', and to call for the country to become 'a true white state in Africa'.[7] This was clearly incompatible with Macmillan's declaration, not only that Britain would support decolonisation, but that decolonisation needed to happen in a certain way, under a process of democratic power sharing, with colonial populations enfranchised and empowered in their new states. The white population of Southern Rhodesia, reading of this speech in their morning newspapers, were especially perturbed. The policy that quickly became known by the shorthand of 'NIBMAR' (No Independence Before Majority Rule) was deeply alarming to these colonial officials and settlers, taken as a sign that they were being actively disempowered by a nation they still thought of as their motherland.

But Macmillan was not only addressing South Africa or British Africa with this speech. He was also talking to a domestic audience that ranged from Conservative backbenchers to communities of people of colour from around the empire, and he was telling these British listeners that the government would no longer resist the impetus towards decolonisation. British newspapers amplified this message, often casting Macmillan in the role of a brave opponent of apartheid. Ironically, this depiction of Macmillan as colonial liberator itself played into racialised attitudes to decolonisation and Black African populations. One *Sunday Express* cartoon by Michael Cummings depicted Hugh Gaitskell, the leader of the opposition, flapping helplessly as his 'propaganda' was blown away by Macmillan, using bellows branded 'wind of change speech': the offending papers, swirling in the wind, labelled Macmillan as an 'imperialist', the 'black man's burden' and (most alarmingly) the 'cannibal of the jungle', dressed in a grass skirt and bone jewellery and preparing to eat a smartly suited Black African man from a large cooking pot.[8] The implication, that all accusations of imperialism or racism from the left aimed at the Conservatives had been proven unfounded by Macmillan's speech, was somewhat undermined by the aggressive racial stereotyping of Cummings's cartoon itself.

Not everyone in Britain was cheered by Macmillan's speech. The Monday Club – so-called to memorialise the 'Black Monday' on which the speech was delivered – was formed by Conservative Party members who had been galvanised by Macmillan's speech in South Africa to reject what they saw as a perniciously 'wet', modernising influence within the Conservative Party. The Monday Club was open to party members under the age of thirty-five (this age restriction was dropped in 1965) who were drawn to the group because they were angry at the stance the party seemed to be taking both abroad and at home. This included abandoning the British empire in favour of a smaller world role and a turn towards European markets and politics, and a perceived left-wing swing on welfare issues. They were particularly keen to counter the influence of the Bow Group, a Conservative think tank that called for decolonisation in pamphlets such as 'Race and Power' published in 1956. The club met on Mondays to discuss political issues and produced pamphlets, often through its study groups, which were formed around topics including African affairs and the Common-wealth, as well as domestic issues such as education or labour and industrial relations.

Although it was theoretically concerned with a broad range of pol-itical issues, the Monday Club became especially associated with its support for Ian Smith's newly independent white nationalist colony of Rhodesia and the apartheid government of South Africa. One of its pamphlets produced in 1969, 'Who Goes Home? Immigration and Repatriation', argued against the immigration of people of colour to Britain and against race relations legislation, casting all activism in the opposite direction as the sinister and self-interested activity of Com-monwealth migrants themselves. The front cover featured a cropped picture of a political demonstration showing mostly people of col-our, labelled 'immigrants protesting in London against the 1968 immigration legislation'.[9] In 1970, in the run-up to the general elec-tion, the club described the race relations acts as 'blows against the traditional British right to freedom of expression' and argued in favour of a scheme for voluntary repatriation for immigrants (which found its way into the Conservative Manifesto), an end to the ban on selling arms to South Africa and Portugal, recognition for the Rhode-sian government and the development of an 'oceanic defence strategy' with Australia, New Zealand and Southern Africa.[10]

The club claimed a great deal of popular support, with branches established at several universities and local groups across the coun-try.[11] But there was also significant resistance to an organisation which was seen as overly influential in its reach and bordering on fascist in its policies. Patrick Wall MP, who was intimately involved with the group, had a meeting at the University of Kent invaded by a hundred student protesters; in Leeds, members of the university audience shouted 'fascist pig' as he delivered a talk on Rhodesia and he was spat on by students and his wife was 'knocked down and trampled on' as they tried to leave.[12] Duncan Sandys – another prominent Monday Club member – had his talk at the University of Bradford disrupted by students who shouted 'Sandys go home!' and 'racialist!' as he tried to speak.[13]

Regardless of this resistance, the Monday Club counted thirty-five MPs and thirty-five peers as members in 1971, and it was to be especially influential on the Conservative Party in the Thatcher years. The party formally severed its links with the club in 2001, because of its adherence to policies such as the (supposedly voluntary) repatriation of people of colour from Britain to their apparent countries of origin; at the time, three MPs were still members of the club and were forced to resign in order to keep their Conservative affiliation.

The Monday Club was not the only British organisation opposed to the end of empire. The League of Empire Loyalists (LEL) had been established in 1954 with the avowed intention to halt the process of decolonisation. The LEL's leader, A. K. Chesterton, had been born in South Africa and had been sent to Britain by his parents at the start of the Boer War. He was a member of the British Union of Fascists in the 1930s and had also been associated with the antisemitic Right Club, which had been founded in 1939 with the explicit intention of freeing the Conservative Party from imagined shady networks of Jewish elites that its founders believed had the party in a stranglehold. Chesterton, in other words, was a committed far-right activist and had obvious sympathies with Nazi ideals; nevertheless, on the outbreak of war, he rejoined the British Army and served in Kenya and Somaliland (Somalia) before being forced to give up his commission in 1943 because of his heavy drinking.

According to both the LEL and the Monday Club, the empire was the last bastion of British power, identity and *whiteness*; decolonisation was a betrayal of all three. Both drew heavily on antisemitic conspiracy theories of fifth columnists within the British state, while blaming social change in Britain more widely for the end of empire and thus, apparently, the end of British power and prestige.

When Chesterton set up the League of Empire Loyalists, he expressed his aims for the organisation in its constitution:

1. The maintenance and, where necessary, the recovery of the sovereign independence of the British Peoples throughout the world.

2. The strengthening of the spiritual and material bonds between the British Peoples throughout the world.
3. The conscientious development of the British Colonial Empire under British direction and local British leadership.
4. The resurgence at home and abroad of the British spirit.[14]

Added to this in many LEL publications was a generalised call to 'fight for British survival'. 'Stand by the Empire' (1954) was a fairly typical pamphlet, gathering together A. K. Chesterton's articles that had previously featured in the LEL magazine *Candour* and containing a number of warnings that the empire might disappear as part of an 'internationalist' conspiracy without ordinary British people even being fully aware of its loss. According to this same thinking, the Second World War happened only because of an international Jewish plot to destroy Germany. Decolonisation is perceived as part of the same giant conspiracy: Gandhi was decried as a 'madman', a 'liar' and a 'colossal clown', and various other governments and organisations were accused of working behind the scenes to bring down the British empire for their own nefarious ends.[15] Those who sympathised with the LEL were not just working to sustain the empire, they were living in fear that the empire and, with it, their sense of Britain and Britishness were about to be torn away from them.

Despite the work of groups like the LEL and the Monday Club, decolonisation only picked up pace. Ghana had become independent in 1957. Nigeria followed in 1960, Tanganyika (Tanzania) in 1961, Uganda in 1962, Kenya in 1963, Northern Rhodesia (Zambia) in 1964, (the) Gambia in 1965. The West Indies had been pushed into an unpopular political federation in 1958, which collapsed in 1962, with Jamaica and Trinidad and Tobago gaining independence in that year; Barbados followed in 1966 and the remainder of the 'little eight' West Indian territories in the 1970s and 80s. In the Far East, Malaya had become independent in 1957; Singapore, North Borneo and Sarawak had continued to be administered as Crown colonies until 1963, when they had joined with Malaya to form Malaysia (from which Singapore broke away in 1965). The British territories in the Middle East had largely become independent in the late 1960s, and in 1968 the government made the decision to withdraw the remaining British troops, in 1971, from the Middle and Far East; this area was collectively known as 'east of Suez', encompassing the Persian Gulf, Malaysia, Singapore and the Maldives.

By 1966, the empire had been transformed into 'a loose and somewhat vocal and troublesome Commonwealth'; one Mass Observer believed that this had led to 'anxious years' for the British public.[16] Philip Larkin's poem 'Homage to a Government', first published in the *Sunday Times* in 1969, captured the way that some felt decolonisation had diminished Britain, not just in terms of power and influence overseas, but in terms of a less tangible, but still potent, sense of loss. The narrator of the poem tries half-heartedly to justify withdrawal by saying that 'The places are a long way off, not here, / Which is all right, and from what we hear / The soldiers there only made trouble happen.'[17] But the nation's children would grow up seeing statues in 'tree-muffled squares' that would only look *nearly* the same as before, and would 'not know it's a different country'. The final line, 'All we can hope to leave them now is money', undercut the balance sheet approach to imperialism; for Larkin, there was a purpose to empire that went beyond profits. Of course, for many others in the metropole, and more importantly around the colonies, imperialism's balance sheet was firmly in the red.

The Labour MP Fenner Brockway, a long-standing opponent of imperialism, had been working to bring together groups like the League of Coloured Peoples with representatives of nationalist and independent movements at conferences in Paris and London since the late 1940s. In 1954, Brockway spearheaded the formation of the Movement for Colonial Freedom, which had the support of seventy Labour MPs including Barbara Castle and Tony Benn, as well as activists such as George Padmore, Oliver Tambo, Ruth First and Leon Szur. The group worked for freedom for the British colonies, gave solidarity to other independence movements, and campaigned against the Vietnam War and in support of Fidel Castro. (In 1970, the group was renamed Liberation.)

The Movement for Colonial Freedom (MCF) disseminated its message against imperialism with enthusiasm, writing a multitude of pamphlets, putting on public events, and generally agitating for an end to formal empire as well as a rejection of the ways in which imperial power structures continued to shape the world even as it decolonised. On the front cover of one pamphlet introducing the organisation to newcomers, the epigraph read: 'Colonialism is not dead. Neo-colonialism is very much alive. We must end both to reach human equality and peace.'[18]. In 1959, the MCF joined together with the Committee for African Organisations to put on a concert at St Pancras Town Hall to mark Africa Freedom Day. The concert included performances from the Guyanese calypso singer and actor Cy Grant, the American singer and actor Paul Robeson, and the English folklorist and singer A. L. Lloyd, as well as 'West Indian songs' performed by Stanley Jack (who would also be the choreographer for the 1959 St Pancras Carnival, the precursor to Notting Hill), and an 'Indian Trio' comprising T. K. Nandi on sitar, K. Khare on tabla and Ayana D. Angadi on tamboura. The event opened with a speech from the Tunisian ambassador to the UK and the evening's entertainment was interspersed with political speeches from Fenner Brockway, Oginga Odinga of the Kenyan Legislative Council, Kanyama Chiume of the Nyasaland Legislative Council and G. H. Doughty of the Association of Engineering and Shipbuilding Draughtsmen.[19]

This event typified the MCF approach to activism. In their introductory pamphlet, they modestly said that they did 'not wish to claim over-much for the MCF' and that the rising support for decolonisation in Britain and globally was 'mainly due to the strength and vigour of the movements for freedom in Africa and Asia and to the liberation which they have brought about. We have been proud to be their voice in Britain.'[20] Crediting and centring activism by people of colour from the colonial and former colonial territories was an important element of the MCF's rejection of and resistance to colonial inequality.

*

Between 1948 and 1960, two atrocities showed a cornered Britain lashing out against its colonial population. Both were declared 'states of emergency' by a British government that wished to avoid the language of civil war within its empire, but those fighting the British colonial state were not fooled by this rhetorical sidestep. In each case the British state worked hard to cover up the true extent of its violence from both the international community and the voters at home.

The first took place in Malaya, where the British sought to resist the Communist forces of the Malayan National Liberation Army (MNLA); the British were reliant on tin and rubber resources in Malaya and unwilling to be pushed into decolonisation by what they perceived as an insurgency campaign. Between 1948 and 1957, the British fought a drawn-out and bloody war against MNLA's guerrilla forces. British troops used a number of tactics that skirted or simply broke outright the rules of war set out in the Geneva Convention: the use of Agent Orange to defoliate forests (the first time this had been used as a weapon of war) as well as the massacre of civilian populations and the destruction of property and land. The British also forced around half a million people from their homes into internment camps, dubbed 'new villages', to punish civilians for apparent collusion with the MNLA and to make it harder for them to materially aid the insurgents.

These tactics would become familiar as part of the American war in Vietnam in the 1960s – in fact, the Americans were explicitly replicating the British approach in their campaign – but they were also strongly reminiscent of techniques used in the Boer War, at the turn of the twentieth century, when Britain had employed a 'scorched earth' policy to destroy Boer homes and farms and had rounded up women and children and put them in concentration camps. The Boer War, and particularly these attacks on civilians, had been the focus of significant criticism in the British metropole from anti-war forces, ranging from Emily Hobhouse, who travelled to South Africa to take charitable donations of clothes to women and children and ended up writing an influential report on the conditions in the camps, to George Cadbury, who used the funds from his successful confectionary company to print anti-war leaflets and even buy a newspaper and install an anti-war editor to further spread his pacifist message. But the Malayan Emergency received comparatively little contemporary condemnation, partly because the role of Communists in the insurgency split opinion on the left in Britain. The war was certainly followed by newspaper readers at home; the *Daily Mail* opened its coverage in 1948 with a bloodthirsty promise that 'Malayan Violence is to be "Smashed"' and concluded with a piece in 1957 that depicted a grateful Malayan nation, its independence duly enabled by British troops indeed 'smashing' the terrorist threat.[21] But many of the worst excesses of the conflict went unreported.

In fact, it was not until 1970, twenty-two years after it occurred, that the press got wind of the Batang Kali massacre, in which twenty-eight unarmed Malayan villagers were murdered by the Scots Guard. The revelation was precipitated by coverage of an eerily similar atrocity, the My Lai massacre by American forces in Vietnam, which shocked American audiences profoundly enough to turn wider popular opinion against the Vietnam War. It also inspired a Scots Guard soldier, William Cootes, to confess to what had happened at Batang Kali to a journalist for the *People*. Cootes claimed that he and other soldiers had been 'incensed' by rumours that three British soldiers from the King's Royal Hussars had been soaked in petrol and burned to death by enemy 'terrorists'. He claimed that his commanding officer had said they would have to go to a village and 'wipe out everyone found there' because it was suspected of harbouring terrorists. The soldiers had arrived at Batang Kali in a state of excitement and after a night of terrorising the inhabitants had eventually shot dead twenty-eight civilians without provocation.

The commanding officer later told the soldiers that the colonial administration in Kuala Lumpur would be conducting an inquiry and that they should get together and fabricate a cover story.[22] They duly appeared in front of the investigation and, in the words of

Allan Tuppen, another of the soldiers who had shot the civilians, 'told the story we had agreed to tell, knowing it was not true'. The inquiry accepted the cover-up, although one official remarked that if the men had been trying to run away when they were shot, it was strange that the bodies had been found in groups; in fact, the soldiers had separated the twenty-eight men into four groups of seven, before taking them to the edge of the village near to a stream and shooting them dead.[23]

To corroborate Cootes's testimony, journalists William Dorran and William Kenneth Gardner tracked down several other of the ex-soldiers involved, who all made statements supporting Cootes's version of events and naming the same commanding officer, Captain Ramsay, who had 'briefed them to kill'. Dorran and Gardner also travelled to Malaysia and interviewed Cheong Hung, who had been an eyewitness to the massacre and had seen many of his own friends killed, escaping himself only because he fainted and was presumed dead before the shooting began. The journalists approached the Ministry of Defence for comment, but it tried to suppress the reporting of the story, largely because it was concerned about possible repercussions for British troops in Northern Ireland.[24]

The story ran in the *People* on 1 and 8 February 1970 and led to widespread public interest in and outrage at the events. The Director of Public Prosecutions was asked by the minister for defence, Denis Healey, to look into it and a formal investigation began in mid-March. The DPP's team expected to spend a significant amount of time in Malaysia speaking to witnesses and undertaking forensic investigation but the work was brought to an abrupt close at the end of June after the DPP's office met with the attorney general, Sir Peter Rawlinson QC; apparently the investigation was being halted because of the difficulty of accessing historic documentation or reliable testimony. Few of those involved at the time were deceived. DCS Frank Williams, the officer who wrote up the report for the Metropolitan Police, noted that it was 'patently clear' that the decision to stop the investigation had been due to the 'political change of view' caused by the election of Heath's Conservative government that month.[25] It later transpired that the British High Commission in Kuala Lumpur had also written to the government forcefully expressing their concerns about the investigation.[26]

In 1993, 2004 and 2008 the Malaysian survivors of the Batang Kali massacre petitioned the government to hold a new inquiry. In 2009, following the publication of a book exploring the massacre, the solicitors Bindmans LLP threatened to sue the British government on behalf of Tham Yong, then the sole surviving eyewitness to the killings, a woman who had seen her fiancé shot and killed by the British forces.[27] In 2015 the UK Supreme Court ruled that although 'wholly innocent men were mercilessly murdered' by British soldiers, too much time had passed since the event for an investigation to be required; in dissenting, Lady Hale argued that despite the passage of time, the value of establishing the truth of what happened was 'overwhelming'.[28] Tham Yong, meanwhile, had died in 2010, without ever seeing justice for her fiancé's murder.

At the same time as the Malayan Emergency was unfolding, the British military were embroiled in a campaign in Kenya, motivated largely by the wishes of the substantial settler population there, who were resistant to the forces of decolonisation and wished to remain in a colonial land that they considered their rightful home. The British settlers' presence in Kenya, in the richest agricultural lands, at the top of a racial hierarchy underpinned by casual violence and structural inequality, was incompatible with the demands of the independence movements in the country. The Mau Mau movement, which began in the 1940s, comprising predominantly Gikuyu fighters, wanted to take back land that had historically been associated with their community and to drive the British colonial state from the region. Started as the Land and Freedom Army under the leadership of Dedan Kimathi, the etymology of 'Mau Mau' is unclear, was never universally adopted by the fighters themselves, and may well have been imposed by British authorities in an attempt to delegitimise the movement by making it sound more 'tribal'. At any rate, Mau Mau was only part of the independence movement of Kenya: the Kenya Africa Union (KAU, later the Kenya African

National Union or KANU) was the main political organisation devoted to independence. KAU was led by Jomo Kenyatta, who had studied in London (under surveillance by the secret services) and Moscow and who would become the country's first leader after independence.

Mau Mau had been banned by the British colonial authorities in 1950, but continued to recruit and agitate against British rule; by 1952, as in Malaya, the government had declared a state of emergency in the country. Kenyatta and five other independence activists, known as the Kapenguria Six, were arrested and charged with being leaders of a proscribed organisation – although there was little evidence that five of the six were even members of Mau Mau – and were each sentenced to seven years in prison. In 1954, the British launched Operation Anvil, aimed at suppressing Mau Mau fighters using cordons and searches: around 16,000 prisoners were taken captive in Nairobi, and many more were deported to reserves – essentially concentration camps – in rural areas. The 'villagisation' system, also in use in Malaya, sought to cut off support for the fighters by moving civilians into geographic 'villages' surrounded by barbed wire; meagre Red Cross rations were unable to sustain these communities in the face of malnutrition and disease. Meanwhile, those suspected Mau Mau fighters who were detained by the British were routinely tortured as part of their 'interrogation' about the movement; this torture was exceedingly brutal and included prisoners being set alight with paraffin, being castrated, and in some cases being flogged to death. In 2013, the British government agreed to pay £19.9 million in compensation to 5,228 Kenyans who had been tortured at the hands of the colonial administration, although they continued to deny liability for this torture or to accept that other former colonies might have cause to bring similar claims.

Compared with the reporting of the Malayan Emergency, the British media coverage of Kenya stands out as particularly lurid. The British press dwelled lasciviously on the threat of Black African violence, feeding the hysteria of the British reading public with tales of home invasions, kidnappings and murders, all happening safely in the distance of empire, but all the more shocking for involving victims who were white and apparently familiar. Two stories above all shaped domestic perceptions of Mau Mau. In January 1953, the murders of the Ruck family – Roger, his pregnant wife Esme and their six-year-old son Michael – and a number of their Black servants were explored in gory detail in the British tabloids, illustrated with a number of graphic photographs showing the bodies slashed with pangas, the long knives used by Mau Mau fighters. In October 1954, the murder of Gray Leakey and his wife Bessie also attracted horrified attention in Britain. Leakey was the cousin of Louis Leakey, a famous British anthropologist, and he had been killed in what was assumed to be a symbolic manner; after witnessing his wife's murder, he had been carried several miles to a place of sacrifice before being tortured and buried face down in a shallow grave. The Ruck family murders were described by the *Daily Mail* as the 'Worst Mau Murder', the family noted as 'the sixth, seventh and eighth European victims of race hate'.[29] The *Mirror* recorded that the three had been 'slashed to death', using this phrase several times to emphasise the brutality and barbarism of the killings.[30] The *Illustrated London News* carried a photograph of the room in which the six-year-old Michael was killed and his body later found, with their caption focusing on his toys and model railway 'left ready for another day of play which never came' alongside pictures of a smiling Michael, with his shining blond hair.[31] This was not even the most in-depth of the coverage. That came in the *Daily Telegraph*, which devoted a number of stories to the murders of the Ruck family and, later, Gray Leakey and his wife. It printed the picture of Michael Ruck's bedroom 'in which he was killed by Mau Mau terrorists',[32] and reported that Leakey's murder was a 'sacrifice' and a 'ritual', that 'wild animals' had apparently dug up Leakey's grave and that the police had searched for his killers in 'almost impenetrable forest'.[33]

Pro-imperial, far-right forces leapt on the reported violence to argue for white supremacy and the civilising force of empire. The newspaper *Black & White News*, which was edited by the neo-Nazi Colin Jordan, claimed to have full details of the Mau Mau rituals but said that their 'revolting sexual obscenities' prevented them from being published.[34] A. K. Chesterton, meanwhile, printed a supplement to *Candour* that detailed, he claimed, the oath taken by Gikuyu people before joining Mau Mau. Chesterton prefaced this supplement with the warning that 'ON NO ACCOUNT should this supplement be allowed to fall into the hands of children or adolescents. It should not be read by subscribers, especially women subscribers, who lack strong nerves and tough minds.' Despite this, he argued that it was vital that the British people understood 'the kind of mentality to which their kith and kin . . . may be sacrificed' if territories such as Kenya and Northern Rhodesia were to be granted independence.[35] The publication included graphic testimony about Mau Mau activities, as well as a number of photographs of dead Mau Mau and British soldiers.

In total, thirty-two white settlers lost their lives at the hands of the Mau Mau fighters. The number of Black Kenyans who died is still contested but undoubtedly far greater. According to the official figures of the British state, 1,819 Black Kenyan civilians were killed by Mau Mau, and 11,000 rebels were killed by British forces: around 10,000 in military action and 1,090 sentenced to hanging. These numbers are certainly far too low. The demographer John Blacker has determined that there were around 50,000 'excess' Kenyan deaths, more than half of them children under ten; the historian David Anderson believes that 20,000–30,000 were killed by British policies, with many women also suffering rape and sexual assault at the hands of the British security services; the historian Caroline Elkins had calculated the death toll far higher, somewhere between 130,000 and 300,000 people.[36]

It is a common assumption that the British public were often shielded from the truth about colonial violence, that violent events were so successfully hidden that nobody knew, or could have known, about them or should be expected to know about them now. This may be true in some cases – the cover-up of the Batang Kali massacre for several decades demonstrates that the British state was certainly motivated to bury the truth about colonial violence where it could – but in the case of Mau Mau the cover-up was not successful. Politicians such as Barbara Castle and Fenner Brockway, stalwarts of the MCF and the anti-colonial movement, fought to expose the 1959 Hola Camp massacre, in which eleven detainees were clubbed to death by guards working for the colonial administration; it was initially claimed that the men had died from drinking contaminated water. Even before the events at Hola Camp, Labour MPs had been demanding more oversight into events in Kenya. One debate in the House of Commons the year before concerning Lokitaung Prison showed the extent to which the government was trying to shut down information from the colony. In this debate, Castle revealed that she and other were receiving letters 'almost weekly' from Lokitaung; Brockway revealed that in one of these letters it had been alleged that 'prisoners were compelled to draw their water from a well condemned by the doctors and in which dogs' carcasses and filth had been thrown for years'; and Kenneth Robinson and John Stonehouse demanded that Kenyan MPs be allowed to visit the prison to see conditions for themselves. The Colonial Secretary Alan Lennox-Boyd dismissed these accusations as 'all part of a campaign to try to smear the security forces and the Administration in Kenya'.[37]

After the events of Hola came to light, Castle and other Labour MPs fought to have a judicial inquiry into the killings; a disciplinary meeting eventually pushed the Commissioner of Prisons and the Commander of the Camp into early retirement, the latter without a pension. The government was forced to concede that this had been a terrible regrettable moment in colonial rule, but were quick to discount it as an aberration rather than an indictment of British colonialism more generally. In fact, in an interview with the *Daily Mail*, Lennox-Boyd claimed that 'The Hola Camp affair has at least highlighted the tremendous amount of good rehabilitation work being done in Kenya'; upon reading this, Kenneth Robinson remarked drily in the House of Commons, 'Are we to believe that this rehabilitation work might have gone unnoticed but for the brutal beating to death of eleven Africans?'[38] In the same session, Enoch

Powell, later infamous for his 'Rivers of Blood' speech, was one of the only Conservative MPs to hold his own government to task, after what Castle described as a 'nauseating parade of complacency' among his colleagues. In a much-celebrated speech, Powell said that although Hola Camp was in Africa – 'and things are different there' – Britain could not have 'African standards in Africa, Asian standards in Asia and perhaps British standards here at home'. The massacre was not, he maintained, 'how Englishmen act': an indictment of colonial violence, wrapped up in a defence of British values.[39]

Many within the British media and British public reacted with disgust and distaste to the news from Kenya. The Colonial Office collected examples of the numerous letters sent by the general public to Members of Parliament expressing anger at the revelations: one, from a Mr Butlin in Twickenham to his MP Gresham Cooke, said that although it had been 'easy to disagree' with some of the actions of the post-war Labour government, he thought it was 'fair to say that it is only under the Conservatives that a considerable number of Englishmen have been made to feel actually ashamed of their nationality'.[40] Another, from Ron and Hilda Hitchcock to Lennox-Boyd, argued that the atrocities in Kenya differed 'not in principle but only in number from those of the Nazis against the Jews'.[41] In fact, as early as 1955, Castle had visited the colony and had described the 'Nazi attitude towards the Africans' that she found there. Only a decade since the Second World War, these comparisons to Nazi atrocities were a powerful rhetorical puncturing of British pretensions to liberal humanitarianism.

Despite the disgust, these events – and the anger they inspired – soon drifted from public view and into obscurity. In 2002, when five elderly Kenyans began the complex and laborious process of suing the British government for their complicity in torture, the BBC's Kenya correspondent John McGhie fronted a documentary, *Kenya: White Terror*, evidently designed for an audience largely ignorant of this period of imperial history; McGhie claimed that the supposed 'revelations' of torture in the programme went 'far beyond what was known at the time', even though campaigners in the 1950s had been explicit about the treatment of Kenyan prisoners, and the British colonial administration and government had full knowledge about what was going on.[42]

In the case of the crisis over Southern Rhodesia in the 1960s, a similar feat of forgetting was so successful that by the time of Zimbabwe's economic collapse and political unrest in the 1990s and early 2000s, it barely occurred to most Britons that their country held any responsibility for its former colony's perilous position. In 2017, when Robert Mugabe resigned after thirty years of increasingly controversial rule over the country, Theresa May could say without any apparent irony that Zimbabwean people finally now had the chance 'to forge a new path' which was free from 'oppression', blithely characterising Britain as 'Zimbabwe's oldest friend'.[43]

In the late 1950s, Southern Rhodesia was being run as it always had been along strict racial lines, with a system of government entirely run by the white settlers who comprised roughly 5 per cent of the population. The white Rhodesians, with their bitter fears of Black nationalism and communism, were known to be radically right wing and committed to a very traditional version of imperialism and Britishness overseas. From outside, the colony was thought of as 'the home of old jokes, old songs and one of the last outposts of fox-trotting ballroom dancing'; the settlers were referred to by the British people who had to work with them as 'Surrey with the lunatic fringe on top'.[44]

This nostalgia and tradition was sustained by a firm commitment to the tenets of white supremacy and colonial rule. In 1959, a Labour MP had been deported from the country because he was seen as a threat to this white authoritarianism. John Stonehouse had given a speech to 1,500 Southern Rhodesian African National Congress activists in which he had actually asked them not to use violence, but his call for them to 'Hold your heads high and behave as though this country belonged to you' had led Rhodesian newspapers to decry the politician as a traitor anyway. When he invited three Black Africans to eat with him in the Meikle's Hotel (where Barbara Castle had also broken the colour bar by having dinner with a Black politician the year before) this proved too much for the colonial administration and Stonehouse was sent to Tanganyika in disgrace.

Back in Britain, MPs voted on a motion to criticise Macmillan's government for not supporting Stonehouse and to argue that British citizens should have the right to freely enter British colonies whether the local government wanted them to or not.[45] The motion fell 237 to 293 against, with Conservative MPs largely unwilling to stand up for a Labour MP against their allies in Salisbury (as the capital, now Harare, was then known). The future Labour leader Michael Foot used the idea of imperial duty to defend Stonehouse, arguing that MPs 'should assert our responsibility for the dependent territories', framing this responsibility not in terms of continuing white colonial rule but of defending the rights of Black Africans to work towards independence.[46]

In the early 1960s, those in the colony responded to the rising tide of decolonisation by writing letters to the *Daily Telegraph*, the paper of choice for settlers in the remaining colonies and ex-colonial officials in the metropole. One correspondent from Salisbury described in glowing terms the work that settlers were doing to educate African children, irrigate African land and pass judgement on African court cases with 'enormous kindness and humour', before concluding – in a sentiment that would not have seemed out of place in Victorian colonial literature – that the colonial state was working hard to 'bring the African into true and responsible adulthood'.[47] Another writer from the Rhodesian capital mocked British pretensions to superiority over the territory, pointing to the recent disturbances between mods and rockers and asking whether the UN should send a peacekeeping force comprising Kenyan, Cypriot, Congolese and Indonesian troops into the 'trouble-spots' of Margate, Brighton and Clacton; the editor headlined this letter 'Darkest Britain', which readers of the paper no doubt found very amusing.[48] The *Telegraph* was itself strongly committed to Southern Rhodesia as a last bastion of British colonial rule overseas. One November 1964 article, headlined 'Rhodesia Faces the Hard, Hard Realities', criticised those settlers who had moved to the region not 'to fight a crusade but only to double or treble their income' and lamented that as a result 'white supremacy' would 'ebb away' until there was a Black majority government in the colony.[49]

In fact, the Rhodesian settlers responded to perceived pressure from the British to decolonise by following their government in entrenching their position. On 11 November 1965, the Rhodesian cabinet pulled together under Smith to issue a 'UDI', a unilateral declaration of independence, the first in the empire since the thirteen American colonies had broken away in 1776. The Rhodesian UDI differed from that of the revolutionary Americans', however, in its ending: at the bottom of the document was a respectful 'God Save the Queen'. As far as Smith and his acolytes were concerned, it was the British government, not the Crown, from which they were breaking away, because it was the Rhodesians, not the people in the metropole, who represented the real spirit of British patriotism.

The Wilson government responded severely by imposing trade sanctions: an embargo on Rhodesian tobacco and sugar, asbestos, copper, lithium, chrome, iron, steel and meat, along with a ban on Rhodesian citizens drawing on British interest payments, dividends and pensions.[50] But this strong stance was tempered with frequent attempts to reach out to and negotiate with Smith. Wilson at one point asked for plans to be drawn up for military force against the territory, but ultimately was unable to countenance making war on British 'kith and kin'.[51] Anti-colonialist groups such as the MCF despaired; pro-empire groups such as the Monday Club, meanwhile, sent delegations to UDI Rhodesia and agitated for sanctions to be lifted. It was not until 1980 that the Southern Rhodesians were forced to surrender power to Black majority rule in newly created Zimbabwe; Peter Carrington, Foreign Secretary in the new Thatcher government, negotiated the handover of power.

Rhodesia retains a specific position in British imperial history: British newspapers frequently covered the descent of Mugabe's regime into dictatorship in lurid detail, although with very little acknowledgement that this might have anything to do with imperial legacies. British coverage was so prevalent partly because it could focus on the violence directed at white farmers as part of the 'land reform' programme of reclamation, in which the land owned by the white colonial settlers was being seized and redistributed to Black farmers; the long period of UDI meant that the transition from colony to independent nation was far messier than in other places. The murder of the first farmer, David Stevens, was even covered in a five-page spread in *Hello!* magazine, in which his tearful widow talked about living in the 'troubled country' with her husband.[52] In her memoir *Don't Let's Go to the Dogs Tonight,* Alexandra Fuller recounts her childhood spent in a reasonably poor, very chaotic family living in Rhodesia before and after independence, stricken by the tragedy of the deaths of three siblings and marred by the alcoholism of their parents. The breakdown of the family is plotted against the breakdown of the colony, as war rages outside the various farms of the white protagonists. Fuller recounts learning to shoot a gun to protect herself from the African 'terrs', or terrorists, who were coming, '*they said,* to chop off the ears and lips and eyelids of little white children'. When the revolutionary forces win the war and the white families flee, her boarding school becomes mostly Black overnight; she meets one little boy, Oliver Chiweshe, and marvels at him having a surname, having 'not known the full name of a single African' until that moment.[53] The book won a number of literary prizes in 2002, a time of increasing political instability in Zimbabwe under the dictatorship of Robert Mugabe, and attracted a wide readership. Perhaps the reading public were responding to a more complex depiction of the relationship between Britain and its colonies, in which white families were not universally wealthy, powerful or privileged. Perhaps it also appealed to an unspoken desire among them to downplay the power and violence of white supremacy in the region at a time when Mugabe was demonising British rule.

As decolonisation unfolded, many white British people came 'home' from Kenya, Rhodesia and other former colonies to a new life and a nation that was no longer familiar. The retired colonial colonel who settled in Cheltenham Spa and wistfully read the *Telegraph* for news from overseas needed to deal with 'pensioned idleness', while his wife would have to adapt to a new life without servants, nursemaids or cooks. As W. P. A. Robinson, an ex-army officer, wrote in *How To Live Well on Your Pension* in 1955, the colonial official's 'wife *never* retires' but must instead, newly bereft of kitchen staff, learn how to regard 'the very dead glare of a dead cod on a plate and . . . turn it into lunch'.[54]

Robinson's guide reveals the quotidian concerns of a returned colonial family, from advice about which cocktails to serve with lunch to which vegetables to grow in an English cottage garden. Throughout the book there runs a continual worry about (lack of) money and reduced status; the cottage garden is, in fact, repeatedly suggested as a way to supplement income. Given this anxiety, there also features a discussion of whether Britain is the most affordable place to retire, although it is never seriously considered that people would go elsewhere (such as, horror of horrors, to France). The benefits of the NHS for the necessary treatment of 'Bombay belly' and other chronic colonial conditions is cited as one reason to stick to Britain, but more broadly there is a sense that coming back to Britain is the patriotic thing to do.

At the heart of the book is a tension. Those returning or retiring from the colonies often felt deeply uncomfortable in an increasingly egalitarian and permissive British society and with the new position of Britain in the world. They were faced with a choice: was it more befitting of a colonial gentleman to exclaim that 'the country is going the dogs' and throw up his hands in horror, or to embrace the still reassuringly familiar Britain of 'the Village Church, the British Legion, the Women's Institute and other ways of "pulling your weight"'?[55] Did patriotism mean supporting the country as it changed and evolved with decolonisation, or bemoaning a lost past of imperial greatness? In his conclusion, Robinson manages somehow to take both positions simultaneously, in a defence of Kipling as a poet of empire against imagined criticism from the 'long-haired boys and short-haired girls of Bloomsbury'. His passionate outburst – 'And wasn't the world a damned sight better place when the Empire of which he sang (and for which we now apologize) swept the seas and kept the peace?'[56] – summarises the frustrated political nostalgia of a colonial class returning to a motherland that seemed infuriatingly ambivalent about the service to which they had devoted their lives. It is difficult to feel much sympathy for those facing the terrible task of preparing lunch without kitchen help or the comparative privation of a colonial pension, but the contrast with the luxury and privilege of imperial life was undoubtedly stark. British colonial officials' roles in the empire were often complicated and tiresome, sometimes lonely or upsetting, but they had been supported by hierarchies of class and race. For every administrator who had loved their colonial subjects there was another who had ruled with an iron fist. More to the point, all served to sustain imperial ideas about civilisation, identity and Britain's place at the top of the largest empire the world had ever seen; these ideas came home to Britain with the returning colonial officials, perpetuating imperial myths about class, gender and race in modern Britain even after decolonisation.

For however much these colonial figures felt that their service went unheralded, their contribution unknown or even disavowed, they remained undeniably part of the British political establishment and their continued efforts to uphold their colonial networks and connections had a strong influence on British political culture. In March 1966, the Queen unveiled a memorial stone at Westminster Abbey that commemorated all those who served the British Crown in the colonial territories. Six years previously, the Overseas Services Pensioners' Association (OSPA) had been formed as an amalgamation of existing associations from Ceylon, Malaya, West Africa and East and Central Africa, primarily to protect the pension rights of colonial service retirees from around the empire, who had worked in territories under the Colonial Office but had not been employed by the British government and so were not guaranteed pension payouts. They eventually succeeded in their aims in 1973 with the passing of the Overseas Pension Act. Until that point and well beyond it, the association continued – in the words of its final chairman – to 'provide the record of our Service in the colonial territories and to uphold our reputation'.[57] Through this associational life, aimed at maintaining connections forged in empire, they also conserved the imperial outlook. The authors in *Overseas Pensioner*, the OSPA journal, frequently discussed topics such as whether to emigrate to places like Tenerife – pros: warm, cheap, affordable domestic help; cons: Spanish – and how to encourage younger relatives to pursue careers in industries such as metal mining in the former colonies.[58] One issue extracted a piece that had run in the *Sunday Express* about the Colonial Office becoming the Commonwealth Relations Office, which valorised colonial service as work that had 'shone the light of Christianity' where there had been merely 'dark superstition and savagery', and lamented the retirees' existence 'eking out their pensions in humble guest houses in Cheltenham or Bournemouth'.[59] Throughout the OSPA community there was a strong sense of grievance about a nation who no longer appreciated the pensioners' colonial contribution, who felt judged, instead, by the new cultural dominance of a group described by the *Sunday Express* as 'stay-at-home progressives'.[60]

The new Labour government was indeed busily reimagining Britain's official relationship with its empire and former empire. The creation of an Overseas Development Ministry had been a key manifesto pledge for Labour in the 1964 election; the new department was duly established, with Barbara Castle as the first Cabinet minister overseeing 'overseas' (rather than 'colonial') aid and development policy, which had previously been split between multiple departments. Not everyone in Britain was happy with the shift to working alongside people from the Global South rather than ruling over them, or with the government budgeting foreign aid for recipients in former colonies rather than spending this money at home. When Castle was pictured at a conference on development with the Malawian politician Hastings Banda, who had held her in an awkward hug for the cameras, she received some of the worst hate mail of her career – 'a shoal of the filthiest letters I have ever received'.[61] The letter writers sent in newspaper clippings of the story anno- tated with their hatred. Castle was described as a 'cheap cow', Banda (who had criticised British policy in Africa) as 'an enemy of this wonderful country' and 'decent white people', and aid generally was denigrated as being provided at the expense of 'old pensioners' in Britain.[62] One letter writer compared Castle to Dusty Springfield as a fellow lover of 'n****r boys', as the singer had recently been deported from apartheid South Africa after she had insisted on per- forming to mixed audiences.[63] Castle responded by engineering a photo shoot a few months later in Tanzania in which she was pic- tured 'smiling broadly' as she held a 'little black baby close'.[64] For the British public, a white woman cuddling a 'black baby' was far more palatable than a white woman being embraced by an African man, and the response was overwhelmingly positive, with the *Daily Express* covering the story with the headline 'A Cuddle in the Sun'.

For many British people, overseas development aid offered a reassuring continuity with imperialism; for some, it extended the opportunities once offered by empire for work, travel and adven- ture. Young men and women whose colonial careers had been cut short by decolonisation found new work in new institutions like Oxfam, the FAO and the UN. Oxfam advertised many job openings in this period in the *Guardian*, with one advert for the position of 'assistant personnel officer', aimed at women, describing it as 'a job of real value to people in developing countries' and 'genuinely inter- esting' work.[65] The Overseas Development Ministry was itself also keen to recruit, advertising positions for 'teachers, doctors, profes- sionally qualified engineers, agriculturalists, veterinary surgeons, architects, town planners' as well as more specific roles such as the head of the Economic Planning Unit for the government of Mauri- tius. The adverts proclaim that the jobs are 'doubly rewarding' – they came with the 'rich reward of helping developing countries in their fight against hunger, disease, poverty and illiteracy', but more tangi- bly included benefits including 'attractive pay with overseas allowance, accommodation at low rental, children's education allowances' and a series of marketable skills for future employers, many of whom 'regard overseas service', to use a distinctly imperial phrase, 'as a plus mark'.[66]

Many young Brits pursued opportunities as volunteers through charitable organisations. One of these was Voluntary Service Overseas (VSO), which had been set up by Alec and Mona Dickson in 1958. It was launched with a letter in the *Sunday Times*, written by the Bishop of Portsmouth, which addressed school leavers looking to fill their time before university and called for them to travel to 'the underdeveloped territories of the Commonwealth', to have the dual opportunities of 'doing something worthwhile, where it is most genuinely needed, and seeing a bit of the world into the bargain'.[67] This letter, and those that followed it over the coming weeks and months from supporters of the plan, such as the headmaster of Marlborough College, referred to this time as 'the year between'; the bishop had invented the gap year. The first eighteen volunteers travelled to Ghana, Nigeria, Northern Rhodesia and Sarawak, contributing their skills through activities like teaching in schools and digging wells. By the later 1960s, around 1,400 young people were travelling abroad each year with the organisation. VSO functioned explicitly as a way to provide opportunities for young British people in the newly independent developing world which would previously have been enabled through imperial networks.

The *Guardian* was a key mouthpiece for this work: as well as coverage of parliamentary debates on VSO, and pieces supporting the organisation (including letters to the editor written by Dickson himself), in 1968 the paper published a number of diaries written by VSO volunteers in a series called 'Adventures Overseas'. This followed individuals like Vic Sutton, nineteen, who taught English in French Cameroon, and David Cooke, twenty-two, who volunteered in India. These diaries often showed the volunteers to be somewhat out of their depth: the nineteen-year-old Miranda Mosscrop, who had travelled to the Solomon Islands for a year and was trying to set up a Women's Club craft shop, juxtaposed the beautiful samples of fans, mats and baskets sent by local women around the islands with her efforts at making pawpaw jam, and how she had 'really made a mess' in her demonstration of the recipe.[68] The diaries also inspired the *Guardian*'s schools competition that year. Students from primary school to sixth form were invited to submit 'essays, poems, drawings, paintings, scrapbooks, small models or research work of any kind' that related to VSO in some way. Students and teachers could also send off for a leaflet about the work of VSO and a desk map showing the countries where the charity worked, reminiscent of the maps of empire that used to adorn British classrooms.[69]

Despite attempts to present this new approach to the 'developing world' as humanitarian, modern, forward-looking and egalitarian, the world views of many British people heading abroad were very similar to those of their imperial peers from twenty or fifty years earlier. The organisation Scripture Union showcased the stories of twelve VSO volunteers who had been selected for their Christian faith, depicting them as something akin to a modern imperial missionary, committed to 'the unchangeableness of Jesus Christ in every nation and every situation'.[70] The former empire could still be a place for adventure, a place that Britain could dominate, lead or even civilise.

But also in 1968, activists working across several British humanitarian organisations, including Youth Against Hunger, Christian Aid, the Overseas Development Institute and perhaps most notably Oxfam, gathered in the small Surrey town of Haslemere to share their frustrations about the way that humanitarian action replicated many of the tropes of imperialism. One particular focus of theirs was the new term 'developing world', often applied to the newly independent former colonies, as a supposedly apolitical label. They argued that 'the developing world is not developing'; it was being held in poverty by the same global economic structures that had shaped and been shaped by imperialism. In the ensuing years, the Haslemere activists worked to highlight the politics of humanitarianism, arguing for interventions that challenged rather than replicated the structures that caused global poverty, and to call for global justice rather than a system built on charity and inequality.

University towns established their own Haslemere groups, holding film nights and discussion evenings, as well as taking part in activism such as campaigning against South African apartheid. In April 1969, the national group held a 'Poverty is Violence' country-wide convention at the Roundhouse in Camden, London, to 'educate themselves and the public about the problems of the Third World in order to create a large and vibrant force to join the struggle to end economic domination'.[71] The event included speakers such as the Reverend Trevor Huddleston, the seasoned campaigner against apartheid, the co-founder of the Black Panthers Bobby Seale, and Bishop Hélder Câmara, a Latin American liberationist theologian who argued passionately in his speech that the only real violence in the world was the poverty of the people – and who went straight from Camden to the Catholic church in Kew to baptise the infant son of the journalist Jan Rocha, in return for a lift to Gatwick Airport.[72]

Haslemere was a watershed because it pushed British charity workers into confronting the politics of the work that they were doing, rather than hiding behind the hitherto accepted values, set by the Red Cross in the nineteenth century, of 'impartiality' and 'neutrality'. It also spawned other groups, for example Third World First, which comprised Oxfam and Christian Aid workers who committed to give 1 per cent of their income to fight global inequality; they encouraged around a thousand Oxford undergraduates to make the same commitment, as well as founding the magazine *New Internationalist* to bring news of the Global South to British readers. As this generation became more influential in humanitarian work, they were often able to persuade their organisations to channel their work more explicitly into political campaigning against poverty and inequality, to the chagrin of British politicians who would rather they 'stick to their knitting'.[73]

In 1949 the London Declaration had allowed India to remain in the Commonwealth despite its status as a republic, and therefore set the precedent for nations to be part of the organisation without recognising the monarch as their head of state. The London

Declaration had also dropped the 'British' from the Commonwealth's title, and the modern Commonwealth of Nations was supposedly an equal federation of states with historic, political and economic interests in common. But the continuation of Britain's imperial identity through the Commonwealth was important: it tied Britain to its colonial heritage and it connected the British people to the rest of the world. Some British people were dismayed to discover that Britain was not the leader of the Commonwealth, but simply one of many member nations; this became apparent when the organisation became a forum in which other countries could air their criticisms of British foreign policy, especially its support for apartheid South Africa. But many British people embraced the Commonwealth too, particularly its cultural events.

The Imperial Institute had been established by royal charter, by Queen Victoria, in 1888. In 1958 it was renamed the Commonwealth Institute and in 1962 it was moved from Imperial College Road to a brand-new building on Kensington High Street. The building was constructed with materials from around the empire-Commonwealth, including wooden flooring in the galleries from Australia, East and West Africa, and Guyana, an auditorium stage made of New Zealand timber, and aluminium window frames made in Canada from bauxite mined in Guyana and Jamaica.[74] The commemorative handbook produced for its opening proudly explained that the project manager, A. J. Potts, was an Australian, and the construction team included men from India, Pakistan, Canada, New Zealand, the West Indies and Cyprus.[75] Beneath its self-consciously modern, swooping parabolic roof,[76] exhibitions were arranged geographically over three levels around a central atrium, with floating floors that made it look more like a giant spaceship than a museum. In order to 'stimulate and excite the imagination',[77] the galleries had varying colour schemes, lighting and soundscapes, and tactics of 'concealment and surprise' were used to avert boredom or complacency.[78] The Canada gallery was crowded with real tree trunks, the Ghana gallery contained a diorama of fishermen dragging a boat ashore, and in the Mauritius gallery, in front of a mural of a market, a set of life-size models depicted the four main racial groups in the colony buying and selling produce native to the region. In the India gallery there was even a figure of Gandhi, by the sculptor Ralph Brown, better known for his large sculptures of meat porters created for Harlow New Town. According to its handbook, written in 1966, the intention was to show 'The Commonwealth Under One Roof' and instil the idea that 'the Commonwealth is not merely an historic survival from the days of Empire' but 'an association of people whose eyes are on the future'.[79] The institute was not, in other words, a museum, nor was it interested in litigating the rights and wrongs of colonialism: it was a shrine to a new relationship, in which the peoples of the Commonwealth – depicted in varying stages of modernity, but all moving inexorably forwards – could find themselves on equal footing.

The 1965 Commonwealth Arts Festival had a similar aim, bringing people from around the Commonwealth to share their culture with the British. For over a fortnight events in Glasgow, Cardiff, Liverpool and London featured singing, dancing, poetry and theatre from Sri Lanka, Canada, Jamaica, Sierra Leone, Australia, Nigeria and New Zealand. As the narrator on the Pathé News broadcast 'Commonwealth Goes Gay' had it: 'London was invaded, and London loves it!'[80] The newsreel showed a crowd watching a performance in Trafalgar Square, first awkwardly clapping and then gradually joining in, as steel bands from Trinidad and Tobago played up on stage.

But this glorification hid significant divisions within the festival itself. The white dominions had been allowed and encouraged to send more artists than poorer Black nations, and the types of performance chosen to be showcased betrayed an implicit hierarchy of cultures. Australia sent the entire Sydney Philharmonic Orchestra, in a display of 'high' Western culture that ignored its Aboriginal community, and was gladly accommodated by the British organisers. But when Sierra Leone decided to send a traditional dance troupe in which female artists would perform topless, the hosts were thrown into a panic; the performance was moved from its intended location under Nelson's Column to the Royal Festival

Hall, where it was hoped that nudity would draw less attention and be rendered more acceptably 'artistic'.[81]

In 1966, the British Empire and Commonwealth Games were held in Kingston, Jamaica. The games had first been held in 1930 as the British Empire Games, and, except for during the war, had been staged every four years since.[82] The changing name of the games said much about the shifting and waning of British power: from 1954 until 1966 they were known as the British Empire and Commonwealth Games; from 1970 to 1974 they were the British Commonwealth Games, before becoming simply the Commonwealth Games in 1978.

The 1966 games were the first held outside Britain or the white dominions. A Pathé news clip described 'a day of uninhibited gaiety, with a splendid evening to follow' as the games coincided with Jamaica Independence Day; the opening parade footage showed bands and parade floats from around the Commonwealth, watched by Jamaicans eating ice cream, riding bicycles and dancing to the music. One of the big stories of the games was the victory of Naftali Temu, who beat the world record holder Ron Clarke to win gold in the six-mile run (the pre-decimalisation equivalent of the 10km); Temu would go on to become Kenya's first Olympic gold medal winner at the 1968 Mexico Olympics.[83] The news footage of the time did highlight Temu's achievement, but mostly focused on the success of white athletes and swimmers from Britain and the dominions, with a great emphasis on how difficult the heat was for them to cope with (a classic concern of imperial literature); one runner, Bill Adcocks, is shown running the twenty-mile race in ninety-degree heat with a knotted handkerchief on his head, every inch the Englishman abroad.[84] British medical reports from the games echoed the old anxiety of empire that the weather was a bad influence on Brits overseas; as well as disapproving references to the number of athletes suffering sunburn, there is consternation that some of the British competitors had injured themselves by running around in tropical 'topless sandals'.[85]

Meanwhile, empire continued to permeate British experience in more quotidian ways. A set of recipe booklets produced by the Women's Gas Federation to promote domestic gas ovens offered housewives a variety of meals that drew on imperial inspiration (as well as other British regional and European dishes). The recipes varied in appeal: 'A Maori Favourite', for example, was a shoulder of lamb stuffed with pork mince and tinned sweetcorn, while 'Ceylon Curry' was a surprisingly authentic recipe for dal, albeit with cautious instructions about the amount of curry powder to be added only 'according to taste'.[86] In one specially themed pamphlet, home cooks were brightly told that Australia produced 'sunshine fruits' for winter meals, and were encouraged to cook dishes such as 'Turkey Orientale', a mixture of turkey, sultanas, onion, almonds and curry powder rolled up in scone dough, while being reminded that 'Australia supplies Britain with more sultanas than the rest of the world put together'.[87]

Children's books continued to promote imperial values in the nursery too, even though the empire itself had almost entirely dissolved by the end of the 1960s. Alongside titles such as *The Story of Captain Cook* (1958), *David Livingstone* (1960) and *Christopher Columbus* (1961), Ladybird published a 'Travel Adventure' series annually from 1958 to 1962 in which Alison and John and their father take 'flights' around six regions: Australia, Canada, the USA, India, Africa and the Holy Land. In *Flight Four: India*, the trip takes in 'the land of temples and tigers, elephants, parrots and monkeys', an 'exciting country of ancient mystery and modern industry'. Gandhi is described as a 'great man' and the demand for independence 'quite natural', although the British colonists who 'devoted their lives to India' are also celebrated. At the end of the book, the two children summarise their experience in India:

'It's such a kind country' said Alison, thoughtfully, 'and peaceful, too. It's horrid to see so many beggars and very poor people, of course. But so many people are gracious and good-looking.'

'I like the great mountains', said John, 'and the valley of the Ganges, full of people and colour and excitement, and all the old temples. And I like to think of the British people who lived here and helped to make India a great nation. And I like the animals – especially that tiger!'[88]

Africa is presented somewhat differently: an entire 'dark continent of desert, great rivers and mighty jungle'. As in India, 'great industries are being developed' while 'the throb of native drums can still be heard', but here the history of British intervention is sanitised beyond any accuracy: 'Britain took a stand against slavery in the eighteenth century, and other countries followed suit. Britain came here to stop the slave trade, and eventually we took over East Africa.' The narrative of African 'progress' is also distinctly mixed, with John and Alison's father explaining that African people 'still believe in witch doctors and millions can't read or write', and the story of decolonisation is deliberately fudged: as their father explains, 'in all the countries which were under British control [the Africans] have been given their independence because they are able to manage their own affairs'. In fact, of all the places visited in the book – the Sudan, Uganda, Kenya, Tanzania, Malawi, Zambia, Rhodesia, South Africa, the Congo, Nigeria, Zanzibar and Ghana – only Ghana, Nigeria and Tanzania had gone through formal decolonisation at the time of its publication in 1961. Again, the children summarise their reactions at the end: 'I like Africa, and the Africans!' says Alison, and John concurs: 'I like the wild animals, too.'[89]

Of course, many parents passed their own childhood books and toys down to their offspring, and these cherished possessions came with a side order of imperial patriotism. This was sometimes an unthinking reflex, and for others a conscious attempt to instil their values in the next generation, but these old-fashioned attitudes did not always pass without comment. Lena Jeger MP, writing in the *Guardian* in 1966, recounted her recent experience of reading an Enid Blyton book to a child she knew and being horrified at the racist message she found in its pages: a child, Matty, has been given a toy, Little Black Sambo, who cannot be loved because of the colour of his skin, and whose only chance at redemption comes when some magic rain washes him pink. As Jeger said, this was an 'insidiously dangerous' message, which she felt should be rejected by parents and even censored by the government as liable to promote racism.[90]

But for many audiences empire remained a source of excitement, fascination and nostalgia. The films *Zulu* (1964) and *Khartoum* (1966) both provided a nostalgic vision of Britain's nineteenth-century imperial expansion at the cost of hundreds of African lives. *Zulu*, which featured Michael Caine in his first major role, is a sprawling epic depiction of the Battle of Rorke's Drift, in which 150 British soldiers fought off 4,000 Zulu forces. The latter are depicted (entirely fictitiously) singing a song that honours the British as fellow brave warriors before they retreat. *Khartoum* shows the doomed attempts of Charlton Heston's General Gordon to defend British Khartoum from the invading Sudanese forces, whose leader the Mahdi is played by Laurence Olivier in blackface. *Zulu,* in particular, was extremely popular with British audiences, playing at cinemas for twelve years after its release; it is still frequently listed in best British film lists. The production was shot mostly in apartheid South Africa, an experience which apparently unsettled Michael Caine to the extent that he refused to work in the country again until the regime was lifted; he later starred in a film with Sidney Poitier, *The Wilby Conspiracy* (1975), in which the two men team up to resist the apartheid state, although this was nowhere near as popular with the British public as the imperial apologia of his first film.

In 1968, another hugely popular film drew on imperial inspiration in a different way. *Carry On Up the Khyber* was the second biggest box-office film of the year; in 1999 it made it onto the list of 100 best British films in a survey conducted by the BFI of British film and TV professionals. The film satirised the imperial fantasies that lay behind *Zulu* and *Khartoum* in a complex story that was, even so, still saturated with stereotypical assumptions about British imperial masculinity and racial identity. A *Variety* review at the time praised the finale of the film in which 'the tribal chiefs launch a full-scale attack on the government residence while the governor and his guests with unshaken poise nonchalantly continue dinner amid the turmoil', and singled out Sid James's 'bluff, vulgar British governor' as its most compelling character; they also praised the 'nubile "native" lasses' who added to 'the scenery, the comedy and the sexiness'.[91]

In October 1959, readers of the *Daily Mail* might have been pleased to see a surprising good-news story over their tea and toast. Sandwiched between adverts for Courvoisier brandy and Prudential Insurance was a piece proclaiming that, for the first time in the twentieth century, 'nobody is shooting at a British soldier'. It had been six months, apparently, since the last death of a Tommy by enemy fire. That month, the final boatloads of young British men were returning home from colonial conflict in Cyprus, after more than fifty years of British military action, from the Boer War and the two world wars, to Kenya, Malaya, Palestine and Suez. There were 'no frontier wars. No colonial wars. No UN wars . . . just no wars at all where a British soldier is risking his neck.'[92]

Some British people, in other words, were not so sad to see Britain's international role diminish. For every person who lamented the loss of empire, prestige, power and glory, there was another who embraced the idea of decolonisation as a moment of reparative justice; but perhaps the abiding feeling for many was simply that Britain was better off out of it. The 1960s would not be a quiet time, internationally – the Vietnam War was brought home to the British people on their television screens and in the protests that raged in their capital city – but the British themselves could perhaps feel somewhat detached from what was happening over there. They could not, however, stay complacent in isolation from the wider world. As the empire gradually broke free from British rule, the people who had once been colonial citizens became something different. Many of them chose to make their way to Britain, the former metropole, their former motherland, to build new lives. These new lives were based in communities that were painstakingly constructed in an unfamiliar, often hostile environment.

5

No Dogs, No Blacks, No Irish:
Migration and Racism in the 1960s and 1970s

In 1963, the sociologist Pearl Jephcott conducted a research study in Kensington, one of the largest, most densely populated and wealthiest boroughs in London. The borough was known for its affluence, including as it did the large houses of Holland Park (one seven-bedroom flat had recently been advertised to rent for £55 a week and was thought to be the most expensive apartment in the country), the ornate exhibitions of the Victoria and Albert Museum, and numerous embassies and diplomatic residencies. But as well as diplomats and debutantes, it was also home to much poverty, mostly concentrated in the North Kensington region of Notting Dale, a council ward which forms part of Notting Hill. This area contained the slums of Harrow Road, the densely populated Golborne Ward, and numerous junior schools that were coping with severe deprivation (with 17 per cent of their pupils receiving free school meals compared with the London average of just 5 per cent).

Published in 1964 as *A Troubled Area: Notes on Notting Hill*, Jephcott's book was inspired by the 1958 race riots which had 'brought North Kensington into the limelight as a district where people lived because they had to and left as soon as possible because they wanted to'.[1] On top of the riots, the area had also experienced sporadic but disruptive activity by the far right, and the housing problems had been heightened by exploitation and intimidation by landlords engaged in 'Rachmanism', named after the rogue landlord Peter Rachman who had housed West Indian migrants at vastly inflated rents and pitted Black and white tenants against one another. Jephcott's study was partly aimed at disproving the lazy assertion by many politicians, local authority workers and white community activists that the problems of North Kensington were caused by the influx of West Indian migrants to the area. Jephcott situated this within a much longer history of migration to the area – including Irish navvies in the nineteenth century who had also been depicted as a troublesome and disruptive community – and downplayed the idea that these newer migrant groups were either especially problematic or taking resources from white residents of the area. Instead, she focused on the squalor and poor housing conditions that these people were forced to live in, the lack of amenities for children, and the lack of incentives or help provided for these communities to improve their environment.

It was certainly true that people in Notting Dale were more likely to live in poverty and poor housing – Jephcott's study found that three-fifths of the West Indian migrants were living in single rooms. But what was also clear was that as well as experiencing severe hardship, these groups were caught in a double bind: they were being blamed for the poor conditions in which they were forced to live, and they were not being given the tools or resources needed to improve their lives. When the council responded to Jephcott's survey, they did so by saying that the main problem faced by the area was the 'invasion' by immigrants, and protested that their previous attempts to provide amenities such as playgrounds had simply been met with vandalism.[2]

These realities of life in Notting Hill for the Black community are captured in a different way in the photographs of Charlie Phillips. Charlie had moved from Jamaica to London in 1956, at the age of eleven, to join his parents; he had been an altar boy at St Michael and All Angels, which had held the funeral for the murdered Kelso Cochrane in 1959, although his parents had been so worried that there might be a race riot at the church that he did not join the procession.[3] He became a photographer after being given a Kodak Brownie as a gift, working as a photojournalist and among paparazzi across Europe, but some of his most striking work is that documenting the bright and bustling life of the Black community in west

London in the 1960s, 70s and 80s. Ten of his pictures are currently held by the V&A: one shows a dapper Black man standing on the platform at Westbourne Park, dressed in a blazer and dark glasses; another shows a mixed-race couple, Anita Santiago and Osmond 'Gus' Philip, poised and beautiful, staring down the lens at a house party in Notting Hill.[4] One picture, though, has no people in it. It is a photograph instead of a scrap of lined paper, pinned on a notice-board, with a handwritten notice advertising a flat to let. The entire text of the advert, before the phone number to call, reads:

FLAT TO LET
3 rooms K+B [kitchen and bathroom],
Married Couple Only
No Coloured.[5]

In response to the race riots in Notting Hill of 1958, the following year saw the first British Caribbean Carnival, organised by Claudia Jones and held in St Pancras Town Hall. It was directed by Edric Connor, who had had a hit in 1957 with the 'Manchester United Calypso' ('A bunch of bouncing Busby Babes / they deserve to be knighted') and in 1958 was the first Black actor to join the Royal Shakespeare Company in Stratford-upon-Avon. The BBC televised its filmed footage from the day-long event as 'Trinidad Comes to Town' in a half-hour programme that evening, described in the listings as a celebration of the 'annual Trinidad fete'.[6] The carnival included a beauty queen parade to choose the Carnival Queen, and a photograph from 1959 shows ten contenders, lined up in their swimsuits in the town hall and looking a little chilly.[7] The first prize was donated by Grimaldi–Siosa Lines and was a round trip to the West Indies on one of the company's 'luxury liners', and the novelists Sam Selvon and George Lamming were among the judges.[8]

In 1966, the British Caribbean Carnival moved to Notting Hill and became a celebration of diversity and local unity; a local social worker, Rhaune Laslett, wanted to organise a fete to bring together the various communities living in the area and developed the idea of carnival that Jones had showcased in St Pancras. The first year included the London Irish Girl Pipers, a New Orleans-style jazz band, Ginger Johnson (a well-known Nigerian jazz drummer, part of the swinging London music scene) and his band the African Messengers, and Russell Henderson's Trinidadian steel band.

It was not just carnival that grew out of the racism of the Notting Hill riots. Claudia Jones was also the editor of the *West Indian Gazette*, which gave a voice to the capital's West Indian community and created a platform for countless writers. Donald Hinds, whose own career started on the paper, pointed out that the British press mostly covered West Indian people as cricketers, or in 'sensational reporting' about the West Indian community and immigration: the only way to see themselves covered more accurately was to start their own publications.[9] Jones described the paper as 'a catalyst, quickening the awareness, socially and political, of West Indians and Afro-Asians in Britain', which had fought against 'imperialist outrages and indignities to our peoples'.[10] The paper was much in demand, frequently selling out its standard 30,000 copies in its heyday from 1958 to 1962, but struggled to survive much past the mid-1960s because of the constant financial and political pressures on the publication. When Jones died in 1965, her funeral procession marched behind a huge banner reading 'WORLD PEOPLE UNITE FOR FREEDOM AND PEACE'. Hundreds of people, including George Lamming, Dr David Pitt, and diplomatic representatives from Africa, Asia, the West Indies and Cuba, but also many ordinary people, made up a vast, multiracial congregation, come to mourn the unofficial 'national leader of the Afro-Asian Caribbean peoples in Britain', as Donald Hinds wrote in Jones's obituary in the paper to which she had dedicated the latter years of her life.[11]

Migration from the Caribbean did not begin with the *Empire Windrush*, nor did it end there, continuing steadily into the 1960s – between 1947 and 1970, almost half a million people came from the West Indies to the United Kingdom. This migration had a profound effect on

British life, both through the migrants' lives in particular neighbourhoods and their effect on wider British culture. And the West Indies was not the only region sending people to start new lives in the former metropole. Britain was increasingly a nation of immigrants, which included a significant proportion of people from what was then known as the 'new Commonwealth', an official euphemism for those countries in the former empire that did not have a majority white population. In the 1971 census, over 1.1 million people living in the UK were recorded as having been born in one of these countries.

The context of this immigration was more and more troubled. After the full employment of the Second World War, and the prosperity of the 1950s, there was rising unemployment in the 1960s. More and more, migrants were seen as competitors for jobs and housing, of which there had also been a pressing shortage since the Blitz, and benefits, which, under the welfare state, were becoming increasingly expensive for the government with a rising population. By 1967, Gallup found that 60 per cent of people surveyed thought that Britain had been harmed by immigration from the 'new Commonwealth' and 55 per cent thought that 'immigration' or 'coloured people' were a 'serious social problem'.[12]

In the 1960s and into the 1970s, anxieties about 'integration' and increased diversity led to intense scrutiny not just of the number of migrants entering the country but also of the areas where they were choosing to settle. This extended beyond places that had been traditionally multicultural, such as the dock cities of Cardiff, Glasgow, London, to Lancashire, the Midlands and Yorkshire – places like Birmingham, Bradford, Oldham. Zaiba Malik's parents came from Pakistan and settled in Bradford, where she and her siblings were born in the 1960s; her father worked long shifts in the textile mills that had attracted many Pakistani migrants with the promise of familiar work, and so 'the city that was once called Worstedopolis, on account of its production of fine worsted wool, the best in the world, was now Bradistan'.[13] Indeed, the city sign was frequently doctored to reflect this new nickname, which could either be a racist slur or a mark of local pride, depending on who was using it.

Pearl Jephcott's *A Troubled Area* was followed by other sociological studies, such as Sheila Patterson's *Dark Strangers*, devoted to exploring the issue of 'integration' and worrying about how communities would absorb mass migrations. Patterson was hopeful that the West Indian community in Brixton, south London, would eventually be assimilated as the Irish had been before them, but she opened her book by writing about the shock of encountering a Brixton street in which 'apart from some shopping housewives and a posse of teddy boys in tight jeans outside the billiards room, almost everybody had a coloured skin'; from 'two dozen black men' waiting outside the employment exchange to 'half of the exuberant infants playing outside the prefab nursery' with their *'cafe noir* or *cafe au lait'* colouring.[14] Patterson believed that most people in Britain 'knew that the majority of inhabitants of the Commonwealth' were people of colour, and 'were even used to the idea that there were old-fashioned coloured communities tucked away in dock and port areas of Britain itself', but that the presence of large communities of people of colour in the centre of large industrial cities led to what she had herself experienced as a 'colour shock'.[15]

Her research used jobs, housing and social activities to explore how the West Indian community – and their white neighbours – had experienced a process of assimilation and familiarisation. Patterson documented the attitudes of white British people in south London to their Caribbean neighbours: the local Labour Party constituency worker who said that it was unfair that Black migrants 'reap all the benefit' of the working-class fight for a welfare state 'without any effort on their part'; the personnel manager at the Pneumastic Company Ltd factory, who said they preferred the Caribbean workers to the overly mobile Irish but also dismissed many Black applicants as 'right out of the jungle' and 'barely literate'; the middle-aged man who said he was afraid to let his daughter walk down Coldharbour Lane because it looked like 'darkest Africa'.[16] And yet Patterson also uncovered through her interviews a West Indian community that was becoming more solidly embedded in south London, feeling more at home, and gradually gaining acceptance among their white neighbours and colleagues; Thelma, for example, who gave an account of steady employment, an attractive flat with 'a good deal of expensive new furniture', a happy marriage and a strong feeling that Brixton was her home (albeit a home with a 'trying' climate).[17] Patterson argued that good race relations, particularly the acceptance and support of new migrant communities, was critical for the development of Britain's post-imperial identity: it was vital that 'the coloured members of the new multi-racial *familia* feel and are made to feel as much at home economically and socially in Britain and elsewhere as the foundation members of the old white family have long felt'.[18]

In order, supposedly, to facilitate this, in 1967, the Home Office produced a booklet, 'Introduction to Britain: A Guide for Commonwealth Immigrants'. This was intended to give potential migrants to the country a basic introduction to British laws and customs; these booklets were periodically updated into the 1980s. The guide opened by saying that it 'welcomes you to Britain and tells you some of the things about life in this country which might not be familiar to you'; it covered housing, education, health and social security, employment, exchange control, entry of dependants, customs control, elections, income tax, and told the reader to get in touch with the Citizens Advice Bureau or local community relations council if they needed more support. The booklet is informative but also gently chiding of its readers, who it assumes to be both somewhat clueless and also possibly on the take: housing, for example, starts by saying that 'before you decide to come to Britain you must make sure that you will be able to find both a house and a job'. It finishes with a section on climate: 'Do not forget that Britain is often cold and wet, particularly from November to April. Make sure that you travel with enough clothes to keep you warm and that you have enough money to buy more warm clothes when you arrive.'[19]

However, despite the lip service paid to supporting migrant communities coming to Britain, integration was very much a burden placed on people of colour, who were expected to accept, without questioning, British norms and customs and to ignore the ways in which they were made to feel unwelcome. Dipak Nandy, in his work at the Runnymede Trust (a think tank devoted to racial justice), pointed out that there was a continual political demand for people of colour to 'integrate' into British society and their local communities, but the places they found themselves in often lacked any meaningful community structures. Instead, they found themselves living in places where 'young people who are waiting to move out and old people who never will, "problem families" and poor families, the Irish, the coloured, jostle one another in the streets, and that is all there is by way of contacts between them'.[20] Because migrants mostly made their homes in places that were already experiencing poverty and dislocation, because this was where they could most readily afford to live and often the only places where they found landlords willing to rent to them, there was nothing tangible into which they could integrate. Instead they stuck out: a useful scapegoat for politicians who wished to avoid speaking about poverty and inequality and who could instead blame the deprivation in these communities on an influx of immigrants.

First Conservative and then Labour governments became increasingly concerned with keeping these numbers as low as possible. Legislation was passed to limit immigration, which was often framed around general questions of migration but which undeniably aimed at limiting migration first and foremost from the 'new Commonwealth', immigrants who were overwhelmingly people of colour. The 1962 Commonwealth Immigrants Act was the first piece of legislation since 1948 to place any limitation on migration from the empire. It decreed that those citizens whose passports were not directly issued by the United Kingdom – anybody from a colony or dominion, any of the citizens supposedly bound to Britain through the Commonwealth – were subject to immigration control, and introduced employment vouchers for people in desired industries; would-be immigrants were graded on their apparent employability.

Claudia Jones railed against the 1962 Act. She used the front page of the *Gazette* to decry the 'hypocrisy and pretence' of it, which existed 'primarily and solely' to prevent the entry – and enable the ejection – of people of colour from the Commonwealth. As such, the Conservative government was turning its back on the myth of a multiracial Commonwealth; despite its 'window dressing', the Act would become 'an official colour bar against the coloured and the poor', from 'Kingston or Port-of-Spain, from Karachi or New Delhi'.[21] The bill had been opposed by a number of Labour MPs, trade unionists, church groups, cooperative organisations, as well as organised protest groups such as the Indian Workers' Association and the Movement for Colonial Freedom. But it was no use: the Act was passed and the controls came into force. The government instructions to immigration officers stated that no obstacle should be presented to Commonwealth citizens who were 'genuinely wishing to visit the United Kingdom', for a holiday or for 'social, family, cultural or business reasons'. Presumably mindful of the furore about the new restrictions, the document opened with the directive that immigration officers should do their job 'without regard to the race, colour or religion of the Commonwealth citizens who may seek to enter the country'[22] But, of course, some groups found themselves far more impacted by this Act than others.

One person directly caught up with these changes was Carmen Bryan. Carmen was twenty-two years old in June 1962 when she walked into a shop in Paddington, London, and stole £2 worth of items, including a packet of tomatoes, four tins of milk and five pairs of nylon tights.[23] She pleaded guilty to a first offence of petty larceny, and was conditionally discharged. However, instead of being released, she was taken straight to Holloway Prison and remained there for five weeks with no legal advice, waiting to hear the ruling from the Home Secretary, Henry Brooke, on whether she should be deported for her crime. This was a possible punishment – despite the minor nature of her actions and the fact that it was her first offence – because Carmen was Jamaican, and because of the passage of the 1962 Commonwealth Immigrants Act. This gave courts the power to deport any Commonwealth citizen who had been living in the

United Kingdom for less than five years if they had been convicted of a crime that might carry a prison sentence.

Carmen's case was championed by the press, by the Jamaican Migrants Service and the Jamaican High Commission, which all lobbied the Home Office not to deport her. Many arguments were given: she had come to Britain on a long journey to make a new life in the country; being sent back to Jamaica would cause her hardship beyond that necessitated in punishment for her crime; the journey would cost the British government £75. Ultimately, Carmen's supporters were victorious, and she was released from prison back to her life in London; the Home Secretary claimed, in making this decision, that deportation had only been considered because the courts believed she might be happier in Jamaica and, once they realised her preference was to stay in Britain, they were happy to reconsider. The next year, Carmen married a Black British welder and they decided, voluntarily, to move to Jamaica; a story in the *People* reported that they wanted to raise their family in the Caribbean sunshine.[24]

Not every story turned out so happily. After the passage of the Act, the threat of deportation was wielded by courts and politicians as part of an increasingly explicit conversation about policing the boundaries of the British nation and preserving the idealised conception of 'British' people: law-abiding, assimilated within British society and ideally (although this often went without being said) white. It was not only Caribbean migrants who were targeted – in fact, in the context of anti-Irish, anti-Catholic prejudice, and scares around IRA terrorism and Irish criminality, the Irish made up somewhere between 60 and 70 per cent of all deportations in the 1960s. But the threat of deportation was more meaningful the further people would be transported – and in reality, almost a third of Irish deportees were known to immediately return.[25] For African, Caribbean and Asian citizens, the threat of deportation – on top of a racist state that was increasingly hostile to their presence – felt more tangible and more oppressive.

In 1965, the new Labour government produced a White Paper

which explored immigration under the subheadings of Housing, Education, Employment and Health, the key areas that were seen as under pressure from new arrivals; the White Paper determined that quotas should be imposed and that the numbers of migrants to the country should be reduced. In 1968, the Asian community in Kenya found their livelihoods increasingly curtailed; despite being a small minority of the Kenyan population, this community was economically dominant, but most had failed to take up the offer of Kenyan citizenship on independence, preferring instead to keep their British passports. This led to distrust by the Kenyan government which implemented 'Africanisation' policies that saw non-citizen civil servants sacked in favour of Black Africans and which curtailed non-citizens' rights to trade and own businesses. Increasingly, the Kenyan Asians turned to Britain for their future, with 13,000 arriving from East Africa in the first two months of the year; in response, at the end of February the Labour government rushed through an updated Commonwealth Immigration Act which extended controls on immigration to anybody whose parent or grandparent had not been born in, or was not a citizen of, the UK. The British High Commission in Kenya estimated that 190,000 Kenyan Asians were entitled to a British passport. However, by taking away the right to residence from 'non patrials', the British government effectively rendered these passports worthless and these people stateless. Those travelling to Britain found themselves stripped of citizenship, sometimes in mid-air.

The *Guardian* stated that 'No previous British immigration legislation has ever been quite so plainly discriminatory as this', and noted that most *white* Kenyans would still be able to enter Britain under the Act.[26] The Archbishop of Canterbury criticised the Act for the way that it 'formally embodied' racial classification into UK law, for rendering a whole class of people 'virtually stateless', and for introducing 'a measure of injustices and indeed bad faith' that could only serve to damage community relations in the UK.[27] Protesters marched through London against the Act, with Asian families carrying handmade placards reading 'Kenya Asians are

Britain's Responsibility' alongside young people marching under the banner of the Union of Liberal Students and pledging to 'Fight Wilson's Race Bill'.[28] Despite these pockets of resistance, the bill stood, with a great deal of popular support; a poll conducted in April recorded that 93 per cent of British people wanted immigration to be curbed even more.[29]

In 1971, the Conservative government extended these immigration controls further, replacing the employment vouchers with work permits that limited stays in Britain to temporary residence, and even including some provisions to enable (voluntary) repatriation; those with close inherited ties to the UK, the patrials, were exempt, as were women married to patrial men (but not, until 1983, men married to women with British citizenship). The Asians expelled from Uganda in 1972 were a small exception to this tightening; because of the government's opposition to Idi Amin, the Ugandan Resettlement Board was established to permit and manage the entry of 27,000 people. Among them was Mahmoud Mamdani, who wrote about his experiences in his book *From Citizen to Refugee* (1973): housed in a camp, sleeping for two and a half months in a room with four other men, incongruously dressed against the cold winter weather in a Parisian cape and a bowler hat from Harrods that had been donated by the Women's Royal Voluntary Service. Mamdani felt strongly that the experience of the Ugandan Asians (who had, in Uganda, been referred to as the British Asians) demonstrated that 'History was catching up with England': 'The colonial child had come to the mother-land. And he had brought with him England's colonial past. Past had become present.'[30]

From 1962 onwards, the apparent 'ties' of Britain to the Commonwealth, so beloved of politicians when speaking as delegates at heads of government meetings or enjoying the hospitality at the Commonwealth Games, no longer translated into a welcome to its citizens. In response, it inspired a significant resistance movement, acting continuously to resist further limitations and to stand up for the rights of migrant communities. Referring to the White Paper of 1965, Fenner Brockway MP wrote of his 'sense of shame' at belonging to a Labour Party that could embrace the restriction of Commonwealth immigration, and the Movement for Colonial Freedom launched 'a New Campaign Against Racialism' and against the 'abject submission to the racialists' that the immigration White Paper represented.[31]

There were more marches and protests too. One picture from February 1968 shows a number of men in turbans walking through London streets holding placards that say 'Stand for Human Equality' and 'Mergers Create Unemployment Not Immigration';[32] another from December of that year shows Black and Asian protesters shouting as one holds a placard demanding that 'Black People Unite Against Racism and Imperialism'.[33] Two hundred students protested against the Act by heckling the Labour Home Secretary Jim Callaghan when he came to speak at Oxford, even going so far as threatening to throw him into the Nuffield College goldfish pond.[34] This fight continued among anti-racist activist groups well into the 1970s. The East London Local Labour Campaign Against Racialism, for example, produced a leaflet headlined 'You Don't Want Race War in Our Streets, so DEFEAT RACIALISM NOW', which urged its readers to fight against this legislation that created a 'second class citizen' status for non-white immigrants, and which rejected some of the common tropes about immigrants being to blame for unemployment and housing shortages.[35]

For hand in hand with the concern about immigration was, of course, an escalating anxiety and anger at the threat it was felt to pose to the exclusivity and whiteness of British identity. As in the 1940s and 50s, there were periodic race riots across the country, often sparked by a particular incident which ultimately became the occasion for a venting by white communities of their anger and frustration at the growing communities of New Commonwealth migrants in their towns and cities. In 1961, for example, there had been an outbreak of white violence against the local Asian communities of Middlesbrough. This violence had been rumbling all summer: on 18 July, a white crowd had attacked a Pakistani landlord who had evicted some white tenants; on 31 July, a large white crowd gathered to protest about the opening of the Taj Mahal cafe, owned by Mr Meah, a Pakistani man, and his white wife. The cafe remained the centre of hostilities for weeks, coming to a head on 19 August when it was the target of an arson attack in retribution for the stabbing of a white man, John Joseph Hunt, the night before; the next day, an Indian butcher's shop was also attacked. The *Daily Mirror* screamed from its front page that 'POLICE FIGHT MOB OF 500 IN RACE RIOT TOWN'.[36] But while they were excited by the prospect of mob violence, British newspapers tried to downplay the racism in these riots, which were being reported in Russia, India, Pakistan and the USA. The *Observer*, for example, claimed hotly that the violence 'did not originate from racial trouble and has never been truly racial', because the local community comprised only 4,000 people of colour among 150,000 in total, with 'hardly a West Indian among them';[37] the racist stereotype of Caribbean immigrants as more inherently troublesome than those from Indian or Pakistani backgrounds meant that the paper literally could not conceive of racial violence targeting the latter.

Day to day, the racism that people of colour faced was less visible but more insidious, built into the structure of the education system, their interactions with the welfare state, their places of work and their relationship with their employers and their colleagues. In April 1963, people in Bristol boycotted the bus company after it came to light that it was unwilling to employ Black and Asian workers as drivers or conductors. The campaign, led by Roy Hackett, Paul Stephenson, Owen Henry and Guy Bailey – and supported by figures like Learie Constantine – was the first Black-led labour campaign in Britain. It had long been informally understood that the buses operated a colour bar in their employment, but the men were moved to do something – first to approach the council, and then, when this did not get them anywhere, to organise the boycott – when Ena Hackett, Roy's wife, was turned away from a job as a 'conductress'. Their campaign was supported by Labour politicians including Tony Benn ('I shall stay off the buses, even if I have to find a bike!'), Fenner Brockway and even the Labour leader Harold Wilson, who spoke out against the colour bar at a rally against apartheid; it soon became clear, however, that the Transport and General Workers' Union (TGWU) had been colluding with the bosses to protect their white unionised workforce.

The boycott began after Ian Patey, the general manager of the bus company, refused to change the policy against employing workers of colour (which was perfectly legal until the second Race Relations Act in 1968). He defended the company's position, arguing that 'the labour supply gets worse if the labour force is mixed'.[38] The campaign was supported by local university students, members of the Campaign for Nuclear Disarmament (CND), the Campaign Against Racial Discrimination (CARD), and the left political parties, who marched in protest to the bus company headquarters and to the TGWU head office; it was opposed, most vocally, by the white bus workers themselves, who turned out to heckle the protests and marches and declared to any journalist who would listen that they would not work with West Indian crew members.[39] Many local people engaged with the debate on a purely practical level, as typified by one woman who wrote to the *Bristol Evening Post* to say that all she cared about when the bus pulled up to her stop was that the conductor was 'one of the helpful ones who will step down and pick up the pushchair for me'.[40] Ultimately, the boycott and surrounding protests were extremely effective; by August 1963, the colour bar had fallen, and Raghbir Singh became the first person of colour to work on the buses as a conductor.

Despite the success of the Bristol bus campaign and other anti-racist activism that followed in its wake, race became more, not less, of a focal point for British politics over the course of the 1960s and into the 1970s. This was true at both ends of the political spectrum. Although they had supported the Black and Asian workers of Bristol, the Labour Party establishment pandered to anti-immigration rhetoric because they were anxious about being seen as soft on the issue compared with the Conservatives. Those fears seemed to be decisively confirmed in the general election of 1964.

Labour won the election with a 3.5 per cent improvement on

their previous showing, but one of their most prominent Shadow Cabinet members, Patrick Gordon Walker, the Shadow Home Secretary, lost his West Midlands constituency of Smethwick with a swing of almost 8 per cent against him. In fact, Gordon Walker had told Hugh Gaitskell as early as 1962 that he was worried he might lose his constituency to an anti-immigration candidate. Smethwick had become richly multicultural after the Second World War, with a large number of migrants coming from the West Indies and the newly decolonised Indian subcontinent; in the 1961 census, nearly 3,000 Smethwick residents were recorded as having been born overseas. But the election was not lost organically or as the result of a grassroots community turn against the Labour Party.

Instead, there was a determined campaign by the Tory candidate Peter Griffiths which saw the widespread use of a racially inflammatory slogan: at its mildest, it was rendered as 'If you want a coloured for a neighbour, vote Labour; if you've already got one, vote Conservative', with 'coloured' often replaced with the N-word. This campaign had not been run by the Conservative Party, officially, but neither had it been rejected by Griffiths, who said he thought the slogan demonstrated 'popular feeling'; 'I would not condemn any man who said that,' he said, when asked about its use. The slogan echoed stickers that were posted around North Kensington in the same election, which proclaimed 'Don't vote: a vote for Tory, Labour or Liberal is a vote for more Blacks!' and which were the work of Colin Jordan's far-right National Socialist Movement. The difference in Smethwick was that this far-right rhetoric was being used in support of a mainstream Conservative candidate. It was claimed in a Channel 4 documentary that the originator of the slogan was in fact the nine-year-old daughter of Griffiths' campaign agent, who based it on the racist rhymes sung in her school playground.[41]

Before the election, the BBC filmed an episode of *Panorama* which had explored the potential 'race problem' in two constituencies in the West Midlands: All Saints in Birmingham and Smethwick. A BBC representative explained that 'rather than make racial problems worse, we thought it better not to go ahead'.[42] This was understandable, given concerns about unduly influencing election results, but was also interpreted in some quarters as a decision borne of cowardice. It was the *Sunday Telegraph* that argued 'the BBC, having given such prominence to racial troubles in the United States and Africa, had some duty to deal with Britain's treatment of its coloured people candidly and fully'.[43] Many British voices in the 1960s were critical of segregation and apartheid, and arguably turning their attention to domestic racial issues was somewhat overdue. (The BBC was anyway at the heart of a controversy about the Smethwick campaign, as Harold Wilson had condemned the Conservative electoral slogan as 'utterly squalid and degrading' on television and had challenged Alec Douglas-Home to issue an immediate repudiation, which he had declined to do.)

It is clear, in any case, that Griffiths was not only sympathetic to, but was in fact explicitly supportive of, the anti-immigration rhetoric of the far right and the racist grievances of the white community in Smethwick. This was a key part of his victory. But he was helped in this campaign by his opponent. Gordon Walker was condemned for having voted against the 1962 Commonwealth Immigration Act – he had been reported as saying that it was 'the wrong solution to the wrong problem' – and for his history of supporting immigration and diversity through his roles in the Commonwealth Relations Office and as Shadow Foreign Secretary. His upbringing, spending most of his childhood in the Punjab where his father had been a member of the Indian Civil Service, and that of his wife, who was the daughter of a coconut plantation owner in Jamaica, was also used against him, with accusations that he was more sympathetic to the predominantly Punjabi Sikh immigrants in the constituency than white Britons.

Gordon Walker clearly did have a nuanced and careful approach to race, immigration and imperial legacies. He had been a broadcaster for the BBC during the Second World War and had toured Germany extensively immediately after the conflict ended. One of the first British people to reach the Bergen-Belsen concentration camps at the end of the war, he later published a short book, *The Lid*

Lifts, drawn from his diaries at the time, in which he made comparisons between the Holocaust and the slave trade: 'The slave ships, driven from the Atlantic, have anchored at Dachau, Belsen and Buchenwald, in the midst of Europe.'[44] He condemned the failure of morality, the 'long descent into degradation' that included the British concentration camps during the Boer War and the atrocities committed by fascists at the Spanish Civil War as well as the Nazi regime. This critique stands out for its willingness to explore the wider context of the horrors of the Holocaust; it meant nothing in the 1964 election.

The party would previously have been confident in their ability to win a seat in a working-class Midlands constituency like Smethwick, and the idea that racism might be the key that unlocked these voters for the Conservatives was deeply concerning. Ernest Lowry, the chair of the local Labour Party, said that he was 'bitter and sorry' about the result which meant that Smethwick had become known as 'the Midlands "Little Rock"', referring to the Alabama town that had seen racist violence in opposition to school desegregation in 1957.[45]

The electoral results did not cauterise the racism of the campaign; instead, tensions were heightened. In the months after the election, one group of white residents petitioned the council to buy up houses on one street and rent them only to white families; this story made it across the Atlantic, with the *New York Times* reporting that Griffiths and the white community were trying to prevent the area from becoming 'a ghetto'.[46] ITN visited Smethwick, and the voice-over on the news story sympathetically described white residents' desire to 'halt the coloured invasion'; a white woman was interviewed and claimed that her Black neighbours 'use the back gardens for toilets'. Griffiths, who was the council alderman as well as the local MP, supported this plan for segregated housing, a plan which was only thwarted when the Labour housing minister refused to approve the funds.

The racism faced by the people of colour in Smethwick went beyond this institutional discrimination. The Campaign Against

Racial Discrimination were concerned in 1964 that Smethwick was 'in danger of becoming as notorious as Little Rock, Sharpeville and Birmingham, Alabama', because of a four-year-long campaign to imply that 'all the problems facing the Smethwick people stem from the presence of 4,000 Afro-Asian immigrants'; it believed that Griffiths and Don Finney, the local councillor, bore 'a large measure of responsibility for the strained and tense atmosphere' in the constituency.[47] Griffiths' victory certainly meant that racists felt empowered to amplify their attacks on the Asian, mostly Sikh, community. In the early summer of the next year, there was a 'spate' of burning crosses in the region, which a government minister tried to dismiss as 'the work of a small lunatic fringe'.[48] A month later, the first British chapter of the Ku Klux Klan was established locally by a Birmingham man called George Newey, who was heavily engaged in far-right politics already, having been arrested in December 1964 along with three other men for painting swastikas and other racist slogans on walls in Warwick.[49]

The situation was so fraught that the Indian Workers' Association had invited Malcolm X, who was in Britain to give talks at LSE and the University of Birmingham Student Union, to come to Smethwick to offer solidarity and support. Malcolm X warned reporters that the Black and Asian populations were being treated 'as the Jews were under Hitler', and urged them not to wait until the 'local fascist element' erected gas chambers.[50] Instead, they should take action to protect themselves and their rights. Television footage from the tour shows Malcolm X standing in front of the sign to Marshall Street, the street which Griffiths intended to segregate, looking at the houses with their For Sale signs (some of which were explicitly marked 'Whites Only'), and talking animatedly in a pub, presumably the Blue Gate, one of the only local public houses that didn't operate a full colour bar. Even then, it only served Black and Asian customers in the 'bar room', ejecting Malcolm X and his guide Avtar Singh Jouhl from the 'lounge room' because they were not white – Jouhl described this as 'one of the most quiet, sombre half-pints I have ever drunk'.[51] The footage is made more poignant by the fact that, nine days later, Malcolm X would be dead, assassinated in the Audubon Ballroom in New York.

Griffiths' election did not go unchallenged. When he attended a meeting of the Conservative Party in Sutton in January 1965, young socialists organised a demonstration outside where they marched with placards reading 'Ban Racialism Now' and 'The Tories created the housing problem, not the immigrants'.[52] In October 1965, his home was the target of a bomb, pushed through his letter box, which caused significant damage inside the house while he and his wife were at a Chamber of Trade dinner.[53] Griffiths blamed the act on 'the work of a maniac';[54] responsibility was never claimed.

In the House of Commons, too, Griffiths was initially ostracised, with Harold Wilson famously declaring him to be a 'parliamentary leper'. But the Conservative Party was unwilling to meaningfully shun its victorious colleague. In June 1965, it was rumoured that Robert Skelton, a prominent American member of the KKK, might try to gain entry to Britain. The Labour Home Secretary, Frank Soskice, said firmly in Parliament that he would be barred from the country, as would any foreign citizens who tried to take part in these activities. But there followed a commotion, as Michael Foot shouted out that Griffiths should also be condemned, as 'the major Member of the House who has conducted racialist propaganda'. Conservative MPs were outraged at such 'aggressiveness' towards their honourable friend, while Foot refused to take back the accusation. 'It is quite impossible for me to withdraw a charge of racialist propaganda against the hon. Member for Smethwick, since everybody knows that he does it.'[55] So it is too simple to argue that Smethwick was an anomaly or that a principled House of Commons shunned Griffiths for his racist tactics; in fact, once he found his place in Parliament, he was absorbed into the political establishment, rejected only along partisan lines.

In fact, Smethwick was not that unusual. Labour lost in three other constituencies, too, in the 1964 election. One, North West Norfolk, was trending away from Labour and had been won by only seventy-eight votes in 1959. The other two were, like Smethwick, seen by the party as a sign that immigration had become an issue they could not ignore. Charles Howell lost Perry Barr, also in the West Midlands, to the Conservative Wyndham Davies, who had distributed leaflets reading '300,000 immigrants if you vote Labour – It's up to you on Thursday!'[56] Meanwhile Fenner Brockway, leader of the Movement for Colonial Freedom (MCF), lost his seat in Slough; as well as his work with the MCF, Brockway had been personally supportive of the West Indian migrants who had been settling in his constituency.

It is certainly true that this election scared Labour, and the party was not immune from appealing to white voters at the expense of immigrant communities, in the 1960s or in the following decades, despite their frequent rhetoric since about their role as a party committed to anti-racism and inclusion. But the story of Smethwick is more complex than this. In 1966, Harold Wilson called a second election only two years after his first victory; he had lost half of his already tiny four-seat majority in two by-elections, and any widespread social reform would require significantly more MPs. The gamble paid off, and Labour won the election with a landslide, and a 98-seat majority. One of the seats newly won was Smethwick. More importantly, the party did not achieve this victory by pandering to racists.

Instead, Labour ran a celebrity candidate, the actor Andrew Faulds. Born in Tanganyika, the child of Scottish missionaries, Faulds had been a political activist since he and his wife had hosted the Black American actor Paul Robeson at their home when he travelled to play Othello in an RSC production in 1959. Robeson had urged Faulds to put his anti-apartheid and pro-social justice views to better practical use, and he had duly joined the Labour Party. He had stood initially for Stratford-upon-Avon in 1963 (in the by-election caused by the resignation of John Profumo over the eponymous affair) and in 1964, both unsuccessfully, before being selected as the Labour candidate for Smethwick in 1966. It was clearly appealing to the local electorate; he represented the area until 1997. He became known for his outspoken views and his activist politics. He was vocally anti-Zionist (and indeed faced significant criticism for antisemitic views and arguments during his time in Parliament) and actively anti-apartheid, signing numerous early day motions and amendments criticising British government policies towards South Africa and Palestine. When Ian Smith issued the unilateral declaration of independence that represented Southern Rhodesia rejecting calls for democratic elections and Black majority rule, Faulds's suggested solution was to 'hang him'. He rejected Enoch Powell's 'Rivers of Blood' speech as 'unChristian . . . unprincipled, undemocratic and racialist'; he was one of only a small number of Labour and Conservative MPs (including Iain Macleod, Ian Gilmour, Shirley Williams and Michael Foot) to reject the 1968 Commonwealth Immigration Act as a shameless act of cowardice in the face of hysterical racism aimed at the Kenyan Asian population.[57]

Losing Smethwick undoubtedly pushed the Labour Party towards a more aggressively anti-immigration stance; it definitely represented a deeply rooted and increasingly vocal and explicit racism in British politics that was the precursor to the 'new racism' of the late 1970s and 80s. But the election of Faulds showed that racism was not the final word when it came to winning and wielding political power, and it could be successfully opposed. In fact, some within the Labour Party were extremely uncomfortable with the party's increasing embrace of racism and immigration controls as a vote winner, committed as they were to socialist internationalism that resisted the nationalism of borders. Many more were happy to reduce migration but concerned with protecting the well-being of immigrants already settled in the country. And so, alongside the laws being brought in to limit migration, the 1960s also saw the first legislation to try to address racism and protect the rights of people of colour.

The Race Relations Act, first passed in 1965 and then amended in 1968 and 1976, eventually made racial discrimination unlawful in employment, training, housing, education and the provision of goods, facilities and services. In its first iteration, however, it did not include the two sectors where people were most likely to face racist discrimination: housing and employment. Wole Soyinka's poem 'Telephone Conversation', written in 1962, gives a glimpse of that discrimination and humiliation in its depiction of a Black student trying to rent a room and being asked by a white landlady, 'How dark – are you light or very dark?'[58] Housing and employment were sidestepped precisely because they would have brought so much daily activity within the bounds of the new legislation and because – Labour's lawyers believed – it would be impossible to prove in these areas whether people of colour were experiencing discrimination based on race or on other subjective measures.

Race relations boards were set up and people could report instances of discrimination, although little action was taken in response. The Indian Workers' Association in Birmingham organised a series of 'pub crawl' protests, sending groups of white students from Birmingham and Aston Universities, followed by groups of people of colour from the IWA, to pubs suspected of racial discrimination, and lodging complaints with the race relations boards whenever the latter were refused entry; they also organised pickets of pubs that dodged the somewhat ineffectual sanctions of the new legislation.[59] In some ways, then, this legislation gave a new tool to activists against racial discrimination, but it was a poor attempt at addressing the extent of racism and injustice directly.

In 1967, the think tank Political and Economic Planning (PEP) conducted a survey that was, unusually, later a bestselling book, *Racial Discrimination in England*. The survey was based on an experiment in which three men – one Black Briton, one white Briton and one white Hungarian – were sent to enquire about various jobs, housing situations and commercial services. Not only did the report show that Black British people were likely to face discrimination in these sectors that were outside the remit of the 1965 Act, but it argued convincingly that this discrimination operated 'on a substantial scale', systemically worse across the country than was suspected by many people of colour based on their own experiences.[60]

A similar report that focused on the areas of Batley and Dewsbury, Spenborough, Bradford, Halifax, Huddersfield, Keighley and Leeds concluded that the lives of Pakistani, Indian and West Indian immigrants were shaped irrevocably by social conditions. These communities faced difficulties in their employment, health and housing situation. The last was amplified by the poor housing conditions in West Yorkshire – which had the highest level of 'obsolescent' dwellings in the country – which meant that migrants were moving into areas that were already suffering from overcrowding, and competing for small, decrepit back-to-backs often lacking basic amenities such as hot water or an indoor toilet.[61] Employment for immigrants in these areas was often precarious or exploitative – it was said, for example, that 'the night-shifts of many woollen mills in West Yorkshire depend on migrant labour' – but at the same time the report was keen to stress that these communities were in work, and were not (despite 'the fantasies of those who think they come here to live off state benefits') drawing the dole.[62] In fact, one of the biggest issues faced by this community was that they were employed in positions far below their qualifications and abilities. One major group for whom this was the case were teachers who had qualified in their countries of origin but who were informed, in a letter from the local education authority, that they were 'not prepared to appoint . . . teachers whose English both in speech and in writing is not readily intelligible to schoolchildren'; as the report pointed out, this was as much 'a consequence of the accents of local people' as it was the fault of the Commonwealth teachers.[63]

While people of colour lamented the limitations of the Race Relations Act that left them unprotected in the central areas of their lives, many white people objected fiercely to what they saw as overbearing control over their personal attitudes and choices. Enoch Powell's 1968 'Rivers of Blood' speech was prompted by his fury at the proposed 1968 extension of the Act to cover housing and employment. The speech was delivered in the West Midlands Area Conservative Political Centre, close to Powell's Wolverhampton constituency, and was tipped off to local journalists the night before. Powell reputedly said to Clem Jones, a journalist on the Wolverhampton *Express and Star*, that he was going to deliver a speech that would 'go up like a rocket' and 'stay up'.[64]

To a friendly audience of local Conservative activists, Powell set out his opposition to the extension of the Race Relations Act as part of a much wider ranging attack on immigration and the existence of the multiracial communities that had developed across the country, including in his own constituency. He framed this partly through a competition for resources and services, including hospital beds, school places, houses and jobs. He explicitly invoked his constituents and their anxieties about immigration to their area in deeply racialised terms: a 'middle aged, quite ordinary man' who told him, unprovoked in the street, that he wanted to emigrate because in fifteen to twenty-five years 'the black man will have the whip hand over the white man'; a little old lady, apparently destitute despite owning a seven-bedroom house, who refused to rent her spare rooms to people of colour and had her windows broken and was called a 'racialist' by children in the street.[65] Powell used these stories to argue that white British people – whom he did not name, explicitly, as white, but instead as 'ordinary, decent, sensible' – were already second-class citizens in their own country. He further predicted that immigrants would soon 'overawe and dominate' Britain using the 'legal weapons' of anti-discrimination legislation. A classics scholar, Powell quoted from the *Aeneid*, saying that he seemed to see before him the River Tiber 'foaming with much blood' (the only glancing reference to 'rivers of blood' in the speech) if the country continued to allow mass immigration and to commit to these race relations programmes.

William Rees-Mogg, the editor of *The Times*, condemned the speech as 'evil . . . shameful . . . disgraceful . . . [and] calculated to inflame hatred between the races'.[66] It is also remarkable because it demonstrates a clear moment when an MP in an area with extensive immigration chose only to represent those constituents he found racially acceptable. MPs for diverse constituencies have often championed them, and these areas have often been places that have seen people of colour rise to elected office, such as the former MP for Southall, Piara Singh Khabra, who was the first Sikh to be an MP when he won the seat for Labour in 1992. Powell drew a line around his 'constituents' to include only those who were white, despite the fact that the people of colour who were supposedly harassing the little old lady he cited in his speech must surely have been his constituents as much as she was. This was consistent with Powell's history as a little Englander, resistant to empire and imperial connections, but it was also something new: a type of racism that developed in the later 1960s, which specifically rejected the notion of a post-colonial multicultural society and which was increasingly fixated on limiting migration from the 'new Commonwealth'.

When Powell was sacked from the Shadow Cabinet, dockers and porters from Smithfield market marched to Downing Street to deliver a petition in support of him. This may not have been entirely spontaneous: the British security services identified the leader of the dockers as Harry Pearman, a well-known anti-Communist activist who had been influenced by the far-right 'moral rearmament' movement, and the leader of the porters as Herbert Harmston, who had stood as a parliamentary candidate for Mosley's New Party of Europe in 1966.[67] But support for Powell was not limited to these specific labour forces; immigration officers at Heathrow, for example, had signed a petition in support of Powell, an action for which the ringleader was suspended.[68] And over 100,000 people wrote Powell letters of support. One man wrote that 'as an Englishman, I would like to think that my son and grandchildren will also be Englishmen, and what's more, look like English men and women'; another asked him to respond to the public desire for an end to immigration by forming a new 'British National Party'.[69]

Powell's speech was a subject of much debate in British universities. In response to the student Conservative Association of University College (London) inviting Powell to attend their annual dinner, the UCL Communist Party produced a leaflet, 'Who Is Enoch Powell?', which summarised his anti-immigration and racist views, as well as his reactionary comments on issues such as overseas aid, the position of Rhodesia, housing, pensions, education and the Second World War. The leaflet authors used Colin Jordan and Oswald Mosley's praise of Powell to condemn the MP as the 'intellectual justification for racialism' and questioned why the Conservative Association wished to 'associate themselves with those views'.[70] Other university groups took direct action: students at the University of Essex damaged the car of Anthony Buck, the Conservative MP for Colchester, as he drove Powell away from addressing a meeting on the new campus. Two students were fined by the university for the damage caused, although Buck pushed for harsher penalties.[71]

Powell quickly became a figure of renown, a symbol of a particular conservative (if not Conservative) position in British politics that sought to defend the white, the 'traditional', the 'ordinary'. He entered British pop cultural consciousness as a shorthand for a set of reactionary views, by those who both approved and disapproved. A novel published in 1970, *Who Killed Enoch Powell?*, took as its starting point Powell's assassination, seemingly by the far left, but really as a false flag operation used to justify a coup by the British military.[72] Meanwhile the *Enoch Powell Fireside Book* annotated pictures of Powell with apparently humorous captions: a picture of Powell riding a chestnut horse with a white horse behind and the caption 'Colourwise, I should be on the *Other* horse'; a photograph of Powell in an election car with loudspeaker, driving past a family with two Asian women in headscarves and asking 'Driver . . . are you *sure* we're in the right street?' Those who enjoyed such humour might also have owned other titles in the series: *The Wit of Prince Philip*, *The Wit of Sir Winston*, *More Wit of Prince Philip* or, more unexpectedly, *The Wit of the Catholics*. And the idea that 'Enoch was right' was asserted in smoky rooms in pubs and clubs, chanted in school playgrounds, and daubed on walls in any area where people of colour lived, worked or played.

Ultimately, Powell's outburst made it less likely that other

Conservative MPs would vote against the new legislation, and the Race Relations Act of 1968 passed by 182 votes to 44. The Act extended the powers of the 1965 legislation to apply to employment and housing (although not public services such as the police), and also set up the Community Relations Commission, which sought to promote 'harmonious community relations' between people of different races. But despite this move to institutionalise racial tolerance, imperialist and racist attitudes were still deeply ingrained in British society and culture.

In 1965, Johnny Speight's *Till Death Us Do Part* premiered on the BBC; it would run until 1968, before being revived in the 1970s and again in the 1980s (this time on ITV). Alf Garnett, the central character was an East Ender, a West Ham fan, a Conservative voter and a dock worker. He was xenophobic, racist, antisemitic, misogynistic, and was embraced by many viewers for these positions, despite the fact that Warren Mitchell, who played the character across all of the series, was a Jewish socialist, and despite both Speight and Mitchell claiming that the character was intended to function as a parody of these attitudes. A subsequent Johnny Speight sitcom, *Curry and Chips*, starring Spike Milligan in blackface as a Pakistani who believed himself to be an Irishman, was cancelled in 1969 after only six episodes when the Independent Television Authority forced London Weekend Television to take it off the air because of numerous complaints of racism, including from the Race Relations Board. Speight protested that the show, as with his other programmes, was intended to satirise racist attitudes, but newspaper reviews at the time questioned whether such programmes would be allowed to be made about other minority groups. Bill Hardcastle, presenter of the BBC radio programme *The World At One*, mused that the outrage was perhaps justified given that 'the coloured communities in Britain are far less secure' and the establishment relationship with them far 'touchier' than with Jewish or Roman Catholic communities, although he praised Speight's 'transcription of the vocabulary of working-class prejudice' as 'faultless'.[73]

*

Enthusiasm for these themes continued into the next decade. In 1974, Jimmy Perry and David Croft – who between them created *Dad's Army, Are You Being Served?* and *'Allo 'Allo* – wrote a sitcom based on their own experiences serving as entertainers in the British empire during the Second World War. *It Ain't Half Hot Mum* was immensely popular, running to eight series, fifty-six episodes in total. It was set in Deolali, a hill station in India, and a fictional village called Tin Min in Burma, in the period between VE Day in May 1945 and the defeat of Japan in August. The main characters are members of a 'concert party', an entertainment troupe of soldiers drawn from the Royal Artillery. The show was intensely imperial – as well as often racist and homophobic – in its outlook, most notably in the diatribes of Sergeant Major Williams about the impossibility of Indian home rule and the achievements of the British empire to date, but also in its depiction of Indian and Burmese characters who are shown generally as cringing, obsequious and often supportive of, or grateful towards, their British rulers. One of the Indian characters was played by Michael Bates, an actor who had been born in India, had grown up speaking Hindi and Urdu, and had served in the Second World War in the Brigade of Gurkhas, but who was, in fact, of entirely white heritage. These programmes have become more controversial since their original transmission; in 2012 it was announced in the tabloid press that the BBC had decided not to repeat *It Ain't Half Hot Mum* on television, and despite its contemporary popularity, the show, along with *Till Death Us Do Part* and its ITV competitor *Love Thy Neighbour*, is absent from the nostalgic collection of sitcoms available on the BritBox service launched in 2019.

This was not the whole story. The history of race relations in Britain is not complete without the vibrant and motivated civil rights movement that countered and exposed this cultural, institutional and governmental racism. The British Black Power Movement, led by figures like Darcus Howe, Obi Egbuna and Altheia Jones-LeCointe, fought back against racist hatred and oppression through a variety of different organisations. The Universal Coloured

People's Association (UCPA) was one of these; in 1967, it produced a manifesto which outlined key concerns and demands. 'Black Power in Britain' was angry, proud and revolutionary, with a clenched fist raised in salute and a black panther on the front cover. The authors responded to the recent declaration by James Callaghan, then the Labour Home Secretary, that he wished to avoid the racial violence being seen in the USA from spreading to Britain by pointing out that this was merely an attempt to protect white people from 'Black defence'. As they argued, 'the Home Secretary has not said that racial discrimination must be discontinued because it is evil, inhuman and immoral. He couldn't. To call racism immoral would be to call his own government immoral. It was his country which legalised racism in this country with the Commonwealth Immigration Bill.' The UCPA's critique of British state racism went further: 'it was the slavery of the Black man that provided the capital for the Industrial Revolution of the west. It was the Black sweat that built the white civilisation . . . it was the exploitation of Black lands that made Britain great.'[74]

The UCPA constitution included a list of aims and objectives that ranged from a global united Black solidarity movement to 'immediate action . . . to do everything in our power to assert our rights here in Britain . . . to settle our political, social, economic and other imperialist problems';[75] there was a tear-off form on the final page of the manifesto where readers could apply for membership at a cost of five shillings. Those who did included 'factory workers, lawyers, railworkers, nurses, plumbers, students, secretaries, road sweepers, priests, novelists, actors, playwrights and Health Visitors, and wherever and whatever profession our coloured brothers and sisters can be found in this country'. The organisation was keen to stress its modernity and democracy: 'we are new, we are young, we are essentially Grass Root'.[76]

In the 1970s, this activism continued through the work of the UCPA and of other organisations such as the Black Liberation Front (BLF), who drew the same connections between the American civil rights movement, anti-colonial and post-colonial activism in the Global South, and anti-racist activism in the United Kingdom. In the late 1970s, the BLF produced a set of pamphlets, the 'Black Liberation Series', born out of discussion groups and exploring topics such as pan-Africanism, the Black community in Britain, and capitalism and socialism. One, which explored the origins of racism in modern Britain, asserted that 'As Britain was the leading power in practising both slavery and colonialism, its relationship with Black people has always been racist'.[77]

The education system came under particularly sustained criticism from many Black activists and other anti-racist campaigners. In 1971, Bernard Coard published *How the West Indian Child Is Made Subnormal in the British School System*. This book was a detailed, careful exposure of the scandal of Black children being deemed 'educationally subnormal', and suffering academically – and therefore 'in their job prospects for life' – because of this mistaken classification. Coard explored how this might happen: teachers could discriminate against Black children by 'being openly prejudiced; by being patronizing; and by having low expectations of the child's abilities'.[78] These attitudes also affected Black teachers in mainstream schools, who were themselves discriminated against by their white colleagues. Coard recounted, for example, a report from two West Indian teachers in a south London school who reported 'the cases of white teachers who sit smoking in the staff-room, and refuse to teach a class of nearly-all-Black children. When on one occasion they were accosted by one of the Black teachers, they stated their refusal to teach "those n****rs".'[79]

On the day the book was published, Coard debated with the head of the Inner London Education Authority live on television and the *Guardian* reprinted the whole of the fifth chapter – 'What the Education System Does to the Black Child' – as an editorial; the BBC followed the publication by making a series of documentary films about the experiences of Black children in British schools.[80] Black communities around the country took matters into their own hands and set up supplementary schools to help to support Black students within and against the British education system. Countless more reports were written: the Newham Monitoring Project explored racist violence in schools in the borough, for example, while the Black People's Progressive Association examined the position of West Indian pupils in Redbridge.[81]

A survey conducted in 1975 by the National Union of Students found that many schools were still using the 1960s Ladybird book *Flight Five: Africa*, which they determined to be 'slightly to the right of Genghis Khan' in its depiction of African peoples.[82] Other books being used in schools and published more recently were no better: one history of Rhodesia written in 1970 stated that the colony had been peopled by 'primitive' tribes but had been brought 'from a wilderness to a republic – in only eighty years'; a geography textbook about rainforests published in the same year described colonialism as merely 'British influence and encouragement', and argued that 'the white man is still needed' even in independent African countries to help to 'modernise' these places.[83] The National Front was also active in schools in this period, distributing leaflets to pupils that asked whether they were 'tired of lessons where the teacher has to go at a snail's pace to allow immigrant kids who don't speak English to keep up' and advised them to join the National Front Students' Association to get a 'decent education for British school kids'.[84]

When John Berger won the Booker Prize in 1972, he used his speech to draw attention to the continuing connections between modern British culture and its roots in empire. Specifically, he denounced Booker McConnell Ltd, the company that had created the prize, for their historic links to slavery and colonial exploitation. 'Booker McConnell have had extensive trading interests in the Caribbean for over 130 years,' he said, and 'the modern poverty of the Caribbean is the direct result of this and similar exploitation'. Berger also stated plainly that 'the industrial revolution and the inventions and culture which accompanied it and which created modern Europe was initially financed by profits from the slave trade'. In a symbolic (and real) act of redistribution, Berger gave half his prize money to the British Black Panthers, 'because, through their Black People's Information Centre, they have links with the struggle in Guyana, the seat of Booker McConnell's wealth, in Trinidad and throughout the Caribbean'.[85] He handed the money over to Darcus Howe in a pub on Great Portland Street, who used it to fund the purchase of a headquarters for the group in Finsbury Park and to start a newspaper.[86]

While Berger drew attention to the links between contemporary racial oppression and Britain's history of colonial slavery, other activists were making connections in other directions: between racism and gender, for example. Black women felt frustrated at the mainstream feminist movement for not acknowledging the particular ways in which their experience of sexism was shaped and compounded by racism. As Valerie Amos and Pratibha Parmar pointed out, while white and predominantly middle-class feminists were talking about 'destroying the family' as a means of liberating women from patriarchal oppression, Black women were trying to assert their right to traditional Caribbean family structures in the United Kingdom, and Asian women were fighting against racist border policing so that their relatives, including their children or husbands, might join them in Britain.[87] In Amos and Parmar's view, the white feminists' desire 'to "help" Asian women liberate themselves from their role' was indicative of the 'imperial' nature of their feminism.[88]

The Brixton Black Women's Group was founded in 1973 by women who had been active in the Black Power Movement and who wanted to have a more practical and ideological focus to their feminist activism than the 'consciousness raising' groups of the Women's Liberation Movement of the 1970s. The Brixton Black Women's Centre was opened in 1980 and became an important place for activists to congregate and provide support and advice to countless women of colour in relation to immigration law and family planning, for example. The centre included an information and advice service, meetings, seminars and film nights, a craft workshop, a crèche and a library with a particular focus on women's literature and Black history.

*

In 1979 a scandal at the Home Office showed just how badly resources like the Black Women's Centre were needed. At that time women from South Asia could be granted special visas to join their fiancés in Britain as long as they married within three months of arrival. The Home Office became suspicious that women were exploiting what they believed to be an immigration loophole, and were not 'really' engaged to be married to men already in Britain. They attempted to crack down on this by administering invasive physical tests at the border to check whether the women who travelled on these visas were virgins, on the assumption that if they were not then they must already be married (or unmarriageable) and thus exposing their claim to engagement as false. The *Guardian* broke the story when a 35-year-old teacher from India, travelling to Britain to join her fiancé, told the paper she had been given a painful internal examination by a male doctor on arrival in the UK. The woman, who asked to remain anonymous, had been told to sign a consent form for 'a gynaecological examination, which may be vaginal if necessary'; she had done so because she was unfamiliar with the British immigration system and was frightened that she might be forced to return to Delhi. She was made to strip naked, before being internally examined by a male doctor who claimed to be checking whether she was pregnant or had been pregnant before; when she objected to this, the doctor had told her that there was 'no need to get shy'.[89]

When approached by the paper, a Home Office spokesman claimed the woman had 'been given only a cursory examination that was not internal', while simultaneously repeating the medical officer's claim that he had 'very quickly and decently established that she was virgo intacto'. (Dr Robert Winston, who was then working as a gynaecologist in Hammersmith, confirmed to the *Guardian* that this test – which he thought was 'scandalous and almost obscene' – had no way of proving whether the woman was pregnant, had ever been pregnant, or was a virgin.[90] Of course, the fact that a woman was or was not a virgin also had no bearing on whether she was or was not married.) The paper followed up the story with further investigations. Mary Dines, who had helped to establish the Joint Council for the Welfare of Immigrants before becoming the Director of War on Want, testified that in 1968 she had been told by immigration officers that they had 'found out whether two immigrant girls were virgins or not'; horrified, she had approached Merlyn Rees at the Home Office, who had claimed that he would do something about it.[91] Alex Lyon, who had been an immigration minister at the Home Office between 1974 and 1976, told the *Guardian* that he had discovered that women in Dacca who wanted to come to Britain were also being subjected to this form of 'virginity testing' before departure as part of the visa process and had instructed all British immigration and entry certificate officers that this should cease.[92] In other words, this was not the first time border control had been involved with the practice, and knowledge of its participation went all the way to the top.

The *Guardian* story horrified readers. Flyers collected by the Home Office to monitor public opinion called on people to join a protest against the 'inhumane and vicious practice', decrying as spurious the idea that virginity could be assessed through physical examination or that it would in any case be evidence for or against a genuine immigration claim, and pointing out that women who were engaged to men who were already living in Britain had an 'absolute right of entry' to the UK.[93] The Organisation of Women of African and Asian Descent (OWAAD) and the Asian women's collective Awaz organised protests at Heathrow, followed by a sit-in. The Commission for Racial Equality (established by the 1976 Race Relations Act) and the Equal Opportunities Commission (set up by the Sex Discrimination Act of 1975) took the unprecedented action of issuing a joint statement against the practices; as these examinations effectively established virginity as a condition for Asian women looking to enter the UK, the CRE argued that this constituted racial discrimination, the EOC said it was discrimination on the grounds of sex.[94]

In Parliament, Jo Richardson, the Labour MP for Barking, raised the fact that potential immigrants, including pregnant women, had been subject to X-rays by border control, a story also covered by the *Guardian*, which reported concerns that those conducting the procedures were not medically trained. She set these scandals within the context of a wide range of indignities and obstacles encountered by families trying to reunite across the British border. One man in Richardson's constituency had been unable to bring his wife to Britain, after ten years' separation, because in the immigration interview there were 'discrepancies between his story about the number of buffalo on his father's smallholding and his wife's story about the number of buffalo' that supposedly proved they were not in a real relationship; a young woman's nineteen-year-old fiancé had been forced to submit to X-ray testing to gauge his age and had then been caught in a Kafkaesque nightmare as the Home Office insisted – against the evidence of his valid birth certificate – that he was only thirteen and thus ineligible to enter the country to marry.[95]

The Home Office responded quickly to the outrage: a press release the day after the first story broke said that the Home Secretary had given instructions that immigration officers should not use the medical officer to try to ascertain whether a woman had given birth or had sex.[96] In internal files, however, Home Office civil servants were defensive about this virginity testing, and their files describe, casually and in some detail, this sexual violence being perpetrated by the British state on Commonwealth citizens of colour: 'the doctor says that penetration of about half an inch made it apparent that she had an intact hymen and no other internal examination was made'. The North London Women Against Fascism pointed out that although this was in theory a general immigration policy, in reality 'we know of no white women who have suffered from similar assault'.[97]

Although the Home Office maintained that the scandal was a minor event, recently released files reveal it is likely that almost one hundred women were affected.[98] And in truth it had an extensive history of similar activity, for sex and race were always at the heart of imperial anxieties. Under the Contagious Diseases Acts of the late nineteenth century, women who were suspected of being sex workers were forced to submit to physical examination and were locked up if they showed signs of venereal disease. When this legislation was exported to India under the British Raj, Indian women protested, while feminists in Britain travelled to 'protect' their Indian 'sisters' from this indignity.

Border control was not the only area of the British state where racism and imperialism were interwoven. Racism within the police was rife during this era, and often entailed the harassment of young Black and Asian men, or the downplaying of racist incidents and unwillingness to investigate racist crimes. In August 1970, 150 people marched through Notting Hill in protest against the harassment by police of the local Black community; between January 1969 and July 1970, the local Black-owned restaurant the Mangrove had been raided by police twelve times, without any evidence being uncovered of illegal activities on the premises. The protest became a riot, and the Mangrove Nine – including Darcus Howe and Altheia Jones-LeCointe – were arrested and charged with riot, incitement to riot, and affray. After fifty-five days of trial, the jury found them not guilty of twenty-three of the thirty-two charges. Judge Edward Clarke, in his ruling, said that there had been 'evidence of racial hatred on both sides',[99] a literal both-sides argument that equated the actions of a minority community being harassed by the state with the police force that was violently targeting them, although at least with the acknowledgement that this police force was acting out of a deep and abiding racism.

Police violence shaped the experience of anti-racism campaigners throughout the 1970s. Blair Peach was a young teacher from New Zealand who had moved to Britain and started working at a school in Hackney. He was active in left-wing politics, including the Socialist Workers Party and the Anti-Nazi League (ANL). In April 1979, he took part in a protest against the National Front in Southall, an area of London which had been a site of much Asian migration, especially from Indian Sikh communities, ever since partition. Southall had become a thriving, diverse borough but also attracted a large amount of harassment from racists and the far-right movement. Three years previously, eighteen-year-old Gurdip Singh Chaggar had been stabbed to death outside the Southall offices of the Indian Workers' Association, leading to the formation of the Southall Youth Movement (SYM) to fight back against the racism experienced by young Asian people in the borough. In 1978, the SYM had organised a picket outside the Hamborough Tavern because the pub was operating a colour bar and hosting music nights for skinhead groups; the group had also demonstrated against Enoch Powell when he spoke in the area.[100] The protest in April 1979 had been organised by the SYM alongside groups like the ANL in order to prevent, or at least disrupt, a meeting of National Front activists in Southhall Town Hall.

On 23 April, depending on the report, between five hundred and two thousand protesters, Blair Peach among them, surrounded the hall. Initially, the police – nearly 3,000 of whom had been drafted in to deal with potential violence – tried to contain the protesters behind a cordon, before trying to disperse them and threatening with arrest anyone who remained. The atmosphere was febrile and explosive. Earlier in the day, police had forcibly entered a house being used as a first-aid post and two officers had been stabbed. In response, the police had used their truncheons to smash up the contents of the house and the people giving and receiving first aid; Clarence Baker, a local youth worker and the manager of the reggae band Misty in Roots, was beaten into a coma by 'ten or twelve' officers who called him a 'black bastard'.[101]

At around 7.30 p.m. Peach was trying to leave the protest when he was also hit over the head by 'a rubber cosh, or a hosepipe filled with lead shot or a similar weapon'; he died in hospital later that night.[102] An internal report into his death, extracts of which were printed in the *Sunday Times*, revealed that he had probably been attacked by a member of the plain-clothes police Special Branch, the Special Patrol Group (SPG), and that other SPG members had colluded to cover this up. There had been an 'explosive atmosphere of violence' on the day, originating not among the ANL marchers but from the police; just before Peach was murdered one officer was heard to shout 'give them a spanking'.[103] It was discovered that SPG members had in their lockers a number of brutal weapons, which they had used in the march, including a leather-encased metal truncheon, a knife with a six-inch blade, two three-foot crossbars, two sledgehammer handles and a rhino whip.[104] Despite having seen this report, the coroner who conducted the inquest directed the jury to reject the idea that a police officer had killed Peach and they recorded a verdict of death by misadventure.

Blair Peach's partner, Celia Stubbs, campaigned tirelessly for the SPG to admit wrongdoing; it would later emerge that this had provoked the Metropolitan Police to spy on her, and her campaign, for more than twenty years, beginning with the surveillance of mourners at Peach's funeral.[105] During that time, his memory became an important touchstone for campaigners against police violence and harassment. The west London local paper *Punjab Times* argued in an editorial that 'Southall has been reduced to the status of a British Imperial Colony' by the police violence, while the Punjabi-language paper *Des Pardes* drew parallels between the actions of the police against the protesters with the imperial violence at Amritsar in 1919.[106] The poet Linton Kwesi Johnson wrote a song, 'Reggae Fi Peach', which memorialised 'Blair Peach the Teacher', who had come from New Zealand, a Commonwealth territory, to fight against fascism in the metropole, and ended by asking how long English people would continue to tolerate these 'great injustices' on English soil.[107] The Southall Black Sisters was an activist and campaign group set up in 1979 in the aftermath of Peach's murder and the ongoing context of racism and violence in Britain. As well as campaigning against the Home Office virginity tests, the group offered support to Asian women in their fight against racial discrimination, domestic violence and religious oppression.

That same year, Rock Against Racism organised a pair of concerts under the title 'The Southall Kids Are Innocent' to raise money to defend the 342 people who had been charged with offences at the protest at which Peach was killed. Musicians Red Saunders, Roger Huddle, Jo Wreford, Pete Bruno and others had formed Rock

Against Racism in response to Eric Clapton's drunken declaration of support for Enoch Powell onstage in 1976, when he had praised the MP and demanded that the country should 'get the foreigners out'. Saunders and his friends wrote an open letter to Clapton that was published in the music press and the *Socialist Worker*: 'you've been taking too much of that *Daily Express* stuff, you know you can't handle it'. As well as calling Clapton 'music's biggest colonist' (because of the influence of R&B and blues on his sound), the musicians stated their intention to launch 'a rank and file movement against racist poison in rock music' and asked for interested supporters to write to them for more details.[108] In the ensuing years Rock Against Racism organised 'carnivals against racism' and around five hundred music concerts across the country to promote racial equality and fight against racist injustice. They also organised political events: for example, in 1977 the National Front had held an 'anti-mugging' march, to amplify the media hysteria that connected young Black men with violent street crime, and Rock Against Racism held a counter-protest, at which Darcus Howe addressed the crowd and the police used anti-riot shields for the first time in mainland Britain. But it was the concerts that really caught the public attention. In April 1978, Rock Against Racism staged what would become a famous gig in Victoria Park in London's East End. Pictures, such as those taken by the photographer Syd Shelton, show the Clash performing onstage and 100,000 people singing along in the crowd, many raising a fist in an anti-fascist salute. Shelton maintained that the manager of the Clash, Bernie Rhodes, initially said he would only let them play if the organisers bought 'a tank for Zimbabwe' to support the anti-colonial freedom fighters there, but this suggestion was eventually dropped when it transpired that the event was not-for-profit and none of the acts were being paid.[109]

In the run-up to the 1979 general election, Rock Against Racism also took musicians around the country on a 'Militant Entertainment Tour' to dissuade young voters from backing the National Front. In September 1978, they held 'Carnival 2' in Hyde Park, with a bill featuring Aswad, Sham 69, and Elvis Costello and the

Attractions. Promo material for the event explained that the NF intended to put up three hundred candidates in the upcoming election which would guarantee the party coverage on television and across newspapers. The flyer showed how the party took inspiration 'directly from Hitler's Nazis in Germany' in its rhetoric, which attempted to 'make scapegoats of black people', and argued that it was trying to 'exploit the real problems of unemployment, bad housing and declining welfare services' to whip up anger and violence towards communities such as the Bengali population of Brick Lane, who had faced increasing levels of attacks and assaults from far-right thugs.[110]

Thanks to their efforts and those of many other grassroots community groups and coalitions of organisations on the left, the general election was a wipe-out for the National Front, who got only 0.6 per cent of the vote. Historian Stuart Hall credited this result to 'local campaigns, anti-fascist work in the unions, trades councils, women's groups, the mobilisation behind the Anti Nazi League, the counter-demonstrations, above all Rock Against Racism'.[111] But, of course, the same election saw one of Britain's most radical right-wing prime ministers take power. A few months after the election, Hall expressed his concern that support for the NF had not gone away, it had simply been co-opted by Margaret Thatcher who had secured her victory by pushing the Conservative Party to the right: 'I would be happier about the temporary decline in the fortunes of the Front if so many of their themes had not been so swiftly reworked into a more respectable discourse on race by Conservative politicians.'[112] In their own campaign materials the year before, the Anti-Nazi League had pointed out that 'Thatcher's remarks about "black people swamping this country"' were one of many pieces of evidence – including recent decisions in the courts, and the continual drip of scare stories about immigration in the tabloid press – that the NF's central ideas had gained a significant foothold in mainstream culture and politics.[113]

In the 1960s, the Smethwick by-election and Enoch Powell's 'Rivers of Blood' speech were critical moments in anti-immigration 'anxiety' among the white British electorate. In the 1970s, the growing movement in support of anti-racist activism must be set against the discrimination and oppression – often at the hands of the state – that they were fighting. Migration had brought imperial citizens 'home' to the former metropole, but the violence of colonial rule overseas had also been brought 'home' through the racism of the British border forces, the British police force and the wider British state. As Stuart Hall made clear, Thatcher's election, in many ways, saw the movement of a pernicious strain of hard-right activism from the periphery to the centre of British politics. Against all of this, the Falklands conflict was a moment of rejuvenated and sustained imperial sentiment in Britain – but this last hurrah for empire was resisted, not least by the anti-apartheid campaigners who yelled slogans on the streets of Glasgow during the Commonwealth Games. As Thatcherism saw a profound shift in domestic politics, Britain's relationship with its empire and its imperial past was also still changing.

6

Britain's Troubled Conscience:
Empire, War and Famine in the 1980s

'Britain is at war with Argentina!!! Radio Four has just announced it. I am overcome with excitement. Half of me thinks it is tragic and the other half of me thinks it is dead exciting.'[1]

So Adrian Mole wrote in his diary, on the morning of Saturday 3 April 1982. When he heard the news, he immediately woke up his father, who shot out of bed, under the impression that the Falkland Islands were located somewhere off the coast of Scotland. Adrian somewhat smugly informed him that the islands were in fact thousands of miles away, but that evening at teatime he tried and failed to locate them on a world map. Eventually his mum uncovered them, under a crumb of fruit cake, in the sea off the coast of Argentina.

A teenage boy living in Leicester, Adrian Mole could be forgiven his ignorance. But despite being a fictional character, the comic creation of Sue Townsend, his response to the Falklands War – a mixture of anxiety and excitement, shaded with confusion – is a good barometer of the British population's as a whole. The three-month campaign, which Britain fought on the other side of the world to defend territories that most British people had never heard of, was perhaps the last gasp of twentieth-century British imperialism. It was used by Margaret Thatcher to tell a story about British identity that evoked nineteenth-century imperial adventure yarns, as well as the spirit of the Second World War. More than anything, it shows how imperial culture continued to suffuse British society long after many people had stopped thinking consciously about empires at all.

Although the Falklands were a less obvious emblem of British imperialism than the jewel in the crown of India or the pith-helmeted settler colonies of East Africa, they had in fact been part of the British empire for far longer than either of these regions. An English naval captain made the first recorded landing on the islands in 1690, and they were declared a Crown colony in 1833. Today these 778 islands are one of the fourteen remaining British Overseas Territories, the last crumbs of empire left over after decolonisation. Most of the population of the Falklands lives on East and West Falkland, and most are descended from British settlers. There is no indigenous population. The islanders were originally mostly whalers and seal hunters, but by the end of the nineteenth century the economy was heavily dependent on sheep farming; today there are half a million sheep spread across the islands, over 140 for every human Falklander.

The British claim to the islands was disputed even before they were formally recognised as colonies: they lie only three hundred miles off the coast of Patagonia, and so Argentina had made a territorial claim to the islands, which they call Las Malvinas, since their own independence from Spain in 1816. The dispute over sovereignty of the islands continued into the twentieth century, but only at a high politics level of diplomacy; the islanders themselves, who spoke English, taught their children about Queen Victoria, Charles Dickens and the Lake District, and ate mutton and fruit cake, believed themselves to be British.

From the 1960s to the 1980s, at various times, the British government had been theoretically happy to cede the islands to the Argentine government: the archipelago was not tactically important, and was difficult to defend, thousands of miles away from the UK in the South Atlantic. Unfortunately, nobody had asked the Falklanders if they actually wanted to be turned over to Argentina. In November 1968, a junior government minister, Lord Chalfont, visited the islands to present proposals for handing the Falklands over. He remembered a very hostile response: 'the quay side was alive with fluttering Union Jacks, punctuated only by a few rather dispiriting messages saying "Chalfont go home". Things of that kind! Some of them rather less polite than others.'[2] After Margaret Thatcher came to power, the government in 1980 again considered ceding the islands to Argentina; again, the islanders and the Falklands lobby in Westminster rejected this proposal.

In March 1982, a party of Argentine scrap metal merchants landed on South Georgia, a small and inhospitable island six hundred miles east of the Falklands. The men had landed to dismantle a whaling station, a lucrative undertaking once the material had been removed and sold. But the British government, whose diplomatic representatives in Buenos Aires had okayed the project, were suspicious. It was reported – perhaps erroneously – that the men had planted the Argentine flag and were singing their national anthem.[3] A group of marines were dispatched to investigate.

Much of the British press, and people, responded with amusement. As the *Guardian* said, it seemed ludicrous that 'the long arm of customs and immigration' should reach all the way to 'the desolate disused whaling station at Leith harbour'. The *Mirror* mocked the 'gaggle of Steptoes' who had made the effort to raise an Argentinian flag over 'a bleak rock near the Antarctic inhabited by reindeer and penguins'. The *Sun* was one of the only British newspapers to really become animated about the South Georgia landings; their assertion that 'the Falklands were British, are British and will REMAIN British' led columnists at the *Mirror* to point out that the two groups of islands were in fact around eight hundred miles apart.[4]

It is possible that the men really were just scrap metal merchants; they had certainly signed a contract with the Scottish owners of the derelict whaling station to dismantle and sell the remains. It is also possible that the party had been infiltrated by, or was knowingly hiding, Argentine special forces. Either way, the Royal Marines sent to investigate ended up detaining the thirty-nine men. Stories appeared in the British press that a submarine had been dispatched from Gibraltar to defend the islands; this was untrue, but the MOD believed that a show of strength might be useful diplomatically and refused to issue a statement to correct the newspapers, to the horror of the Foreign Office who rightly predicted that this would lead to an escalation in hostilities.[5]

Argentina was run by a military dictatorship led by General Leopoldo Galtieri, who had always maintained that Argentina had sovereignty over the islands and who needed to bolster domestic support for his unpopular, violent and undemocratic government. This apparent British aggression in the South Atlantic was a perfect excuse. Argentine forces were dispatched, theoretically to free the thirty-nine imprisoned men; on 2 April, they landed on the Falkland Islands. Governor Rex Hunt armed himself with a pistol and, along with his wife, refused to leave his command post, instead taking refuge under a heavy desk in his office. Argentine forces surrounded Government House and fired on the flimsy building before gaining entrance to the office and asking the governor to surrender. The five-foot-six Hunt, in his smart suit, tried to bluster it out – 'This is British territory. We don't want you here. You're not invited and I want you to go and take all your men with you' – but was forced to accept the overwhelming numbers of the Argentine invasion force and ordered the Royal Marines to surrender.[6]

The next day, in the first Saturday emergency session of Parliament since the Suez Crisis, some MPs were already calling for an armed response. Sir Bernard Braine (Con, Castle Point) protested that the 'very thought that our people . . . of British blood and bone, could be left in the hands of such criminals is enough to make any normal Englishman's blood . . . boil'.[7] Newspapers echoed this language, not least the ever-patriotic *Sun*, which evidently felt itself vindicated; that morning's edition, with the triumphant headline 'It's War!', dismissed the possibility of UN intervention in favour of a Royal Navy strike. In the House of Commons, Thatcher described the invasion as an act of 'unprovoked aggression', and committed the government 'to see that the islands are freed from occupation and are returned to British administration at the earliest possible moment'.[8]

Some MPs were publicly critical of the war: Denis Healey (Lab,

Leeds East) and Tony Benn (Lab, Bristol South East) both called for a negotiated settlement rather than fighting, and Tam Dalyell (Lab, West Lothian) remained a staunch critic of the campaign. Others were hotly in favour. Peter Mills, the Conservative MP for the naval constituency of West Devon, cheered on the prime minister in public and in private was even more enthusiastic, saying that his constituents 'wanted blood'. But many other Conservative MPs also expressed private doubts. Ian Gilmour (Con, Chesham and Amersham) warned that a military campaign would be 'a big mistake' that would 'make Suez look like common sense'; Ken Clarke (Con, Rushcliffe) wanted to avoid war and hoped that it would be enough for Britain to 'blow up a few ships'.

The problem faced by even those British people with the most anti-imperial sympathies was that Galtieri was a brutal right-wing dictator, running the country by military junta, with an appalling human rights record. Amnesty International had been collecting information on his crimes for some time, and these had been taken up by the Falklands lobby in Parliament. Bernard Braine remembered 'compiling a list' of crimes committed by the junta: 'priests were abducted for protesting against this violation of human rights, their bodies found on the roadside a day or two later, with their eyes gouged out, and when the local bishop objected to it, he too was run off the road in his car, and left to die by the roadside. Former Argentinian diplomats who raised their voices were killed. University professors, teachers were killed. Students who protested were killed. Argentina became a graveyard.'9

This made it difficult for even staunch opponents of Thatcher to oppose her war, for to do so would be to side with Galtieri. Michael Foot, leader of the Labour Party, condemned the Argentine invasion as 'an act of naked, unqualified aggression' and committed the party to supporting a British military response. He pre-empted possible criticism by arguing that 'there is no question in the Falkland Islands of any colonial dependence or anything of the sort': in other words, the Falklanders were entitled to self-determination and their national impulse to remain British should be respected and protected.[10] In this way, politicians who felt morally repulsed by colonialism managed to elide the fact that this naval war fought to protect the right of white settlers far away was, in the words of left-wing political activist and academic Stuart Hall, 'an imperial adventure that would have seemed out of date in 1882'.[11]

There was also the problem of the tabloid press, whose coverage of the conflict was intensely jingoistic and influential. The constraints of distance and the conditions – including heavy government censorship – meant that this was, unusually, a modern war without television coverage. Newspapers, especially the tabloids, which were predominantly supportive of the Conservative government, found themselves with an immense degree of power to set the narrative and tone of the war. To express any criticism of Thatcher or any doubts about the war was to risk seeming unpatriotic, letting down the brave boys sailing from Southampton to beat the 'Argies'. Even the Queen's own son, Prince Andrew, would be co-pilot of a Sea King helicopter for the Royal Navy. The *Sun* was the most excitable of them all. On the first day of the conflict, its headline read 'WE'LL SMASH 'EM' and was presented over pictures of a British bulldog and Winston Churchill. (The military was more circumspect; Lieutenant Commander Raymond John Adams remembered encouraging his sailors to make a will, and take out life insurance.)[12]

The *Sun* would end up being one of the victors of the Falklands. It had long encapsulated a particular type of British chauvinism – xenophobic, often racist, homophobic and sexist, with the Page Three girls a constant thorn in the side of the British feminist movement. The Labour MP Clare Short would later introduce a bill in Parliament to try to ban pornographic pictures from British newspapers: the *Sun* responded by calling her 'Killjoy Clare', sending busloads of Page Three girls to park outside the house of her elderly mother, and mocking up pictures of her as an unattractive topless model.[13] In the early 1980s, the paper was in a circulation battle with the left-leaning *Mirror*; by the end of the war, the *Sun* would have won the race to 1 million sales, beating its rival, and underwriting the Murdoch media empire for years to come.

The paper was the preferred read of the young squaddies being sent out to fight, and die, for Britain, and its focus on girls, goals and guns helped it soar in popularity. It juxtaposed bloodthirsty narratives of the military campaign with heart-warming stories about the sacrifices made by British families sending their sons overseas to fight. In a coming-together of the paper's two main interests – soft pornography and rampant jingoism – it reported that 'thousands of women with loved ones aboard the Navy's Task Force . . . are sporting specially-made underwear embroidered across the front with the proud name of the ship in which a husband or boyfriend is serving', with a spread of semi-naked women in illustration.[14] The Page Three girls, the topless models that graced the *Sun*'s pages every day, were also militarised, with captions referring to the campaign, and posters of the 'girls' sent out to sailors on the boats.

More importantly, it set the tone for the British experience of the war, not by dragging other papers down into the gutter – in fact, one editorial in the *Mirror* proclaimed that 'the Sun today is to journalism what Dr Josef Goebbels was to truth' – but by normalising and dominating the narrative of the war with its relentless, screaming nationalism.[15] At the start of the conflict, it rejected the possibility of a peaceful solution with 'STICK IT UP YOUR JUNTA!' and excitedly heralded the start of a British counter-invasion with 'IN WE GO!'. Later in the campaign and most infamously, the *Sun* responded to the sinking of the Argentine light cruiser the ARA *General Belgrano*, in which 323 Argentine men lost their lives, with the headline 'GOTCHA'. These campaigns were devised in a newsroom that had been decked out as a replica war room, with the news editor 'Commander Petrie' wearing a tin hat at his desk and the editor Kelvin MacKenzie marching, saluting and barking orders around the office in the style of a sergeant major.[16]

Other newspapers resisted the urge to descend into a parody of military men but were no less supportive of the war, repeatedly evoking both the Second World War and the British empire and inscribing the Falklands into the canon of great British military campaigns. On 5 June, after the Battle of Goose Green in which British forces had regained control of an airfield on East Falkland and two weeks before the end of the war, *The Times* ran an editorial headlined 'We are all Falklanders now', drawing a parallel between defence of the Falklands and the moment in 1939 when Britain had had to stand up to Nazism. The *Daily Mail* also repeatedly used imagery that invoked the Second World War and earlier imperial campaigns. Perhaps these constant invocations were why 24 per cent of people surveyed by Ipsos Mori in April 1982 thought that Argentine citizens living in Britain should be interned for the duration of the war.

On the other side, the *Mirror* was concerned with the speed and fervour with which Britain was embracing warfare. One front page, 'MIGHT ISN'T RIGHT', warned against 'mounting hysteria' and concluded that 'the killing has got to stop', calling on Britain and Argentina to compromise to bring peace.[17] The *Guardian* went further, consistently refusing to support the war, drawing opprobrium from politicians and the wider public. The paper's opposition was partly based in a principled commitment to peace and resistance of British neo-imperialism, but it was also pragmatic: the Falklands had little contact with Britain and little to offer the world other than 600,000 sheep. In an editorial entitled 'Taking Leave of Our Senses' published in early April, the paper argued that the Argentine invasion made little difference to the British on a practical level and that responding with military force was both inappropriate and illogical.[18] The left-wing historian E. P. Thompson wrote a column for the paper in which he warned that the military action on South Georgia had again associated Britain with 'the stereotypes of her own imperial history', and that this would reduce international support for the campaign.[19] It was certainly true that the American press saw the war as an anachronism: as *Newsweek* had it, a 'nineteenth-century showdown in twentieth-century battle dress', while the *New York Times* attributed the campaign to a 'nostalgic yearning for the proud old days of empire'.[20]

Margaret Thatcher kept a stern eye on media coverage. She was greatly concerned that the British people should feel themselves to be at war, despite the fact that the fighting was happening thousands of miles away, and was furious that the BBC aimed for neutrality in their coverage. In her autobiography, she bemoaned the 'chilling use of the third person' in its news bulletins, which talked about 'the British' instead of her preferred term, 'our soldiers'.[21] But BBC guidelines unrepentantly instructed reporters to remain neutral during the campaign. 'We should try to avoid using "our" when we mean British. We are not Britain,' they argued. 'We are the BBC.'[22] At any rate, their right to report the war freely was curtailed. Thatcher expressed concern that the BBC's speculation about future military manoeuvres might put British soldiers at risk, and the British people agreed: 65 per cent believed the MOD had the right to censor journalist reports. The BBC was forced to accept this censorship – not least because their war correspondents relied on navy wires to transmit reports back home.

For many people, though, the BBC television coverage was the way they experienced the war. The moment when correspondent Brian Hanrahan, banned by the MOD from reporting the exact numbers of British Harrier jets involved in a mission, reassured viewers that 'I counted them all out, and I counted them all back in', quickly became emblematic of the British campaign as a whole. His reporting that the pilots had been in high spirits and giving thumbs-up signs to the watching media helped to create an image that was brave and jubilant.[23]

Away from the cameras, ordinary soldiers had a more ambivalent attitude to the campaign. The HMS *Glamorgan* had on its crew a number of men who did not want to go to the Falklands, or were critical of the use of military force to retake the islands; their commander, Captain Michael Ernest Barrow, was careful during informal chats with his men to point out that 'the military must always carry out the wishes of the government when diplomatic means fail'.[24] Many sailors were unprepared for war after a long period of relatively peaceful manoeuvres. Petty Officer Brandon

Christopher Smith, on HMS *Fearless*, recalled 'one young lad who'd jumped ship from the *Hermes*, under the impression that as he'd missed his ship he wouldn't have to go' who had to hitch a ride down to Ascension Island where he could rejoin his crew; the 'frightened boy', as Smith remembered, asked 'Do you think we'll be hit?' so many times that he started to affect the morale among the other men.[25] Private Graham Carter, from 2 Para Regiment, said later that 'you don't particularly join the army these days to actually go to war, but for a career', and that he, like most of the men he knew, 'really wasn't looking forward to the prospect of going down to the Falklands in that respect'.[26]

Collectively, the British people shared some of this ambivalence. Among them, there were of course those who did not think any bloodshed could be justified and who attended anti-war protests. The Ad Hoc Committee for Peace in the Falklands was set up to bring together groups that opposed the fighting: the Peace Pledge Union, the National Union of Students, the Roman Catholic peace movement Pax Christi and the Ecology Party (the precursor to the Green Party). The Campaign for Nuclear Disarmament, which was not keen on the partisan implications of opposing the war, somewhat reluctantly joined the coalition after the news broke that the British Task Force was carrying tactical nuclear weapons. Most of these groups opposed the fighting on pacifist grounds, but there was some political activism as well: many far-left groups, such as the Revolutionary Communist Party, believed that the Malvinas belonged to Argentina and that the Falklanders were themselves anachronistic imperialists.

The Ad Hoc Committee organised marches in London as well as meetings, vigils and events in other parts of the country. The Peace Pledge Union produced leaflets, constantly updated with the number of dead and injured soldiers on both sides, as well as the news that three civilian Falklander women had been accidentally killed by the Royal Navy. Activists poured fake blood on the steps of the MOD, and held protests where they tore up Union Jacks and Argentine flags and paraded fake coffins, leading to a number of arrests (including briefly of the coffin itself).[27] There was a March for Peace on 23 May which ended in Trafalgar Square and was addressed by speakers including Tony Benn and Harriet Harman. Opposition to the war was particularly focused on the British sinking of the *Belgrano*, which had been outside the official exclusion zone during the attack by British submarines. In the election campaign of the following year, a PE teacher from Cirencester named Diana Gould memorably confronted Thatcher during a live appearance on the current affairs programme *Nationwide*, repeatedly asking her why did she 'give the orders to sink it' when it was outside the zone and sailing away from the Falklands; the interview became an iconic moment of television history and led Denis Thatcher to complain to the producer that the BBC was run by 'a load of pinkoes'.[28]

Even among those who supported the war were many who felt conflicted. In Mass Observation surveys collected at the time, people were encouraged to write about their emotions as the conflict unfolded. A woman in her late sixties lamented that, although she supported the Task Force, it was 'altogether, a sad and unnecessary thing, so many lives lost, so young too'. On the other hand, an ex-serviceman wrote that 'for once we are returning to the bygone standards of protecting Britons wherever they may be' – the war, with its simplistic narrative of right and wrong, enabled people to feel pride again in Britain in the world and what British values represented to them. One woman explicitly connected her feelings about the Falklands with her feelings for empire, reminiscing that 'When I was a child, today would have been Empire Day. We would sing patriotic hymns in the morning, wore little bunches of daisies tied with red, white and blue ribbon, then out came the may pole for our old English dances . . . our young men are still patriotic and brave, ready to defend the honour of the land of our birth.'[29] For some British people who had lived through empire and decolonisation, as well as the Second World War, the Falklands represented more than just a rocky outpost far away, and the war was more than a skirmish in the papers. Perhaps the fact that, compared with the civilian horrors of the Second World War, this was an old-fashioned war that happened 'over there' meant that people felt that they could celebrate British military prowess from a safe vantage point. The seemingly unambiguous morality of the campaign, the fact that the Falkland Islanders *wanted* to remain part of the British empire, might also have come as a welcome relief after decades of colonial warfare in which Britain's position had been altogether more murky.

This rediscovered patriotism and the resurgence of British imperial feeling meant that, once again, empire and identity saturated British mass media and popular culture. Stockport County football club had changed their kit to a pale blue and white stripe with black shorts in homage to Argentina after it won the 1978 World Cup. Come the Falklands War in 1982, they decided this was no longer appropriate, and returned to their traditional dark blue and white. Ossie Ardiles and Ricky Villa had been part of the Argentine team in 1978, and had started playing for Tottenham Hotspur that autumn. Ardiles in particular was popular with fans: Chas and Dave recorded 'Ossie's Dream (Spurs are on their way to Wembley)' to mark the team's FA Cup campaign and the player responded by scoring a famous goal in the final. But after Argentina invaded the Falklands, the two men faced scrutiny from the British press and hostility from British fans. A game against Aston Villa was marked by jeers and boos, even from some Spurs fans, although the banner that read 'Argentina can keep the Falklands, we'll keep Ossie' has passed into folk memory. The two players found it increasingly difficult to cope, and Ardiles returned to Argentina early to train for the 1982 World Cup, his misery compounded by the death of his cousin José, the first Argentine fighter pilot to be killed in the conflict. His feeling of being torn was impossible to resolve; 'it was incredibly sad how two countries which I loved could be at war against each other', he later said.[30] Villa stayed in Britain but did not play in the Cup Final: a football match in the middle of the war felt too emotionally charged, and he withdrew from the squad. In 1986, when Argentina beat England in the quarter-finals of the World Cup, Diego Maradona celebrated by saying that 'We have beaten a country, not just a football team. They killed a lot of Argentine boys . . . killed them like little birds. And this was revenge.'[31]

The extent to which imperial jingoism saturated much of the mass media in Britain meant that those who were critical or questioning of the war often felt isolated. Many of them were determined to make sure their more ambivalent responses to wartime were not ignored. In the world of pop, Pink Floyd, Crass and Dire Straits all released music inspired by and referencing the war. Dire Straits' 'Brothers in Arms', which imagined the experiences of soldiers on the islands and finished with the exhortation that 'We're fools to make war / On our brothers in arms', can be interpreted as an anti-war ballad. Pink Floyd's *The Final Cut* was a concept album telling the stories of men who had fought for a better future in the Second World War only to see the country descend once again into jingoism; the song 'Southampton Dock' tells a story of women waving men off to fight from Southampton in the Second World War echoed by the wife or girlfriend who 'bravely waves the boys goodbye again' in 1982. The single 'Shipbuilding' written by Elvis Costello, sung by the folk singer Robert Wyatt and released in a sleeve decorated with work by Stanley Spencer, presented the difficulty faced by shipbuilding communities who would benefit financially from the need for warships, while boys from their own towns went off 'to task' to fight and hope to return.[32]

But many British people did embrace the glories of the Falklands War, which felt akin to a nineteenth-century imperial jolly, with career soldiers fighting a safe distance from the British metropole. In this place of nostalgic safety, Britain was great again not only militarily but also morally. But wars always eventually come home, not least in the broken bodies and destroyed minds of those soldiers, many of whom were only young men, who were fighting so far away. Simon Weston was a soldier in the Welsh Guards who had served in Northern Ireland and Kenya before being deployed to the Falklands. He was aboard the *Sir Galahad* when it was bombed by Argentine planes on 8 June, in an attack which saw fifty-six British soldiers killed and three times that number wounded; this was the worst loss of life in a single incident for British forces since the Second World War. Of Weston's platoon of thirty men, twenty-two were killed; he suffered burns to 46 per cent of his body and face, requiring over ninety operations in the following years. The documentary *Simon's War*, broadcast in 1983, documented his recovery, and in the years thereafter he became a leading figure in the campaign to provide better services to British armed forces veterans. Crass's album *Yes Sir, I Will* took its title from Weston's response to Prince Charles when, visiting the soldier in hospital after the bombing, he weakly told him to 'get well soon'.[33]

In 1988, *Tumbledown* presented another bleakly critical view of the conflict. This BBC film followed the story of Robert Lawrence, who was awarded the Military Cross after he was shot in the face and left paralysed with severe PTSD. Ten million viewers tuned in to watch Lawrence, played by a young Colin Firth, deal with the indifference and lack of care shown by the government and British society for returning, wounded Falklands veterans. The film was also controversial because it showed Lawrence attacking and killing Argentine men with a broken bayonet – shocking its audience who had imagined this modern war to have been more sanitised – and presented a lack of remorse among the British soldiers for the Argentine deaths they had inflicted.[34] The MOD demanded that controversial scenes be cut and spread rumours to try to discredit Lawrence's testimony; the film won a BAFTA for best single drama.[35] In truth, many members of the British armed forces returned from the Falklands in shock, traumatised by the loss of their comrades. Linda Kitson, the official war artist, remembers the Welsh Guards who had survived the bombing of the *Sir Galahad* as feeling endless guilt for their lost friends, with 'their faith in religion, the government, the diplomats and all things human' simply gone; she recalls that, on the two-week voyage back to the UK, at least four men every night had to be prevented from jumping overboard.[36]

The war lasted for only ten weeks. Three days after the Argentine air attacks on British ships at Bluff Cove, Britain launched an attack on the Argentine defences outside Port Stanley. On the night of 13 June, British forces advanced on Wireless Ridge and Mount Tumbledown in bitter close-quarters combat. They were eventually victorious, and Pipe Major James Riddell stood on Mount Tumbledown with his bagpipes to play 'The Crags of Tumbledown Mountain', hastily composed 'on the back of a fag packet' to mark their victory.[37] These battles sapped the morale of the remaining Argentine forces, with commanders going missing and soldiers unsure of their orders or status 'streaming' into Port Stanley; a ceasefire was declared, and the Argentine surrender was accepted by Major General Moore. British forces were greeted with enthusiasm by the Falkland Islanders, many of whom had been sheltering in the church hall, and they all had cups of tea; Lt Col. Chris Keeble, who had struggled with 'the paradox between being a Christian and being a soldier' during the campaign, later said that this moment was when his moral concerns about the conflict had been 'blown away'.[38]

At 10.30 p.m., Margaret Thatcher followed a long debate on industrial training in the House of Commons to announce a point of order 'to give the House the latest information about the battle of the Falklands'. In it, she announced erroneously that 'they are flying white flags over Port Stanley', this error caused by Major Bill Dawson having earlier told local reporters that this was the case and that it was 'bloody marvellous' to see. Later it was discovered that there had been no white flags at all, with Dawson acknowledging that it was 'probably someone's washing hanging on a clothes line'.[39] White flags or not, the Argentines had surrendered. After speaking to the media – 'It's *wonderful* news and it's *Great* Britain' – Thatcher excused herself to join in a raucous chorus of 'Britannia Rules the Waves', shake hands with well-wishers, and shout 'Great Britain is Great Again!' to the cheering crowds outside Downing Street. The front page of the *Express* the next morning showed her face caught in a giant V for Victory.

As she wrote in her memoir, Thatcher had a keen sense that Britain 'had come to be seen by both friends and enemies as a nation which lacked the will and the capability to defend its interests in peace, let alone in war'.[40] She saw an opportunity to restore some of the pride and self-confidence that she lamented the British had lost with their empire, and to draw political capital from doing so. She had judged the electorate well. Between April and June 1982, the proportion of people polled by Ipsos Mori who said that they would vote Conservative in the next election rose from 33 to 51 per cent. Opinion polls found that 45 per cent of people reported that their opinion of Thatcher had gone up during the crisis, compared with 47 per cent who felt their opinion of Michael Foot, the Labour leader, had gone down. (In comparison, only 7 per cent felt their opinion of Thatcher had gone down because of the Falklands; but then again, some people had started with a pretty low opinion of her in the first place.)[41]

In the Falkland Islands two holidays commemorate the war: Liberation Day on 14 June, a public holiday, and Margaret Thatcher Day on 10 January, marking Thatcher's first visit to the islands in 1983. The Iron Lady had wanted to be a war leader, and she had succeeded. But she was furious, again, when the service of thanksgiving and remembrance at St Paul's Cathedral in July took on a sombre note of reflection rather than the unbridled gratitude for victory she had envisaged. Afterwards, the Very Reverend Alan Webster argued that the 'traumas of modern war made a triumphalist "Victory Service" a contradiction in terms' and said that his only regret was that he had shied away from his original plan to read the Lord's Prayer in Spanish.[42] Exactly eighty years earlier, at the end of the Boer War, Britain's imperial victory had been praised in sermons across the country, and Thatcher evidently felt this victory was owed the same reception. The Church took a different view in light of the fact that 649 Argentine men, 255 British soldiers, and 3 Falkland Islanders had been killed in the campaign; the Anglican Church had evidently reconsidered its relationship to British imperial victories in the preceding eight decades.

In the June 1983 election, Thatcher's Conservatives won with a landslide, buoyed in the polls against a Labour Party that was cast as increasingly radical, disorganised and irrelevant by a largely hostile press. Two months earlier, the British Nationality (Falkland Islands) Act had been passed, giving full British citizenship to all the islanders. The war had been different from other imperial fights: the enemy was a brutal dictatorship, the people on the ground welcomed British intervention, and while there were some dehumanising, racialised caricatures of the 'Argies', this was not cast as a battle against an uncivilised, inferior other – although, in line with other moments of imperial identity, the whiteness of the islanders was utterly crucial to the British sense of kinship with them. And the pageantry around the war and the way it boosted Thatcher's ratings at home with a bit of 'Land of Hope and Glory'-style patriotism was pure *Boys' Own* imperialism. This energy would continue to suffuse Thatcher's period in power, as she and the right of the Conservative Party invoked narratives of plucky Britain and thought of themselves once more as representatives of a proud island race. Britain's relationship to its old empire had been newly invigorated, and with it some of the 'decline', perceived by those on the British right who saw the fall of the empire as the fall of the nation, had been offset; the Thatcherite project had been renewed, the way paved for ever more drastic attacks on a British state that many on the right believed had become flabby and complacent with decolonisation.

It was not just the right in Britain that had seen its relationship to the empire and to the wider world challenged in this moment. Decolonisation seemed to have finished, with even the old white bastion of Rhodesia having fallen with the Lancaster House Agreement in late 1979 and the election of Robert Mugabe as leader in 1980. *Was* the empire in fact over? Many on the left would argue not – the charge of 'neo-colonialism' was levied against Britain by critics at home and overseas who saw its dominance of organisations such as the UN and the IMF as a continued hangover of its old imperial might. On a more personal level, while the formal empire had been dismantled, for many in Britain the sense of their nation as a global power had not gone away. The Falklands War was, of course, part of this identity. But those ideas that became popular in the 1960s of Britain as a newly post-imperial humanitarian power – and the British as a people with a unique duty to the rest of the world that drew on, but never acknowledged, their imperial past – was also invigorated in this period. The old instincts towards white saviourism that had underpinned the civilising mission of the nineteenth century had never really gone away. The 1980s, which were so close to the end of empire and yet saw so little interrogation of this still-recent imperial past, were a decade marked by British good intentions – and the problems that arise when such intentions are so lacking in self-reflection – on a global scale.

On 23 October 1984, the BBC televised a news report by Michael Buerk from Ethiopia. It opened with his voice-over: 'Dawn, and as the sun breaks through the piercing chill of night on the plains outside Korem, it lights up a biblical famine, now, in the twentieth century.' The accompanying footage, shot by the Kenyan video journalist Mohammed Amin, panned slowly across a huge desolate landscape filled with people starving to death, interspersed with close-ups of men, women and children who were often, unusually, shown looking steadily straight at the camera. By the time Buerk had detailed the death and desolation he had seen in Korem – the three-year-old girl who had died while they were filming her being attached to a drip, the mother who had starved and would be buried wrapped together with her two-month-old baby, the 'tangible' grief in the camp at the thirty-seven people who had died overnight and the knowledge that more would die the next day, and the next – many viewers of the *Six O'Clock News* were unable to look away from their television screens. With his final sentence, 'Ethiopia is turning into the worst human disaster for a decade. A disaster begun by nature but compounded by man,' Buerk made an important intervention. He made clear that the 'famine' was not somehow natural or inevitable but a consequence of the rest of the world's inaction to prevent it. It invoked among many British viewers the feeling that they had a responsibility to act.[43]

Three days after the story was first broadcast, Christian Aid reported that British people had donated £5 million to the Ethiopian Famine Appeal, an amount that was matched by the British government.[44] Different groups made different kinds of donations: British farmers donated grain, for example, as part of the 'Send a Tonne' campaign, to supplement the grain drops organised by Oxfam. Meanwhile, the children's television show *Blue Peter* was forced to have its first 'Double Lifesaver' appeal, having already decided on the Royal National Lifeboat Institution as its beneficiary for the year before its young viewers started writing letters to the programme demanding that they be given the chance to donate to the famine victims; and so children collected stamps to send water and pumps, as well as tools and cooking utensils, to Ethiopia, alongside buttons and postcards to buy six new lifeboats in the United Kingdom. But these were not the most famous charitable responses to the Ethiopian Famine.

The Irish musician Bob Geldof had risen to prominence as the lead singer of the Boomtown Rats, a rock band with a number of hit singles in the late 1970s and early 80s. He too had been watching Michael Buerk's broadcast from Korem, and was as shaken as many other viewers by what he saw. He was moved to action, and to push others in the music industry to get involved. And so, with Midge Ure, Geldof recorded and released a charity Christmas single, 'Do They Know It's Christmas?', with a group of musical superstars that was dubbed Band Aid. The charity single had become an increasingly popular form of musical response to a cause, following George Harrison's 'Bangla Desh' recorded in 1971 to raise funds for the victims of the Bhola Cyclone and the civil war, which was also accompanied by a benefit concert. 'Do They Know It's Christmas?' was largely judged to be a poor musical effort that nevertheless deserved to sell handsomely because of its good intentions: *NME*'s entire review read 'Turkey: millions of dead stars write and perform rotten record for the right reason'.[45] It did, indeed, sell by the bucketload, going double platinum in the UK and with over 11 million copies being sold around the world.

But this was not enough for Geldof, who decided to stage an event to capitalise on global empathy for Ethiopia and build on the single's success. Live Aid took place in July 1985, and more than a billion people around the world watched the day-long concert, held in London and Philadelphia simultaneously, with performances from some of music's biggest stars. In Britain, the concert took place in the middle of a heatwave, and families dragged their televisions into their gardens and sat in paddling pools watching the show, with the sound of Queen, Status Quo and Madonna drifting down suburban streets. Every so often, the music would cut away to appeals from Bob Geldof, who was becoming visibly more tired and anxious as the day progressed. The live performances were paused for the video for 'Drive' by the Cars, which showed CBC footage of starving Ethiopian women and children accompanied by the crooning voice of the band's bass player, Benjamin Orr, asking 'Who's gonna drive you home tonight?'

The visual reminder of the charitable cause behind the day pushed many people to donate; but many also felt an uncomfortable tension with the portrayal of the Ethiopian people as entirely helpless and hopeless without British support. The British empire had a long history of justifying its exploitation with supposed humanitarianism, and furthermore British humanitarian organisations had themselves been key drivers of imperial expansion: British colonisation of Australia and New Zealand, for example, had been heavily influenced by the Aboriginal Protection Society, an early-nineteenth-century example of an NGO which had lobbied the government under the guise of concern for indigenous populations. This 1980s, supposedly post-colonial, relationship between a sentimental British public on the one hand and starving African babies on the other was reminiscent of an imperial narrative in which *all* subjects of British African colonies were children, who must be educated and guided towards civilisation and independence. In 2012, surveys for Oxfam demonstrated that Band Aid and Live Aid had been extremely damaging over the long term to British attitudes to African people; more than half of British people immediately mentioned hunger, famine or poverty when asked to speak about Africa, while over 40 per cent said that they thought conditions in the continent could never improve. In response to this research, the chief executive of the charity, Dame Barbara Stocking, called for the charity to 'shrug off the old stereotypes' of Band Aid and Live Aid and to embrace 'a more nuanced portrait of the continent'.[46] Geldof himself was attuned to this tension, sometimes refusing to have his photograph taken on visits to Ethiopia alongside the recipients of Live Aid because it fed into a 'patronising', 'distasteful' and 'exploitative' press coverage of the issue that he dubbed 'black baby syndrome'.[47]

Contemporary criticism of the British response to the Ethiopian Famine was unusually productive and emotive, with many of the more political charities mobilising not only to raise money for Ethiopia but also to draw attention to the British state's responsibility for poverty and inequality across the Global South, as well as its contribution to the political conditions which had caused the famine in the first place. In May 1985 there was a 'Bread Not Bombs Week', organised by Oxfam and Campaign Against the Arms Trade, to highlight the fact that the British government had sold £1,800 million worth of military equipment to the 'developing world' in 1984. This undoubtedly sustained many conflicts at the costs of many lives, and also put official British aid efforts into the proper context, since the money raised from these sales could have provided 13 million tonnes of grain to feed starving Africans.[48]

Live Aid demonstrated British people's commitment to maintaining a role – a duty, even – in the Global South, which in some ways sought to take the legacy of colonialism and turn it into an active engagement with the challenges faced by those people living in poverty in a recently decolonised world. However, this engagement, generous as it undoubtedly was, took place without much interrogation of Britain's previous role in Africa or the potential culpability of British governments for African poverty, famine or war. The guilt that many British people felt about their relative comfort compared with the deprivation they could see on their television screens was itself a response to Britain's imperial legacy. But it was a response that did not engage with the trickier questions about how and why the poverty of the Global South had come about, not just uncomfortably alongside the material comforts of the British people, but as a direct result of British policies and actions. The fact that Africa was poor *because* Britain was rich, and vice versa, did not seem to occur to those people who rang up to donate their hard-earned money as they watched Paul McCartney play to Wembley Stadium.

But alongside those who embraced the comforting colonial humanitarianism of Live Aid – which told its viewers that a continent could be saved by simply writing a cheque – a whole swathe of people were more intent on working actively to undo some of the worst legacies of British colonial rule. Britain's movement to end racial segregation in South Africa was formed with a far greater understanding of Britain's role in the creation of the South African colony and the responsibility that the British government, multinational companies and ordinary British people had to stop propping up the apartheid state. It was also an endeavour shared with, rather than imposed on, the anti-apartheid movement within South Africa itself. The African National Congress (ANC), the South African liberationist political party banned since 1960, which would eventually form a government under Nelson Mandela's leadership, worked hard to cultivate international networks of anti-apartheid activism to put continued pressure on the white South African government.

The roots of the brutal and violent South African apartheid state lay in the conflicts between the British and Boers almost a century before, when the British defeat of the Boers – the Afrikaner descendants of Dutch colonists – had instilled a sense of racial patriotism. In 1910, the British had passed the South Africa Act, creating the Union of South Africa in which the white settlers – both British and Afrikaner – were formally given political dominance over the Black African, Asian and 'Coloured' (mixed race) populations. The country had been a dominion of the Commonwealth from the 1926

Balfour Declaration until a referendum in 1960 in which the white population had narrowly voted to become a republic. This transition sparked a vote in the Commonwealth, in which other members would have to unanimously assent to South Africa remaining in the organisation; many newly independent nations from Africa and Asia had refused to do this because of the country's apartheid policies. South Africa duly left the Commonwealth in 1961.

From the start of the Union, successive white governments implemented policies of racial segregation which sought to protect the white population against the Black majority. In 1948, the Afrikaner politician D. F. Malan's Nationalist government was elected and the state set about introducing its earliest apartheid legislation, which was closely followed in newspapers such as the *Manchester Guardian*. The paper featured letters from supporters and critics of Malan's policies; 'Blikoor' (a nickname for an inhabitant of the Orange Free State) wrote to defend apartheid as 'essential for the preservation of white South Africa', in a letter that was printed next to one from E. A. Barker from Nqutu, Zululand, arguing that 'only a wise and liberal policy involving the jettisoning of race as a concept' could save the country from 'moral and economic ruin'.[49] The LCP, too, was watching events in South Africa closely, and its newsletter detailed the 'growing avalanche of racial discrimination' faced by Black Africans reported by its contacts and members living in the territory.[50]

Over the years, apartheid in South Africa continued to be reported on in the British media. A BBC documentary, *The Heart of Apartheid*, broadcast in 1968, showed daily life in apartheid South Africa in which interviewees in voice-overs explained the ways that their lives were constrained by racism and oppression. In an early scene, white ('European') South Africans were shown frolicking happily on a beach while South African people of colour spoke of the way that 'the laws of this country are totally, hopelessly unfair and . . . weighted heavily against the non-white people'.[51] Apartheid may have been happening 'over there', but it was happening in the full view of the British people.

By the early 1960s when decolonisation was gathering momentum, there was a lively and sustained British anti-apartheid movement. British activists understood apartheid to be a consequence of imperialism; these activists had seen decolonisation as an urgent moral duty, and so too was ending apartheid. The anti-apartheid movement was also a part of the burgeoning pan-African political movement and the global Black Power movement, leading to some unexpected transnational alliances. In spring 1964, just before the Civil Rights Act finally outlawed segregation in the United States, Marlon Brando flew to the UK to campaign for actors and producers to sign up to a boycott campaign refusing permission for their films to be screened in front of segregated audiences. When he arrived in London, his first stop was to join the picket outside the South African Embassy to demand that political prisoners be freed by the apartheid state, to the surprise of the picket organisers, who read about his appearance in the newspapers the following morning.[52]

Anti-apartheid activism grew steadily in Britain over the next two decades. The Anti-Apartheid Movement (AAM) was formed in 1960 in response to the Sharpeville Massacre, in which the apartheid state killed 99 protesters – ten of whom were children – and injured many more from a crowd who had gathered outside a police station in the aftermath of a protest against the racist pass laws. Within South Africa, Sharpeville led Nelson Mandela to organise uMkhonto we Sizwe, the paramilitary wing of the ANC, to fight actively against the apartheid government; in Britain, the AAM was created in order to put pressure on the same government from an international position. The AAM was both a national and local organisation, with branches up and down the country. One newsletter told its readers 'don't get the idea everything happens in London' and celebrated a variety of activities, from university campaigns in Bristol and Durham, a picket in Crawley organised by the folk singer Mike Rogers at which the local Labour councillor condemned South Africa's 'Neo-Nazi nonsense of racial supremacy', and a public meeting in Edinburgh that had raised £400 for the campaign to release political prisoners.[53]

From 1964 onwards, the AAM encouraged its members to write to all parliamentary candidates in their constituencies and attend electoral campaign meetings, to demonstrate their concern about apartheid and 'make the difference between a strong and feeble policy on South Africa when the new Government takes office'.[54] In 1964, Labour candidates paid lip service to opposing apartheid, promising in their manifesto to end the supply of arms to South Africa, although voters were disillusioned once Wilson's party came to power; only two months after the election, the new Labour government sold a substantial number of Buccaneer aircraft to the South African Navy. In 1979, an AAM pamphlet which asked voters to 'remember the people of Southern Africa' acknowledged that 'of course, every candidate in the election – except those from racist or fascist organisations – will say that they condemn apartheid' and posed a series of specific questions about the region with which candidates could be confronted and pinned down: 'Do you support the UN mandatory arms embargo against South Africa?', 'Will you support the provision of humanitarian aid to the Patriotic Front [of Zimbabwe]?', 'Do you support the United Nations effort to reach a settlement in Namibia which is acceptable to the Namibian people?'[55]

By the 1980s, some local branches of the AAM were especially active. The members of the City of London Anti-Apartheid Group (CAAG) were behind a number of particularly attention-grabbing activities, such as a non-stop picket which ran from 19 April 1986 until 1990. The picket aimed to secure the release of Nelson Mandela, along with all other South African political prisoners, and to close down the South African Embassy in London; the embassy was located in Trafalgar Square, which meant the campaigners had to fight hard to assert their right to protest there. A song sheet – which included the lyrics for 'Freedom Song' ('Mandela says fight for freedom / Mandela says freedom NOW!'), a number of African protest songs, and parodies of pop music ('It's a hard day's night / and I've been shouting like a frog') – also included tips on how to engage with the police and what to do if arrested, as well as strict instructions 'to ignore racists and fascists and not respond to them in any way whatsoever'.[56]

Consumer boycotts were one of the more popular ways to participate in the anti-apartheid movement; the British AAM itself was born out of a campaign launched in 1959 after an appeal from Albert Luthuli, the president general of the ANC, who remained ideologically committed to a non-violent protest movement against apartheid. Luthuli called for an international boycott of South African goods, and so the AAM had printed leaflets asking people to avoid buying South African sherry and fruit, and Craven A cigarettes. The campaign was reinvigorated by the AAM in 1974 and again in 1980, with many British individuals refusing to buy goods from South Africa and pressuring businesses to stop stocking these products. In 1985, the Co-op supermarket and Next fashion chain stopped trading in South African food and textiles. By 1986, a Gallup poll found that 27 per cent of British people claimed to be boycotting South African goods.[57] (Although even with this level of participation, the racial politics of the boycott passed some people by. One greengrocer in Lincolnshire was under the impression that people were boycotting South African fruit because they did not want to eat produce that had been handled by Black workers.)[58] The two biggest targets of the boycott campaign were Shell Petroleum and Barclays Bank, who both continued trading in South Africa despite international sanctions. The Barclays boycott was launched in 1970, with the radical Haslemere group of NGO workers and researchers playing a key role in its instigation and employing innovative tactics such as a mass purchase of shares to gain entry to internal meetings. Boycotting Barclays became a flagship campaign of AAM with an impressive amount of public recognition; a cartoon in the *Daily Star* showed a bank manager and the caption 'Open a student account and you get a free briefcase, diary, pen AND we pull out of South Africa'.[59] The campaign to boycott Shell was launched internationally in the Netherlands, the UK and North America in 1986: posters declared 'No Fuel For Apartheid' and demanded that the company pull out of South Africa and Namibia.

The Trades Union Congress (TUC) pledged its support to the boycott campaign from its inception, and many employers were faced with their unionised employees refusing to handle South African products. But British trade unions had a complex relationship with the AAM: many maintained close connections with the white South African labour movement, much of which supported the apartheid state. Although some smaller groups such as the Draughtsmen's Union and the Musicians' Union took a hard line against apartheid from the start, other more powerful groups such as the Boilermakers and the Amalgamated Engineering Union had whites-only counterparts in South Africa, and the TUC was reluctant to work with the South African Congress of Trades Unions, suspecting it of Communist tendencies. Jack Jones, the veteran leader of the Transport and General Workers' Union, linked the slowness of the trade unions to act on apartheid to 'their attitudes towards race and colour' in Britain, which he blamed explicitly on 'racial discrimination'; as he said, 'there was (a) an attitude that South Africa was far off and (b) an attitude that said "Well, what's wrong, South Africa's quite a nice country."'[60] The TUC did take anti-apartheid action – in 1964, it passed a unanimous resolution demanding a total diplomatic and economic blacklisting of South Africa and calling for an international labour boycott – but it was reluctant to enforce compliance at a local level. So, for example, there was never a wholesale commitment among unionised dockers to refuse to handle South African goods, according to Jack Jones, because this would involve enforcing a boycott of the Union Castle line, which provided the main livelihood of Southampton dockers.[61]

By the early 1980s, many workers within the labour movement were pushing for a response to apartheid, mirroring the radicalisation of unions in South Africa in this period. A trade union conference on apartheid in 1982 included workshops on sanctions, trade, imported South African goods and military cooperation, as well as a lunchtime session for female delegates to find out more about the AAM women's committee.[62] Many workforces took their own decisions to act against apartheid: in 1985 alone, Welsh dockers in Swansea refused to unload South African coal, workers at the Passport Office rejected the dual-citizenship applications of white South Africans, and librarians at the British Library refused to catalogue records from South African libraries. In 1965, over five hundred British academics, including Isaiah Berlin and Iris Murdoch, had committed to a boycott of South Africa; this was sustained into the 1980s when the Association of University Teachers union voted to support the boycott in 1980 and again in 1988. Students were at the forefront of this campaign as well: the National Union of Students supported the academic boycott and worked with the AAM from 1971 to coordinate student activism against apartheid. The student bodies at Liverpool, UEA, Swansea, UCL, Manchester, Durham and many other institutions demanded that their universities disinvest from South Africa and support motions to condemn the regime. In October 1985, students held a rally and sit-in in Trafalgar Square, and the NUS renamed its London headquarters Nelson Mandela House.[63]

In 1970, a joint Labour Party and ANC publication had pointed out that among the parliamentary Conservative Party, eight members of the Shadow Cabinet and thirty-two MPs in total were directors of companies that had South African subsidiaries, and many more had strong connections to the apartheid regime. The headquarters of the UK South Africa Trade Association, the main South African economic lobby in the UK, shared a building with the head office of the CBI.[64] It is not entirely fair to characterise the Conservative Party as pro-apartheid; the Bow Group, for example, had been active in the early formation of the AAM. But for many participants in the AAM, their anti-apartheid activism went hand in hand with criticism of capitalism and the global north–south divide, and support for women's rights, anti-racism and gay liberation. Opposition to apartheid was embraced by many of its supporters, but also dismissed by many of its critics, as an orthodox British left-wing position. In opposing the left, some right-wing British political actors therefore adopted pro-apartheid positions. The far-right

National Front explicitly supported the white South African government and the apartheid state, in 1986 heralding the country as a 'spirit that will not be broken', and 'the only light of civilisation in a dark continent'.[65] The NF engaged in its own consumer action; in 1988, the Haringey branch produced a leaflet asking its supporters to go out of their way to buy South African goods to counter the AAM boycott and promised that surplus produce would 'be used at fundraising wine and fruit parties'.[66] The Federation of Conservative Students wore stickers and stuck up posters saying 'Hang Nelson Mandela', until the Conservative Party banned the organisation in embarrassment in 1986.

There was an important grassroots contingent to the movement, as being 'anti-apartheid' overlapped with other civic organisations and social campaigns. Many of those who were most active in the AAM were seasoned political campaigners, but many too came to the movement via a church congregation, another charitable organisation, or even a social group. As such, anti-apartheid activism echoed earlier humanitarian engagement at the end of empire, something that many people believed to be more an act of conscience than a political statement; at the same time, it could also represent a radical critique of racist geopolitics, and a fundamental rejection of one of the most visible legacies of British imperialism. In 1987, *Anti-Apartheid News* urged its readers to ask 'your youth group, student union, church, union branch, club or office' to circulate and sign a petition to release all apartheid detainees, showing the way that anti-apartheid activism could spread through other networks of charity, solidarity or activism.[67] A conference that year on the position of Namibia in apartheid, for example, was sponsored by British teachers' unions. Other civic connections, such as feminist networks, could also be rallied in support of the cause. In Britain, the AAM Women's Committee organised petitions, marches and letter-writing campaigns, supported South African exiles in London, raised money and staged protests. In late 1985, women who were interested in working against apartheid could attend a Christmas fundraiser, write letters to the families of detained ANC fighters or to the South African president, P. W. Botha, join an AAM women's section based in their local area, attend the Older Women's Group film screening (with tea and cake), or attend a play exploring the life of Ruth First, the Jewish anti-apartheid campaigner who had been assassinated by the South African state in 1982, at the Charter Theatre in Kennington.[68] They could also participate in direct action through a number of affiliated organisations: on 12 November, delegates from the Feminist Library, the London Armagh Women's Group, Brighton Women's Centre, the West Indian Women's Organisation, Jewish Lesbians, WILPF, Outwrite and the Oxford Women's Solidarity Group all attended a march to protest against the apartheid state.

Meanwhile, Black activists in Britain worked to sustain the ANC in exile and to demand that the British state take action on apartheid. *Grassroots: Black Community News*, a newspaper published by the British Black Liberation Front, regularly carried news about Azania (an alternative name for South Africa used primarily by radical Black activists). One issue in 1986 proclaimed from its front page that 'Victory Is Certain' in the fight against apartheid, calling on its readers to 'isolate the racist regime and its imperial backers' by boycotting Barclays, South African imports, and any sporting and cultural events involving the nation; readers were also invited to join the African Liberation Committee to play their part in the destruction of the apartheid regime.[69]

This grassroots activism, in turn, had an effect on political structures such as local councils, demonstrating how anti-imperialism – at a local level, at least – had become embedded in the British state. Many councils organised themselves to express opposition to apartheid formally and to enact their own boycotts against South African goods and services. In spring 1983, Sheffield City Council held the first local authority conference on action against apartheid; representatives from fifty-four councils attended and many more sent messages of support. Fifteen councils around the country – from Great Yarmouth to Aberdeen – had committed to permanent boycotts of South African goods in the 1960s and 70s, although the reorganisation of local authority boundaries towards the end of this period meant that many of these commitments had not been sustained; following the Sheffield conference, a number of councils reinvigorated their anti-apartheid stance. For example, Camden Council made an 'anti-apartheid declaration' in which it called upon the local community to 'help develop and support all measures to combat apartheid', and brought in a series of measures itself: not being officially represented at any function attended by South African politicians, not permitting council facilities to be used for any event involving supporters of the apartheid regime, and supplying anti-apartheid groups in the borough with grant aid, concessionary use of facilities, and publicity through local libraries and exhibition spaces.[70]

Suddenly, it seemed like the AAM was everywhere, including on the radio. In 1984, the Specials reached number 9 in the charts with their single 'Free Nelson Mandela', written by Jerry Dammers after he attended a concert at Alexandra Palace to celebrate the ANC leader's sixty-fifth birthday the year before. In April 1986, the comedy sketch show *Spitting Image* released the song 'I've Never Met a Nice South African' as a B-side to its recording of 'The Chicken Song', which topped the charts for three weeks; the song described (white) South Africans as 'talentless murderers', 'ignorant loud mouths' and 'arrogant bastards who hate black people'.[71] The cultural boycott of South Africa was reinvigorated in the 1980s as well, and those who chose to circumvent it faced significant criticism. Rod Stewart, Status Quo and Queen all played gigs at Sun City, a luxury resort in South Africa that offered huge financial incentives to musicians to break the boycott and play to white audiences. Queen's performance in October 1984 was particularly controversial: the band was fined by the Musicians' Union, and the United Nations added the band to their list of blacklisted artists, despite guitarist Brian May's protests at a press conference that they had 'thought about the morals of it a lot' and that the band – and presumably their decision to break the cultural boycott and support the apartheid state – was 'not political'.

In 1985, Jerry Dammers founded Artists Against Apartheid (AAA), in which musicians and activists came together in protest against the regime. In June 1986, as part of the AAM Festival for Freedom, they organised a concert on Clapham Common; before the concert, 25,000 people held a rally in Hyde Park then marched through the city to south London. On the way, protesters stopped outside a branch of Barclays Bank and a Shell service station to chant 'Barclays is an Apartheid Bank' and 'Shell Fuels Apartheid'.[72] On Clapham Common, tens of thousands of people gathered for the six-hour free concert featuring Billy Bragg, Elvis Costello, Boy George, Gary Kemp, Gil Scott Heron and Sade; across the top of the stage was a huge banner reading 'AAA: NO TO APARTHEID'.

Two years later, the AAM staged an even bigger concert in celebration of Nelson Mandela's seventieth birthday. Freedom at Seventy was held, like Live Aid three years earlier, at Wembley Stadium and featured performances from Dire Straits, Whitney Houston, Sting, George Michael, Annie Lennox, UB40, Aswad and the Bee Gees, among many others. South Africa complained to the BBC to try to stop the concert from being televised; John Carlisle MP (Con, Luton North) supported the apartheid government and argued in the House of Commons that the BBC should not be using licence fee money to promote 'an unashamedly political organisation' such as the AAM.[73] In turn, anti-apartheid campaigners criticised the concert organisers for asking participants not to make any political statements beyond calling for Mandela to be freed – a decision taken to enable the concert to be broadcast across the greatest number of platforms, but one that many artists disagreed with. (The night before the concert, George Michael did a gig at Earls Court during which he 'let fly' at his 16,000-strong audience in a 'four letter tirade', complaining that he had been told not to make any political comments and condemning Britain's stance on apartheid as 'a fucking disgrace'.)[74] The *Mirror* reviewed the ten-hour concert, broadcast to more than a billion viewers around the world, saying approvingly that 'not since Live Aid has so much talent shared one stage in harmony – singing one tune – this time against apartheid'.[75] The concert raised £2 million for the AAM, but the real purpose was awareness raising; Mandela's lawyer said that he had been 'sitting in his cell, dreaming about the concert'.[76]

As well as music, sport was another arena in which British people were forced to confront the existence of apartheid and in which they had to make moral choices about something that many of them might have preferred to ignore as a far-off problem for distant strangers. Inevitably, given the vocal criticism of the South African government in the Commonwealth meetings by African, Caribbean and Asian governments, the Commonwealth Games became an international focus for the anti-apartheid protests. For many British people, the Games were the only context in which they thought about the Commonwealth at all, and so were perhaps their first real understanding of how apartheid was viewed around the world.

In 1986, Edinburgh hosted the Commonwealth Games for the second time since 1970, the first city to host the event twice. The sporting events were soon overshadowed, however, by the calls for nations to boycott the Games in protest against Margaret Thatcher's failure to impose a sporting boycott on South Africa. In the end, thirty-two nations refused to attend, including Jamaica, India, Kenya, Barbados and Cyprus, leading to broadcasts and medal tables dominated by white athletes; before the opening ceremony, the *Guardian* pointed out that when Prince Philip opened the Games, 'most of the non-white competitors left for him to greet are likely to be English'.[77]

The Scottish committee of the AAM, along with trade unionists and church leaders, tried to meet with Malcolm Rifkind, the Secretary of State for Scotland, before the Games to register their concerns, and accused him of trying 'to protect apartheid South Africa rather than the interests of the Scottish people' when he refused.[78] Protests ranged from the subtle to the explicit: Edinburgh City Council unveiled a 'Woman and Child' sculpture dedicated to the freedom fighters of South Africa, while five hundred protesters chose a more direct approach and pelted Thatcher's car with eggs and tomatoes when she arrived for her official visit to the Games. Thatcher was introduced to only one athlete, the English reserve rower Joanna Toch, who was obviously not as carefully vetted as might have been expected: Toch demanded to know why the prime minister had told sportspeople to boycott the Moscow Olympics but was now saying that politics 'should be kept out of sport'. (Thatcher reputedly responded that 'I left you free to choose, dear,' before hissing at her security staff to 'get a move on'.)[79]

It was not just in the context of the Commonwealth Games that sport was dragged into the apartheid battle: given the fanatical sporting culture of South Africa and the way that rugby and cricket, in particular, tied the nation to Britain, this was a critical arena in which British activists could fight the apartheid state. And yet, as with the artists who insisted on their right to play at Sun City, many sporting figures refused to honour the boycott, claiming sport as space apart from politics. The AAM had to work hard to draw attention to the stark realities of these choices.

In 1967, the D'Oliveira Affair had sparked controversy in the cricketing world as British sports fans had been forced to confront the realities of apartheid. Basil D'Oliveira, a 'Cape Coloured' South African citizen with Indian and Portuguese heritage, had emigrated from South Africa to England in 1960 and was at the time the only non-white member of the English cricket squad. The South African government felt strongly that D'Oliveira could not play against the all-white South African teams in England's upcoming tour of the country, and tried to put pressure on the MCC not to select him and even to bribe D'Oliveira not to play. When he was eventually selected, the South African government was vocally hostile and the MCC cancelled the tour. English public opinion had largely supported D'Oliveira, with figures like the commentator John Arlott and the cricket-playing Bishop of Liverpool Reverend David Sheppard speaking out against the apartheid state; Arlott wrote in an early editorial that 'the cancellation of a cricket tour would seem a trifling matter compared with an apparent British acceptance of apartheid'.[80] Even those with less shining anti-racist credentials resented the meddling of another country in English team selection; the *Daily Mail* argued that 'either we play cricket as a team according to our own custom and fashion or we don't play at all' in a piece that also criticised the 'absurdity' of apartheid.[81]

However, despite the outrage at the time, the D'Oliveira Affair did not mark the start of a sustained commitment among British athletes or sporting administrators to boycott South African fixtures. Three years later, a proposed tour of South Africa by the British Lions rugby team had been cancelled only after a hard-fought campaign by the AAM. The year before, the Springboks had toured Britain, and crowds travelling to see their matches had been met with protesters handing out leaflets asking why they were watching the South Africans play: 'Because: You enjoy the game? What happens in South Africa is not your concern? You support racialism?'[82] The Stop the Seventy Tour activists, led by Peter Hain (at that point associated with the Young Liberals), also targeted the South African cricket team after a tour was planned of English grounds that summer. Activists produced campaign material (including a poster proclaiming 'If you could see their national sport, you might be less keen on their cricket' over an image of a policeman beating a protester with a baton), marched to Notts County's cricket ground carrying a coffin, and made plans to dig up the cricket pitch if the match against South Africa went ahead. By May 1970, the British government had instructed the English Cricket Board (ECB) to cancel the South African tour.

In 1977, Commonwealth governments, including Britain, signed the Gleneagles Agreement, in which they had committed to 'discourage contact or competition by their nationals with sporting organisations, teams or sportsmen from South Africa or from any other country where sports are organised on the basis of race, colour or ethnic origin'.[83] Despite this commitment, cricketing and rugby organisations continued to break the ban. In rugby, the British Lions toured South Africa in 1980 and 1984, and hosted reciprocal tours of the UK by the Springboks. In 1992, one of these tours was met by the 'Springbok Reception Committee': these anti-apartheid activists protested at matches holding banners featuring the AZAPO (Azanian People's Organisation, the main Black liberation organisation within South Africa at this time) slogan 'No Normal Sport in an Abnormal Society', alongside demands to 'Put the Racist Springboks on the First Plane Home'. Members of the CAAG, who became known as the Springbok Nine, were arrested outside the Leicester Tigers rugby stadium after police searched their van and found 'bags of broken glass, metal tacks, balaclavas, gloves and two notices which read "Danger, do not play on the pitch" '.[84] After a two-week trial at the local Crown court, the jury returned a hung verdict and the judge bound the activists over for two years to keep the peace, which they interpreted as a political and moral victory.

Despite these moral victories, the AAM continued to have to battle against cricketing complacency about apartheid. The so-called 'rebel tours' were organised by the South African cricketing association to entice international players to break the boycott and travel to South Africa to play for rich financial reward. A team made up of English players – but not approved by the ECB – played the first and last of the seven tours; Graham Gooch led the side in 1982, and in 1990 the team was captained by Mike Gatting. The twelve players of the first tour, who became known as the 'Dirty Dozen' and were derided in the House of Commons for 'selling themselves for blood-covered Krugerrands', were banned from playing internationally for England for the next three years, a ban which effectively ended the international career of several players including Geoffrey Boycott.

Despite this, in 1990 another English team made the decision to travel to South Africa, including the spin bowler John Emburey, who had already served an international ban following the first rebel tour. The first tour had been kept entirely secret until the players landed in Johannesburg; the second became public in advance, which allowed for more sustained protest. Gatting found himself both attacked and ridiculed for his widely reported statement that he did 'not know much about apartheid' (he later clarified 'I know it's bad'), and for his excuse that he was travelling to South Africa to see conditions for himself.[85] The summer before the planned tour, eight members of the CAAG invaded Lord's during a match between Middlesex and Northamptonshire. After their arrest for invading the pitch and 'causing alarm and distress', they announced their intention to call Gatting and Emburey as witnesses for the trial; being summonsed to court would have forced them to miss the first week, at least, of the South Africa tour. Carol Brickley, the convenor of the group, argued that the defendants were calling Gatting and Emburey as witnesses because as the focus of the demonstration 'they were in the best position to see what happened' and to testify as to whether they had indeed been alarmed or distressed by the protest – although she also admitted that 'if that stops them from going to South Africa, naturally we would be delighted'.[86] This tactic was ultimately unsuccessful since the law only really allowed for witnesses to be called who would *support*, rather than undermine, the defence's case, but the invasion of the ground succeeded in drawing attention to the anti-apartheid cause. Following their tour, the team members again found themselves banned from international cricket for three years by the ECB.

The second 'rebel tour' was in fact cut short by two weeks, but not because the cricketers had an attack of conscience. On 2 February 1990, F. W. de Klerk, the new South African president, announced in his first address to parliament that he intended to lift the ban on the ANC, repeal the laws that embedded racial discrimination in the country, restore press freedom and release political prisoners. Nine days later, Nelson Mandela finally walked free after twenty-seven years. The *Sunday Mirror* story marking Mandela's release added 'a footnote to these dramatic pages of history', calling for Gatting and his rebels to immediately return home, as 'an embarrassment to Britain and a distraction from a truly historic moment'.[87] People at home watched a special hour-long broadcast of *On the Record* on BBC1 which showed the release live on air: Mandela, holding hands with his wife, Winnie, walking slowly through a crowd and 'taking his first steps into a new South Africa'

as the narrator would have it. And indeed this was the beginning of
the end of apartheid, although unpicking such an intricately
constructed system of oppression would take time: political negotiations and a period of transitional government gave way in 1994 to
free and fair elections and a landslide victory for the ANC with
Mandela at its head.

British activism had had a part to play in this victory. The networks that had sustained the ANC in exile often found themselves
given support – whether that was financial, political, tactical or
moral – from within Britain. The boycotts of South African goods
and of sport and entertainment had hit the apartheid government
financially and had kept the issue alive in the global media. And the
continual insistence from some British people that their nation had
a duty to fight for the end of apartheid was an important corrective
to the reluctance of successive British governments to take decisive
action. This was a case of imperial legacies – a sense of connected-
ness to the Global South, a belief in British responsibility for South
African politics – being mobilised for good.

The work of the AAM was part of a broader cultural reckoning
with Commonwealth and imperial legacies that took place during
the 1980s and, specifically, a rise in more general anti-racist and
Black community activism. The aim of *Grassroots*, the newspaper
of the Black Liberation Front, was to spread the message of Black
liberation and to build networks of community and activism among
Britain's Black population and with the wider global African diaspora; in doing this, it supported the work the BLF was doing to
establish supplementary schools for Black schoolchildren, to set up
community spaces such as bookshops and to confront the racism
embedded in the British state. *Grassroots*, founded in 1971, owed
much in conception and reach to the pioneering work of Claudia
Jones and her *West Indian Gazette* and was part of a long-standing
history of Black resistance to imperialism in Britain through radical writing and publishing, stretching back to the work of people
like Olaudah Equiano in the eighteenth century. The paper reported

on the experiences of Black people in Britain and their causes and struggles – for example, resisting mass deportations under the British nationality acts and fighting for better housing conditions and stronger workers' rights for people of colour – as well as covering moments of racist violence such as the murder of Loustan Parry in Manchester in 1980. It also carried news of the wider Black diaspora from across Africa and the Caribbean, such as the developments towards independence in Zimbabwe or the American invasion of Grenada.

Some elements of the British political left in this period were particularly active in their support for anti-racist activism, most notably local councils controlled by the Labour Party or under the wider umbrella of the Greater London Council (GLC). In 1984, for example, Camden Council organised a 'Celebrating Africa in Camden' event as part of the GLC's 'Anti Racist Year'; the event included African food, book and poster stalls, and performances by 'radical poets', dancers and musicians.[88] Some of the backlash indicated that the anti-racist movement was perceived as a significant force – indeed, in its critiques of British structures and society, as a threat to Britain on an existential level. The *Islington Gazette* carried a piece proclaiming to its local readers that 'fourteen thousand pounds of your money has been donated by the Labour-controlled Islington council to the African National Congress of South Africa', which it derided as 'terrorist'; arguing that this could never be 'an appropriate use of ratepayers money', the paper urged its readers to register complaints with their local councillor.[89] Other opponents responded by portraying Labour councils as part of a 'loony left', obsessed with token gestures towards political correctness but out of touch with reality and the sentiments of the British public. In the sitcom *Only Fools and Horses*, first broadcast in 1981, the Trotter family live in the fictional Nelson Mandela House, a tower block alongside two others named for Desmond Tutu and Zimbabwe on the 'Nyerere Estate'; canonically, their home was originally named Sir Walter Raleigh House, its renaming a nod to the apparent anti-imperial sympathies of Ken Livingstone's GLC.

In the election of 1987, Diane Abbott, Paul Boateng, Bernie Grant and Keith Vaz all won seats for the Labour Party. Abbott was born in Paddington to Jamaican parents; Boateng's heritage was Scottish and Ghanaian and he had lived in Ghana during his childhood and teenage years; Grant was born in Guyana before moving with his parents to London in 1963; Vaz was born in British Aden to Goan parents before also moving to London in the 1960s. In 1987 these four Labour MPs were the first people of colour elected to Parliament since Shapurji Saklatvala, who had lost Battersea North in 1929. All four were elected with a commitment to improving race relations and fighting for the rights of Black and minority ethnic British voters. Looking back at that moment, Diane Abbott said, 'there was a feeling in Parliament when we arrived that we would be like the 19th-century Fenians and disrupt and cause problems and keep them up at night'.[90] In Paul Boateng's victory speech, he proclaimed from the stage: 'Today Brent South, tomorrow Soweto!' Although this was later dismissed by *The Times* as 'extraordinarily gauche', it clearly illustrated the extent to which many people of colour in Britain connected their political identity to other global anti-imperial movements such as the anti-apartheid campaign in South Africa.[91]

Within the Labour Party, there had been an increasing degree of activism and solidarity among Black candidates and members for several years. The Labour Party Black Sections (LPBS), a caucus within the party that operated between 1983 and 1993, had pushed for formal recognition in order to achieve more 'politically Black' representation at a local and national level; the party was initially hostile to this proposal, as they had generally been able to rely on the votes of people of colour without this formal recognition and some white MPs were concerned that their largely 'ethnic minority' constituencies might try to replace them if the proposals were adopted. Although Black sections were adopted at a constituency level in many regions of Britain, and although there was support from trade unions such as the NUM and NUT and from MPs such as Claire Short, they were never formally endorsed by the Labour Party leadership in the way that the

Women's and Youth sections were. The election of the four 'politically Black' MPs marked, for some people, a victory for the LPBS, although notably some other prospective candidates, such as Martha Osamor, were blocked from standing by the leadership apparently because they were too politically radical.[92]

From its inception, the LPBS had always been concerned to place the struggle of people of colour in Britain within an international context; in a 1988 publication, it tackled racism and fascism, discrimination in the school system and limits on immigration within Britain alongside discussions of Palestine, Ireland and Azania (South Africa). The booklet was dedicated to 'the 500 Black pioneers who sailed to England aboard the Empire Windrush 40 years ago', who had 'launched the final conquest of racism and colonialism in Britain'. Here migration itself was being cast as a political act while racism and colonialism were mutually constitutive.[93]

At the same time, mainstream British popular culture in the 1970s and 80s was somewhat less critical of Britain's imperial past. Although viewers, readers and listeners were often drawn to imperial stories in the 1980s, they generally preferred to engage with empire only as something that had happened long ago with few, if any, contemporary implications. That is not to say that the cultural appetite was only content with entirely positive narratives of British imperialism. The Booker Prize had been awarded to books set during or immediately after the British Raj in India in 1971, 1973, 1975, 1977 and 1981. Almost all of these novels – *In a Free State* by V. S. Naipaul, *The Siege of Krisnapur* by J. G. Farrell, *Heat and Dust* by Ruth Prawer Jhabvala and *Midnight's Children* by Salman Rushdie – undermined and criticised traditional narratives of Britain's history in India. Only one of them, *Staying On* by Paul Scott, was a more sympathetic portrayal of imperial values – even, in some eyes, a gentle celebration of them and the comforting British myth of benign rule on the subcontinent. But perhaps the problem was that British readers viewed all of these books as dealing with something that was dead and buried, seeing empire as a benign setting for historical fiction in the same vein as the court of Henry VIII or a Georgian country house, rather than as a deep injustice that permeated their own society and culture.

In his 1984 essay 'Outside the Whale', Salman Rushdie expressed his frustration that 'the British Raj, after three and a half decades in retirement, has been making a sort of comeback'. He cited not just Paul Scott's *Raj Quartet* (which had also been adapted into a TV mini-series) for which *Staying On* was a sort of sequel, but also M. M. Kaye's *The Far Pavilions*, which was made into a mini-series and film, as well as the big-budget Richard Attenborough film *Gandhi*, the Granada TV documentary about partition, *War of the Springing Tiger*, and even the Bond film *Octopussy*, all infused to a greater or lesser extent with nostalgia for British rule in India. At this point there could have been a retelling of these stories to more accurately portray colonial violence, Rushdie said, but instead they fell back on tired old tropes, continuing to 'provide moral, cultural and artistic justification for imperialism' and to 'conjure up white society's fear of the darkie'.[94]

It was not the first time Rushdie had explored these themes; his writing consistently pulled at the threads of empire. His Booker Prize-winning novel *Midnight's Children* was a postmodern and magical realist treatment of Britain's withdrawal from India and the violence of partition. In 1982, he had proclaimed that Britain had 'never been cleansed of the filth of imperialism'. Rather than accepting the idea that 'Give or take a Falkland Island, the imperial sun has set', he had posited the existence of a 'new empire' of British racism at home: 'in the run-down housing estates of the new Empire, black families have their windows broken, they are afraid to go out after dark, and human and animal excrement arrives through their letterboxes'.[95] His writing took aim at the kind of self-satisfied narratives that superficially acknowledged the ills of empire while tacitly restating the good intentions, respectable values and forgivable human foibles of the imperialists – a new form of British imperial apologia. The irony was that his most controversial work would ultimately be defended with appeals to supposedly sacred and long-held British values, too.

The Satanic Verses was published in 1988 and depicted the journeys of two men, Chamcha and Farishta, who are miraculously saved when the plane they are on is blown up over the English Channel; these form part of a sprawling narrative that uses magical realism, dream sequences and allegory to explore the lives and experiences of Asian immigrants in Britain. The book includes depictions of the life of the Prophet Muhammad and other key elements of the Quran as part of this complex plot, which many Muslims found offensive and even blasphemous. In February 1989, the Supreme Leader of Iran, the Ayatollah Ruhollah Khomeini – who himself appeared in the novel in a thinly veiled depiction of 'The Iman' – issued a fatwa against Rushdie which called for the death of the author and his publishers. The British press reacted with outrage: the *Daily Mail* described the fatwa as an 'invitation to murder' and cried out that 'we must not let the fanaticism of the few menace the liberty of the many', while the *Guardian* criticised the Ayatollah's actions as 'the poison of defeat and of hatred'.[96] Khomeini and his followers were demonised as enemies not just of free speech, but of progress, civilisation and democracy, all values that were, supposedly, bound up with British society (and, for those who were sensitive to history, Britain's former imperial mission). A piece in the *Daily Mirror*, reporting the call from Iranian politician Hashemi Rafsanjani that five Westerners should be killed for every murdered Palestinian in Gaza, took the form of a Q&A which asked 'Are all Iran's leaders mad?' and 'But seriously, are they mentally ill?' before explaining to the reader that Iran's government 'is not a democracy, like ours'.[97]

Rushdie's novel, which had not been selling especially well before this, became a must-buy text after the fatwa; it was still sixth on the bestseller lists in the UK a year after it was first published, and was also spectacularly successful in the United States, Italy and many other countries where readers wanted to express solidarity with Rushdie or simply see what the controversy was all about.

Muslim communities in Britain, mostly of Pakistani and

Bangladeshi heritage, were divided by the novel. In December 1988, 7,000 protesters attended a gathering in Bolton at which copies of *The Satanic Verses* were burned; early in the new year, a similar protest in Bradford attracted double this number. In the spring, coachloads of British Muslims travelled from Bradford, Birmingham and Glasgow to protest in London; an effigy of Rushdie was thrust aloft on gallows, more copies of the book were burned in Hyde Park and 20,000 people marched on Parliament and Downing Street, as the Labour MP Keith Vaz called for Viking to withdraw the book from publication.

Some British Muslims, such as Sayed Abdul Quddus, a retired gas-board worker and secretary to the Bradford Council of Muslims, were radicalised by the Rushdie affair; Quddus had set fire to a copy of the novel at the Bradford protest, and received both death threats and praise for his actions.[98] Zadie Smith's novel *White Teeth*, published in 2000 to critical and popular acclaim, fictionalises these events; one of her protagonists, Millat, becomes so radicalised by the Rushdie protests that he becomes a fundamentalist who is driven to a violent act at the book's conclusion. But many others, like the journalist Yasmin Alibhai-Brown, were irritated by British hand-wringing over 'extremist' responses to the book and frustrated that any critique of Rushdie was immediately assumed to be religious intolerance. A decade later, Alibhai-Brown mourned the way that Western Muslims like herself had become 'orphans', rejected by both a white liberalism that refused to take their concerns about the treatment of their religion seriously, and by an Islam that showed such intolerance for free speech; as someone who 'grew up under the imperial sun', she was frustrated that the British literary establishment still did not think critically about imperial legacies of race and religion in British literature.[99]

Organisations such as the British Muslim Action Front called on Britain to change their laws on blasphemy to give more power to the protesters and better reflect Britain's multi-ethnic, multi-faith population; the English High Court, however, ruled in March 1989 that the law did and should only protect the established Church of

England from insult or ridicule. In July 1989, despite the objections of the Archbishop of Canterbury, the BBC broadcast a film written by the poet Tony Harrison, *The Blasphemer's Banquet*, which compared Rushdie to other writers, such as Molière, Voltaire, Omar Khayyam and Byron, who had been accused of blasphemy, and defended the right to free speech. The film was set in the 'Omar Khayyam Restaurant' in Bradford, sited in a former Presbyterian church.[100] The setting pushed the audience to imagine the imperial, migratory histories that could have led to the establishment of an Indian tandoori restaurant in a former Christian place of worship; it also encouraged viewers to think more critically about the possible tensions and challenges in British multiculturalism, which was so often glibly dismissed only as meaning that white people now enjoyed Indian food on a Saturday night.

The Rushdie affair highlighted the fact that migrant communities were tolerated only if they worked to 'fit in', to 'integrate' and to adopt 'British values', and it showed the resistance they faced when they rejected these demands and made demands of their own, valuing their own traditions equally or above the expectations of the British state. This had always been the case, but the rise of Thatcherism – inherent to which was the power of the selfish individual over collective society – meant it was perhaps inevitable 'integration' and assimilation became the watchword for migrants in Britain; the *individual* immigrant could strive and succeed in a Thatcherite narrative, but the immigrant *community* should not expect any support or protection. Migrants from the Commonwealth had had their right to settle in Britain chipped away over the preceding decades. Now their right to belong to these communities within Britain was being undermined as well. In 1990, the Conservative MP Norman Tebbit said that most migrants would not pass the 'cricket test' – meaning that in a match with England, they would cheer for India or Pakistan or Sri Lanka.[101] He encapsulated many lingering racist fears about migrant communities as 'fifth columnists', traitors hiding within society, undermining British values and Britishness.

The election of Margaret Thatcher and the development of Thatcherism marked the end of the social democratic consensus in Britain, the period since the end of the Second World War in which the policy gap between Labour and the Conservatives had been reasonably small – both parties accepting the role of trade unions in politics, both committing to NHS spending, and (although this is often less acknowledged) both experiencing an uneasy relationship to empire, decolonisation and migration. As Thatcherism dragged Britain to the right, attacking the state and the certainties of postwar society, the Labour Party moved leftwards, and the left in Britain started to embrace the identity politics of feminism and postcolonialism on top of their traditional focus on class. Britain in the 1980s had been confused and conflicted about its recent imperial past: the Falklands War had pushed the nation to fight to protect an empire that many imagined had already dissolved into nothing, while the anti-apartheid movement had demanded that the British take responsibility for imperial legacies that some would rather pretend did not exist. In the 1990s and 2000s, these tensions around Britain's place in the world, and the British people's identity at home, continued to divide British politics and culture.

7

From Cool Britannia to Brexit Britain: Imperialism Since the 1990s

On 30 June 1997, a respectable crowd of British dignitaries – Tony Blair, Robin Cook, Chris Patten, even Prince Charles – gathered together in a foreign clime to pay their respects as, once more, the British lost another part of their empire. At midnight on this day Britain formally withdrew from Hong Kong and completed its handover of the colony to the Chinese government as part of the 'one country, two states' deal first proposed in 1984. The withdrawal was marked musically, with the bugle call 'Sunset' – the tune used in the military to mark the end of the day and commonly played at memorial ceremonies – and with military band renditions of 'Auld Lang Syne' and (less explicably) Rod Stewart's 'Rhythm of My Heart', and with speeches from Patten and Prince Charles on behalf of the British government and Crown. At midnight, the Union Jack and the British colonial flag of Hong Kong were ceremonially lowered. In China, simultaneously, fireworks went off in Tiananmen Square.

Hong Kong was one of the last remaining British imperial territories, although it stood apart from much of the colonial empire because of its extraordinary prosperity. The area had been captured as a colony in 1841 in the aftermath of the First Opium War, one of the repeated conflicts between the British and the Chinese as Britain tried to force China into the sphere of British imperialist trade, and was formally ceded by the Chinese with the Treaty of Nanking the following year. Originally a sleepy fishing port surrounded by farmland, Hong Kong had grown to one of the major financial centres of the world. The Hongkong and Shanghai Banking

Corporation – now more commonly known as HSBC – had been set up in 1865, to further enable British imperial trade in Asia. In 1898, Britain obtained a ninety-nine-year lease on the territory – a somewhat unusual form of time-limited colonialism.

British investment poured into the colony, which by the early twentieth century had a university, an airport and a highly developed financial district. The Second World War saw the colony occupied by the Japanese, but after Britain took back control in August 1945, Hong Kong rapidly rebounded – particularly after 1949, when the Communist Party's rise to power in China meant that many of the wealthiest Chinese businessmen and entrepreneurs fled to the city. The colony did not entirely accept British rule – there were pro-Communist, anti-colonial protests in 1956 and again in 1967, when at least fifty people were killed and almost 2,000 arrested, some of whom had been deported to mainland China. The British colonial government cracked down harshly on pro-Chinese agitation by, for example, banning the publication of left-wing newspapers and shutting down schools suspected of harbouring anti-British sentiment. But the colony's complex relationship with the Chinese government meant that Hong Kong did not see the same type of independence movement as other British colonies. Instead, the country counted down to the end of the ninety-nine-year lease, which would run out in 1997. Britain agreed to step away at this date, as long as the economic and political systems in Hong Kong were protected for fifty years. The region was to become a 'special administrative region' of China, but it would remain a capitalist democracy; this was the sort of imperial legacy that the British government was happy to put its name to.

And so, one of the first acts of the newly elected Blair government was to oversee the retrocession of Hong Kong. For some in Britain and overseas, this 'Final Farewell to Hong Kong' represented the last vestiges of British imperialism being swept from the map at last.[1] For others, the idea that Britain's empire had continued to exist for this long came as a surprise. For a few individuals, such as Prince Charles and Chris Patten (the last governor of Hong Kong), it was an occasion of genuine sadness. In its coverage of the hand-over ceremony, *The Times* reported that tears had mingled with the monsoon rain; the *Telegraph* ran a picture of Patten's daughters crying. The *Daily Mail* recorded 'a tearful salute to the last jewel in the crown', and labelled Charles, wearing his negative feelings on his face, as the 'Prince of Gloom'.[2] Later, when the Prince's diaries were leaked to the press, it was revealed that unlike the Labour politicians present he had not been flown to Hong Kong first class; 'such is the end of Empire, I sighed to myself', he apparently recorded.[3]

The prevailing mood in London's Chinatown was joyful rather than despondent. Sandie Chan, one of three hundred people watching the television coverage of the handover ceremony on the corner of Gerrard Street, cried when she spoke to a reporter about how she had gone that morning to visit the British Museum, to see the artefacts that had been taken from the Tang Ming Dynasty as spoils of war, and to reflect on what it meant for the country to finally be free of British rule.[4] These were tears of sadness, not that Britain was losing a colony, but that Hong Kong had been subject to colonial rule for so long. But as the *New York Times* recorded, the wider British public was largely 'indifferent' to the loss of the colony and any humiliation it represented. A Foreign Office official was quoted as saying that 'It may still exist in a couple of clubs in Pall Mall, but for most Britons the empire is no longer a reality'.[5]

One month earlier, in May 1997, a self-consciously 'new' era had begun with the election of a new prime minister. Tony Blair, only forty-five years old and with three young children, came to epitomise the idea of a new modern Britain, looking forward to the new millennium. Labour worked hard to distinguish themselves, culturally as well as politically, from their Conservative predecessors. The 1997 Labour Manifesto said that 'the clock should not be turned back', praised Britain's modern attitudes to gender, sex and sexuality, and race (the only mention of race in the document), and proclaimed that the party would balance 'change and social stability'.[6]

Labour's proposed role for Britain in the international

community was also explicitly progressive: setting up the International Criminal Court (ICC), rejoining the global cultural and educational organisation UNESCO (which Thatcher had taken Britain out of), and pressing for reform of the United Nations. The Commonwealth was cited as 'a unique network of contacts linked by history, language and legal systems' – although there was no acknowledgement of how this network of law and language developed or the nature, exactly, of this history – and there was a commitment to give 'renewed priority to the Commonwealth in our foreign relations'. And there was also a commitment to creating the new Department for International Development, to uphold Britain's 'clear moral responsibility to help combat global poverty'. Would former colonies really want Britain to grasp 'a real opportunity to provide leadership to the Commonwealth' when they hosted the Heads of Government meeting at the end of the year? Was Britain's moral responsibility to the Global South part of its old imperial identity, or a reckoning with its post-decolonisation debts to its former colonies? Only time would tell.

At home, meanwhile, one of the ways in which the party sought to define itself as new and modern was in its soft-focus celebration of diversity, broadly construed, which it referred to as 'multiculturalism'. One of the more famous aspects of their election-winning campaign had been a party political broadcast, 'Things Can Only Get Better', a cheesy but memorable video of a voter walking to the polling station and collecting a caravan of cheerful Labour supporters on his way. This group of people are pointedly young, photogenic and, importantly, both Black and white. The voter, meanwhile, is ultimately revealed to be Tony Blair.

For this was not just a new Labour government, but a New Labour government. This wasn't the party of the Longest Suicide Note in History, the nickname coined by Labour MP Gerard Kaufman for Michael Foot's radical manifesto of 1983, which had seen the party ridiculed in the press and defeated at the ballot box. It wasn't even the party of the socialist commitments of Clause IV, the section of the original Labour Party rule book adopted in 1918, which had committed the party to common ownership and redistribution of wealth, and which Tony Blair had rewritten and watered down in response partly to the bruises from that heavy 1983 defeat. This New Labour government had moved to the centre in pursuit of electoral success – and voters had responded by giving them a landslide electoral victory, a 'crushing triumph' according to the front page of the *Guardian*, a 'Blair Revolution' according to the *Daily Mail*.[7] But the newness of New Labour was not only about consciously disavowing its own left-wing past. It was also about a broader denial of any connections with, or culpability for, the shadier moments of Britain's history. In the lead-up to the 1997 election, Blair had been advised by his future chief of staff, Jonathan Powell, that he should say he was 'proud of the British empire' in a speech in Manchester; at the last minute, Blair decided against it and skipped the line, although he did profess himself 'proud to be a British patriot'.[8]

Despite this rhetorical flourish, New Labour was not, in its early days, the party of Rule Britannia, Thomas Arne's 1740 battle hymn that had become inextricably linked with the Royal Navy and the Last Night of the Proms. Instead, they were the party of Cool Britannia. This sense of new British cool actually slightly predated the Labour victory. The American magazine *Newsweek* had a 1996 front cover headlined 'London Rules: Inside the world's coolest city';[9] in November 1996, John Major, at the Lord Mayor's Banquet, celebrated Cool Britannia for its success in finance, films, hospitality and education and its ability to attract visitors from around the world.[10] Even earlier, in 1995, the American ice-cream brand Ben & Jerry's had launched a Cool Britannia flavour, comprising vanilla ice cream with strawberries and fudge-covered shortbread. But Labour saw an opportunity and Tony Blair cynically, but successfully, courted the label of 'cool' to go with his image of dynamic youthfulness and the newness of New Labour.

The global success of the Spice Girls – with Geri in her Union Jack dress – and bands like Blur and Oasis had driven a wider renaissance in British fashion, art and other exciting exports. 'Britpop', a term coined by music journalist Stuart Maconie in 1993, became recognised as both a genre and a movement: *Select* magazine, in April of that year, featured the slinky-hipped lead singer of Suede, Brett Anderson, posing on the cover in front of a Union Jack with the headline 'Yanks Go Home', and bands such as St Etienne and Pulp name-checked in an apparent 'Battle for Britain'. This cultural moment was modern but also nostalgic; it echoed the moment in the 1960s when British culture, led by the Beatles, was exported around the world (in fact, the Beatles had received MBEs not for their cultural impact, but for their services, via their mass exports of records, to the British balance of payments). In the 1960s, Carnaby Street in London had become the global centre of 'cool', a counter-cultural hub at the heart of a global hegemon. In the 1990s, Cool Britannia was a similar attempt to reimagine Britain's place in the world, an imperial preoccupation that saw the small island nation as something much greater than the sum of its geographic breadth.

Unlike in the 1960s, though, London was not the only centre of this cultural moment: the pull of 'Madchester' of the late 1980s was sustained by Oasis, and the whole of Wales – in this moment of devolution – was drawn into the cultural maelstrom as 'Cool Cymru'. But perhaps in the 1990s, compared with the 1960s, this cultural moment was more self-conscious and less self-assured; by 1998, *The Economist* was warning that there was nothing so embarrassing as trying too hard to be 'cool'.[11] Ben & Jerry's discontinued their Cool Britannia ice-cream flavour the same year.

The trendy multiculturalism of New Labour, Cool Britannia and Britpop was built on a disavowal of the past and the idea of a fresh and clean new slate. As part of this fresh start, there was a sense that Britain should forge a new place in the world rather than dwell on its position in the past. But Britain could not escape the long shadow of imperial history even as the twentieth century was left behind. In the 1990s and the 2000s, the country was forced to face its recent past, reckoning in particular with one key aspect of the empire story: race and racism.

*

Four years before Labour's election, at half past ten on the night of 22 April 1993, an eighteen-year-old boy had been stabbed to death while waiting for a bus with his friend. The murder of Stephen Lawrence was determined almost immediately to have been racially motivated, as his friend, Duwayne Brooks, had heard the accused gang of men shouting racial slurs before they attacked Stephen, and all five suspects had previously been involved in racist knife attacks on Black and Asian young men. This unspeakably violent act, which ended the life of a teenager in the middle of his A levels, was shocking to the British public; so too was the mishandling of the investigation and trial, which saw the Crown Prosecution Service originally drop the charges against the five suspects, despite evidence including covert police surveillance video showing the accused using violent and racist language. This sparked a media outrage and searching questions about the failure of the police and systemic racism in Britain. Lawrence's funeral was held at the Trinity Methodist Church in Plumstead, and was attended by seven hundred people including Diane Abbott and Paul Boateng. During the service, Reverend David Cruise said that the murder had led many people in Britain to feel 'ashamed to be white' and called for the closure of the British National Party headquarters, located a short distance away in Welling.[12]

Stephen's murder stayed in the public consciousness in large part because of the work of his parents, Doreen and Neville Lawrence, to keep the campaign to catch his killers alive and to fight against racism in the justice system. In 1998, the artist Chris Ofili – born in Manchester in 1968 to parents who had moved from Nigeria a few years earlier – was the first Black artist to win the Turner Prize, awarded to a collection of works that included a large portrait of Stephen's mother Doreen entitled *No Woman, No Cry*; the painting includes, in the teardrops running down Doreen's face, a collage of photographs of Stephen's face. An acclaimed ITV drama, *The Murder of Stephen Lawrence*, written by Paul Greengrass and broadcast in 1999, followed Doreen and Neville as they fought for justice. The film used improvisation and naturalistic filming techniques because,

the producer Mark Redhead said, they wanted the viewers to empa-
thise with Stephen's parents and understand 'what it felt like to be
in their shoes', being told 'virtually nothing' about what was going
on. It was rewarded with the BAFTA for Best Single Drama the
following year.[13] The media came back to the murder again and
again. In 2006, a BBC documentary, *The Boys Who Killed Stephen
Lawrence*, accused senior police officers of taking bribes from the
gangster father of one of the suspects; an Independent Police Complaints Commission (since 2018 the Independent Office for Police
Conduct) investigation found no evidence of this, but the documentary succeeded in keeping the case in the public eye and prompted
the police to review the evidence. In 2011, two of the original suspects were arrested and tried at the Old Bailey as prosecutors
demonstrated that Stephen's DNA had been found on their clothes;
both were found guilty of murder after a six-week trial. The police
continued to face accusations of corruption and mishandling of the
case; when, in 2015, an inquiry was launched into undercover policing, one of its central investigations was into allegations that police
had tried to infiltrate the Lawrence family's campaign for justice.

Famously, even the *Daily Mail* was disgusted by the failure of the
investigation, publishing a front page in February 1997 that presented
pictures of the five suspects under the bold headline 'MURDER-
ERS' and the subheading 'The Mail accuses these men of killing. If
we are wrong, let them sue us'. The *Mail* was outraged at what it
explicitly named as a 'racist attack' going unpunished and has been
publicly self-congratulatory since about its role in eventually bringing Lawrence's killers to justice, for example in its campaigning to
end the double jeopardy rule that meant the suspects could not be
tried twice for the same crime. And yet, in the same issue of the
paper as the MURDERERS headline, an editorial argued that
although Stephen Lawrence's family felt 'betrayed' by the police and
the justice system, Doreen Lawrence's concerns that 'police were
less than assiduous because of Stephen's colour' were 'misplaced'
because the police had 'committed huge resources' to the case.[14]
The *Mail* could accept that the murder of Lawrence was racist; what

the paper was unwilling to accept was that the justice system, and perhaps even more widely British society, might be racist too.

In July 1997, the new Labour Home Secretary, Jack Straw, ordered a public inquiry into the Lawrence case; the results of this were published as the Macpherson Report in 1999. The report explored the various failures of the police force in the investigation of Stephen's murder, which had led 'many people, both black and white, in our Public Gallery and in the community at large' to believe that the police was a racist institution.[15] The report concluded that the failure 'to recognise and accept racism and race relations as a central feature' in the murder had played a part in the 'deficiencies' of the original investigation, noting that 'a substantial number of officers of junior rank would not accept that the murder of Stephen Lawrence was simply and solely "racially motivated" '.[16] The treatment of Duwayne Brooks, Stephen's friend and the key witness to the attack, was also criticised by the investigators, who highlighted that Brooks had faced racism and stereotyping by the police from the moment they arrived on the scene and throughout the investigation.[17] Most damning was the report's assertion that British policing was marked by 'pernicious and persistent institutional racism', specifically and locally in its investigation of the Lawrence murder, but also generally and nationally in the implementation of 'stop and search' policies, the under-reporting of 'racial incidents' and the complete failure of police training to address racism or race awareness in any way.[18] Newspapers seized on this accusation: the *Guardian* described it as a 'devastating critique' of British policing, while the *Mail* reversed its earlier judgement and concluded simply that it was 'because he was black' that Lawrence's murder had not been properly investigated.[19] The inquiry and its conclusions so captured the public imagination that its transcripts were dramatised, distilled into a two-hour play at the Tricycle Theatre in Kilburn, which the *Observer* called 'the most vital piece of theatre on the London stage'.[20]

In Parliament in a debate on the findings of the inquiry, the Labour MP Piara Singh Khabra (Southall) took the opportunity to call for a similar inquiry into the murder of Blair Peach, whose murder had taken place in his constituency. Born in British India, Khabra had come to Britain in the 1960s after fighting for the Allies in the Second World War. He was the first Sikh elected to the House of Commons, in 1992, and by the time of his death in 2007 he was the last sitting MP to have fought in the war as part of the British Commonwealth forces. In the debate, the elderly parliamentarian used his speech to draw attention to the racism that continued to pervade both the British establishment and the wider British population and did so by reading a sample of the hate mail he had received over his career as a politician:

> A letter that I was sent last year stated: 'when we had a Empire trying to make scum like you better, you did not want us in your country' – India – 'but after the British had left, you all realised what a stinking shower you all are, and you all want to come to our lovely country and make it like a pig hole like your own country.' 'Go back to your own country and try to make it better, I believe and hope we British will get a new Enoch Powell who will deport all the stinking curry eating wogs out of Britain. Sooner the better. Union Jack.'[21]

Khabra was clear that the roots of institutional police racism were in the history of British imperialism; the Metropolitan Police was racist, he said, because it had been 'founded during the period when this country was an imperial power'.

Not every Member of Parliament agreed with Khabra's conclusions. Gerald Howarth, the Conservative MP for Aldershot, spent some time objecting to the report, on the grounds that it was overly critical of the police for committing what he dismissed as 'minor' racism – such as referring to Lawrence and Brooks as 'coloured' – and because it was a 'partial' account of racism since, he said, it only acknowledged 'white against black' rather than vice versa. His impassioned speech finished with the call that 'it is time that those with ethnic minority backgrounds, who represent just 6 per cent of the population, tried to be more understanding of us and our centuries-old culture'.[22] Howarth's response demonstrates that it would be premature to herald Macpherson as a sea change in race relations or in the understanding of imperial legacies in Britain.

Macpherson was not the first report that sought to understand and to ameliorate the breakdown of relations between the British police forces and people of colour across the UK. The Scarman Report had been undertaken in response to racialised rioting and violence across British cities in 1980 and 1981, looking into the conditions that had led to such widespread protest and that had been so poorly handled by the police system. In the report, Scarman pointed to the 'social and economic disadvantages that are suffered particularly by black residents, particularly young blacks'. The report stopped short of designating the police as institutionally racist, instead identifying 'racial discrimination' and 'racial disadvantage' at work. But it insisted that the police should undertake racism awareness training and work with a series of community consultative committees to encourage 'continuing dialogue' between the police and Black British citizens. As Stuart Hall pointed out, the emphasis on institutional racism in Macpherson was 'a real advance' on Scarman, but part of the reason that Stephen Lawrence's murder had been such a watershed was that the Lawrence family were so very respectable, presented to the public 'with their own fears and hopes and aspirations', and so white middle-class liberals had seen in them 'people very much like themselves'. This, Hall believed, showed the fragility of the supposed 'rise and rise' of multiculturalism in Britain, which was, in this telling, layering class identity on top of race rather than challenging racial difference altogether.[23]

This much lauded 'rise and rise' of multiculturalism was indeed fragile, and was often challenged by groups who felt threatened by the increasing visibility of people of colour in British society and culture. The rise of the far right in Britain, particularly in areas such as the East End of London, was a trend that had been monitored with anxiety by anti-racist groups and organisers from Commonwealth migrant communities. Although in the 1979 election the National Front had largely seen their vote share squashed – both

because of grassroots anti-racist activism and because NF supporters moved across to vote for Thatcher – the NF had remained an
important cultural force, looming large in the lives of many people
of colour. There was a clear overlap between NF attitudes and
those of many Conservative voters, so that although people were
not turning out for the NF at the ballot box, the party could feel
that many 'ordinary' British voters were sympathetic to their causes.

As well as supporting apartheid, the NF was continually critical
of former colonial nations and their populations. One front cover
of the NF newspaper *The Flag* proclaimed 'It's Time to Unload the
Mango Dictators' and argued that Britain should cut off 'the burden
of the Black Commonwealth', end overseas aid, close Britain's borders to immigration and 'repatriate' people of colour with imperial
heritage; the editorial was sparked by Geoffrey Howe's 1986 tour of
Southern Africa, during which the NF believed the 'feeble' Foreign
Secretary had been humiliated by African politicians.[24] The paper
frequently ran anti-immigration stories that claimed white Britons
had somehow been duped into accepting migrants by politicians
who had changed Britain's identity without their consent. One story
demanded to know, 'was there ever a referendum on whether the
British people wanted to share their country?' before concluding
'NO! Coloured immigration was hoisted on Britain without con-
sulting the British people.'[25] The narrative in many of these stories
echoes Powell's argument that 'native' Britons were being denied
funding, goods and services either because resources were being
stretched thin by an influx of immigrants, or because communities
of colour were actively being prioritised for housing, health care
and education. In this telling, decolonisation had apparently left
Britain in hock to the Commonwealth and unable to defend itself
against hordes of migrants from former colonies; empire might be
something in which the British should take patriotic pride, but the
legacy of imperialism here was one of British decline.

The NF and their successor party the British National Party
(BNP), founded in 1982, remained a threat in specific constituencies
into the 1990s, thanks largely to this dual narrative of national

decline and a migrant influx. In 1993, the BNP won a seat in a council by-election in Millwall, south-east London, after their candidate Derek Beackon ran a campaign around 'Rights for Whites' which was condemned by, among others, the Archbishop of Canterbury; in his acceptance speech, Beackon declared that the BNP was going to 'take our country back'.[26] The BNP proclaimed it would go on to win control of the council and rename the local meeting hall Oswald Mosley House, but sustained campaigning by the Labour Party and anti-fascist organisations meant that Beackon lost his seat in the council elections of the next year. It was not only the BNP that endorsed this racist rhetoric in the East End. In 1996, the Newham South Conservatives had circulated a leaflet titled 'Ethnic Cleansing in South Newham', which had accused the Labour council of 'racial engineering to change the make-up of our local community', supposedly by giving Asian, African and Caribbean people the majority of council houses.[27]

The same charges that had been levelled against Commonwealth immigrants in the 1960s by Powell and others, that they were going to the top of the queue for council houses and swamping nursery school places and hospital beds, was a crucial part of far-right community campaigns in the 1980s and 90s. In Canning Town, the National Front and BNP focused on stoking these anxieties among white residents, for example by setting up a housing advice centre which catered only for them. In 1984, Canning Town Council actually had to evict a white family from council housing because of their sustained harassment of their Asian neighbours; in response, the local director of housing, Barry Simons, had his car smashed up by racist protesters and Fred Jones, the chair of housing, had a coffin sent to his house.[28]

Community groups sprang up in Newham to combat this racist activism. The Newham Monitoring Project (NMP), founded in 1980, ran a twenty-four-hour emergency hotline for people experiencing racism, monitored police violence and unfair policing against people of colour, distributed leaflets around elections, and helped communities mobilise to organise their own responses to poverty and inequality that did not draw on racist, anti-immigrant rhetoric.[29] The NMP also ran specific campaigns, such as a series of actions to support the Newham 8, a group of young Asian men who had been arrested defending Asian schoolchildren from racist attack in Manor Park. In September 1983, 2,000 people, including many schoolchildren, marched through Newham on a National March Against Racism and Fascism, following which the NMP supported the children as they organised a school strike in support of the cause. Uma Bhugtiar, who was fifteen at the time, said that the chance to 'do something constructive, put stamps on envelopes, send out leaflets, go to the courts, walk on marches' was a welcome change to feeling 'angry or hurt' at seeing racism reported on television.[30]

Other community activists worked alongside and with the NMP to fight against racism in the borough. Gilli Salvat, who had come to Britain as a young girl with her family after partition, co-wrote a pamphlet, 'Facts and Fictions in the 1990s: Once Upon a Time in the Docklands', to provide 'community groups, tenants associations, youth organisations and schools' with the ammunition needed to fight against this racist far-right politics. The pamphlet emphasised the imperial history of the region, with the development of the docks to deal with imperial shipping reflected in street names like East India Dock Road, Trinidad Street and Empire Wharf. It was explicit about the roots of migration: 'the links between British colonial exploitation of India, Africa and the Caribbean and presence of black people in Britain are straightforward'. One cartoon showed a skinhead asking an elderly Asian man why 'an old sod like you' had been let into the country, and the older man replying, thoughtfully, that he had been quite young when he had joined the British Army in 1942.[31] The pamphlet, which took concerns about housing shortages and unemployment seriously but argued that the answer was not racist exclusion but inclusive community action, was disseminated throughout east London and helped to defeat the BNP at the 1994 local elections.

These conversations about race and identity were happening nationally, not only in Newham, and in many areas of culture and society, not just politics. One of the most significant arenas was in the world of professional football. The international football championship Euro 96 was the first time that the England flag had been promoted by the English footballing authorities as the appropriate symbol of support for the national team. Despite the four nations being separate footballing entities, the Union Jack had been more commonly used by England supporters to show their affiliation at previous international tournaments. But by the time of Euro 96 it had been tainted by its association with the National Front and other far-right political groups – the chant 'There ain't no black in the Union Jack, send the bastards back' had become commonplace from the 1970s onwards – and the rise in English football hooliganism, and the crossover between these two groups, had rendered it toxic and off-putting to many fans. In addition, England was playing Scotland in 1996, and so the Union Jack was no longer an appropriate flag for England fans alone. As the *Telegraph* asked and answered at the time: 'Does the profusion of crosses of St George rather than Union flags in the Euro 96 football tournament presage an outbreak of English, as opposed to British nationalism? . . . we suspect not.'[32] However, the national identity of Britain, and England, was undoubtedly shifting at this point, and the way that different people and communities understood their place within the nation(s) was also in flux. There was a transition, too, in who might consider themselves an England fan and who might be able to imagine themselves one day on the pitch.

Paul Ince, born in Ilford in east London with Trinidadian heritage, became the first Black England captain in 1993, but in the early 1990s football at all levels in Britain was still an extremely racist environment, both on the pitch and in the stands. This had been a problem for some time, despite the increasing visibility of Black players in the football league, who were largely the descendants of the Windrush generation or other European empires, and who held British citizenship and qualified to play for one of the four nations. Many found themselves the targets of racism that questioned their right to play for British teams and, by extension, their right to call themselves British at all. When Cyrille Regis, who was born in French Guiana, accepted the call-up for England in 1982 over France, he received a bullet through the post and a warning, written in cut-out newspaper lettering, that if he stepped foot on the Wembley turf he would be kneecapped.

Racism was rife within football clubs as well as among supporters, and not only aimed at opposing players. Ian Wright, who earned thirty-three caps for the England team, recalled that in his early career he often experienced abuse in the dressing room from his own teammates; when playing for Crystal Palace in the late 1980s, the training matches would often be 'blacks against whites'.[33] Richie Moran was born in London to Nigerian parents and adopted by a white family, growing up in the mostly white area of Gosport, 'one of only three black kids in a school of 1200'. He was a talented footballer, starting out with local non-league clubs before playing professionally first in Japan and then at Birmingham City. However, he withdrew from playing, in 'a terrible indictment of the football industry', because of the racism he experienced both as a supporter – 'standing in the middle of thousands of people giving the Nazi salute' at Fratton Park because of the rise of the National Front in Portsmouth – and as a player. This was present at every level of the game. When Moran was playing for non-league Gosport Borough, a supporter of the opposing team shouted 'Why don't you go back to Jamaica, you black bastard?', to which Moran replied that, since he was originally of Nigerian heritage, this would be several thousand miles out of his way. When playing for Birmingham City in a game in which Moran was shown a red card, the assistant manager of their opponents Halifax Town followed him into the dressing room and racially abused him; Moran punched him, and was reprimanded by the management at Birmingham City and told that he should instead have tolerated the abuse.[34]

Let's Kick Racism Out of Football was created in 1993 as a joint movement between the Campaign for Racial Equality and the Professional Footballers' Association. They determined a ten-point plan for clubs to follow in an attempt to eradicate racism from the game. These included suggestions such as zero tolerance of racist chanting in the stands and condemning this when it occurred; taking action against racist fans by withholding season tickets; preventing racist literature from being distributed outside grounds on match days; removing racist graffiti from grounds 'as a matter of urgency'; and working with community groups such as schools, youth groups, local businesses and the local racial equality council to 'eliminate racist abuse and discrimination' in the area.[35] Leyton Orient FC developed a play, *Kicking Out*, which toured around all the cities hosting Euro 96 games, visiting schools, civic centres, trade union conferences and the House of Commons; the play focused on a group of five children who wanted to play in a football tournament and their battle against their racist coach, who might have been involved in the racial attack that killed one player's uncle.[36] The Football Supporters' Association produced a one-off anti-racist fanzine, *United Colours of Football*, which combined history – one article explored the legacy of early Black players such as Arthur Wharton – with reporting about recent racist incidents at grounds and the work being done to stamp it out. Another piece suggested things to do if a fan sat next to a racist, including reporting them to a steward or police officer under the 1991 Football Offences Act, writing to the club to complain (making sure to include a description and the offending fan's seat number), but also 'accidentally' dropping your Bovril down the back of his neck or throwing the remains of your pie at him when your team scores ('this is obviously not relevant to Arsenal fans').[37] The free fanzine included a list of supporting publications across the country, from Aberdeen to Yeovil Town, and was distributed outside football grounds on the opening day of the 1995–6 season. The Newham Monitoring Project made a special effort to help distribute it to West Ham supporters because of the infamous extent of the racism that their crowds brought to Green Street on a Saturday, and because of their famed connection to the National Front; the NMP also produced a fixture card, emblazoned with the slogan 'Kick Fascism out of West Ham United FC', which they handed out to supporters at

Upton Park.[38] In 1997, Let's Kick Racism Out of Football became a formal organisation, Kick It Out, funded by the FA, PFA, Premier League and Football Foundation, and expanded to address all forms of discrimination in the game.

The year after England slipped out of the Euros in the semi-finals, the Labour Party were elected in their historic landslide, and led the country for thirteen years – ten under Tony Blair, three under his Chancellor, Gordon Brown. There is a counterfactual history in which the Labour government might have been remembered chiefly for their social democratic reforms to the British economy, and their progressive interventions in British social and cultural life. Their canonical historical legacy might have included the children's programme Sure Start, the Department for International Development, the Millennium Dome and the 1998 Human Rights Act; the cutting of NHS waiting lists and introduction of a minimum wage; devolution in Scotland and Wales, the Northern Irish peace process and the Good Friday Agreement; or the abolition of the Section 28 legislation that prevented local authorities from 'promoting homosexuality', the introduction of civil partnerships and the lowering of the age of consent for gay sex. They might have been criticised from the left for other policies: social welfare reforms that did not go as far as many people wanted, the use of private finance initiative contracts to fund hospitals and schools, the imposition of tuition fees and the abolition of student maintenance grants. But Blair's actual legacy, a legacy which clouded the Brown premiership and turned many on the left against the Labour Party for a generation, was none of these things. It was the war in Afghanistan and Iraq.

The terrorist attacks on the United States in September 2001 were aimed at a nation perceived by many as having quasi-imperial intentions on much of the rest of the world. Only a month before the attacks, the *Washington Post* had published a piece entitled 'Empire or Not?', setting out the 'quiet debate' in Washington DC around US foreign policy. The think tank Project for the New American Century had been espousing a Reaganite, 'expansionistic' foreign policy based on 'a dominating global presence militarily, economically and culturally', an approach described by one conservative American thinker somewhat dismissively as a 'really neat, exciting, return-of-the-Raj adventure'.[39] While the *Washington Post* journalist set out this imperialist fantasy as one that had not been fully embraced by either Secretary of State Donald Rumsfeld or President George W. Bush, the attacks on the World Trade Center only a few weeks later would have a clarifying effect on US foreign policy.

For Britain, America's new imperial crusade put it in a tricky position. The two countries' relationship, dubbed at least in the UK as the 'special relationship' since the Second World War, had been tested over foreign policy before – most notably when Harold Wilson's government refused to join Lyndon B. Johnson in sending troops to Vietnam, but also in the early 1980s when the usually warm Reagan–Thatcher connection was briefly cooled by American reluctance to take sides over the Falklands. Over Afghanistan and Iraq, though, there was no such rupture at the highest level of government. When Harold Macmillan had been prime minister, he and many of his policymakers had imagined that Britain might be the 'Greeks' to the American 'Romans': British historical prestige and foreign policy intellect, particularly its experience of empire, could be used to influence the callow and inexperienced Americans, and harness their hard power and military might to British ends. In contrast, Blair followed Bush so obediently that he famously earned the sobriquet of the president's 'poodle', and Britain went to war in the Middle East as the clearly junior partner in a US-led coalition. Most of the British media supported Blair in this, at least at first: *The Times*, the *Sun*, the *Daily Mail* and the *Daily Telegraph* all published consistently pro-war editorials about action in Afghanistan and Iraq. Even the *Observer* was pro-war, and for a significant period: in January 2003, one editorial made 'the case for decisive action' in Iraq.[40] The *Guardian* was deeply sceptical of calls for invasion – although it did publish a piece by Julie Burchill bluntly headlined 'Why we should go to war' which dismissed opposition as 'prissy, pacifist twaddle'.[41] Among the tabloids, the *Daily Mirror* alone remained hostile to both conflicts.

However, among MPs on both sides of the House, and on the streets of Britain's towns and cities, there was somewhat more resistance. In 1998, America had bombed Iraq with British support as part of Operation Desert Fox; unlike Operation Desert Storm in 1990/91, this had taken place without support from the United Nations. Tony Benn, the veteran Labour MP, had spoken passionately in the House of Commons vote, which had sought to give the government the power to use 'all means possible' against Saddam Hussein. Benn compared the experience of Arab civilians with the terrifying experience of Londoners during the Blitz – 'don't Arab and Iraqi women weep when their children die?' – and evoked the United Nations Charter and its opposition to the 'scourge of war' in explaining why he would vote against the Labour government. But he also spoke about the imperial legacies in the Middle East that, he believed, still contributed to anti-British and anti-American feeling in the region. 'In 1958, 40 years ago, Selwyn Lloyd, the Foreign Secretary and later the Speaker, told Foster Dulles that Britain would make Kuwait a Crown colony. Foster Dulles said, "What a very good idea." We may not know that history, but in the Middle East it is known.'[42] In this debate, Benn drew attention to the way that British politicians and commentators talked as if decolonisation had never happened – 'We are sitting here as if we still had an empire' – and the way that they depended on American strength to maintain this illusion – 'only, fortunately, we have a bigger brother with more weapons than us'.

This critique was sustained, not just by Benn but by many who opposed British participation in the invasion of Afghanistan in 2001 and Iraq in 2003, and the charge of neo-imperialism against both Britain and America remained a key tenet of the anti-war movement in this period. The placards handed out by *Socialist Worker* at the first major demonstration against the invasion of Afghanistan in October 2001 had the strapline 'Fight US/UK Imperialism' under the exhortation to 'Stop This Bloody War'. Two years later, Andrew

Murray, the deputy leader of the Stop the War coalition campaign group, wrote a piece in the *Guardian* in which he heralded the American invasion of Iraq: 'Welcome to the new colonialism.'[43]

And yet some people seemed to embrace the idea of British foreign policy as a continuation of imperial values. In his speech at conference on 2 October 2001, Tony Blair reflected on the still very recent events of 9/11. He told the assembled Labour Party members about meeting the families of British victims of the attacks – 'it was in many ways a very British occasion. Tea and biscuits. It was raining outside' – and his desire to provide them with a 'memorial' for their loved ones via the medium of a 'fight for freedom' and 'fight for justice'. Blair called for international action that would mean 'people everywhere can see the chance of a better future through the hard work and creative power of the free citizen, not the violence and savagery of the fanatic'. Given the timing of conference, it is not surprising that the speech was focused on international affairs, unusual though this is for Labour Party policy discussion. Blair sought to justify the war on terror, still very much in its infancy, by citing other foreign policy interventions that Britain had, or should have, made: praising the action it had taken in Kosovo, lamenting the lack of action taken in Rwanda. These were the same values set out in Blair's famous speech in Chicago in 1999, which established the hawkish 'Blair doctrine' in international relations.

He also contextualised the potential future war in Afghanistan by comparing it to the work he believed the international community must undertake in 'Africa', which would be built on the same values. Listing the things the West could provide – aid free from trade obligations, writing off international debt, training soldiers and giving access to markets – Blair then reeled off what Britain would expect in return: 'true democracy, no more excuses for dictatorship, abuses of human rights', as well as 'proper commercial, legal and financial systems'. There is very little recognition here of Britain's imperial legacies in Africa, which might explain some of these political and economic failings; no recognition, either, of the fundamental neo-imperialism of demanding regime change in exchange for aid. It did not go unnoticed, though, among listeners; one writer in the *Guardian* summarised the vision of the world being presented as 'a moral absurdity based on a colonial delusion'.[44]

In this speech, too, Blair used the women of Afghanistan as a foil for his military intentions. 'Women are treated in a way almost too revolting to be credible. First driven out of university; girls not allowed to go to school; no legal rights; unable to go out of doors without a man.' Those who supported the invasion frequently cited the treatment of women by the Taliban as reason enough to go to war. In an unusually explicit moment of politics for the two women, Cherie Blair and Laura Bush, the wives of the prime minister and US president, both made public interventions in support of the war by citing the treatment of Afghan women; Cherie hosted a reception for Afghan women at Downing Street and called on the British government to 'give back a voice' to the country's female class, while Laura took over her husband's weekly radio address to highlight the 'brutal oppression of women' that she characterised as 'the central goal of the terrorists'.[45] These interventions – by women whose voice in this debate came by virtue of their husbands' jobs – sought to underscore the difference between the independence enjoyed by women in 'the West' and the poor benighted women of the Middle East. As such, they drew heavily on imperial tropes such as the nineteenth- and early-twentieth-century imperial feminist campaigns against sati (widow-burning), purdah (the seclusion of women from public life) and female genital mutilation around the empire, in which British women claimed imperialism could liberate colonial women from the traditional conservative forces of their native lands.

Not everyone in Britain bought into these narratives of war in Afghanistan as a humanitarian moment of liberation. As with previous wars, protests against the invasion and the bombing campaign took place across Britain. The march in London on 13 October 2001 – before military action in Afghanistan had even started – attracted around 20,000 people, with another 1,500 protesting in Glasgow. This continued as bombing began in Afghanistan, with a Campaign for Nuclear Disarmament vigil organised in London in November and smaller events in towns and cities such as Blackburn, Bolton and York. On Sunday 18 November, thousands of people – the police put the figure at 15,000, while organisers believed it was closer to 100,000 – marched through London from Hyde Park to Trafalgar Square, where speakers including Tony Benn (who had stepped down from his parliamentary seat at the election that summer), Bianca Jagger, and the Labour MPs Alan Simpson, Paul Marsden and George Galloway addressed the crowd. Mike Marqusee, one of the organisers of the Stop the War coalition – founded in London in October 2001 at a public meeting of more than 2,000 people in opposition to the 'war on terror' – said that the turnout reflected the 'scale and diversity of anti-war opinion' in Britain at the time.[46]

As well as marches, people could register their opposition to the war in other ways. The international Christian charity Tearfund organised a mass letter-writing campaign to MPs to urge the government to ensure that the humanitarian needs of the Afghan people would be met, and held a public prayer meeting at Westminster Chapel at which prayers asked for open borders to allow food relief to reach the country.[47] Staff and students at the universities of Manchester, Southampton and Leeds held 'teach-in' activities that questioned the basis for war; twenty students in Brighton were arrested after they barricaded themselves inside a Royal Navy recruiting office – trapping a naval recruiting officer alongside them – on the University of Sussex campus.[48] Brian Haw, who had established his 'peace camp' in Parliament Square in the summer of 2001 in protest against the sanctions imposed on Iraq, became a key symbol against war in the Middle East. Haw's camp grew to become the Parliament Square Peace Campaign, displaying works of art by Banksy and hosting anti-war political figures such as Tony Benn and John McDonnell. Haw was joined by Barbara Tucker and others who wished to protest against British foreign policy; the camp survived the 2005 Serious Organised Crime and Police Act, which banned unauthorised protests, and remained in the square until 2012 when it was forcibly cleared by the police. The artist Mark Wallinger won the Turner Prize in 2007 with a full recreation of the peace camp, describing Haw in his acceptance speech as 'a remarkable man who has waged a tireless campaign against the folly and hubris of our government's foreign policy'.[49]

The war in Iraq attracted even greater protest. With a more tenuous connection to the attacks of 11 September, and after two years of bombing Afghanistan without a clear victory in sight, the war was clearly lacking in moral justification for many British people. Military action in Iraq was dogged with controversies before it started, with accusations in September 2002 that the British government was using a dossier to justify a potential invasion of Iraq that included the unproven claim that Saddam Hussein could launch weapons of mass destruction (WMDs) in forty-five minutes, and the production of a second 'dodgy dossier' in February 2003, given to journalists to build the case for action, which was plagiarised from various unattributed sources including a student thesis. This significant public outcry against the war was heightened in the summer of 2003 with a bitter fight between the government and the BBC, after journalist Andrew Gilligan accused the government of having 'sexed up' the September dossier and inserted the forty-five-minute claim themselves, and the subsequent death of Dr David Kelly, the government scientist accused of leaking the information, in circumstances that many found suspicious. In this context, opposition to the war increasingly felt to many like a moral imperative.

The marches against the invasion of Iraq were the biggest pacifist protests ever seen in the United Kingdom. On 15 February 2003, as part of a global day of protest against the looming threat of war, more than 750,000 – perhaps a million, or even more – people descended on central London and marched to Hyde Park; another 90,000 marched in Glasgow. They came to the capital from all over the UK: two hundred coaches from Birmingham, thirty from Bristol, seven from Tyneside, six from Calderdale.[50] Many of these protesters were seasoned pacifists, who nevertheless saw something different in this moment of anti-war fervour. Brenda Burrell, who had been at the Greenham Common feminist protests against American nuclear weapons and who had painstakingly sewn almost every one of the CND banners for the Birmingham contingent, said she was more frightened than ever before by the complete lack of 'social justice' in a war against Iraq; Barbara Green, a retired French teacher who attended weekly 'traffic light' vigils against the invasion in Hebden Bridge, noted that the support for the pacifist movement was significantly larger than when they had protested against the Gulf War a decade earlier.[51]

Many others were protesting against war for the first time in their lives. The *Observer* write-up of the February march noted the attendees as unusually diverse.

> There were nuns. Toddlers. Women barristers. The Eton George Orwell Society. Archaeologists Against War. Walthamstow Catholic Church, the Swaffham Women's Choir and Notts County Supporters Say Make Love Not War (And a Home Win against Bristol would be Nice) . . . One group of SWP stalwarts were joined, for the first march in any of their histories, by their mothers. There were country folk and lecturers, dentists and poulterers, a hairdresser from Cardiff and a poet from Cheltenham.[52]

One poll conducted by ICM for the *Guardian* found that 6 per cent of all British households sent at least one person to the march.[53] Those who reached the end in good time – and many did not as the route was so busy – were greeted in Hyde Park by speakers including civil rights leader Jesse Jackson, Tony Benn, Charles Kennedy (the leader of the Liberal Democrats, who thought this 'the riskiest moment for Britain since Suez'), Mo Mowlam MP, the playwright Harold Pinter and Bianca Jagger. Two days before the march, an advertisement had been taken out in the *Guardian* in protest against the planned invasion signed by a huge array of public figures, including – as well as many politicians, and organisations such as CND and the Muslim Association of Britain – the artist Bridget

Riley, the UK garage star Craig David, the actors Andrew Lincoln, Richard E. Grant and Emma Thompson, the writer Benjamin Zephaniah and the comedian Victoria Wood.[54] On the day, Kate Moss and Alexander McQueen led a fashion delegation on the march; the musicians Billy Bragg and Damon Albarn were pictured carrying CND placards, and Ms Dynamite sang in Hyde Park (six days later, she performed a duet of 'Faith' with George Michael at the Brit Awards, during which they changed the lyrics to criticise the government's war plans). People carried placards, many hand-drawn – the wryly twee 'Make tea not war' on a painted cardboard teapot, the slogan daubed on a bedsheet 'The war on Iraq could kill this many', referring to the crowd and rendered terrifying by the scale of the march – and many more produced by organisations – the CND's 'No War On Iraq' and Stop the War Coalition's 'Not In My Name'. There was a sea of thousands of copies of the David Gentleman-designed, eye-catching placard reading 'NO'; in smaller letters, alongside blood splatters, were listed the things that the marchers opposed, including not only 'war on Iraq', but also 'brute force', 'body bags' and 'imperialism'.

Opposition to the war continued – in early March, hundreds of schoolchildren across the country walked out of their lessons to join protests and marches in their local communities, often in defiance of their teachers, occasionally with their encouragement. In November 2003, George Bush visited the United Kingdom and was confronted with somewhere between 100,000 and 200,000 protesters who took to the streets and marched to Trafalgar Square (pausing to boo loudly at 'Bush House', the unfortunately named headquarters of the blameless BBC World Service), where they toppled an effigy of the US president. Public opinion had not been so solidly lined up against British foreign policy since the Suez Crisis. And attitudes to the wars did not mellow with time. In 2011, the British Social Attitudes survey showed that almost 50 per cent of the British public did not approve of the war in Afghanistan and almost 60 per cent disapproved of the war in Iraq. These wars in the Middle East were, for many Britons, an ideological throwback, an unwelcome reminder of British imperial excursions. But the wars, and the nebulous and pernicious 'war on terror' more broadly, shaped British domestic politics irrevocably.

For the right-wing media, of course, the wars in Afghanistan and Iraq were not unjustified or unwelcome. The invasions had been folded into a media rhetoric of the Middle East as a breeding ground of lunatic religious extremists and bloodthirsty terrorists. The proliferation of these attitudes contributed clearly to a rise in Islamophobia in British society and culture. Following the Rushdie Affair, the British media treatment of Muslims had often been stigmatising or dismissive. The Runnymede Trust produced a report in 1997 which highlighted the pernicious effects of Islamophobia in Britain, particularly the 'vulnerability of Muslims to physical violence and harassment', and called for media coverage to be 'less distorted and negative'.[55] But instead the war on terror dramatically heightened the negative coverage of the Muslim community in Britain.

The Commission on British Muslims and Islamophobia published a report in 2004 that made clear just how dire the situation was for many Muslims in Britain. Like the Macpherson Report before, it demonstrated that Muslim communities faced institutional discrimination from the police; one borough councillor, Murad Qureshi, recalled that 'I went to school in west London with a lot of black lads and I never had the kind of grief that they had from the police. But I am beginning to realise how they felt.'[56] But the report went further in highlighting other areas of British life in which Muslims found themselves stigmatised, attacked or oppressed. The 'Community Cohesion' agenda, for example, was introduced in 2001 by Home Secretary David Blunkett after riots led the Home Office to target Muslims for supposedly failing to integrate into British society; leaflets distributed by the BNP in 2002 had called for the boycott of Muslim-owned shops and takeaways and evoked a Muslim 'dictatorship' in Britain to spur anger among its supporters; Muslim children were more likely to live in households that faced overcrowding or unemployment than any other group.[57]

The report also included testimony from young people in Britain who were torn between their British and Muslim identities because of the stigma they faced and because of their anxiety about British government policies. Fazeela, fifteen, talked about feeling 'angry and helpless' because her 'own government is helping to kill Muslims' but also because she and a friend had been verbally abused on East Ham high street for wearing headscarves, while Yasir, sixteen, shared his frustration that Islam was, at best, depicted as being 'old fashioned' in comparison with 'the West': 'they think Muslims . . . live in tents with camels'. Zainab, fourteen, spoke of her relief at seeing the marches against the war – previously she had felt she couldn't describe herself as 'British Muslim' because of the bombing in Afghanistan – and Khaled, sixteen, was also encouraged that it was not only Muslims opposing the war, although he felt that white English people might have been marching for 'different reasons'.[58]

The report made a number of recommendations to fight against Islamophobia which unfortunately failed to make much impact on British society. In July 2005, just after the 7/7 bombs in London, ICM polling for the *Guardian* found that 20 per cent of Muslims had experienced 'hostility or abuse' from non-Muslims because of their religion. In 2006, Tony Blair could talk about 'the relationship between our society and how the Muslim community integrates with our society' in a press conference without any apparent concern that this dichotomy fundamentally set British Muslims apart from their fellow citizens entirely because of their faith.[59]

The rise of Islamophobia in Britain with these two wars did not easily abate. Instead, the hostility towards Muslim people as outsiders, a threat to the British state and its people and values, bled into other areas of British life. The treatment of refugees in the media, like the earlier treatment of migrants from the empire, made little concession to the fact that these people were here because the British were there. Even as the country became increasingly diverse – even as multiculturalism became increasingly structurally integrated into the British state – there still remained an ambivalence about the role of 'outsiders' and their culture in Britain itself.

Nowhere is this more clear than in the rise of discourse around 'British values', which was present throughout the period of New Labour – the Home Secretary David Blunkett, for example, a keen disciple of these ideas – but especially notable under Gordon Brown. Brown, a historian with a PhD in the interwar history of the Labour Party in Scotland, became steadily more publicly committed to the idea of an explicit set of British values, as a way to bind the nation together. In February 2007, Brown gave a speech at a seminar on 'Britishness' at the Commonwealth Club.[60] In this speech, he argued that the 'long tidal flows of British history', which he characterised as '2,000 years of successive waves of invasion, immigration, assimilation and trading partnerships', had created 'distinctive' British values that fundamentally shaped institutions. The speech is notably light on empire given the setting, containing just one reference to abolishing the slave trade.

Perhaps this was not unexpected. Two years earlier, Brown had visited Kenya, Tanzania, Mozambique and South Africa on a tour intended to highlight poverty issues as part of Britain's new plan for global aid; in Tanzania, the then Chancellor had enthusiastically proclaimed that 'the days of Britain having to apologise for its colonial history are over'. On this trip, Brown had already been thinking about British values: in this iteration, they were 'tolerance, liberty, civic duty' and 'fair play . . . openness . . . internationalism', and he presented them as a gift to the world from the British delivered through their empire.[61] By 2007, he had boiled these values down to 'British tolerance, the British belief in liberty and the British sense of fair play' and lost the explicit imperial references; he believed these values should be inculcated in British people, but especially in migrants to Britain, through various elements of 'citizenship' education.

Brown's British values speech is also notable for the way that he sets out the central challenges to the British 'way of life'; given the same weight as challenges to the union, and Britain's role in Europe, were the need to integrate 'our ethnic communities' and to 'respond to Muslim fundamentalism'. Brown might have drawn these values from his Christian childhood and his brand of left-wing politics, but it is also clear that this speech and others around the same time were fundamentally shaped too by panics about immigration and the fervency of the anti-terrorism agenda.

In 2003, in the context of increasing legislation as part of the domestic front on the war on terror, the Home Office established a counter-terrorism strategy, CONTEST, the most notable feature of which is the first strand, 'Prevent', which seeks to stop people from becoming terrorists or terrorist sympathisers (the others are 'Pursue', 'Protect' and 'Prepare', aimed at countering planned terrorist attacks). Prevent includes a deradicalisation programme, aimed explicitly at Muslims, as well as much broader provisions aimed at identifying people at risk of 'radicalisation'; since 2003, the legislation has been repeatedly strengthened and has required schools, hospitals, youth groups, community centres and many other community or civic institutions to report people who fall under suspicion. Even in the early days of the legislation, it was already being used in ways that led groups such as Liberty to criticise the government for spying on and stigmatising Muslim citizens, including children. A youth project in London revealed that the Metropolitan Police was trying to use Prevent to force them to share the details of young Muslims as a condition of funding, while one London borough required people working with young people to make a special note of whether they were Muslim and to tell the police where Muslim teenagers liked to hang out in the area.[62] The British government increasingly saw Muslim communities as suspicious and potentially dangerous, echoing the anxieties of British colonial officials who saw Islam as a fundamentally anti-colonial force in the empire, and drawing on years of demonisation of Muslim migrants to Britain from the Commonwealth.

On the one hand, the New Labour years were notable for the way that imperial history was obfuscated, denied or forgotten. But there was also a key moment during this period when British society, politics and culture came together in a rare public examination of the history of empire and an explicit consideration of its victims and beneficiaries. The occasion was the 2007 bicentenary of the ending of the British slave trade, commemorated through museum exhibitions, TV programmes, church services and the issuing of a £2 coin.

This moment was fundamentally a celebration of Britain's role in ending the slave trade (not slavery, which would take until the 1830s in the Caribbean and into the twentieth century in many British African territories), while largely avoiding any discussion of Britain's role as an enthusiastic and brutal trader in enslaved peoples, or the long history of rebellions and campaigns by enslaved and formerly enslaved peoples against slavery. Indeed, 2007 became jokingly referred to as 'Wilberfest' by campaigners, because of its focus on William Wilberforce and his white British activism. In a special episode of Radio 4's *In Our Time*, which focused not on abolition but only on Wilberforce himself, Melvyn Bragg visited Westminster Abbey and described the campaigner as 'a man I would contend had more influence than any other individual in this abbey'; at the end of the programme, Bragg doubled down on this 'Great Man' interpretation of abolition, explicitly describing Wilberforce as 'a great man in his time, and all time'.[63] This did not go unchallenged, however. Moira Stuart's documentary *In Search of Wilberforce*, another BBC broadcast, set out explicitly to explore the myths that sustained such hagiography – which she punctured right at the start of the programme by announcing that 'history didn't happen that way' – and included interviews with a number of historians who asserted the agency and importance of enslaved peoples in the fight for abolition.[64]

Many communities explored the legacies of slavery in their local areas. In Bristol, which had been a key port in the slave trade and which had the history of empire engrained into its architecture and local history, there were over a hundred events in 2007 including art exhibitions, talks and debates, performances of plays such as *Slave Ship* (Amiri Baraka, 1967) and *Land* (Edson Burton, 2007), and concerts. 'Breaking the Chains', an exhibition at the Empire and Commonwealth Museum, which closed in 2008 and was liquidated in 2013 amid controversy about the unauthorised sale of many of its exhibits, included a multimedia gallery exploring emotions and memories around the contemporary legacies of the slave trade, and exhibits engaging personal testimony and Black musical heritage.

Alongside these cultural events, attempts were made to engage with the legacies of slavery in a meaningful political way. In January 2007, key figures from Bristol's local leadership signed a 'declaration of regret' about the city's role in the slave trade, and over the weekend of 24/25 March (the exact bicentenary of the signing of the Abolition of the Slave Trade Act) there was a special 'people's service' at Bristol Cathedral with the themes of 'remembrance, reconciliation and healing'.[65] At a debate in 2006, the General Synod of the Church of England had voted to apologise for the Church's role in supporting slavery, with the then Archbishop of Canterbury Rowan Williams saying they shared 'the shame and sinfulness of our predecessors'.[66] In March 2007, Ken Livingstone wept in City Hall as he read a statement apologising for the role of London and its institutions in the slave trade, condemning 'the racial murder of not just those who were transported but generations of enslaved African men, women and children' and its lasting consequences.[67]

These were not the first apologies. In 1999, as its last formal act of the millennium, Liverpool City Council had apologised on behalf of the city for its role in the slave trade. The motion, which was passed unanimously, expressed 'shame and remorse for the city's role in this trade in human misery' and included 'an unreserved apology for [Liverpool's] involvement in the slave trade and the continual effects of slavery on Liverpool's Black community'. Anti-racist groups condemned the use of the town hall for this motion, since the building had images of Black enslaved peoples literally moulded into its plasterwork, while the Liverpool Anti Racist Community Arts Association said the apology was merely 'lipservice' to anti-racism.[68] But the coverage of the apology outside Liverpool was fairly muted – it was not until the wider events of 2007 that the question of if and how to apologise for Britain's slaving past received national attention.

The debate over apologies became increasingly contentious in the intervening years; at the heart of it was Tony Blair's equivocation over whether he would or would not admit culpability and regret on behalf of the nation for its slave history. In 2001 he insisted at a UN summit on racism that Britain would not apologise for its role in the slave trade. 'The position is that slavery has to be condemned in the present and regretted in the past,' his spokesman clarified. In 2006, he had expressed 'deep sorrow' for the 'profoundly shameful' history. Eventually in a meeting with the president of Ghana in 2007 he said that 'I have said we are sorry and I will say it again'.[69]

Naturally, there were plenty of politicians and journalists who believed that Britons were too willing to feel shame about their imperial past, and that Britain's achievements should be celebrated, not condemned. Melanie Phillips, writing for the *Daily Mail*, said that although 'slavery was evil', the 'orgy of breast-beating is utterly absurd'.[70] Her exasperated aside that 'you would have thought . . . that this country actually invented slavery rather than playing such a historic role in stopping it' echoed, presumably unintentionally, Eric Williams's famous observation that the British 'wrote almost as if Britain had introduced Negro slavery solely for the satisfaction of abolishing it'.[71] In 2007, David Cameron, then leader of the opposition, said he did not believe that one generation could meaningfully apologise for the actions of another; a few years later the historian and journalist Dominic Sandbrook lamented that 'apologising for our history has become an almost instinctive reflex'.[72]

But many of those whose families met the British empire in a different way – as the colonised, not colonisers – wondered if this sense of shame really even existed. There were certainly still those who were happy to revel in imperial legacies: in 2009, Emmanuel College Cambridge advertised a May Ball to its students with the theme of the British empire. Students were invited to experience 'the hedonism of 19th-century Hong Kong, the sweltering rainforests of Sri Lanka and the beautiful cliffs as you sail around the Cape of Good Hope. Last, but by no means least . . . the jewel in her majesty's crown: the Great British Isles themselves'. After an outcry by students, marshalled in the Facebook group 'Emma against the Empire', the theme was made less explicit: 'empire' was dropped from the event's title and instead attendees were told they would be celebrating the 'Pax Britannica' while they partied 'like it's 1899'.[73]

But even as the British became increasingly open about and aware of their country's dark imperial past, their government was revealed to have been highly secretive. It had been known for some time – in fact since the moment of decolonisation – that the British had been reluctant to leave evidence of their imperial rule with the newly independent governments and people who had been until recently subjected to it. There had infamously been a 'pall of smoke' over Delhi in 1947, created by the colonial administration's rapid, methodical destruction of government records.[74] The cleansing power of fire was embraced again in the 1960s as Britain pulled out of African colonies.

Years later, in 2011, a well-to-do woman attending a garden party to celebrate the wedding of Prince William and Kate Middleton casually reminisced that, when working as a file clerk at Government House in 'Keeenyaaa', she had personally carried bundles of documents onto the lawn to be burned in fires that 'never ended'.[75] Her indiscretion was perhaps understandable, given that this had been official government policy. Memoranda sent from the metropole to the colonial administrations were clear that potentially controversial or incriminating files should either be burned and the ashes broken up, or packed in weighted crates and dropped at the bottom of deep and ideally current-free water (or the sea). Only files that could or should not be disposed with in this manner were to be marked with a red stamp (W for 'watch' in Kenya and Northern Rhodesia, DG for files that could be seen only by British officials of European descent in Uganda) and removed to England, where they were kept at a secret storage facility known as Hanslope Park. After this had been done, officials were told to destroy the 'W' stamp that they had been keeping hidden in their office, and – of course – burn the document informing them of these instructions. This was Operation Legacy.

The material was a vast archive – Kenya alone sent around 1,500 files in 294 boxes – that was not made available to historians, or to the former colonial territories; the Kenyan government had first requested the files be returned to them in 1967 and had been told that they were the possession of HMG and would not be surrendered.[76] The files sent to Hanslope Park were a sort of open secret: not searched in FOI requests, not shown to researchers, and not spoken about in public. One archivist said that they 'tried to ignore the fact that we had them. We weren't really supposed to have them so it was thought best to ignore them for the purpose of requests.'[77]

In 2001, the historian David Anderson was visiting archives in Nairobi when he was approached by representatives of Kenyan veteran groups who wished to pursue compensation claims against the British government. He eventually became part of a team – 'archives junkies, activists and advocates' – who worked to assemble evidence in support of five Kenyan activists, Ndiku Mutwiwa Mutua, Paulo Nzili, Wambugu wa Nyingi, Jane Muthoni Mara and Susan Ngondi, all suing the British government for the torture they had suffered at the hands of the British forces during the Mau Mau crisis. Anderson's historical research proved vital. In 1999, a file had been declassified – possibly accidentally – which detailed the British government's refusal in 1967 to return the migrated documents to Kenya and inadvertently therefore revealed their existence; in 2003, another historian wrote to Anderson to let him know that he had actually visited Hanslope Park and had seen material relating to Kenya among other colonial documents.[78] Anderson told the law firm Leigh Day about this hidden archive and in 2005 the firm filed the first of many requests to see this material. In 2010, a preliminary hearing was finally fixed for spring 2011.

In early January 2011, after being instructed by the courts, the British government eventually admitted that they had in their possession a number of 'migrated' files from the British colonies. The government had, of course, always been interventionist in the way its imperial history was documented and preserved. In 1993, for example, the Foreign Office had intervened to prevent Interpol from interviewing British citizens as part of a Malaysian government inquiry into the Batang Kali massacre in 1948. Imperial historians had long accepted that the National Archives at Kew were not going to hold the hidden histories of colonial violence, or the voices of colonial people themselves. The fact that many of these documents had been wilfully destroyed in fires, or sent to the bottom of the ocean, was understood to be part of the violence of colonial rule. Instead, researchers had worked to read 'against the grain' and between the lines to find these untold stories. And yet, suddenly, the Hanslope Park disclosure revealed that some of these documents had in fact existed all along and had been sitting, patiently, in a building in the Home Counties, waiting to be found.

In the wake of the admission, these files, FO 141, were 'migrated' back to the National Archives, where historians could explore their contents. Often, the material did not reveal anything that fundamentally changed the narrative historians had already been able to construct about British imperialism, or the testimonies from the former colonised peoples themselves, who had long been able to detail the excesses of the British colonial state and its structures of coercion and violence. More important was the fact that the British state was actively concealing its colonial history, wilfully and systemically, as late as 2011.

The court case that forced the revelation of the existence of the archive ended with the British government agreeing to pay almost £20 million in damages to over 5,000 claimants who had suffered torture at the hands of the colonial administration. The then Foreign Secretary, William Hague, claimed that this did not establish a precedent for any further claims by former colonial territories; the Kenyan abuses must be seen not as indicative of colonial rule, but as a regrettable deviation from the civilised norm. In 2019, the government was forced to pay almost £1 million in compensation to thirty-three Cypriots who had been beaten and tortured by British forces in the late 1950s during the guerrilla campaign by the underground nationalist movement EOKA to overthrow colonial rule. Again, the government stated that this was not 'any admission of liability' and was not a precedent for future claims.

These cases punctured British complacency about imperial violence with the testimony of those who had survived it, but they did not fundamentally reshape the way the British felt about their imperial history. Myths about British history continued to be constructed. And yet those myths did take on a different complexion, and few were explored more publicly or spectacularly than those of the opening ceremony for the 2012 Olympics held in London.

The film-maker Danny Boyle had been given the task of assembling an opening ceremony that represented Britain to a global audience. He saw his creation, entitled 'Isles of Wonder', as 'a sort of civic or national duty'.[79] Working with writer Frank Cottrell-Boyce, production designer Mark Tildesley and costume designer Suttirat Anne Larlarb, and with Rick Smith, from the band Underworld, as the music director, Boyle constructed a multidisciplinary extravaganza exploring overlapping conceptions of Britain and Britishness, drawing on history, society, literature, pop music and culture. The historical sections, titled 'Green and Pleasant Land' and 'Pandaemonium', focused on the transformation of Britain from a pastoral land to a modern industrial society, with the actor Kenneth Branagh delivering Caliban's 'Be Not Afear'd' speech from Shakespeare's *The Tempest* dressed as Isambard Kingdom Brunel. The ceremony then flashed through a series of moments that changed British history: the industrial advancements of the Victorians, the two world wars, the women's suffrage movement, the Jarrow Crusade of 1936 (when two hundred men marched from Tyneside to Downing Street to protest their unemployment and poverty), the arrival of the *Empire Windrush*. The title 'Green and Pleasant Land' was taken from the hymn 'Jerusalem', written by William Blake, with its ambiguous narrative of industrial development; 'Pandaemonium' is the title of a book edited by Humphrey

Jennings, the film-maker associated with Mass Observation in the 1930s and 40s, which collated contemporary accounts of the Industrial Revolution from the mid seventeenth century to the end of the nineteenth century, and which juxtaposed the apocalyptic with the optimistic. As these two titles suggest, the opening ceremony presented Britain's relationship with its history not as an inevitable march of progress but as a more ambiguous process of change and perhaps even loss.

Even so, the overall narrative of the ceremony was a celebration of British culture, portrayed as a tapestry woven from and by different communities around the nation. The multiculturalism of musical traditions were a feature throughout, from the Nostalgia Steel Band (formed in 1964 and integral to the Notting Hill Carnival) to the British DJs of the 1970s, the Grimethorpe Colliery Band to the Beatles, from the Rolling Stones to Millie Small, the Specials to the Prodigy, the Sex Pistols to Soul II Soul, finishing with Dizzee Rascal and Emeli Sandé. The choice of music, as well as the wider cultural narrative constructed, led to a few voices of dissent; the Conservative MP Aidan Burley described the ceremony as 'leftie multicultural crap'. The *Daily Mail* admired the 'brilliant show', but criticised the contents as 'Marxist propaganda', lamenting particularly that there had been 'no references to the achievements of the Empire' and that immigration had been depicted as 'a uniformly liberating force'.[80] But broadly speaking, the media got behind the surprisingly radical, surprisingly progressive message of the opening ceremony. During the Games themselves, there was a sudden and cynical move to embrace and celebrate Team GB's 'multicultural' athletes, even from papers and politicians who had previously spoken critically about 'mass immigration'.

The global reach of the opening ceremony – the fact that it featured the first gay kiss ever televised in Saudi Arabia, for example – was lauded in 2012, as a moment of British soft power unparalleled in recent times. Britain had used the occasion of the Games to reassess its history in front of the world and, in doing so, project and promote some socially liberal values. And yet, the message projected to the world by the leader of Britain's coalition government, David Cameron, was somewhat less revisionist. In 2013 Cameron visited Amritsar, the site of the 1919 Jallianwala Bagh massacre, when 379 Indian men, women and children were murdered by General Robert Dyer and his troops as they tried to peacefully assemble to protest against British rule. The massacre had been condemned in Britain, at least partly because it revealed the lie at the heart of the idea that Britain was committed to a benign form of civilising imperialism. Winston Churchill had been a particularly vocal critic of Dyer, saying that the slaughter was 'an extraordinary event, a monstrous event, an event which stands in singular and sinister isolation'; in fact the vehemence of his critique served as a way to justify imperialism, by insisting that Amritsar stood outside the norms of British imperial restraint and beneficence.[81] Dyer became a scapegoat precisely because his actions had lifted the curtain on the violence that underpinned all imperial rule; he was, however, allowed to resign from the British Army without any formal disciplinary hearing and was presented upon his return to Britain with a large sum of money that had been raised for him by readers of the *Morning Post*, a conservative newspaper later absorbed into the *Daily Telegraph*.

Cameron was the first British prime minister to visit the site of the massacre, but it was noted at the time in both India and Britain that his visit was not accompanied by an apology for British actions. Cameron laid a wreath at the memorial and wrote in the guest book a short message in which he quoted Churchill's statement, calling the massacre a 'deeply shameful' moment for Britain and expressing 'regret'. (This echoed, for example, the speech given by the Queen in 1997 when she had described Amritsar as one of the 'moments of sadness' in British–Indian relations.) This was intentional: at a press conference in Amritsar, Cameron said that the massacre had happened forty years before he was born and that he didn't 'think the right thing is to reach back into history and to seek out things you can apologise for'. He set out a vision of empire as a simplistic sort of balance sheet: there was 'an enormous amount to be proud of in what the British Empire did and was responsible for, but of course there were bad events as well as good events', and 'the bad events we should learn from and the good events we should celebrate'.[82]

At the same press conference, Cameron was asked (not for the first time) about the calls for the return of the Koh-i-noor diamond to the Indian subcontinent. The diamond, one of the largest in the world, is one of the literal jewels in the Crown of the British empire, ceded to Queen Victoria in 1849 when Punjab was annexed by the British East India Company. It was displayed at the Empire Festival in 1851, as part of that huge showcase for British imperial might and wealth. The diamond is now set in the Crown of the Queen Mother; it was placed on the Queen Mother's coffin for her funeral in 2002. The Koh-i-noor diamond is at the heart of a familiar controversy around the return of artefacts that were acquired by the British during imperialism, as war spoils, stolen goods or traded materials. India, Pakistan and Afghanistan all make claim to the jewel, and all have demanded its return. On a previous trip to India in 2010, intended to drum up trade between the two countries, Cameron had been interviewed on ND-TV and was asked about the demands to return the diamond. In a moment of unexpected candour, he said that it was 'going to have to stay put' because 'If you say yes to one you suddenly find the British Museum would be empty'.[83]

When Cameron was asked again in 2013, he stuck by this argument, again citing the British Museum – which does not hold the Crown jewels – in defence of his approach. 'It is the same question with the Elgin Marbles and all these other things. The right answer is for the British Museum and other cultural institutions to do exactly what they do do, which is to link up with other institutions around the world to make sure that the things which we have and look after so well are properly shared with people around the world.' He dismissed what he described as 'returnism' by saying he did not think this approach was 'sensible'.[84] His response was boiled down even further in the *Sun*, who reported, in a piece headlined 'Gem to Stay Put', that Cameron had declared 'they're not having that back'.[85]

Cameron's casual defence of Britain's imperial plunder and his simplistic idea of empire as a collection of good things and bad things were clearly connected. In his conception of imperial legacies, in which the 'bad things' that Britain did should be 'learned from' but never apologised for, imperial history was – like the contents of Britain's museums amassed from the former colonies – simply a way for the British people to enrich their knowledge of the world, guilt-free. Unfortunately, during Cameron's years as prime minister, this simplistic version of imperial history would not only become part of the official canon, it would also have a significant impact on questions of British identity and citizenship, as well as Britain's place in the world.

One aspect of this process was the government's attempt to clarify and control the narrative of Britishness being taught in schools. Michael Gove, education secretary between 2010 and 2014, made clear his opposition to what he described as left-wing 'ideologues' in the education system who had condemned children to the 'prison house of ignorance' with their new, trendy ideas about learning. Gove believed that the curriculum in history – an area that he identified as one of his passions in a speech at the London Academy of Excellence in 2014 – was particularly lacking both in academic rigour and in patriotic fervour. He set about constructing reforms drawing heavily on H. E. Marshall's *Our Island Story*, a book beloved of Conservative MPs including David Cameron, first published in 1905, which presented the development of the British nation as a series of inexorable and unstoppable triumphs, with imperialism as a key component of this rise. (In 2005 the *Daily Telegraph* and the right-wing think tank Civitas had sent a copy of the book to every primary school in Britain.) Initially, the education secretary had enlisted the historian Simon Schama as a consultant on this project, but soon moved on to working with Niall Ferguson, whose cheerleading for imperialism was more in line with Gove's own historiographical foibles.

Gove argued in the House of Commons that history teaching should 'celebrate the distinguished role of these islands in the history of the world' such as 'the role of the Royal Navy in putting down the slave trade'; he was notably less keen on addressing topics such as the role of Britain in slavery itself.[86] In a speech to the Conservative Party conference in 2007, he had identified Britain's historic heroes as those people who had 'ventured to the hidden corners of the globe' (hidden, presumably, from the British rather than from those people who were living in them at the time); he wished to structure the curriculum around these heroes, along with a pedantic focus on chronology and dates. When the initial draft was released, Schama told an audience of history teachers that the new curriculum proposals were 'insulting', 'offensive', 'pedantic' – '1066 And All That, but without the jokes' (somewhat ironically, given that Yeatman and Sellar's book was itself a parody of *Our Island Story*). He highlighted as especially problematic the inclusion of Clive of India as a historic hero for his work establishing the East India Company, given that Clive was a 'sociopathic, corrupt thug' who made 'our most dodgy bankers look like a combination of Mary Poppins and Jesus Christ'.[87] The new curriculum was duly met with 'near-universal derision' among historians and history teachers, and Gove was forced to row back his proposals. The historian Richard Evans, writing in the *Guardian*, welcomed the rowed-back version as 'a world away from Gove's original list of patriotic stocking-fillers', but pointed out that the Labour education spokesman, Tristram Hunt – himself a historian – had been all too keen to embrace the original 'redraft of history teaching as a way of building national identity through a patriotic narrative', instead of standing up for history as a 'myth-busting' rather than 'myth-making' discipline.[88]

The other consequential place where imperial narratives were used to foster a specific attitude to citizenship was at Britain's borders. Since 2005, anybody who wants to become a British citizen has had to take the 'Life in the UK' test. This comprises twenty-four multiple-choice questions, which must be passed with a mark of 75 per cent or above. Prospective citizens who wish to study for the test must purchase a copy of an official handbook in order to learn the required information. First published in 2005 and created under

Blair's Labour government, *Life in the United Kingdom: A Journey to Citizenship* had as its first chapter a historical section, 'The Making of the United Kingdom', but the test only covered material from the second chapter onwards. The history was included, along with other supporting chapters on the law, sources of help and information, and community cohesion, because it was believed to be 'of interest and practical value' to people taking the test. As the first chapter opened, the handbook posited that 'to understand a country it is important to know something about its history'. A narrative from the Roman invasion to New Labour was duly constructed to this end.[89]

The first edition of the handbook focused almost entirely on English history; in March 2007, it was revised to embrace a slightly more four-nations approach. The narrative bounces from king to act to revolution to war in a clear top-down history; there is little space either for ordinary people or for any particularly critical analysis. There are a few surprising moments, though: the description of the slave trade as the 'evil side' to imperial expansion (although this is, notably, the only downside to empire identified); the assertion that the suffragettes 'had to resort to civil disobedience' to achieve the vote (and therefore no narratives about helpful female munitions workers being rewarded for their patience).

Notably the historical section of these early editions of the handbook begins with the statement that 'any account of history, however, is only one interpretation. Historians often disagree about what to include and what to exclude in historical accounts'. Labour's Home Office was taking ownership of its own historiography: it was explicit that the story it told was partial, only one possible route to the present from the past. By presenting one historical narrative alongside a disclaimer highlighting the role of interpretation and the impossibility of finding one single true story, the handbook not only acknowledges but subtly emphasises the fact that history is inherently political.

In 2013, however, a new edition of the handbook was developed, which is used to this day. Theresa May had become Home Secretary and the approach taken was very different. For a start, the historical material was much expanded – fifty-five pages – and became part of the information covered by the citizenship test. The section on contemporary society also included plenty of references to British traditions, culture and heritage that drew on historical examples. History, under this new regime, explicitly became part of British citizenship and was assessed as such.[90]

The section of the new handbook dealing with Britain's past was titled 'A Long and Illustrious History'. There are no references here to interpretation or to the idea that histories might be multiple, diverse and contested: this history exists to celebrate, to justify and to exculpate. It provides a reason to embrace Britishness and the British, who – the reader is told – have been 'at the heart of the world's political, scientific, industrial and cultural development'. (Although historians of empire would certainly agree with this, they might note that 'developments' can be either positive or negative.)

The history presented is a march towards progress: the creation of a modern, dynamic, united nation. Certain aspects of this history might not have been quite as positive. The slave trade is mentioned, although downgraded from 'evil' to 'horrible'. The British opponents of slavery, Wilberforce predictably at the centre, are celebrated for their work towards abolition, and the humanitarian efforts of the Royal Navy in policing the seas are lauded. Figures like Olaudah Equiano, the eighteenth-century writer and activist for abolition who had himself been enslaved by a Royal Navy officer, are absent. The reader is told that Indian and Chinese workers were 'employed' to 'replace the freed slaves', but learns nothing of their poor conditions in indentured servitude. The freed slaves themselves disappear from the story, entirely excluded from this narrative of the British nation.

Under Victoria, it is written, Britain 'increased its power and influence abroad' as the British empire 'grew to cover all of India, Australia and parts of Africa'. It becomes 'the largest empire the world has ever seen', curiously passive in its construction – a reader might ask who built it, and what violence or coercion or resistance was sparked by its growth, but would not find the answers here. The Boer War is covered – a regrettable event – and then, by the end of the twentieth century, 'for the most part, an orderly transition from Empire to Commonwealth'. In the box at the end of 'A Long and Illustrious History', readers are told to check they understand the growth of the British empire, but there is no mention of its decline and fall.

They are told, later, that immigrants were invited to come to Britain to help rebuild after the Second World War; new laws to restrict immigration were apparently passed in the 1960s to make sure immigrants would have 'a strong connection to Britain' but, 'even so', Britain admitted 28,000 people of Indian origin who had been expelled from Uganda in the 1970s (their history as citizens of the British empire and their resulting very strong legal and cultural connections to Britain therefore wholly elided). Given that the people reading this book and taking this test are themselves by definition immigrants to the United Kingdom, this partial history is particularly ironic.

It is the Second World War, rather than the British empire, that is at the heart of this narrative. The familiar spirits, Dunkirk and Blitz, are explicitly invoked. Britain (and the empire) 'stood almost alone' against Nazi Germany. Churchill remains 'a much-admired figure', who made many famous speeches, some of which are quoted. Churchill is one of a number of key historical figures who are set aside in little boxes, their potted biographies showing their achievements. There are nineteen of these boxes in the history section. Thirteen of them are reserved for white men, from Isambard Kingdom Brunel to Alexander Fleming to Dylan Thomas to Roald Dahl. There are five boxes for women – one showing the six wives of Henry VIII and their various fates, and then Florence Nightingale, Emmeline Pankhurst, Margaret Thatcher (the reference to her being a 'divisive figure' removed somewhere between the 2007 and 2013 versions of the handbook) and Mary Peters, the pentathlete. One person of colour is featured: Sake Dean Mahomed, who apparently introduced curry and shampooing to the British in the nineteenth century.

Life in the United Kingdom is not intended to test existing knowledge among applicants to the citizenship process: it is both teacher and examiner, and must be read and absorbed before being regurgitated. The historical material is vital in demonstrating what Britishness means to the Home Office as it determines who belongs and who must be excluded, deported, denied. A research project by the University of Essex in 2021 surveyed 270 British people and found that 66 per cent of them were unable to correctly answer 18 out of 24 questions needed to pass the test. In 2020, a group of historians wrote an open letter to the Home Office protesting against the 'on-going misrepresentation of slavery and Empire' in the test, and calling for the history section of the test to be 'corrected and rewritten'.[91] But the test itself does not seek to be accurate, and nor does it matter to its aims that British people themselves could not pass. Instead, the test seeks to inculcate certain values and beliefs in the prospective British citizen by means of a particular narrative, built on a very partial history that excludes many people even while it purports to build citizenship and belonging. And that is in fact the point of the entire exercise: history is not being explained or examined, but used as propaganda.

In the last few years, these history wars have spilled over from curricula and test centres into British politics, society and culture, most notably in Britain's referendum on its membership of the EU. Empire was ever-present during the Brexit campaign. Many Leavers – such as Daniel Hannan, a Conservative MEP from 1999 to 2020 and one of the longest and loudest supporters of exiting the EU – explicitly invoked the Commonwealth as an alternative trading partner for Britain. In the 2015 leaders' debate before the general election, Nigel Farage of the UK Independence Party (UKIP) described leaving the EU as a chance to reconnect with other global partners, 'starting with our friends in the Commonwealth'. CANZUK – a fantasy trading bloc between Canada, New Zealand, Australia and the UK – was invoked repeatedly during the Brexit campaign. Hannan even had a mocked-up version of the CANZUK flag as his Twitter header photograph; two years after the referendum, he wrote an article for the *Telegraph* in which he argued that the only people resistant to CANZUK were those on the 'far left, who were determined to find evidence of colonialism and racism everywhere . . . When you say "CANZUK", they hear "Empire" '.[92] Of course, CANZUK is not empire, but a reimagining of imperialism with all the difficult points removed: a federation of white, English-speaking countries, who come together in a mutually beneficial arrangement of freedom of movement, free trade and international cooperation.

The empire was not financially or politically viable as a future for Britain in 1973 when the country first joined the EEC; it was never likely that it could be revived as such in the twenty-first century. But that was not the point. Brexit, like empire, originated among the British elites who stood best to profit from it, before being sold to a wider public particularly targeting those voters who felt 'left behind'. Whether Leavers were those from poor communities who resented competing with cheaper workforces from the EU and whose local economies, such as in Grimsby, were visibly suffering in a globalised world, or those from the Home Counties who were financially comfortable but felt that the nation had nevertheless seen a 'decline' in its finances, its culture and its place in the world, they were voting based on the idea that being part of the EU had been detrimental to British success, compared with the victories and (perhaps more importantly) certainties of empire.

Some of the early critiques of the EU, made by groups such as the Anti-Federalist League, attacked the organisation as pedantic and overmighty, with arguments for Leave focusing on what was seen as legislative overreach and red tape imposed from Brussels; the Anti-Federalist League had been set up in 1991 to campaign against the adoption of the Maastricht Treaty which sought far greater political, as well as economic, unity between its members. But in 2016, the campaign was fought quite blatantly on the topic of immigration. In 1975, the question of immigration had barely featured in the referendum on whether to stay in the EEC, both because freedom of movement was not fully introduced until Maastricht, but also because immigration in this period was thought of primarily in terms of people of colour arriving from Commonwealth countries, not white migrants from Europe. The referendum of 2016 saw the Brexiteers effect a remarkable inversion of these assumptions and prejudices.

In February 2016, Vote Leave published on their website a letter signed by eighty 'community and business leaders' with links to the Commonwealth who lamented that EU membership meant that Britain had to 'turn away qualified workers from the Commonwealth so as to free up unlimited space for migrants from the EU'. The letter bemoaned the fact that 'descendants of the men who volunteered to fight for Britain in two world wars must stand aside in favour of people with no connection to the United Kingdom'. In response, the Britain Stronger In Europe campaign accused Vote Leave of looking back at Britain's history 'with rose-tinted spectacles' and pointed out that many Commonwealth leaders had indicated they would prefer the UK to remain part of the EU.[93] Of course, the idea that Commonwealth immigrants were somehow 'connected' to the UK and should be welcomed to the country had been entirely missing from narratives around immigration in the 1960s and 70s, when successive Conservative and Labour governments had passed laws to limit their entry to the country.

It was a curious irony of the Brexit campaign that its aggressively weaponised narrative about immigration from the EU had long roots in Britain's imperial and post-imperial demonisation of Commonwealth migrants as unwanted, disruptive and un-British. When Farage, for example, unveiled a poster that screamed 'BREAKING POINT' over an image of mostly non-white, mostly male refugees crossing the Croatia–Slovenia border in 2015, he was drawing on this imperial legacy, even though his notional target was migration from the European Union. The contradictions and ironies made the strategy no less effective, forcing the debate away from practical and economic concerns and onto the emotive territory of belonging and identity, security and self-determination. A *Guardian* editorial the week of the vote, which argued that the 'wise vote is for Remain', worried nonetheless that the referendum 'risked descending into a plebiscite on whether immigrants are a good or a bad thing'.[94]

As the name implied, the Stronger in Europe campaign saw the need to mount a positive campaign rather than a defensive one. It celebrated Britain as a global nation, a country with a proud history of reaching beyond its borders and playing a leadership role in the international community. Leave was denigrated as being small-minded, Little England, wanting to cut Britain off from the wider world. Remainers invoked supposed British values in defence of a liberal internationalism: the ideals of tolerance, diversity, humanitarianism were espoused as proudly and historically British, and the campaign to leave the EU was depicted as going against this proud history. An impassioned editorial for the *Financial Times,* for example, written by Simon Schama, was headlined 'Let us spurn Brexit and remain a beacon of tolerance', although the piece itself acknowledged that the Britain of Enoch Powell's Rivers of Blood and the *Daily Mail*'s cry of 'Hurrah for the Blackshirts!' was not uncomplicatedly tolerant of diversity or welcoming to migrants.[95]

It was a difficult trick to pull off. For centuries, Britain's global role had frequently been shaped by greed, and violence, and naked expansion; the British at home had often been intolerant, uncomfortable with migration from the empire, unhappy about British taxes being used to fund adventures – or even aid – overseas. The benign past of a happy, tolerant, internationalist Britain was just as much a construction as the image of Britannia ruling the waves.

As Britain lurched towards the day of the referendum, the question of what it meant to be British became ever more potent and politicised. The outcome certainly did not resolve any of them. If anything, in the years since, the debate over who belongs in Britain and who does not, who in its past should be celebrated and who demoted, which aspects of its history might still be in need of revision and which should remain untouched, has only grown more fervent and more divisive.

Conclusion

Where We're Going, We Don't Need Rhodes

On 8 September 2022, a little after midday, BBC1 interrupted *Bargain Hunt* to cut abruptly to a newsreader announcing that the Queen was under medical supervision at her Scottish residence, Balmoral. The rolling coverage continued all afternoon, as a variety of studio guests proceeded to fill time with speculation about the monarch's health, and commentary about her life and reign. At 6.30 p.m., a shot of the Union Jack flying at half-mast was followed by veteran broadcaster Huw Edwards, sombre in a black tie, announcing that Queen Elizabeth II had died peacefully at the age of ninety-six. She was the oldest and longest-reigning monarch that Britain had ever seen.

Over the coming days, the new prime minister, Liz Truss, and countless newspaper and magazine headlines spoke of a 'second Elizabethan age', in which the Queen had overseen a fundamental transition in British politics, society and culture. The seventy years of her reign had indeed seen great change. But while narrating the history of Britain from the 1950s to the beginning of the next century from the perspective of the Queen and royal family might make for an immensely popular Netflix series, for any modern historian such an insistent framing of British politics through the life and reign of a constitutional figurehead struck a jarring note. It overlooked prime ministers and politics ('the Attlee years', the 'social democratic consensus'), social changes and movements (the welfare state, the women's movement), cultural and demographic upheaval (the 'Swinging Sixties'). But this was not a mistake, or a coincidence. The Queen was being celebrated for her unchanging steadfastness, as the only constant in a world full of change. As the

Archbishop of York, Stephen Cottrell, said in his tribute in the *Yorkshire Post*, she had been a 'constant anchor' in the lives of the British people, 'through the turbulence and changing waters of the postwar period'.[1] The Queen was the antidote to the historical twists and turns that made so many British people feel uneasy.

Such feelings were very much to do with empire and decolonisation. The Queen was frequently credited with having 'championed the development of the Commonwealth', as Liz Truss said in her speech from Downing Street when the news was announced: 'from a small group of seven countries to a family of fifty-six nations spanning every continent of the world'. In other words, the Queen kept the spirit and to some extent the reality of empire alive. The news coverage of world leaders paying their respects highlighted statements from Justin Trudeau (Canada), Jacinda Ardern (New Zealand) and Anthony Albanese (Australia), and this 'kith and kin' Commonwealth was again emphasised during the funeral coverage – at one point, Trudeau and Ardern were picked out of the procession by the BBC commentary for the viewing public, ignoring entirely the presence of the Jamaican prime minister, Andrew Holness, walking between them. The BBC also produced a video package for social media highlighting the Queen's 'longstanding relationship with Africa', a characterisation of the relationship between monarchy and empire that at best sanitised and at worst obfuscated the nature of imperial rule. It was mostly international media outlets that drew any connection between the Queen and the reality of Britain's imperial legacy. American media, with its love–hate relationship to the British monarchy, was especially keen on this angle: the *Washington Post*, for example, mentioned the 'ugly truths' about British colonial brutality under her reign, NBC pointed out that the Queen was not a 'gentle figurehead' for people in former colonies with reporting from New Delhi, while Sunny Hostin, the co-host of *The View*, described the monarchy as 'built on the backs of black and brown people'.

The British monarchy and the British empire have always been fundamentally intertwined. Much of Britain's imperial expansion was undertaken in the name of Queen Victoria, Empress of India from 1877, whose birthday was adopted as Empire Day. Filmed footage of her funeral – which took place in the middle of the Boer War, the first royal military and state funeral, setting the tone for royal burials since – was screened across the empire in London, Bombay, Cape Town, Auckland and Singapore. When Queen Elizabeth ascended to the throne in 1953, she did so as the head of an empire that was diminished but not yet defeated. In the days following her death, the speech she had made on her twenty-first birthday, in which she declared that 'my whole life, whether it be long or short, shall be devoted to your service and the service of our great imperial family to which we all belong', became one of the overwhelming symbols of the Queen's reign. It was quoted on the order of service for an event of 'prayer and reflection' at St Paul's Cathedral that was attended by Liz Truss and 2,000 mourners the day after the Queen had died, and was repeatedly featured in broadcast news, magazine pieces, and tweets by organisations such as English Heritage and the Royal Collection Trust.[2]

Simon Schama, in his piece for the *Financial Times*, was one of the only people to mention that this speech had been made during a trip to Cape Town.[3] The rest of the speech, in which she recounted her recent travels around the two white bastions of South Africa and Rhodesia as the 'great privilege belonging to our place in the world-wide commonwealth', in which she and her family could find 'homes ready to welcome us in every continent of the earth', did not become part of the memorial soundbite. By many accounts the Queen took her role as the Commonwealth leader seriously, having Commonwealth symbols embroidered on her coronation gown, encouraging the holding of multi-faith services in Britain to mark Commonwealth Day from the 1960s, and generally taking an interest in Commonwealth affairs that went beyond her constitutional duties as head of the organisation. But to describe her as the benign architect of this transition from empire to Commonwealth is to ignore the very obvious fact that the main engines of this shift were the victories of decolonising movements across the colonies and the gradual defeat of Britain as an imperial power.

The role of the monarch in the Commonwealth is itself not without controversy. The Queen was head of the organisation, but this was not a title with a clear line of succession: it was not until 2018 that it was confirmed that Prince Charles would take over its leadership at the point of her death. Fifteen of the countries in the organisation are Commonwealth realms, meaning that they had the Queen – and now the King – as their head of state; thirty-six are republics, while Brunei, Eswatini (Swaziland), Lesotho, Malaysia and Tonga have their own monarchies. The process by which countries in the Commonwealth might shift from monarchy to republic often forces a confrontation with the legacies of imperialism and the monarchy's role within it. In November 2021, at the ceremony at which Barbados became the sixteenth Commonwealth nation to shrug off the British monarch's leadership, Prince Charles made a sympathetic speech in which he condemned the 'appalling atrocity of slavery' that 'forever stains our history'; despite this, the royal family has never officially apologised for its role in British imperialism.[4] On the death of the Queen, the debate over republicanism was immediately reinvigorated in Jamaica and Australia.

Just as the Queen Mother's coffin had been adorned with a crown decorated with the Koh-i-noor diamond, so the Queen lay in state under the Sovereign's Sceptre and the Imperial State Crown; both contain stones cut from the Cullinan Diamond, the 'Great Star of Africa' that is the largest gem-quality rough diamond ever discovered, presented by Louis Botha to Edward VII in 1905. The Queen made more than two hundred visits to Commonwealth countries during her reign, and these visits had been covered in Britain with a strong sense that her presence was welcomed and encouraged by her loving subjects; a trip to Jamaica in 1994, for example, was depicted in the *Daily Telegraph* as a chance for the country – which had already indicated its desire to become a republic at this time – to 'indulge in a little star-struck nostalgia'.[5] In fact, it was more obviously the royal family itself that was indulging in imperial nostalgia, with a sustained relationship to the British empire that could see Prince William's twenty-first birthday party, for example, adopt the theme 'Out of Africa', set in a specially created 'jungle at Windsor Castle' and featuring guests swathed in leopard print and sporting pith helmets.[6] And yet, what the Queen's death made starkly apparent is that they were not alone. For all those whose attitudes to and experiences of empire might have changed over the last fifty years, there are many for whom imperialism has remained an unwavering constant.

Since 2016, there has been much discussion in Britain about its imperial history. Some argue that it has been hidden, whitewashed and ignored; others that it has been misunderstood, misjudged by anachronistic standards and misrepresented. Those on both sides of these debates believe that history has been twisted and that Britain runs the risk of losing or erasing its historical identity. In truth, history can be rewritten – it should be rewritten, and this is the job of historians – but the past cannot be erased. And as many of these recent debates about Britain's past and its heritage have shown, British history and imperial history cannot be separated.

The retrocession of Hong Kong on 1 July 1997 was the final act of formal decolonisation of the twentieth century. But this did not mean that the empire was over and done with. British imperialism still exists – and not just in the sense of British soft power or a cultural hangover in films, television programmes and interior design choices. Britain is still a colonial power because Britain still administers an empire: there are currently 270,000-odd people around the world living in the fourteen remaining British Overseas Territories (BOTs). These vary hugely in size and population, from around 68,000 people in the Cayman Islands, that offshore financial haven for so many British companies, to around fifty people in the Pitcairn Islands, which were originally settled by the descendants of the mutiny on the *Bounty*. Three of the BOTs have no permanent inhabitants: the British Antarctic Territory, which hosts scientists from around the world but has no indigenous population; South Georgia and the South Sandwich Islands, administered as a Falklands Island Dependency until 1985 and still strongly connected to the Falklands by economics and shipping; and the British Indian Ocean Territory, midway between Tanzania and Indonesia. Another name for the British Indian Ocean Territory is the Chagos Peninsula. It was not always uninhabited. And the story of the people who lived there shows that violence of empire continues to reverberate to this day.

There had been a British imperial presence in the Chagos Peninsula from 1814; the islands were largely used as plantations to produce copra, the dried white flesh from coconuts processed into fats and animal feed. Rooted in this history, the population of the islands included a migrant workforce, originally from Mauritius or the Seychelles, and those who had been born on the islands, who called themselves Chagossians. In 1962, the Salomon Atoll, and the islands of Diego Garcia, Peros Banhos, and Agaléga – all part of the British Mauritius colonial territory – were acquired by Chagos-Agalega Company Ltd, who wished to revitalise the coconut plantations, in an echo of the nineteenth-century history of imperial 'companies' that had run the islands and many other colonial regions a century before. But two years later, the British and American governments began to discuss a different fate for the peninsula as part of the US–UK defence strategy. In November 1965, the British government purchased the islands, splitting them off from Mauritius – which would be granted independence three years later – to form the British Indian Ocean Territory (BIOT); the next year, Britain agreed to lease the BIOT to the Americans for fifty years to use as a military base, in return for a discount on the Polaris missile system.

The fate of the Chagossians in all of this was essentially disregarded by the British. One minute produced by the UK mission to the UN claimed that the islands had 'no indigenous population except seagulls who have not yet got a [UN] committee (the Status of Women Committee does not cover the rights of Birds)'. Denis Greenhill, then assistant undersecretary to the Foreign Office, scribbled on the memo that this wasn't quite correct: 'along with the birds go some Tarzans or Men Fridays whose origins are obscure'.[7] But despite knowing that around a thousand people lived on the islands, the government spent little time thinking about their future. Once the United States had taken possession of the peninsula, the British employed a variety of tactics to make the Chagossians leave; those who had temporarily left the islands, for example on holiday, were not allowed to return, food and medical supplies were restricted, all of the pet dogs on the islands were killed as part of the process of 'sanitising' the territory for the United States. Eventually, the Chagossians were forced to leave, first going to Peros Banhos and then to Mauritius; the people born on the islands and their children born between 1969 and 1982 held British citizenship, with this right being reiterated in the 2002 British Overseas Territories Act, and many of them made their way to the United Kingdom. Today, there are around 10,000 people from the Chagos Islands split between Britain and Mauritius, with around 3,000 settled in Crawley, in West Sussex.

The Chagossians have been fighting against British imperialism on two fronts ever since: firstly, the right of their children born after 1982 to claim British citizenship, and secondly, their right to return to the islands. In 2000, the UK High Court ruled that the Chagossians could return to the islands; in 2004 the British government used royal prerogative to overturn this ruling; in 2007, in turn, the High Court ruled that this royal prerogative was itself unlawful. In 2009, the UK government established a 'marine protection area' around the peninsula. Leaked government cables from the US Embassy in Britain showed that the British government was using this environmental concern as a smokescreen – 'BIOT's former inhabitants would find it difficult, if not impossible, to pursue their claim for resettlement on the islands if the entire Chagos Archipelago were a marine reserve' – and recorded the FCO's director of overseas territories, Colin Roberts, stating firmly that the UK did 'not regret the removal of the population'.[8] In 2019, the United Nations accepted a judgement from the International Court of Justice that the Chagos Islands had been unlawfully detached from Mauritius upon independence and that the British had no continued right to use the islands.

In February 2022, five Chagossians made the first trip to the islands unsupervised by British authorities; Olivier Bancoult, who took his parents' birth certificates to the islands in a symbolic gesture of exile, made a comparison with the much more favourable treatment of the Falkland Islanders by the British government, asking, 'Is it because we are black?'[9] The Chagossians have also faced discrimination in the UK based on their claim to citizenship, as the British government argued that citizenship could only be conferred to one generation abroad. This left young people such as Taniella and Nesta Moustache, who had lived in Milton Keynes since childhood, facing deportation to Mauritius when they turned eighteen; the girls' grandmother had been forcibly evicted from the islands, their mother had been born with British citizenship, but the UK government insisted that they must apply for the right to hold a UK passport or leave the country.[10] In 2022, in response to constant campaigning from the community, the government passed the Nationality and Borders Bill which clarified the Chagossian entitlement to British nationality. Adult direct descendants of those expelled from the islands were given five years in which to apply for British citizenship without a fee, while those under the age of eighteen or born before 2028 would have until they turned twenty-three to make this claim.

The Chagos Islanders have been caught between Britain's imperial history and its commitments to the Anglo-American 'special relationship'. The callous disregard for their identity as British *imperial* citizens by a series of governments who refuse to allow them either to return home or to remain in the metropole is an important reminder of the continuing legacies of imperial power in British politics and culture. This community and their struggle demonstrate the way that empire functions in twenty-first-century Britain: an Empire 2.0, in which Britain simultaneously denies its own imperial heritage and continues to operate as an empire both at home and overseas.

The fate of the Chagos Islanders provides an important parallel for another seismic moment in Britain's reckoning with its recent imperial past. In October 2017, the journalist Amelia Gentleman was contacted by the Refugee and Migrant Centre, a small charity in Wolverhampton, with a story about one of their clients. Paulette Wilson, a retired chef who had worked at one time in the House of Commons, was being threatened with deportation by the Home Office. Paulette had lived in Britain since 1968, when she was ten years old. She had been to school in Britain, raised her daughter in Britain, worked and paid tax and national insurance for thirty-four years. She was a stalwart community volunteer who now spent her time making weekly meals for homeless people at her local church. But the Home Office was unconvinced that she had a right to live in the UK, and Paulette was detained in Yarl's Wood, the infamous women's immigration detention centre, for a week, before being sent to an immigration removal centre at Heathrow Airport for deportation. At the last minute, her MP and the Refugee and Migrant Centre were able to convince authorities that she should be allowed to return home – but she was told that she would have to report to the Home Office again in December. The charity had contacted Gentleman because they were worried that this second meeting might again result in Paulette being detained and eventually deported to a country she had not lived in for fifty years.[11]

It has been estimated that roughly 50,000 former colonial migrants were swept up in the government policies, started under Theresa May's tenure as Home Secretary and continuing into her time as prime minister, which aimed to make the UK a 'hostile environment' for illegal immigration.[12] Harassed about their right to work in Britain when getting a new job, forced to prove their citizenship before being allowed access to medical care, or threatened with deportation, a whole generation – almost universally people of colour – found themselves suddenly unable to live comfortably in the country they had called home for decades. Eventually, the scandal – driven in large part by the reporting in the *Guardian* by Gentleman and Gary Younge, but also by the work of charities such as Praxis and politicians such as David Lammy and Jamaican High Commissioner Seth George Ramocan – forced a government climbdown. May apologised to the 'Windrush generation' and Caribbean leaders in April 2018, saying she did not want 'anybody to be in any doubt about their right to remain in the United Kingdom'. A little more than a week later Amber Rudd, the Home Secretary when the scandal was exposed, resigned after a leaked document showed that she had been aware of deportation targets, taking the bullet for her leader. In May 2018, Rudd's successor, Sajid Javid, admitted to a Home Affairs Select Committee that more than sixty people might have been wrongfully deported under the scheme. In November 2021, it was reported in a document produced by a cross-party group of MPs that only 5 per cent of eligible Windrush victims had received compensation from the government.[13]

The name Windrush evokes something positive – hard-working Commonwealth citizens who wanted to come to the 'motherland' and help reconstruct it after the horrors of the Second World War. For the activists working to support the people whose citizenship was under threat, it made strategic sense to refer to these people as the 'Windrush generation'. But the fact is that most of those concerned had arrived in Britain at least a decade after 1948, and many of them had come not from Jamaica or even the wider Caribbean but from India, Pakistan, Sierra Leone, Uganda, Nigeria.

Other misconceptions are apparent in the arguments used to support their continued life in the UK. Often the stories focused on what 'good immigrants' they had been, working hard, paying taxes to the British state, often caring for British patients, teaching British children or building British homes. Many narratives focused on the length of time that people had been living in Britain, and spoke about the disparity between these thirty-, forty- or fifty-year experiences and the much shorter time period – seven years – required for a naturalisation application. These details helped convey the moral injustice of being deported 'home' to a country you have not visited in decades, and the iniquity of having to prove your citizenship to a state which has been happily taking your taxes for years. But this elided the fact that almost all of the 'Windrush generation' who were being discussed in the press were not 'immigrants' to Britain, nor did they need an invitation to come to the country, or to prove their worth to remain through tax receipts and clean criminal records. They were Citizens of the United Kingdom and Colonies (CUKCs): when they arrived, they had the right to live in Britain as citizens. And yet they had been trapped in a Kafkaesque nightmare, in which they had to prove that they had the right to live in a country that had been their home for decades, and in which their right to remain had been so fundamentally accepted that they were without documents to prove this was the case.

Then, partway through the Windrush Scandal news coverage, the *Guardian* made its discovery that the Home Office had destroyed the original Windrush landing cards, as well as landing cards of other arrivals from the Caribbean and other former colonies, in October 2010. The destruction of these records was sparked by the closure of a Home Office site in Croydon; the department claimed in a public statement that they had destroyed the material in line with data protection laws. But this act of elimination was also symbolic of the British state's relationship to its own past. It dealt a terrible blow to individuals who might have been able to use these documents to prove their citizenship, but it also removed the link between these 'ordinary' people and their past, erasing their ability to point to an archive and say, look, there I was: here I am.

From the perspective of a historian, the Windrush Scandal showed the consequences of Britain's hiding, erasing and failing to understand the gritty details of its own imperialism. Even many of those who were sympathetic to the plight of the deportees did not properly understand the imperial context that had given these people the right to live and work in Britain. In 2022, it was revealed that the Home Office had commissioned, and then suppressed, a report by an unnamed historian that had explored the 'historical roots' of the Windrush Scandal. The report had concluded that the Home Office's 'deep-rooted racism' had originated in the fact that 'during the period 1950–1981, every single piece of immigration or citizenship legislation was designed at least in part to reduce the number of people with black or brown skin who were permitted to live and work in the UK'.[14] The report, which was made available internally but was not seen by outsiders – even after repeated FOI requests – until it was leaked, was completed in the context of the Home Office's commitment to teaching its 3,500 staff about the history of the British empire and of Black British people. In 2022, it was also discovered that the government department had tried to 'sanitise' a module on race, empire and colonialism created by the University of Coventry for this purpose; Professor Jason Arday, who had been contracted to contribute to the module said that academics were 'being asked to engage in historical amnesia'.[15]

Britain's historical amnesia when it comes to empire was challenged during the summer of 2020 when, in the midst of global protests following the murder of George Floyd by a white police officer in Minneapolis in May 2020, activists threw a bronze statue into Bristol harbour and sparked a national conversation about how history should be marked, how the past should be remembered, and who could make, defend or amend the historical record. The removal of this statue was in fact the culmination of many years of local protest and controversy about its presence, and the act represented a reimagining of the relationship between Bristol's imperial past and the local community.

Edward Colston, born in Bristol in 1636, was a cosmopolitan merchant; from an already wealthy family, he increased his capital by importing oils and wine from the Iberian peninsula, and trading textiles from London to Tangiers and cod from Newfoundland to Naples. He was an imperial and a global subject, a reminder that the British have always looked outwards as well as inwards. But describing Colston as a 'merchant' elides one of the most profitable of his enterprises. From the 1680s, Colston was also a slave trader. He was a member of the Royal African Company (RAC), which held a monopoly on the slave trade until 1698, serving on its Court of Assistants and briefly acting as its deputy governor. He played key roles in the work of the RAC, for example leading the negotiations with the Spanish government over the 'Assiento for Negroes', the contract for supplying slaves to the Hispanic new world colonies. During Colston's tenure, the company enslaved almost 90,000 men, women and children and exiled them from West Africa to the Caribbean. Almost 19,000 of them did not survive the journey; the rest were forced into slavery, on plantations owned by British companies that provided the metropole and the world with sugar, molasses, rum.

Colston grew rich from the profits of this brutal economy, and used this wealth to control – and whitewash – his reputation in life and his memory in death. He spent his money on workhouses and almshouses to support the poor and needy; hospitals to treat the sick and churches to save their souls; schools to educate the young, particularly those in his home city of Bristol, where he was also an MP for several years. On Colston's death in 1721, much of his fortune was left to charities, to be spent in Bristol and around the nation; he was remembered, in the eighteenth century and perhaps particularly by the Victorians, as a philanthropist.

The statue of Colston standing in Bristol harbour was a figure cast in bronze by John Cassidy, and had been erected in 1895 by the Anchor Society after the president, James Arrowsmith, decided it would be fitting to commemorate Colston as an early imperial hero. Several appeals were made to the public, including the pupils and alumni of the Colston School, to raise the necessary funds, but donations were slow; eventually a wealthy anonymous donor (possibly Arrowsmith himself) made up the shortfall. Other organisations including the Society of Merchant Venturers were persuaded to contribute after the statue was unveiled by the mayor on 13 November (declared 'Colston Day'). The statue portrays Colston in middle age, and there are three decorative reliefs around the plinth; one shows him dispensing charity to poor children, one depicts him at the harbour where the statue is located, and one is a sea scene, with mermaids and anchors, to represent his seafaring history.

There is no particular indication that the statue of Colston was venerated by the people of Bristol for whose benefit it had been erected, although photographs of the unveiling show a substantial crowd. The statue was erected, of course, at the height of Victorian imperial fervour, when the state sought to embed imperialist and patriotic ideals among its domestic population. In 1899, Britain went to war in South Africa against the Boers and the country exploded in a feverish display of jingoism and colonial excitement. Statues went up around the country, including one in Bristol on Queen's Road, to celebrate the British imperial forces; a Boer War soldier stands on a plinth in the middle of a traffic island, holding a rifle in his left hand, retrieving a cartridge with his right. The unveiling of this statue also drew a crowd, much larger than the one attending Colston; the plinth below the soldier lists 251 names of men who died fighting for the Gloucestershire Regiment.

In 1920, a progressive Anglican vicar, Reverend H. J. Wilkins, went into the archives and published a study into Colston's life, which highlighted his role in the slave trade and questioned whether it was appropriate that he be commemorated so enthusiastically in Bristol. By this point, it was not just the statue that held up Colston's memory; many streets were named for him, and so was the concert hall, which had been built using Colston's money in 1867 but had been acquired by Bristol Corporation (later the city council) at the end of the First World War. Wilkins stated baldly in his book that 'Colston engaged in the African slave trade'.

> Still, it has been written that from the latter part of the seventeenth century, when the nature of the slave trade began to be understood by the public (Colston must have known very much earlier) all that was best in England was adverse to it. The wish cannot but arise that Edward Colston had been found among 'all that was best in England'. But Colston was not a 'man of vision'. His sympathies were narrow and did not go out to mankind in general.[16]

In 1977, the statue was listed, and therefore protected in heritage and planning laws from being defaced, amended or removed. But there remained a significant degree of criticism. In 1992, the cities of Liverpool, Hull and Bristol joined together to host an artist commission entitled 'Trophies of Empire', intended to explore the legacies of imperialism for the three port cities. At the Arnolfini gallery in Bristol, Carole Drake – who had been educated at Colston Girls' School – exhibited a mixed-media piece, *Commemoration Day*, directly addressing Colston's legacy. Drake projected an image of schoolgirls climbing on Colston's statue on the wall of the gallery, above a sea of chrysanthemums (Colston's favourite flower, worn by the girls at his eponymous school every year on Commemoration Day) left to die over the course of the exhibition. From the ceiling, a replica of Colston's statue was hung by its neck, casting a grim shadow over the projection. Drake explained that her piece was addressing Bristol's amnesia about Colston and his violent imperial history: 'into this dark hole had been sucked the histories of thousands of black children, men and women, sacrificed a second time in order to present an uncomplicated, unsullied image of Colston as a benign patriarch'.[17]

In 1998, the plinth below Colston's statue was graffited with the words FUCK OFF SLAVE TRADER. That same year, Massive Attack refused to play a gig at the Colston Hall, with band member Robert Del Naja arguing that 'it should be renamed and not celebrate someone who took part in the slave trade'.[18] Local politicians were also active in this debate. Ray Sefia had been elected to the council in 1995, where he served as the only Black councillor until 2000. In the discussions about how to respond to the graffiti, Sefia said: 'If we in this city want to glorify the slave trade, then the statue should stay. If not, the statue should be marked with a plaque that he was a slave trader or taken down.'[19] In his view, it was as inappropriate to have a statue of Colston in the city as it would be to have a statue of Hitler.

The citizens of Bristol did not unanimously agree. As late as 2014, the *Bristol Post* surveyed its readers to see their feelings about the statue: 56 per cent of the 1,100 respondents wanted it to stay, compared with 44 per cent who wanted it gone. And yet there were many who made their dislike of the statue, and what it represented, visible. In 2017, white paint was daubed over Colston's face; in 2018, a red knitted ball and chain was attached to his leg. That year, local campaigners sought to add a second plaque to the statue that included a description of Colston's trade in enslaved peoples; this followed the removal of an 'unauthorised' plaque, modelled on the English Heritage blue plaques, which proclaimed that Bristol was 'capital of the Atlantic Slave Trade 1730–1745' and sought to commemorate the '12,000,000 enslaved of whom 6,000,000 died as captives'.

The proposal for an authorised second plaque went through three separate drafts. The second version, which stated that Colston 'played an active role in the enslavement of over 84,000 Africans' was criticised by a Conservative councillor for being 'revisionist' and 'historically-illiterate'.[20] The wording was duly watered down until it said only that 'a significant proportion of Colston's wealth came from investments in slave trading, sugar and other slave-produced goods', which meant that its installation was vetoed by Marvin Rees, Bristol's mayor at the time. Rees criticised the charity in charge of the changes for trying to bypass 'the mayor of a city whose wealth has been inseparable from slavery and plantations and who is himself the descendant of enslaved Africans'.[21]

And so the statue remained unaltered, the centre of local controversy but rarely puncturing national consciousness until, on 7 June 2020, protesters put a noose around its neck, daubed it in paint, pulled it down, rolled it along Anchor Road, and pushed it into Bristol harbour. When called upon for comment, Rees said he felt 'no sense of loss' at its removal.

In contrast, the Home Secretary, Priti Patel, condemned the protest as an 'utterly disgraceful' act of 'sheer vandalism'.[22] There was much hand-wringing over whether the removal of the statue was an attempt to erase and destroy history itself; the right-wing think tank Policy Exchange conducted opinion polling which they argued showed that more than three-quarters of Britons 'believe we should learn from history rather than rewrite it' and in which the people surveyed complained they had had enough of a 'minority' of people having a say in whether monuments were preserved. To address this, the influential organisation launched their 'History Matters' project in which they encouraged people to report to them 'examples where public memory is being rewritten', for instance when 'certain historical subjects, or people, are deemed to be too controversial for a public setting such as a museum or town square', or examples of 'one-sided' textbooks, curricula or museum exhibits.[23] The one-sided nature of a statue celebrating a slave trader did not seem to occur to them.

In January 2022, the four campaigners charged with criminal damage for toppling the Colston statue were acquitted in a surprise verdict in their trial by jury. In the closing statements, the defence for one of the activists, Liam Walker, argued that 'The removal of the statue was not an attempt to erase history, the erection of the statue was an attempt to erase history'. This type of argument had short shrift with the prime minister, Boris Johnson, who blustered that removing a statue was 'like some person trying to edit their Wikipedia entry – it's wrong' and that 'you can't . . . go around seeking retrospectively to change our history or to bowdlerise it or edit it in retrospect', seemingly ignorant of the fact that historians do indeed edit material on Wikipedia and in published books.[24] History is, at its heart, the work of constantly re-evaluating accounts of the past.

The Colston Must Fall campaign was a moment of spontaneous historiographical intervention, rooted in a local community. But it also drew heavily on the work of another campaign, which started in 2015 in South Africa, where a large statue of Cecil Rhodes stands at the University of Cape Town, and which was taken up in other locations, notably Oriel College, Oxford, which has a prominent statue of Rhodes affixed to its building overlooking the high street. In 2016, despite a committed campaign of student protests, a report was leaked that showed Oriel felt unable to remove the statue because it risked losing £100 million in funding from alumni donations. Polling by YouGov, which explained that 'Cecil Rhodes was an important British colonialist, politician and businessman in the

19th century, largely responsible for Britain's colonisation of southern Africa' but that 'Some people think that Rhodes is symbolic of the racism and unfairness of British colonialism, and that is inappropriate to continue to have statues and memorials to him', found that 59 per cent of British people wanted the statue to remain in place.[25] In 2020, after new protests in the context of the Black Lives Matter movement, the college agreed to remove the statue but then immediately backtracked because of the threat of 'regulatory and financial challenges'.[26]

These challenges were posed largely by the British government. In response to the lively debates about which parts of British imperial history should be allowed to loom over public spaces, the Conservative government made adjustments to planning law that made it harder to remove material heritage. Paragraph 198 of the National Planning Policy Framework, inserted in 2021, now says:

> In considering any applications to remove or alter a historical memorial or monument (whether listed or not), local planning authorities should have regard to the importance of their retention in situ and, where appropriate, of explaining their social and historical context rather than removal.

It was partly these changes, proposed by the government in 2020, which made Oriel College so concerned about the removal of the statue, which would be subject to planning permission as part of a listed building. And if an enterprising protester felt that, like Colston, perhaps Rhodes could be induced to fall from the building without Oriel's permission, they would be subject to the new provision in the Police, Crime, Sentencing and Courts Act 2022 which increased the potential prison sentence for damaging a memorial from three months to ten years. This enormous increase was justified by the Home Office because previous law did 'not provide enough powers to allow the court to deal effectively with the desecration of war memorials and other statues', with an explicit statement that 'the issue re-emerged during summer 2020 when many statues and memorials were damaged causing great concern to the wider public'; there had previously been 'insufficient consideration given to the emotional or wider distress caused by this type of offending'.[27]

There is of course an intentional blurriness here between a statue and a 'memorial'; criminal damage to a statue of a slave trader surely has a very different emotional register than vandalism of a war memorial, for example. But the government justifies its heavy-handed protection of such statues, not as sites of heritage or commemoration, but as the protection of the truth: destroying or removing a statue has become synonymous with destroying history itself. And so Rhodes is caught in limbo, always falling, but never fallen.

The government maintains that its preferred approach to the past is to 'retain and explain': objects, statues and other historical artefacts should not be removed from display but should be annotated with more up-to-date analysis of their place in history and their complex connections to topics such as empire and slavery. So for example the British Museum has produced a 'Collecting and Empire' trail, which visitors can follow by using a specially produced guide, which states clearly that the museum's 'history and collection are intimately linked to that of the British Empire', which was sustained by 'the transatlantic slave trade and the colonial exploitation of people and resources'. The trail itself stops short of really interrogating this history, however: one item, a West African drum, 'was taken' to Virginia 'during the period of the slave trade' before it 'came' to the British Museum; another, a shield from New South Wales, was 'collected' during 'the early days of the British colony at Sydney' before it was 'received' by the museum.[28] Neither of these descriptions really unpick the ways in which colonial violence shaped the acquisition of these two items, nor the ways in which the continued possession of them might itself represent a form of continued violence or imperialism.

But the government is not really interested in the 'explain' element of retain and explain, as was shown by the outcry when the National Trust published their 'Interim Report on the Connections between Colonialism and Properties now in the Care of the National Trust,

Including Links with Historic Slavery' in 2020. This report sought to establish and contextualise the connections between National Trust properties and the transatlantic slave trade. A week after it was released, Oliver Dowden, the culture secretary, warned museums that they 'should not be taking actions motivated by activism or politics', hinting that if they removed 'contentious' artefacts they might find their funding cut in the upcoming Government Spending Review.[29] On 13 February 2021, he announced to the *Telegraph* that he had summoned twenty-five heritage organisations to a meeting at which they would be told 'to defend our culture and history from the noisy minority of activists constantly trying to do Britain down'. It was also hinted that the government might intervene to stop heritage organisations or academics from doing research on these topics, because 'public funds must never be used for political purposes'.[30] Again, the definition here of 'political' is simply any work with historical narratives that go against the government's preferred interpretation of the past.

It seems that when the British government, and much of the British museum establishment, thinks of Britain's cultural heritage, the empire is included as a benign provider of objects for display cases, paintings for gallery walls, and curiosities for family heirlooms. Britain is seen as the best place for them, and the British as the only people who can either protect or appreciate these items properly. The idea that these objects should be returned – that they might belong to anyone other than the British – is treated as laughable; the notion that they might have been acquired in anything other than the most understandable of circumstances is dismissed as offensive. It is particularly galling to remember that much of this material is not actually on display: when the British refuse to return colonial items, they are arguing that their desire to hold material in a cold storeroom is more important than a community's wish to have returned their cultural heritage that was stolen as spoils of war. But the fact that some institutions are starting to question these received wisdoms indicates a tangible shift in public opinion, occasioned at least partly by a wider understanding of which voices are allowed to be included as part of the 'public' in the first place.

For as long as Britain is committed to a version of history that doesn't tell the whole truth, it will be a nation trapped in its past. The world today does not map onto the future Britain once imagined for itself, and British politics, culture and identity are still being worked out under the shadow of an empire that has not existed, really, for half a century. Understanding Britain's past – as a nation, as an empire, and most of all as a collection of millions of messy, tangled individual lives – can help us to understand who we are today, and how we got here. The British people as a whole tend to be resistant, when asked outright, about any reappraisal of their nation's imperial past; YouGov polling from 2016 showed that only 19 per cent felt that the empire was 'a bad thing' and 44 per cent felt that the nation should be 'proud' of its imperial history. Around the same number of people agreed with the statement that 'Britain tends to view our history of colonisation too positively – there was much cruelty, killing, injustice and racism that we try not to talk about' as agreed with the idea that 'Britain tends to view our history of colonisation too negatively – we talk too much about the cruelty and racism of Empire, and ignore the good that it did' – 29 to 28 per cent – and another third felt that the British got the balance 'between the good and bad sides' about right.[31] And yet hidden within these statistics are many people who dearly wish that these conversations about our ancestors could be more nuanced, and capture more completely their own family histories of empire, migration and identity.

The Royal Docks closed for general cargo handling in 1981, in which year the London Docklands Development Corporation was established to aid the regeneration of an isolated, impoverished and desolate area of London; just down the road, the creation of the new financial centre and shrine to neoliberalism in Canary Wharf began in 1988. Blocks of housing now crept right up to the edges of the water, along with London City Airport (opened in 1987) and the Excel Centre, opened in 2000, a vast conference centre intended to replace Earls Court and owned since 2008 by the Abu Dhabi National Exhibitions Company. The area is connected to the rest of the London transport network by the Docklands Light Railway, which has several stops that run along the top of the old docks, and the Jubilee Line at Canning Town as well as local bus services.

In 2012, a month before the opening ceremony of the Olympic Games, a new mode of transport was introduced to the area. The London Cable Car connects Custom House to North Greenwich, site of the Millennium Dome, and takes passengers high above both the docks and the River Thames. The name of the cable car for its first decade in existence was the Emirates Air Line, as it was sponsored in a ten-year, £36 million deal by the Dubai-based airline; both the cable car and the Excel Centre thus reflected the dominance in London finance markets of the United Arab Emirates, a British protectorate until 1971. Empire can come home in many forms.

The cable car is largely a tourist attraction rather than a feasible mode of transport, given that it connects two areas already essentially linked by the Jubilee Line. But the views over London are undeniably impressive, even on a grey day: the docks, the airport, Canary Wharf, the green edges of London to the south and the urban centre to the west. Gently swinging above the water, passengers can also choose to soundtrack the journey by listening to an audio installation created by the British-Ghanaian artist Larry Achiampong as part of The Line art walk and sculpture trail. *Sanko-time* is an audio collage that is 'infused with the sounds and rhythms of Accra and London', two cities connected by the meridian line that, Achiampong points out, was itself a mechanism of imperial control. The material used includes oral histories taken from the Museum of London archive, snippets of workshops with the pupils of St Mary Magdalene C of E Primary School in nearby Greenwich, and field recordings from London and Accra, including the lapping water of both the fishing harbour in Accra and the docks over which the cable car is suspended.[32] The sounds 'rise and fall to reveal the imprints of histories and the colonial past in our present'; the title comes from the Twi word 'sankofa', which implies using the past to prepare for the future.

The audio is supported with a second artwork, a flag, entitled *What I Hear I Keep*, although visitors in the autumn of 2022 who wanted to see the flag would be disappointed. A note on the website explained that, 'following the death of Queen Elizabeth II', it had been temporarily removed and would be reinstated after the funeral had been held; none of the other artworks on The Line were affected by the death of the monarch and there was no explanation as to why this was the case for the Achiampong piece.

Perhaps it was simply that flying a flag, any flag, at full mast after the death of a monarch felt distasteful. It may have been coincidence that the *Sanko-time* audio does much to interrogate the connections between the docks, the monarchy and the empire. Stating that 'these royal docks were previously a celebrated global centre for innovation and industry. But for many, they still represent the stink of colonialism', Achiampong's narration goes on to list some of the major institutions – Tate & Lyle (located right next to the docks) but also Oxford and Cambridge universities, Lloyds of London, the British Museum 'and so much more across this island nation' – who had built their fortunes on slavery.

What *Sanko-time* makes so brilliantly clear is how the docks remain a space where the history of Newham and the history of the British empire are intertwined and overwritten. Where there was once a busy trade route funded and enabled by a brutal and overwhelming empire, now the water quietly laps in front of hotels and cafes as wild swimmers brave the cold and dive in off a wooden dock. But the imperial history remains; the docks are soaked in it.

In 2022, after years of existing only as a periphery to the real London, the Royal Docks regained some of the city's political power. The Greater London Authority, the mayor's office and the London Assembly, formerly located in a Norman Foster-designed spherical building near the Tower of London, moved to a new angular glass home right in front of the docks, next to the cable car and the wild swimming pontoon. Overseeing this move was Sadiq Khan, whose family moved to London from Pakistan in 1968 and who was a human rights lawyer fighting cases that – among other things – highlighted institutional racial discrimination in the Metropolitan Police, the NHS and Oxford University before becoming a Labour MP and, in 2016, London

Mayor, the first Muslim mayor of a major Western capital city. The relocation of London City Hall from the south bank of the Thames to the Royal Docks was largely a financial decision, intended to save the Greater London Authority money on rent. But it was also symbolic, moving the centre of the capital's power from the literal centre to a space that had until recently been so neglected. And yet of course the docks had once, too, been at the heart of a London that was itself the heart of an empire.

July 2021 was the centenary of the completion of the docks, and to mark the occasion the local history society and a local bookshop were invited to work with the dockland authorities to rename the street on which the new City Hall stands. More than 1,500 people voted, rejecting the anodyne 'World's Gate Way' and 'People's Way' for a name that explicitly reflected the local history of empire, migration, race and community. Imperial statues still stand in the same tree-muffled squares – for now – but London's new City Hall stands on Kamal Chunchie Way.

Acknowledgements

First I have to thank my agent, Carrie Plitt, who has worked with me from the very beginning of this proposal and has been the best, most encouraging stage mom any writer could ever want; I could not have done it without her. My editor at Bodley Head, Will Hammond, has been a beacon of enthusiasm, clever ideas and sympathetic support, and his suggestions have made this book infinitely better. With thanks to Katherine Fry, too, for her sensitive and thorough copy-editing.

I have to thank the staff at a number of archives and libraries for their help and guidance in accessing their collections: the Bishopsgate Institute, the Bodleian Library, the National Archives, the British Library, the Black Cultural Archive, the Churchill Archives Centre, the Mass Observation Archive and Eastside Community Heritage. This book has also benefited from the collections at the Imperial War Museum, the British Museum and the Museum of London.

History research and writing is a collaborative art and (at its best) a sustaining community. I owe many thanks to the historians who encouraged me to write this sort of book: Chris Jeppesen, Andrew Smith, David Edgerton, Antoinette Burton, Jean Smith, Catherine Hall, Lawrence Black, Lucy Robinson, Katie Donington, Stefan Visnjevac, Jack Saunders, Lucy Dow, David Sim, Agnieszka Sobocinska, Lyndsey Jenkins, Helen Glew, Camilla Schofield, my past and present co-convenors at the IHR seminar, and many more people besides. My PhD supervisor Kathleen Burk made me into a historian; my annoying historic idiosyncrasies are, however, mine alone.

I have been employed at the history department at Southampton since 2015 and my past and present colleagues there have made me immeasurably better at my job. Particular thanks to Chris Fuller, Helen Spurling, Kendrick Oliver, George Gilbert, Priti Mishra, Tony Kushner, Hannah Young, Rachel Herrmann, Elisabeth Forster, Julie Gammon, Eleanor Quince and Maria Hayward for their support. Extra special thanks to Eve Colpus for being the best co-teacher anyone could ever want. And to my PhD students and all the students I have taught, whose ideas have often moved mine forwards when I've been gloomy or stuck.

Historians exist in cohorts and I wouldn't still be an academic without the support and solidarity of mine: Emily Baughan, Anna Bocking-Welch, Tehila Sasson, Kara Moskowitz, Emma Lundin, Sarah Crook, Jenny Crane. May all of our children grow up not to be historians. Particularly emotional thanks to Emily and Emma for the literally daily words of encouragement and love.

I am immensely grateful to the people who kept my life going around the edges of this book. Love and thanks to Louise and Julia Peart, Michelle Morris, Kirsty Strawbridge, Stefan Visnjevac (again), Stephanie Boland, Kirsty Rolfe and Sarah Broadhurst, Jen Sutcliffe, Chris Cook, Sian Redwood, Nicola Salmon, Angharad Fletcher and Rhian Bird. To my parents, Rita and Andrew, and my siblings, Georgie, William (and Valeria), Alice (and Tom) and Alfie. And to the group of mothers and babies who have kept me sane and happy during my maternity leave: Katie and Evie, Elise and Marina, Jen and Luca, Ursula and Delia, Priya and Harlyn, Ada and Rudi, Louisa and Bertie, Beth and Henry, Katrina and Elijah, Anna and Oscar, Maggie and Lucy, Beth and Ada.

The only thing worse than being locked down in a small flat during a global pandemic while you are trying to write a book is being locked down in a small flat during a global pandemic with somebody else who is trying to write a book. David Maguire deserves all my thanks for taking the photograph at the end of the conclusion, for explaining planning law to me, and for so much else besides. Towards the end of the writing process we had a baby, Raphael. His arrival inadvertently delayed the book's completion by so many months that I could include the Queen's funeral in its epilogue. For this historiographical intervention, for his willingness to sleep in the car while his father drove him around Essex and I frantically typed, and for all the joy he has brought to our lives, I have dedicated this book to him.

Bibliography

Some especially good recent books that explore empire, race and migration in Britain include Priyamvada Gopal, *Insurgent Empire: Anticolonial Resistance and British Dissent* (Verso, 2019); Kojo Koram, *Uncommon Wealth: Britain and the Aftermath of Empire* (John Murray, 2022); David Olusoga, *Black and British: A Forgotten History* (Pan Macmillan, 2016); Clair Wills, *Lovers and Strangers: An Immigrant History of Postwar Britain* (Ebury, 2017); Hakim Adi, *African and Caribbean People in Britain: A History* (Allen Lane, 2022); Sathnam Sanghera, *Empireland: How Imperialism Has Shaped Modern Britain* (Viking, 2021); Kennetta Perry, *London is the Place for Me: Black Britons, Citizenship and the Politics of Race* (Oxford University Press, 2016); Rob Waters, *Thinking Black: Britain, 1964–1985* (University of California Press, 2019); Stuart Hall, *Familiar Stranger: A Life between Two Islands* (Penguin, 2017); Hazel V. Carby, *Imperial Intimacies: A Tale of Two Islands* (Verso, 2019). Peter Fryer's *Staying Power: The History of Black People in Britain* (Pluto Press, 1984) remains a classic for a reason.

Sonya Rose's *Which People's War?: National Identity and Citizenship in Wartime Britain 1939–1945* (Oxford University Press, 2004), more than any other text, disrupts the popular Blitz-spirit narrative of Britain during the Second World War. Some of the most illuminating books on the Black British experience in the Second World War are by Stephen Bourne, including *War to Windrush: Black Women in Britain 1939–1948* (Jacaranda, 2018) and *Under Fire: Black Britain in Wartime 1939–1945* (History Press, 2020). Max Arthur's *Forgotten Voices of the Second World War: A New History of the Second World War in the Words of the Men and Women Who Were There* (Ebury, 2005) is one of several 'Forgotten Voices' books that showcase the Imperial War Museum oral history collection to great effect. On Mass Observation, James Hinton has written several interesting books that examine the documents and diaries produced, including *The Mass Observers: A History 1937–1949* (Oxford University Press, 2013) and *Nine Wartime Lives: Mass Observation and the Making of the Modern Self* (Oxford University Press, 2010). Simon Garfield, *Our Hidden Lives: The Remarkable Diaries of Post-war Britain* (Ebury, 2005), showcases a number of MO diarists once the conflict was over. On the Attlee government, David Kynaston's *Austerity Britain 1945–51* (Bloomsbury, 2010) is a rich and detailed narrative (as are the following books in the series exploring the 1950s and early 60s). On Indian independence, Kavita Puri's *Partition Voices: Untold British Voices* (Bloomsbury, 2019) brings the narrative of partition home to Britain through the people who migrated to this country after independence. Colin Grant's *Homecoming: Voices of the Windrush Generation* (Vintage, 2019) shares similar stories from this community.

On Suez, Alex von Tunzelmann's *Blood and Sand: Suez, Hungary and the Crisis that Shook the World* (Simon & Schuster, 2016) tells the story in a rich and fast-moving narrative. Jean Smith's *Settlers at the End of Empire: Race and the Politics of Migration in South Africa, Rhodesia and the United Kingdom* (Manchester University Press, 2022) teases out the different factors that drove British people to move out to empire in the twentieth century. Wendy Webster's *Englishness and Empire 1939–1965* (Oxford University Press, 2005) explores how English identity was formed through having and losing an empire. Philip Murphy's *Monarchy and the End of Empire: The House of Windsor, the British Government, and the Post-war Commonwealth* (Oxford University Press, 2013) explores how the empire was made by and made the British Crown. Anna Bocking-Welch's *British Civic Society at the End of Empire: Decolonisation, Globalisation, and International Responsibility* (Manchester University Press, 2018) is a detailed and thoughtful exploration of how ordinary people navigated the end of empire. Jordanna Bailkin's *The Afterlife of Empire* (University of California Press, 2012) argues persuasively that the British welfare state and decolonisation are intertwined. Emily Baughan's *Saving the Children: Humanitarianism, Internationalism, and Empire* (University of California Press, 2021) uncovers how British humanitarianism and empire were connected, not least in Kenya during the time of Mau Mau. Caroline Elkins's *Britain's Gulag: The Brutal End of Empire in Kenya* (Jonathan Cape, 2005) and David Anderson's *Histories of the Hanged: The Dirty War in Kenya and*

the End of Empire (Weidenfeld & Nicolson, 2005) remain vital histories of
the Mau Mau 'emergency'.

Camilla Schofield's *Enoch Powell and the Making of Post-colonial Britain*
(Cambridge University Press, 2013) sets Powell within a vital historical
context. Panikos Panayi's work, especially *Migrant City: A New History of
London* (Yale University Press, 2020) and *An Immigration History of Britain:
Multicultural Racism since 1800* (Longman, 2010), does much to explain the
experience of multiculturalism and racism in British history. John Solo-
mos's *Race and Racism in Britain* (Palgrave Macmillan, 2022) mixes imperial
history with political theory. Dilip Hiro's *Black British, White British: A History of Race Relations in Britain* (Grafton, 1991) has gone through multiple
editions and is another comprehensive text.

On the Falklands, Helen Parr's *Our Boys: the Story of a Paratrooper* (Penguin, 2018) gives a human face to the history of the conflict. Hugh
McManners's *Forgotten Voices of the Falklands* (Ebury, 2007) showcases the
Imperial War Museum oral histories from the war. Simon Peplow's *Race
and Riots in Thatcher's Britain* (Manchester University Press, 2019) explores
how Thatcherism developed alongside a politics of whiteness. On apartheid and the Anti-Apartheid Movement, Roger Fieldhouse's *Anti-apartheid:
A History of the Movement in Britain: A Study in Pressure Group Politics* (Mer-
lin, 2005) is a comprehensive study of the movement in Britain. Elizabeth
M. Williams's *The Politics of Race in Britain and South Africa: Black British
Solidarity and the Anti-apartheid Struggle* (I.B. Tauris, 2015) explores the
important transnational racial politics of anti-apartheid activism. Stuart
Hall's *The Hard Road to Renewal: Thatcherism and the Crisis of the Left* (Verso,
2021) has recently been reiussed and remains a vital analysis of the 1980s in
Britain.

Amelia Gentleman's *The Windrush Betrayal: Exposing the Hostile Environment* (Guardian Books, 2019) details that newspaper's investigation into
the Windrush Scandal and provides more stories of those people who
were caught up in its trap. Philippe Sands, *The Last Colony: A Tale of Exile,
Justice and Britain's Colonial Legacy* (Weidenfeld & Nicolson, 2022), tells the
story of the Chagos Islanders' dispossession and persecution at the hands
of the British state through the lens of the legal battle for their rights.
Danny Dorling and Sally Tomlinson, *Rule Britannia: Brexit and the End of*

Empire (Biteback, 2019), and Stuart Ward and Astrid Rasch (eds), *Embers of Empire in Brexit Britain* (Bloomsbury, 2019), examine Brexit in the context of British identity and imperial hangovers. Hannah Rose Woods's *Rule Nostalgia: A Backwards History of Britain* (Ebury, 2022) sets this imperial nostalgia within a much longer chronology to remind us that the British have always had a tricky relationship with their own history.

Notes

Introduction: Empire's Shadows

1. Geoffrey Bell, *The Other Eastenders: Kamal Chunchie and West Ham's Early Black Community*, Eastside Community Heritage, 2002.
2. Rozina Visram, 'Chunchie, Kamal Athon', *Oxford Dictionary of National Biography* (online edn), Oxford University Press.
3. *Newham: The Forging of a Black Community*, Newham Monitoring Project / Campaign Against Racism and Fascism, 1991, pp. 3–4.
4. Arthur Lewis (MP), 'Slum Clearance (Newham)', 28 February 1967, Hansard, Vol. 742, cc. 64–5.
5. Tim Buttler and Chris Hamnett, *Ethnicity, Class and Aspiration: Understanding London's New East End*, Policy Press, 2011, p. 44.
6. Ibid., p. 46.
7. Neil Berry, 'Britain's Asians', *London Review of Books*, Vol. 9, No. 19, 29 October 1987.
8. ONS, 'Ethnic Group, England and Wales: Census 2021', November 2022.
9. Stephen Jivraj, 'Local Dynamics of Diversity: Evidence from the 2011 Census', ESRC Centre on Dynamics of Ethnicity, October 2013.
10. David Low, 'Very Well, Alone', *Evening Standard*, 18 June 1940.
11. Cyril Fougasse, 'So Our Poor Old Empire Is Alone in the World', *Punch*, 17 July 1940.
12. E. P. Thompson, *The Making of the English Working Class*, Vintage, 1963, p. 12.

1. Home and Away in the Second World War

1. James Hinton, *The Mass Observers: A History, 1937–1949*, Oxford University Press, 2013, p. 14.
2. Directive Questionnaire, Mass Observation, February 1942.
3. File Report 1158, 'Feelings about the British Empire', Mass Observation, 16 March 1942.
4. League of Nations Union, *National Canvass for a Strong and Enduring League of Nations: Canvassers' Answers (c.*1935), pp. 26–8.
5. 'Ovation in London', *The Times*, 1 October 1938.
6. 'Premier Appears on Palace Balcony', *Manchester Guardian*, 1 October 1938.
7. E. M. Andrews, *Isolationism and Appeasement in Australia*, ANU, 1970, p. 140.
8. 'German Colonial Claims: Concern in Tanganyika', *Manchester Guardian*, 7 October 1938.
9. Letter, 'Future of Tanganyika', *Daily Telegraph*, 16 February 1938.
10. 'The Natives of Tanganyika', *Manchester Guardian*, 13 October 1938.
11. Student Christian Movement, 'Youth and the Colonies' Student Christian Movement Press, 1939.
12. 'Record of conversations between British and French Foreign Ministers held at No. 10 Downing Street on November 29 and 30 1937', no. 354, *Documents on British Foreign Policy, 1919–1939*, HMSO, 1946, pp. 608–9.
13. Miss Akhurst to Winston Churchill, 27 September 1938, CHAR 7/107A/38, Churchill Archive.
14. Mary Agnes Hamilton, diary entry 30 September 1938, HMTN 1/1 1938 Diary, 6 January 1938–3 January 1939, Mary Agnes Hamilton Papers, Churchill Archive Centre, Cambridge.
15. Malcolm MacKinnon, *Independence and Foreign Policy: New Zealand in the World since 1935*, Auckland University Press, 2013, chapter 2.
16. D 5437, diary for August 1939, Mass Observation Archive, pp. 1–2.
17. Loleta Jemmott, interview with Stephen Bourne, 20 February 2008, in Stephen Bourne, *Mother Country: Britain's Black Community on the Home Front 1939–45*, History Press, 2010, p. 118.

18. Mercedes Mackay, quoted in Charles Allen, *Plain Tales from the British Empire*, Abacus, 2008, p. 433.

19. Inter-Imperial Relations Committee, 'Report, Proceedings and Memoranda', Imperial Conference, London, November 1926.

20. Stephen Leacock, 'Canada and the Monarchy', *Atlantic*, Vol. 163, No. 6, June 1939.

21. J. V. T. Baker, 'War Economy: Food Crisis in Britain', *The Official History of New Zealand in the Second World War*, Historical Publications Branch: Department of Internal Affairs, 1965; New Zealand National Film Unit *Weekly Review* No. 249, *New Zealand and World War II* (dir: Oxley Hughan), 1946.

22. *Food from the Empire* (dir. Theodore Thumwood), Ministry of Information, 1940.

23. File Report 11, 'Evacuation Report', Mass Observation, November 1939.

24. Women's Group on Public Welfare, *Our Towns: A Close Up*, 1943.

25. Paul Stephenson, *Memoirs of a Black Englishman*, Tangent Books, 2011.

26. Claire L. Halstead, '"Dear Mummy and Daddy": Reading Wartime Letters from British Children Evacuated to Canada During the Second World War', in Shirleene Robinson and Simon Sleight (eds), *Children, Childhood and Youth in the British World*, Palgrave Macmillan, 2016.

27. Letter from the Office of High Commissioner for the UK, Ottawa, Canada, to the Director General of CORB, London, 23 September 1940, DO 131/45, National Archives.

28. 'Belmont School Goes to Nassau, Bahamas', amateur film, 1941, Imperial War Museum.

29. A. H. Trelawny-Ross to Mr Anderson, 22 June 1940, Sherborne School archive.

30. 'Recruitment of British Subjects from the Colonies in the Armed Forces of the Crown', 1939, ADM 1/10818, National Archives; Frances Houghton, '"Alien Seamen" or "Imperial Family"? Race, Belonging and British Sailors of Colour in the Royal Navy, 1939–47', *English Historical Review*, 2023.

31. Women's Land Army (Colour Discrimination), HC Debate, 23 September 1943, Hansard, Vol. 392, cc. 390–1.

32. 'Coloured Girl Joins Land Army', *Oxford Times*, 1 October 1943.

33. 'West Indian ATS volunteers being served tea at the Colonial Office in London', 21 September 1944, Photo by Reg Speller/Fox Photos/ Getty Images; 'Garden Party for West Indian ATS: Rest and Relaxation in Bicester, Oxfordshire, England, UK, 1944', Ministry of Information Photo Division, Imperial War Museum, D 21329.

34. William Vanderson, 'The first group of Indian pilots arriving at London Station to be greeted by Louis Greig, right, 8th October 1940', William G. Vanderson/Fox Photos/Getty Images.

35. Rozina Virsam, 'Pujji, Mahinder Singh (1918–2010)', *Oxford Dictionary of National Biography*, Oxford University Press, 2014.

36. J. F. Cody, *The Official History of New Zealand in the Second World War, 1939–45: 28 Māori Battalion*, Historic Publications Branch: Department of Internal Affairs, 1956, chapter 2.

37. Gus John, 'Cy Grant Obituary', *Guardian*, 17 February 2010.

38. 'Obituary: Sam Martinez, Forester and Oldest Hibs Fan', *Scotsman*, 5 October 2016.

39. Dorothy Connor, 'Heroic Scot's Amazing Letters Home Reveal the Hardship of Gruelling Burma Campaign During World War II', *Daily Record*, 29 August 2015.

40. Spike Milligan, *Rommel? Gunner Who?*, Michael Joseph, 1974.

41. Lt Palmer, 'Cheerful British Soldiers on Board a Troopship Arriving at Singapore, October 1941', War Office Second World War Official Collection, FE 97, Imperial War Museum.

42. Selwyn Selwyn-Clarke, *Footprints: The Memoirs of Sir Selwyn Selwyn-Clarke*, Sino-American Publishing Company, 1975.

43. Rose Hunt, 'Letters to the Editor: Hong Kong Prisoners', *Manchester Guardian*, 2 November 1942.

44. King George VI, Empire Day message, in Wendy Webster, *Englishness and Empire 1939–1965*, Oxford University Press, 2007, p. 26.

45. Winston Churchill, Speech receiving the Freedom of the City of London, Guildhall, 30 June 1943.

46. Daniel Coetzee, 'Fires and Feathers: Acculturation, Arson and the Jewish Community in Oudtshoorn, South Africa, 1914–1948', *Jewish History*, Vol. 19, No. 2, Springer, 2005, pp. 143–87. www.jstor.org/stable/20100950.

47. 'The British Commonwealth of Nations', 1942, Imperial War Museum, Art. IWM PST 15786.

48. 'Your Planes and Your Work Defend Your Empire', 1942, Imperial War Museum, Art. IWM PST 14397.

49. 'Playing their Part: The War Effort of the British Colonial Empire', No. 5, Ministry of Information, 1944.

50. Frederick J. Ney, *Some Notes on the Proposed Empire Youth Movement*, Empire Youth Movement, 1938.

51. Amateur film, 'Empire Youth Sunday 1944', Nottingham, 1944, BFI, player.bfi.org.uk/free/film/watch-empire-youth-sunday-1944-1944-online

52. David Reynolds, 'Zest: The Real Mrs Miniver', *London Review of Books*, Vol. 24, No. 8, 25 April 2002.

53. Cumberland Clark, *The British Empire At War*, Henbest Publicity Service 1940.

54. Leonard Barnes, *Empire or Democracy? A Study of the Colonial Question*, Victor Gollancz, 1939.

55. 'A Charter for Coloured Peoples', LCP, *News Letter*, Vol. X, No. 59, August 1944.

56. Anthony Burgess, 'In the Other England, the Land of Cotton, Nobody Says "Baaaaath"', *New York Times*, 28 January 1973.

57. Linda Hervieux, *Forgotten: The Untold Story of D-Day's Black Heroes, at Home and at War*, Harper, 2016, p. 157.

58. 'From a London Diary', *New Statesman and Nation*, 22 August 1942.

59. 'Vicar's Wife Insults Our Allies', *Sunday Pictorial*, 6 September 1942.

60. 'Colour Bar: Use of the City's Amenities', *Birmingham Mail*, 15 May 1945.

61. 'Conclusions of a Meeting of the War Cabinet held in the Prime Minister's Room, House of Commons, S. W. 1, on Tuesday, October 13, 1942', Cab 65/28, National Archives.

62. Sylvia McNeill, 'Illegitimate Children Born in Britain of English Mothers and Coloured Americans: Report of a Survey', League of Coloured Peoples November 1945.

63. M. Romyn, ' "We could be anything we wanted to be": Remembering Jimmy Rogers', *Race & Class*, 61(2), 2019, pp. 62–84.

64. 'Coloured Illegitimate Children in Britain', *League of Coloured Peoples Newsletter*, Vol. XIV, No. 80, May 1946.

65. 'Holding the Baby', *League of Coloured Peoples' Review*, Vol. 1, No. 1, January 1951.

66. 'The Coloured Brat', *League of Coloured People's Review*, Vol. 1, No. 1, January 1951.

67. *Burma Bugle*, August 1945 (D/DLI 2/2/83), Durham Record Office.

68. 'The Election Scene Landslide for Socialists', Pathé News, Film ID: 1159.07, 30 July 1945.

69. 'Volunteer Observer: The Forces Vote in West Africa, 1945', in Angus Calder and Dorothy Sheridan (eds), *Speak for Yourself: A Mass Observation Anthology 1937–1949*, OUP, 1985, p. 219.

70. File Report 2270A, 'The General Election 1945', Mass Observation, July 1945.

71. Edie Rutherford, quoted in Simon Garfield, *Our Hidden Lives: The Remarkable Diaries of Post-war Britain*, Ebury, 2005, p. 65.

72. 'Freed War Prisoners Return to Africa', *Colonial Cinema*, September 1945, pp. 53–4.

2. The People's Peace:
the Attlee Government, 1945–51

1. 'To-day, as we celebrate victory', HMSO, 1946, Imperial War Museum, LBY K. 04/2304.

2. 'Victory Parade', Colonial Film Unit, 1946, 21304, BFI.

3. 'Victory Celebrations: Special Supplement', *The Times*, 10 May 1946.

4. NEB [Ronald Niebour], Untitled, *Daily Mail*, 29 October 1948.

5. Joseph Lee, 'Terrifying Days', *Evening News*, 20 July 1949.

6. Jean Mann, 'Overseas Resources Development Bill', HC Debate, 6 November 1947, Hansard, Vol. 443, cc. 2079–80.

7. File Report 3010, 'Public Opinion on Colonial Affairs', Mass Observation, May and June 1948.

8. Giles, 'Letter Here . . .', *Daily Express*, 13 December 1948.

9. Alan Wood, *The Groundnut Affair*, Bodley Head, 1950, p. 9.

10. Maurice Webb, 'Book "The Groundnut Affair"', HC Debate, 20 March 1950, Hansard, Vol. 472, c. 1537.

11. 'Dan Dare', *The Eagle*, 29 September 1950.

12. 'Sir Stafford Cripps in India', British Pathé, 27 April 1942.

13. Ibid.

14. File Report 1401, 'Morale in August 1942', Mass Observation, September 1942.

15. 'The Riots in Calcutta', *Manchester Guardian*, 22 August 1946.

16. Ibid.

17. 'India: the British Raj is Dead', *Manchester Guardian*, 15 August 1947.

18. 'Comment', *Observer*, 17 August 1947.

19. Letter from Mr Clifton H. Stephenson to Sir John Anderson MP, 10 March 1947, Churchill Archive, CHUR 2/43A-B/82-83.

20. John Hall, 'Rift? No Says Peggy Cripps', *Daily Mail*, 4 March 1957.

21. James Proctor, 'Empire Windrush: Forgotten Archive Material Reveals Who Was on Its Outward Voyage to the Caribbean', The Conversation, 14 June 2018, theconversation.com/empire-windrush-forgotten-archive-material-reveals-who-was-on-its-outward-voyage-to-the-caribbean-97905

22. Goldsmiths, University of London, 'Windrush: Arrival 1948. Passenger List', www.gold.ac.uk/windrush/passenger-list/

23. Peter Fryer, 'Five Hundred Pairs of Willing Hands', *Daily Worker,* 23 June 1948.

24. 'Why 492 West Indians Came to Britain – Not All Intend to Settle Here', *Guardian*, 23 June 1948.

25. Ibid.

26. Ivor Cummings, 'Short Address to West Indian Workers on HMT "Empire Windrush"', 1948, Employment of Jamaicans from the S.S. Empire Windrush, CO/876/88, National Archives.

27. Peter Fryer, 'The Men from Jamaica are Settling Down', *Daily Worker*, 14 July 1948.

28. Michael Banton, 'Recent Migration from West Africa and the West Indies to the United Kingdom', *Population Studies* 7, No. 1, July 1953, p. 10.

29. Stuart Hall, 'Postscript: The Windrush Issue', *Soundings*, Autumn 1998, Issue 10, p. 188.

30. Tony Kushner, *The Battle of Britishness: Migrant Journeys 1965 to the Present*, Manchester University Press, 2012, pp. 179–80.

31. Profiles: Allan Wilmot, Windrush Foundation, windrushfoundation. com/profiles/allan-wilmot/

32. Samuel Beaver King, Oral History Interview 2007–8, Imperial War Museum, 30021.

33. Gilli Salvat, interviewed by Allegra Damji, 29 June 1986, Hall–Carpenter Oral History Archives, British Library.

34. Letter from Prime Minister Attlee to J. D. Murray, 5 July 1948, HO 213/715, National Archives.

35. These communities later worked with the African American sociologist St Clair Drake to produce a response to Little, in which they objected to their status as subjects of observation and raised their 'distrust' of people who would write about them in an attempt to 'reform and lead' them. L. James & D. Whittall, 'Ambiguity and Imprint: British Racial Logics, Colonial Commissions of Enquiry, and the Creolization of Britain in the 1930s and 1940s', *Callaloo*, Vol. 39, No. 1, 2016, p. 180.

36. Kenneth Little, 'Advisory Committee on Imperial Questions. No. 320, The Colour Problem in Britain and Its Treatment', July 1948, Labour Party, Modern Records Centre, MSS.292/805.9/1/151.

37. Derek Bamuta, 'Report on an Investigation into Conditions of the Coloured People in Stepney, E1', *c.* December 1949, HO 344/32, National Archives.

38. Basil L. J. Henriques JP to Clement Attlee, 9 December 1949, HO 344/32, National Archives.

39. 'Indian Hemp in the UK 1947–48', Drug Branch Home Office, November 1948, 'Colonial Subjects, Illegal Activities: Traffic in Drugs and Practice in London', HO 344/32, National Archives.

40. C. B. Selby-Boothroyd, HM Deputy Chief Inspector, Home Office (Drugs Branch), 'The Illicit Traffic of Indian Hemp in Great Britain since the War', 1 April 1947, 'Colonial Subjects, Illegal Activities: Traffic in Drugs and Practice in London', HO 344/32, National Archives.

41. 'A Giant Led Bandaged Procession', *Daily Mirror*, 3 August 1948.

42. Christopher Fevre, ' "Race" and Resistance to Policing Before the "Windrush Years": The Colonial Defence Committee and the Liverpool "Race Riots" of 1948', *Twentieth Century British History*, Vol. 32, Issue 1, March 2021, pp. 1–23.

43. 'The Cook, with his Sabre, Held the Stairs', *Daily Mirror*, 4 August 1948.

44. 'Racial Riots – First Charge', *Daily Mirror,* 28 October 1948.

45. Fevre, pp. 1–23.

46. File Report 3010, 'Public Opinion on Colonial Affairs', Mass Observation, May and June 1948.

47. Graham Stanford, ' "Lincs a Colony" Shocks Quizzers', *Daily Mail*, 21 December 1948.

48. This level of knowledge can be compared with the results of a questionnaire conducted in 1940: 54 per cent of men knew the difference between a colony and a dominion, compared with only 12 per cent of women. Many of the incorrect answers related to size – dominions, generally, were thought to be larger. One person stated that 'Dominions are what we've conquered in battle and Colonies are the places where our ancestors have settled. They are generally British.' Knowledge about other aspects of colonial politics were similarly blurred; upon being asked to identify the Statute of Westminster (the document which gave the Dominions their legislative independence), one respondent said, 'Isn't it in the middle of the road in front of the House of Commons?' before adding, somewhat redundantly, 'I don't know anything about it.' File Report 514, 'Colonies Questionnaire', Mass Observation, 3 December 1940.

49. 'Colonial Month' *Guardian*, 22 June 1949.

50. 'Colonial Month', *Listener*, 23 June 1949.

51. 'King Opens Colonial Month', Pathé News, 27 June 1949.

52. Arthur Creech Jones, 'Colonial Affairs: Publicity', HC Debate, 9 March 1949, Hansard, Vol. 462, c. 119.

53. Public Record Office, *Special Exhibition of Documents Relating to the Colonies*, May 1949; 'Colonial Month', *The Times*, 20 June 1949.

54. 'Colonies Show for a Month', *Daily Telegraph*, 20 June 1949; 'Gentoo Penguins Arrive by Air', *The Times*, 24 June 1949.

55. 'Colonial Month', *The Times*, 20 June 1949.

56. Wyndham Lewis, 'The London Galleries', *Listener*, 14 July 1949.

57. H. Winston Greenwood, Letter to the Editor, *Manchester Guardian*, 30 June 1949.

58. John M. Mackenzie, *Propaganda and Empire: the Manipulation of British Public Opinion 1880–1960*, OUP, 2017, p. 120.

59. Milton Brown, 'An African at the Colonial Exhibition', *Daily Worker*, 29 June 1949.

60. 'The Colonial Month', *Corona: the Journal of His Majesty's Colonial Service*, Vol. 1, No. 7, August 1949, pp. 4–11.

61. Rees Williams, 'Colonial Month', HC Debate, 27 July 1949, Hansard, Vol. 467, c. 71.

62. *The Official Book of the Festival of Britain*, HMSO, 1951, p. 3.

63. Ibid., pp. 6–10.

64. Alayna Heinonen, 'A Tonic to the Empire?: The 1951 Festival of Britain and the Empire-Commonwealth', *Britain and the World*, 8.1, 2015, pp. 95–7.

65. *The Official Book of the Festival of Britain*, HMSO, 1951, p. 62.

3. Never Had It So Good? Britain in the 1950s

1. *The Colonies in Pictures*, HMSO, 1956.

2. Katharine Whitehorn, 'The Best of Times', *Guardian*, 10 October 2007.

3. Boy Scouts Association, *The Call of Empire*, Migration Department, 1939, pp. 1–2.

4. Ibid. pp. 7–8.

5. 'Empire Settlement Bill', HC Debate, 21 April 1952, Hansard, Vol. 499, cc. 53–162.

6. Marilyn Barber and Murray Watson, *Invisible Immigrants: The English in Canada since 1945*, University of Manitoba Press, 2015, chapter 1.

7. 'Emigrate to New Zealand for a New Way of Life', *c.*1949, New Zealand Government, nzhistory.govt.nz/media/photo/emigration-poster

8. Megan Hutching, *Long Journey for Sevenpence: Assisted Immigration to New Zealand from the United Kingdom 1947–1975*, Victoria University Press, 1999, pp. 93–4.

9. 'Australia: Build Your Children's Future', Australian Migration Office, 1955–60, Museum of Applied Arts and Sciences, Sydney, collection. maas.museum/object/52927

10. Wendy Webster, *Imagining Home: Gender, Race and National Identity 1945–64*, Routledge, 2005, p. 31.

11. *First Annual Report of the Oversea Migration Board*, HMSO, 1954.

12. 'Thousand Migrants, Many Children Arrive by the Ormonde', *Western Australian*, 8 November 1947.

13. Aida Edemariam, 'Saturday Interview: People should sort out this mess', *Guardian*, 20 February 2010; Melissa Davey, 'Abused and Publicly Flogged: The UK Child Migrants Sent for a Better Life in Australia', *Guardian*, 16 June 2016.

14. Alexis Jay et al., *Child Migration Programmes: Investigation Report*, March 2018, www.iicsa.org.uk/reports-recommendations/publications/investigation/child-migration

15. 'A Million-to-One Chance brings Fame to Barbara', *Daily Mirror*, 7 September 1955.

16. 'Australia brings out the best in you', 1967, National Film and Sound Archive of Australia, www.nfsa.gov.au/collection/curated/australia-brings-out-best-you-advertisement

17. Oliver Williams, *Kaffirs are Lively*, Victor Gollancz, 1948.

18. Migration Council, 'Operation British Commonwealth', October 1951.

19. 'The Flowing Tidal Wave of Supply', British Pathé, 1942.

20. 'Ex-Leaders in Egypt Lose Public Rights', *Daily Telegraph*, 17 April 1954.

21. Ibid.

22. '2 Britons on Suez Malaria Duty Vanish', *Daily Telegraph*, 25 January 1954.

23. Ronald Camp, 'The Commons Speak for Britain', *Daily Mail*, 3 August 1956.

24. 'What We Think: No More Adolf Hitlers!', *Daily Herald*, 28 July 1956.

25. 'Balcony Bravado', *Daily Mirror*, 29 July 1956.

26. 'Cassandra', *Daily Mirror*, 30 July 1956.

27. 'Call to Arms', *Picture Post*, 18 August 1956.

28. Ibid.

29. Ibid.

30. Mrs A. Yates, '. . .and the British in Suez', *Picture Post*, 26 November 1956.

31. Gallup: Social Surveys, *News Chronicle*, 6 November 1956.

32. Suez Crisis 1956, 'A Stage Camel Makes a Useful Prop in a Protest over the Suez Situation', 23 8 56 H7479, 23 August 1956, Mirrorpix.

33. 'Mightiest Lobby Since War Says: No!', *Daily Worker*, 13 September 1956.

34. 'Miners' Leaders Were There', *Daily Worker*, 13 September 1956.

35. 'Thousands in Night March', *Daily Worker*, 13 September 1956.

36. James Griffiths, 'Egypt and Israel', HC Debate, 1 November 1956, Hansard, Vol. 558, cc. 1631–8.

37. Ibid.

38. 'Eden Meant War All Along', *Daily Worker*, 1 November 1956.

39. 'British Bombers Blitz Egypt', *Daily Worker,* 1 November 1956.

40. Peter Rawlinson, 'British Broadcasting Corporation (News Broadcasts)', HC Debate, Hansard, 14 November 1956, Vol. 560, cc. 1023–102.

41. Nicklaus Thomas-Symonds, *Nye: The Political Life of Aneurin Bevan*, I.B. Tauris, 2015, pp. 1-3.

42. 'Sir Anthony Eden Resigns', *Guardian*, 10 January 1957.

43. Oscar Gish, 'Color and Skill: British Immigration, 1955–1968', *International Migration Review*, Vol. 3, No. 1, 1968, pp. 19–37, *JSTOR*, doi.org/10.2307/3002179

44. Beryl Gilroy, *Black Teacher*, Faber, 2021, p. 13.

45. Ibid., p. 45.

46. Ibid., p. 240.

47. Donald Hinds, *Journey to an Illusion: The West Indian in Britain*, Bogle-l'Ouverture Press Ltd, 2001 (second edn), pp. 46-7.

48. 'Working Party to report on the social and economic problems arising from the growing influx into the United Kingdom of coloured workers from other Commonwealth countries', February 1957, HO 344/122, Police Reports, March 1957, National Archives.

49. Grimsby, 22 February 1957, HO 344/122, Police Reports, March 1957, National Archives.

50. Glasgow, 1 March 1957, HO 344/122, Police Reports, March 1957, National Archives.

51. Bolton, 25 February 1957, HO 344/122, Police Reports, March 1957, National Archives.

52. Essex, 9 March 1957, HO 344/122, Police Reports, March 1957, National Archives.

53. 'Working Party to report on the social and economic problems arising from the growing influx into the United Kingdom of coloured workers from other Commonwealth countries: Extracts from reports submitted from the Home Office by the Chief Constable of the under-mentioned districts', February 1957, HO 344/122, Police Reports, March 1957, National Archives.

54. Middlesbrough, 18 March 1957, HO 344/122, Police Reports, March 1957, National Archives.

55. 'Racial riots at Notting Hill between 31 August and 3 September 1958', 1958–9, MEPO 2/9838, National Archives; Simon Peplow, ' "Cause for Concern"? Policing Black Migrants in Post-War Britain (1945–68)', *Immigrants & Minorities*, 40:1–2, 2022, pp. 177–209.

56. Afro-West Indian Union, 'Statement on Racial Violence', 4 September 1958, Socialist Party: 'Colonial work': circulars, correspondence, etc., Modern Records Centre, 601/B/3/2/1/1

57. Anonymous letter attacking Trades Union Congress statement following the Notting Hill riots, 4 September 1958, Modern Records Centre, MSS.292/805.7/3/197.

58. 'The Habit of Violence', *Universities & Left Review*, Autumn 1958, pp. 4–5.

59. Ibid., p. 4.

60. 'Funeral of Kelso Cochrane', British Pathé, 6 June 1959.

61. Hinds, p. 121.

62. *Going to Britain?*, BBC Caribbean Service, 1959.

4. *Losing an Empire: Decolonisation, 1950s–60s*

1. 'High-Life!', *Daily Mirror*, 20 November 1961.

2. 'S. Africa Critic of Queen', *Daily Telegraph*, 25 November 1961.

3. 'Happiest Moment', *Sunday Pictorial*, 12 November 1961.

4. Leonard Harris, *Long to Reign Over Us: The Status of the Royal Family in the 1960s*, Mass Observation/Kimber, 1966, pp. 51–2.

5. Douglas Hurd, 'No Going Back', *Guardian*, 24 April 2007.

6. 'Souvenir of visit of the Rt Hon Harold Macmillan Prime Minister of the United Kingdom to the Houses of Parliament Cape Town on 3 February 1960', Cape Times Ltd, 1960.

7. Ibid.

8. Michael Cummings, 'My Goodness – My Propaganda!', *Sunday Express*, 7 February 1960.

9. George K. Young, 'Who Goes Home? Immigration and Repatriation', Monday Club, May 1969.

10. 'The New Battle of Britain', Monday Club, 1970.

11. Young, 'Who goes home?'.

12. 'Militants and Moderates in the Universities', *Minerva*, Autumn–Winter 1968–69, Vol. 7, No. 1/2, pp. 290, 296.

13. Ibid., p. 300.

14. A. K. Chesterton, 'Britain's Graveyard: Dangers of the Common Market', League of Empire Loyalists, 1957.

15. A. K. Chesterton, 'Stand by the Empire', League of Empire Loyalists, 1954.

16. *Long to Reign Over Us*, p. 189.

17. Philip Larkin, 'Homage to a Government', *Sunday Times*, 19 January 1969.

18. Fenner Brockway, 'What is the M. C. F.?', Movement for Colonial Freedom, *c*.1966.

19. 'African Freedom Day Concert, April 19th 1959, at 7.30pm, St Pancras Town Hall', Committee for African Organisations and MCF, 1959.

20. Brockway, 'What is the M. C. F.?'.

21. 'Malayan Violence to be "Smashed"', *Daily Mail*, 14 June 1948; Noel Clark, 'Thank You Britain', *Daily Mail*, 31 August 1957.

22. Central Officer's Special Report to Commander C. 1, 'Alleged Massacre in Malaya', Criminal Investigation Department, New Scotland Yard, 30 July 1970.

23. John Halford and Stephen Grosz, 'A Very British Cover-up. A briefing for members of the House of Commons and the House of Lords on the Government's response to calls for an inquiry into the 1948 Batang Kali massacre', Bindmans LLP, 28 August 2009.

24. Central Officer's Special Report.

25. Ibid.

26. Halford and Grosz.

27. 'I Survived Batang Kali', *Guardian*, 9 December 2009.

28. Judgment Keyu and others (Appellants) *v* Secretary of State for Foreign and Commonwealth Affairs and another (Respondents) before Lord Neuberger, President, Lady Hale, Deputy President, Lord Mance, Lord Kerr, Lord Hughes. Judgment given on 25 November 2015, Heard on 22 and 23 April 2015, [2015] UKSC69 On appeal from [2014] EWCA Civ 312.

29. 'Worst Mau Murder', *Daily Mail*, 26 January 1953.

30. '3 Slashed to Death', *Daily Mirror*, 26 January 1953.

31. ' "A Vile, Brutal Wickedness": The Murder of the Ruck Family by Mau Mau Terrorists in Kenya, a Shocking Crime Redeemed Only by the Heroism of an African Houseboy', *Illustrated London News*, 7 February 1953, pp. 190–1.

32. 'Family of 3 Britons Killed by Mau Mau', *Daily Telegraph*, 26 January 1953; 'Mau Mau Murder Scene', *Daily Telegraph*, 26 January 1953.

33. 'Body of Mr. A. G. Leakey Found', *Daily Telegraph*, 23 November 1954.

34. Colin Jordan (ed.), *Black & White News*, 1958.

35. A. K. Chesterton, Introduction, *Candour* Supplement, 22 July 1960.

36. John Blacker, 'The Demography of Mau Mau: Fertility and mortality in Kenya in the 1950s: a demographer's viewpoint, *African Affairs*, Vol. 106, Issue 423, April 2007, pp. 205–27; David Anderson and Julianne Weis, 'The Prosecution of Rape in Wartime: Evidence from the Mau Mau Rebellion, Kenya 1952–60', *Law and History Review*, 36(2), 2018, pp. 267–94; Caroline Elkins, *Britain's Gulag: The Brutal End of Empire in Kenya*, Jonathan Cape, 2005.

37. 'Lokitaung Prison', HC Debate, Hansard, 17 June 1958, Vol. 589, cc. 869–75.

38. 'Hola Camp, Kenya Report', HC Debate, Hansard, 27 July 1959, Vol. 610, cc. 181–262.

39. Ibid.

40. Butlin to R. Gresham Cooke, MP, 29 May 1959, 'Representations about conditions in detention camps in Kenya', CO 822/1260.

41. Ron and Hilda Hitchcock to Alan Lennox-Boyd, 31 May 1959, 'Representations about conditions in detention camps in Kenya', CO 822/1260.

42. *Kenya: White Terror* (producer: Giselle Portenier), BBC2, 17 November 2002; John McGhie, 'Kenya: White Terror', 9 November 2002, BBC News, news.bbc.co.uk/1/hi/programmes/correspondent/2416049.stm

43. 'British PM May says Mugabe's resignation gives Zimbabwe a chance to be free', Reuters, 21 November 2017.

44. Charles Mohr, 'Time May Be Catching Up With Rhodesia', *New York Times*, 22 December 1974.

45. 'Southern Rhodesia: The Munt Lover', *Time*, 16 March 1959.

46. Michael Foot, Hon. Member for Wednesbury, 'Federation of Rhodesia and Nyasaland', 4 March 1959, Hansard, Vol. 601, c. 436.

47. K. E. Pridham, 'Training of the African', *Daily Telegraph*, 2 January 1964.

48. D. I. Coles, 'Darkest Britain', *Daily Telegraph*, 31 May 1964.

49. Douglas Brown, 'Rhodesia Faces the Hard, Hard Realities', *Daily Telegraph*, 1 November 1964.

50. 'Rhodesia: Some Planes Arrive', *Time*, 10 December 1965.

51. Wilson to Secretary of State for Defence, 8 January 1966, DEFE 32/17, National Archives.

52. 'The widow of murdered Zimbabwean farmer David, Maria Stevens, tells how she's finding the strength to cope with the loss of her husband and her feelings towards her troubled country', *Hello!*, No. 612, 23 May 2000, pp. 98–102.

53. Alexandra Fuller, *Don't Let's Go to the Dogs Tonight*, Picador, 2002.

54. W. P. A. Robinson, *How To Live Well on Your Pension*, Faber & Faber, 1955, p. 72.

55. Ibid., p. 21.

56. Ibid., p. 208.

57. David Le Breton, speaking at OSPA's 'Farewell Event' held in London on 8 June 2017.

58. *Overseas Pensioner*, No. 15, May 1968.

59. Ibid., No. 12, September 1966.

60. Ibid.

61. Barbara Castle, *Fighting All the Way*, Macmillan, 1993, p. 357.

62. MS. Castle 261, Correspondence and Papers, October 1964–December 1965.

63. *Witness History*, 'Dusty Plays South Africa', BBC News World Service, 25 December 2012.

64. Castle, p. 358.

65. Display Ad, 'Oxfam Needs An Assistant Personnel Officer', *Guardian*, 18 April 1969.

66. Display Ad, 'Government of Mauritius: Head of Economic Planning Unit', *Guardian*, 30 December 1964; Display Ad, 'Senior Economist Tanzania', *Guardian*, 20 January 1966; Display Ad, 'Help Build a Better World', *Guardian*, 9 February 1965.

67. Launcelot Fleming, 'The Year Between', *Sunday Times*, 23 March 1958.

68. Miranda Mosscrop, 'Glad to Have a Rest', *Guardian*, 9 July 1968.

69. 'Contest Based on the Work of VSO', *Guardian*, 17 May 1968.

70. Scripture Union, *We All Volunteered: Twelve VSOs Write About Their Experiences,* Scripture Union, 1967.

71. 'Poverty is Violence', *International Times*, No. 52, 14–27 March 1969, p. 14.

72. 'Hélder Câmara: Brazilian Cleric Who Eschewed Pomp in His Battle against Injustice and Inequality', *Guardian*, 31 August 1999.

73. John Stevens, 'Avoid Politics and Stick to Knitting, Tory Minister tells Charities after Oxfam Rails against Government's Flagship Policies', *Daily Mail*, 4 September 2014.

74. *Commonwealth Institute*, Commonwealth Institute, 1973, pp. 30–1.

75. *Commonwealth Institute: A Commemorative Handbook Issued on the Occasion of the Opening of the New Institute, 6 November 1962*, Commonwealth Institute, 1962, p. 34.

76. Ibid,, p. 22.

77. *A Handbook describing the Work of the Institute and the Exhibitions in the Galleries*, Commonwealth Institute, 1966, p. 42; *Commonwealth Institute: A Commemorative Handbook*, pp. 36–8.

78. *Commonwealth Institute: A commemorative handbook*, pp. 36–8.

79. *A Handbook describing the Work of the Institute*, pp. 34–6, 23.

80. 'Commonwealth Goes Gay!', Pathé News, 19 September 1965.

81. Radhika Natarajan, 'Performing Multiculturalism: The Commonwealth Arts Festival of 1965', *Journal of British Studies*, 53(3), pp. 705–33.

82. The first para-athletic games were in 1962, and were repeated until 1974, when they fell into abeyance due to the cost; there were exhibition para-athletic events in 1994, and the Commonwealth Games became fully integrated in 2002.

83. 'Jamaica, Commonwealth "Olympics" – Colour by Technicolor', British Pathé, 1966.

84. 'Farewell to the Games – Technicolor', British Pathé, 1966.

85. 'VIIIth British Empire and Commonwealth Games, Kingston, Jamaica 1966', Report by the British Empire and Commonwealth Games, Council for England, 1966.

86. 'I Pass This On To You: Empire Roundabout', Women's Gas Federation 1946–51; 'I Pass This On To You: Horoscope Birthday Recipes', Women's Gas Federation, 1962–5.

87. 'I Pass This On To You: Sunshine Fruits in Winter Meals', Women's Gas Federation, 1962–5.

88. David Scott Daniel, *Flight Four: India*, Ladybird Books, 1960.

89. David Scott Daniel, *Flight Five: Africa*, Ladybird Books, 1961.

90. Lena Jeger, 'In Large Print', *Guardian*, 24 May 1966.

91. 'Carry on . . . Up the Khyber', *Variety*, 25 December 1968.

92. Noel Monks, 'For the First Time This Century Nobody Is Shooting at a British Soldier . . . ', *Daily Mail*, 23 October 1959.

5. No Dogs, No Blacks, No Irish:
Migration and Racism in the 1960s and 1970s

1. Pearl Jephcott, *A Troubled Area: Notes on Notting Hill*, Faber, 1964, p. 11.
2. J. Waring Salisbury, 'Comments by the Town Clerk of the Royal Borough of Kensington on the Foregoing Study', 20 February 1964.
3. Charlie Phillips, in Ashleigh Kane, 'Documenting London's African Caribbean Funerals', *Dazed*, 6 November 2014.
4. Charlie Phillips and Mike Phillips, *Notting Hill in the Sixties*, Lawrence & Wishart Ltd, 1991, p. 13.
5. Ibid., p. 11.
6. 'Trinidad Comes to Town', *Radio Times*, 25 January 1959.
7. 'Carnival Queen Contestants', January 1959, Chris Ware / Stringer via Getty Images, British Library.
8. 'Caribbean Carnival Souvenir 1960: televised by BBC Television, organised by the West Indian Gazette', Andrew Salkey, Archive Dep 10310 Box 33, British Library.
9. Donald Hinds, *Journey to an Illusion: The West Indian in Britain*, Bogle-L'Ouverture Publications, 2001 (second edn), p. 149.
10. Claudia Jones, quoted in Hinds, p. 150.
11. Donald Hinds, 'People of All Races Pay Homage to Claudia Jones', *West Indian Gazette*, December 1965–January 1966.
12. Marcus Collins, 'Immigration and Opinion Polls in Postwar Britain', *Modern History Review*, 18(4), 2016, pp. 8–13.
13. Zaiba Malik, 'Bradistan', *Granta*, 2 November 2010.
14. Sheila Patterson, *Dark Strangers: A Study of West Indians in London*, Pelican, 1965 reprint, p. 13.
15. Ibid., p. 14.
16. Ibid., pp. 136, 112, 216.
17. Ibid., p. 275.
18. Ibid., p. 357.
19. 'Introduction to Britain: A Guide for Commonwealth Immigrants', HMSO, 1967.
20. Dipak Nandy, *Race and Community*, University of Kent, 1968, pp. 10–11.

21. Claudia Jones, 'Butler's Colour Bar Mocks the Commonwealth', *West Indian Gazette*, November 1961.

22. Home Office, 'Commonwealth Immigrants Act 1962: Instructions to Immigration Officers', presented to Parliament by the Secretary of State for the Home Department by Command of Her Majesty, August 1966, Cmnd 3064.

23. Jordanna Bailkin, 'Leaving Home: The Politics of Deportation in Postwar Britain', *Journal of British Studies*, Vol. 47, No. 4, October 2008, pp. 852–82.

24. Ibid.

25. 'Minutes', 22 March 1963, 'Return of citizens of Eire to UK in defiance of deportation order', 1963–68, HO 344/74, National Archives.

26. Editorial, 'Bill Speeded to Curb Flow of Immigrants', *Guardian*, 23 February 1968.

27. 'Statement by the Archbishop of Canterbury, Chairman of the National Committee for Commonwealth Immigrants, February 27 1968', HO376/125 Immigration: Asian Immigrants from East Africa.

28. 'New Immigration Bill: Asians Leave Kenya', British Pathé, 29 February 1968.

29. Lord Elton, 'Immigration and Public Opinion Poll', House of Lords, debated on 14 May 1968, Hansard, Vol. 292, c. 206.

30. Mahmoud Mamdani, *From Citizen to Refugee: Uganda Asians Come to Britain*, Frances Pinter, 1973, p. 80.

31. Fenner Brockway, 'Appeasement to Racial Prejudice', *Colonial Freedom News*, July–August 1965, p. 2.

32. 'United Kingdom: Protest March Over the Immigration Curbs in London on 25 February 1968', Photo by Keystone-France/Gamma-Keystone via Getty Images.

33. 'Great Britain England London – During a demonstration against the migration politics, 31 December 1968', Photo by Henning Christoph/ullstein bild via Getty Images.

34. 'Militants and Moderates in the Universities', *Minerva*, p. 284.

35. Local Labour Campaign Against Racialism, 'You Don't Want Race War in Our Streets, so DEFEAT RACIALISM NOW', 1976.

36. 'Police Fight Mob of 500 in Race Riot Town', *Daily Mirror*, 21 August 1961.

37. Christopher Brasher, 'Nothing Racial in this Riot: "Fun" in Cannon Street', *Observer*, 27 August 1961.

38. Madge Dresser, *Black and White on the Buses: The 1963 Colour Bar Dispute in Bristol*, Bristol Broadsides, reprint 2013, p. 18.

39. Ibid., p. 23.

40. Ibid., p. 43.

41. Elliot Ross, 'Britain's Racist Election', *Africa is a Country*, 16 March 2015.

42. Jack Bell, 'BBC Cuts "Race Hate" Probe from Television Show', *Daily Mirror*, 18 September 1964.

43. 'BBC: Whiter than White?', *Sunday Telegraph*, 20 September 1964.

44. Patrick Gordon Walker, *The Lid Lifts*, Victor Gollancz, 1945.

45. Ray Hill, 'Parsons Slam Race-Town Poll', *Daily Mirror*, 17 October 1964.

46. 'Smethwick Given Anti-Ghetto Plan: British Town Focus of Rift Over Colored Immigrants', *New York Times*, 13 December 1964.

47. These comparisons to American civil rights battles show the strength of feeling in Britain but also a certain distaste for recognising racism as a central part of the British imperial state, as much as the American segregated south. CARD, *Smethwick – Integration or racialism?*, CARD, 1964.

48. '"Take Smethwick out of the Headlines" – Lunatic Fringe at Work – Minister', *Guardian*, 12 June 1965.

49. Paul Jackson, *Colin Jordan and Britain's Neo-Nazi Movement: Hitler's Echo*, Bloomsbury Academic, 2017, pp. 128, 133.

50. 'Exclusive: The Day I Called Malcolm X to Fight Racism in Birmingham's White-only Pubs', *Daily Mirror*, 14 February 2015.

51. Avtar Singh Jouhl, 'Afterword: Smethwick, Pub Crawl Protests and Malcolm X', in Sandra Alland et al., *Protest: Stories of Resistance*, Comma Press, 2017.

52. 'Young socialists demonstrate at a meeting held by Conservative MP for Smethwick, Peter Griffiths in Sutton', 27 January 1965, Photo by Jobson/Mirrorpix/Getty Images.

53. 'Explosion at Home of MP', *Midlands News*, ATV, 27 October 1965.

54. 'Bomb at Smethwick MP's Home', *Daily Telegraph*, 27 October 1965.

55. 'Mr Robert Shelton (visit)', HC Debate, 15 June 1965, Hansard, Vol. 714, cc. 240–7.

56. Herbert Bowden, 'Debate on the Address Sixth Day, House of Commons, 10 November 1964, Hansard, Vol. 701, c. 968.

57. Michael White, 'Obituary: Andrew Faulds', *Guardian*, 1 June 2000.

58. Wole Soyinka, 'Telephone Conversation', in Gerald Moore and Ulli Beier (eds), *Modern Poetry from Africa*, Penguin, 1963.

59. Jouhl, 'Afterword'.

60. W. W. Daniel, *Racial Discrimination in England (Based on a PEP Report)*, Penguin, 1968, p. 13; 'A PEP Report on Racial Discrimination in Britain', Political and Economic Planning, 1967.

61. Eric Butterworth, *Immigrants in West Yorkshire: Social Conditions and the Lives of Pakistanis, Indians and West Indians*, Institute of Race Relations special series, 1967, pp. 7, 12.

62. Ibid., pp. 12, 17.

63. Ibid., p. 18.

64. Nicholas Jones, 'Enoch Powell: A Personal Insight', *Political Quarterly*, Vol. 89, Issue 3, September 2018, pp. 358–61.

65. Enoch Powell's Speech of 20 April 1968, Roy Jenkins' of 4 May 1968, et al., *Race*, 10(1), 1968, pp. 94–103.

66. William Rees-Mogg, 'An Evil Speech', *The Times*, 22 April 1968.

67. Security Service [written after consultation with Special Branch], 'Demonstration of Dockers against the Race Relations Bill on 23 April 1968', 24 April 1968; Security Service, 'March of Smithfield Market Porters to the House of Commons on 24 April 1968 in support of Mr Enoch Powell, MP', 25 April 1968, PREM 13/2315 Race Relations, National Archives.

68. Note to PM, 24 April 1968, PREM 13/2315 Race Relations, National Archives.

69. Amy Whipple, 'Revisiting the "Rivers of Blood" Controversy: Letters to Enoch Powell', *Journal of British Studies*, Vol. 48, No. 3, 2009, pp. 717–35.

70. University College Communist Party, 'Who Is Enoch Powell?', 1968.

71. 'Militants and Moderates in the Universities', *Minerva*, p. 290.

72. Arthur Wise, *Who Killed Enoch Powell?*, Weidenfeld & Nicolson, 1970.

73. William Hardcastle, 'Beastly Beauties', *Listener*, 4 December 1969.

74. 'Black Power in Britain: A Special Statement', Universal Coloured People's Association, 1967.

75. UCPA Constitution, 22 June 1968.

76. 'Black Power in Britain'.

77. Black Cultural Archive, 'Black Liberation Series, No. 3 – Racism', *c*.1978.

78. Bernard Coard, *How the West Indian Child Is Made Subnormal in the British School System*, Caribbean Education and Community Workers' Association, New Beacon Books Ltd, 1974 (first published 1971), p. 18.

79. Ibid.

80. Bernard Coard, 'Why I wrote the ESN Book', *Guardian*, 5 February 2005.

81. 'Cause for Concern: West Indian Pupils in Redbridge', Black Peoples Progressive Association & Redbridge Community Relations Council, 1978; *Racism and Racist Violence in Schools: Towards Establishing Effective Anti-Racist Policies and Practice in Newham*, Newham Monitoring Project, 1990.

82. Chris Proctor, 'Racist Textbooks', NUS, 1975, p. 30.

83. Ibid., pp. 26–32.

84. Ibid., p. 12.

85. John Berger, Speech on Accepting the Booker Prize for Fiction, Café Royal, 23 November 1972.

86. Tom Overton, 'Art and Property Now: Room 2: Ways of Seeing and G at 40', Inigo Rooms, Somerset House, 2012.

87. Valerie Amos and Pratibha Parmar, 'Challenging Imperial Feminism', *Feminist Review*, 17, 1984, pp. 10–11.

88. Ibid., p. 9.

89. Melanie Phillips, 'Virginity Tests on immigrants at Heathrow', *Guardian*, 1 February 1979.

90. Ibid.

91. Ibid.

92. Melanie Phillips, 'I Knew about Virginity Tests, Says Former Minister', *Guardian*, 2 February 1979.

93. P&P Women from North London Women against Racist and Fascism, 'This Immigration Control Must Stop', leaflet, *c.* February 1979, HO 418/29, National Archives.

94. Commission for Racial Equality and Equal Opportunities Commission, 'Virginity Testing: Joint Statement by CRE and EOC', 1 February 1979, HO 418/29, National Archives.

95. Jo Richardson, 'Immigration Procedures', HC Debate, 19 February 1979, Hansard, Vol. 963, cc. 216–17.

96. 'Medical Examinations at Ports', 2 February 1979, HO 418/29, National Archives.

97. P&P Women from North London.

98. Alan Travis, 'Ministers Face Calls for Apology as Extent of 1970s "Virginity Tests" Revealed', *Observer*, 8 May 2011.

99. John Cunningham, 'Short Order for the Law: John Cunningham on the Mangrove Nine Trial', *Guardian*, 17 December 1971.

100. Campaign Against Racism and Fascism, *Southall: The Birth of a Black Community*, Institute of Race Relations/Southall Rights, 1981, pp. 54–6.

101. Jay Rayner, 'Blair's Britain', *Observer*, 14 March 1999.

102. Michael Dummett, *The Death of Blair Peach: The Supplementary Report of the Unofficial Committee of Enquiry*, National Council for Civil Liberties, 1980, p. 38.

103. 'Blair Peach Killing – Top Yard Men Urged Charges', Insight Exclusive, *Sunday Times*, 16 March 1980.

104. Campaign Against Racism and Fascism, *Southall*, p. 59.

105. Rob Evans, 'Met Police Spied on Partner of Blair Peach for More Than Two Decades, Inquiry Hears', *Guardian*, 6 May 2021.

106. Campaign Against Racism and Fascism, *Southall*, p. 58.

107. Linton Kwesi Johnson, 'Reggae Fi Peach', *Bass Culture*, 1980.

108. Red Saunders et al., 'When We Read about Eric Clapton's Birmingham concert When He Urged Support for Enoch Powell We Nearly Puked', *NME*, 11 September 1976.

109. Killian Fox, 'Rock Against Racism, the Syd Shelton Images that Define an Era', *Observer*, 6 September 2015.
110. Anti-Nazi League Rock Against Racism 'Carnival 2' flyer, 1978.
111. Stuart Hall, 'The Great Moving Right Show', *Marxism Today*, January 1979, p. 15.
112. Ibid., p. 20.
113. 'Carnival 2' flyer.

6. Britain's Troubled Conscience:
Empire, War and Famine in the 1980s

1. Sue Townsend, *The Secret Diaries of Adrian Mole Aged 13¾*, Methuen, 1982.
2. Denys Blakeway, *Channel Four: The Falklands War*, Sidgwick & Jackson, 1992, p. 11.
3. Simon Scott Plummer, 'Argentines Hoist a Flag on Falklands', *The Times*, 23 March 1982; 'Battle for the Falklands', *Newsweek*, 12 April 1982.
4. 'Scrapping of a Scrap-heap', *Guardian*, 31 March 1982; 'Marching through South Georgia', *Daily Mirror*, 1 April 1982; 'The Sun Says', *Sun*, 30 March 1982; 'Marching Through South Georgia', *Daily Mirror*, 1 April 1982.
5. Blakeway, p. 35.
6. Mike Norman and Michael Jones, *The Falklands War: There and Back Again, The Story of Naval Party 8901*, Pen & Sword Military, 2019, p. 105.
7. Bernard Braine, 'Falkland Islands', HC Debate, 3 April 1982, Hansard, Vol. 21, c. 659.
8. Margaret Thatcher, 'Falkland Islands', HC Debate, 3 April 1982, Hansard, Vol. 21, c. 633.
9. Bernard Braine, quoted in Blakeway, p. 15.
10. Michael Foot, 'Falkland Islands', HC Debate, Hansard, 3 April 1982, Vol. 21, c. 638.
11. Stuart Hall, *The Hard Road to Renewal: Thatcherism and the Crisis of the Left*, Verso, 1988, p. 69.

12. Raymond John Adams, Imperial War Museum Oral History, quoted in Hugh McManners, *Forgotten Voices of the Falklands: The Real Story of the Falklands War*, Ebury, 2008, p. 37.

13. Clare Short, *Dear Clare . . . this is what women feel about Page 3*, Hutchinson Radius, 1991.

14. 'Knickers to Argentina', *Sun*, 16 April 1982.

15. 'The Harlot of Fleet Street', *Daily Mirror*, 8 May 1982.

16. Chris Horrie, 'Gotcha! How the Sun Reaped Spoils of War', *Observer*, 7 April 2002.

17. 'Might Isn't Right', *Daily Mirror*, 5 April 1982.

18. Peter Jenkins, 'Taking Leave of Our Senses', *Guardian*, 7 April 1982.

19. E. P. Thompson, 'Why Neither Side Is Worth Backing', *Guardian*, 29 April 1982.

20. 'Britannia Scorns to Yield', *Newsweek*, 19 April 1982; 'Britons and Argentines Squaring Off', *New York Times*, 31 March 1982.

21. Margaret Thatcher, *The Downing Street Years*, HarperCollins, 1993, pp. 173–85.

22. Jean Seaton, *Pinkoes and Traitors: The BBC and the Nation, 1974–1987*, Profile, 2015, chapter 7.

23. Brian Hanrahan and Robert Fox, *I Counted Them All Out and I Counted Them All Back: Battle for the Falklands*, BBC Books, 1982.

24. Michael Ernest Barrow, Imperial War Museum Oral History, quoted in McManners, pp. 37–8.

25. Brandon Christopher Smith, Imperial War Museum Oral History, quoted in McManners, p. 49.

26. Graham Carter, Imperial War Museum Oral History, quoted in McManners, p. 93.

27. 'Falklands War: 40th Anniversary', Peace Pledge Union; Symon Hill, *The Peace Protestors: A History of Modern Day War Resistance*, Pen & Sword History, 2022.

28. 'Diana Gould: Obituary', *Daily Telegraph*, 9 December 2011.

29. 'The Falkland Island Crisis: War with Argentina', April 1982, Directive no. 5; Falklands/Malvinas Postscript 1982; 'Falklands War Aftermath: Reactions to the Falklands Parade of October 1982', September 1982, Directive no. 9.

30. Peter Lennon, 'Famous Then: Ossie Ardiles', *Guardian*, 25 February 2002.

31. Simon Kuper, 'No Peace Until He Dies', *Observer*, 22 October 2000.

32. Mark Knopfler, 'Brothers in Arms', Vertigo, 1985; Roger Walters, 'Southampton Dock', Harvest Records, 1983; Elvis Costello/Robert Wyatt, 'Shipbuilding', Rough Trade, 1982.

33. *Simon's War*, BBC, 1983; Crass, 'Yes Sir, I Will', Crass Records, 1983.

34. *Tumbledown* (dir: Richard Eyre), BBC, 1988.

35. Seumas Milne, 'MP Challenges Younger over Tumbledown Victim', *Guardian*, 31 May 1988; 'Tumbledown: The Only Truth', *Daily Express*, 31 May 1988; 'Dirty Tricks and the Art of War', *Independent*, 31 May 1988.

36. Linda Kitson, Imperial War Museum Oral History, quoted in McManners, pp. 453–4.

37. Sharkey Ward, *Sea Harrier over the Falklands: A Maverick at War*, Leo Cooper, 1992, p. 266.

38. Chris Keeble, quoted in Blakeway, p. 136.

39. Margaret Thatcher, 'Falkland Islands', HC Debate, 14 June 1982, Hansard, Vol. 25, cc. 700, 'White Flags Over Stanley', *Merco Press*, 12 November 2002

40. Thatcher, *The Downing Street Years*, p. 173.

41. Ipsos Mori, 'The Falklands War – Trends', 30 June 1982.

42. 'Obituary: Very Rev Alan Webster', *Daily Telegraph*, 6 September 2007; 'Dean Planned Memorial Service in Spanish', *Daily Telegraph*, 28 December 2012.

43. Michael Buerk, 'Report from Ethiopia', BBC News, 23 October 1984.

44. Derek Brown, Michael Simmons and Paul Keel, 'Famine Aid Outcry Spurs Europe into Action', *Guardian*, 26 October 1984.

45. Biba Kopf, 'Singles', *NME*, 8 December 1984.

46. Press Release, 'Show Africa's potential not just its problems, says Oxfam', 28 December 2012; YouGov Survey Oxfam/Africa, 8–9 November 2012.

47. David Blundy and Paul Vallely, *With Geldof in Africa: Confronting the Famine Crisis*, Times Books, 1985, p. 30.

48. 'They Can't Eat Missiles', *Third Way*, Vol. 8, No. 5, May 1985, p. 3.

49. 'Letters to the Editor', *Manchester Guardian*, 25 February 1949.

50. 'South Africa', *League of Coloured People's Review*, Vol. 1, No. 1, January 1951.

51. *The Heart of Apartheid* (dir. Hugh Burnett), BBC1, 1968.

52. 'Brando against Apartheid', *Anti-Apartheid News*, March 1964.

53. *Anti-Apartheid News*, March 1964.

54. Ibid.

55. AAM, 'On 3rd May When You Vote, Remember the People of Southern Africa', 1979.

56. 'NON-STOP PICKET' 19 April 1986 Onwards, CAAG/28 Anti-Apartheid Campaigns and Demonstrations, Bishopsgate Institute.

57. Gallup, June 1986.

58. The source for this story is my mother, Rita Riley, who received this response when she realised some grapes she had been planning to buy were from South Africa when she was already at the till.

59. Bill Caldwell, 'Open a student account and you get a free briefcase, diary, pen AND we pull out of South Africa', *Daily Star*, 25 November 1986.

60. Interview with Jack Jones, former General Secretary of the Transport and General Workers' Union, 17 February 2000, reproduced on the Anti-Apartheid Movement Archives Committee Forward to Freedom project website, www.aamarchives.org/

61. Ibid.

62. *Isolate Apartheid: Report of the Anti-Apartheid Movement Trade Union Conference held on November 27, 1982*, AAM, 1982.

63. Poster, 'South Africa Must Be Free!', NUS, October 1985.

64. Labour Research Department and the African National Congress – South Africa, *South Africa Apartheid and Britain*, Labour Research Department, 1970, pp. 11–16.

65. 'South Africa: A Spirit that Will Not be Broken', *The Flag*, September 1986.

66. Haringey National Front, Press Release, 'National Front Supports South African Goods', 22 October 1988, AAM Archives.

67. *Anti-Apartheid News*, October 1987.

68. *AAM Women's Committee Newsletter*, No. 23, November/December 1985.

69. *Grassroots: Black Community News*, No. 2, 1986, Black Cultural Archives.

70. 'London Borough of Camden Anti-Apartheid Declaration', 7 December 1983.

71. John Lloyd and Peter Brewis, 'I've Never Met a Nice South African', Virgin Records, 1986.

72. Lee Stokes, 'Anti Apartheid Demonstration in London', United Press International, 28 June 1986.

73. 'BBC Is Criticised over Mandela Birthday Concert', *Daily Telegraph*, 26 May 1988.

74. 'George's Four Letter Fury at Apartheid', *Daily Mirror*, 11 June 1988.

75. 'Stars Shine for Nelson', *Daily Mirror*, 13 June 1988; Keith Richmond and Neil Taylor, 'Thanks a Billion', *Sunday Mirror*, 12 June 1988.

76. Richmond and Taylor, 'Thanks a Billion'.

77. 'The Wrong Side of the Moral Divide', *Guardian*, 14 July 1986.

78. 'Press Statement: Malcolm Rifkind Refuses to Meet Anti-Apartheid Leaders over Games Crisis', CAAG/76 Commonwealth Games in Edinburgh, Scottish Committee of the Anti-Apartheid Movement, 22 July 1986.

79. Derek Douglas and Derek Bateman, 'Games Athletes snub Thatcher', *Glasgow Herald*, 2 August 1986.

80. John Arlott, 'The d'Oliveira Decision', *Guardian*, 22 October 1968.

81. 'Colour and cricket', *Daily Mail*, 26 January 1967.

82. Stop the Seventy Tour campaign, 'Why Watch the Springboks?', Anti Apartheid Movement, 1969.

83. Commonwealth Heads of Government Meeting, London, 8–15 June 1977, Final communique.

84. *Leicester Mercury*, 24 March 1990.

85. David Townsend, 'The Reluctant Rebel', *Evening Standard*, 16 January 1990.

86. Sean Poulter, 'Gatting's Tour hit by call to court', *Daily Mail*, 16 January 1990, CAAG 52/Anti-Apartheid Demonstration at Lord's Cricket Ground, Bishopsgate Institute.

87. 'First Stride Towards Sanity', *Sunday Mirror*, 11 February 1990.

88. Camden Council, 'Celebrating Africa in Camden', 1984.

89. *Islington Gazette*, 12 January 1989, CAAG/28 Anti-Apartheid Campaigns and Demonstrations, Bishopsgate Institute.

90. 'Diane Abbott: My Struggles and Triumphs', *Conversations*, BBC Parliament, December 2016.

91. Tom Baldwin, 'From Hackney to Pretoria for Nowhere Man', *The Times*, 15 March 2005.

92. Harmit Athwal and Jenny Bourne, 'It Has To Change: An Interview with Martha Osamor', *Race & Class*, 58(1), 2016, pp. 85–93.

93. Labour Party Black Section, 'The Black Agenda', 1988.

94. Salman Rushdie, 'Outside the Whale', *Granta*, 1 March 1984.

95. Salman Rushdie, 'The New Empire within Britain', *Imaginary Homelands: Essays and Criticism, 1981–1991*, Granta Books, 1991, pp. 129–38.

96. 'Fanaticism in a free country', *Daily Mail*, 16 February 1989; 'Poison of Defeat and Hatred', *Guardian*, 15 February 1989.

97. 'Is This Man Mad?', *Daily Mirror*, 8 May 1989.

98. Richard Rayner, 'Mills & Boom', *Daily Telegraph*, 16 September 1989.

99. Yasmin Alibhai-Brown, 'Liberalism and its Limits', *Prospect*, 20 May 1998.

100. *The Blasphemers' Banquet* (dir. Peter Symes), BBC, 1989.

101. 'Tebbit Seeks Cricket Test of Asian Loyalty to Britain', *Daily Telegraph*, 20 April 1990.

7. From Cool Britannia to Brexit Britain: Imperialism Since the 1990s

1. 'Final Farewell to Hong Kong', *The Times*, 1 July 1997.

2. Simon Jenkins, 'Tears Mingle with Monsoon Rain as Retreat is Beaten', *The Times*, 1 July 1997; Graham Hutchings, 'Britain's Farewell to Hong Kong', *Daily Telegraph*, 1 July 1997; Ann Leslie, 'A Tearful Salute to the Last Jewel in the Crown', *Daily Mail*, 1 July 1997.

3. 'The Diaries of a Dissident Prince Revealed', *The Times*, 23 February 2006.

4. Jojo Moyes, 'Cheers and Tears in Gerrard Street', *Independent*, 1 July 1997.

5. Warren Hoge, 'Britain Leave Hong Kong in Sour Kind of Grandeur', *New York Times*, 27 March 1997.

6. Labour Party, 'New Labour: Because Britain Deserves Better', 1997.

7. Michael White, 'Blair's Crushing Triumph: Majority Is Projected at over 180', *Guardian*, 2 May 1997; 'The Blair Revolution', *Daily Mail*, 2 May 1997.

8. Richard Gott, 'The Third Crusade', *New Left Review*, May/June 2005, p. 155.

9. Stryker McGuire, 'This Time I've Come to Bury Cool Britannia', *Observer*, 29 March 2009.

10. 'Cool Britannia: Major Claims the Credit', *Independent*, 12 November 1996.

11. 'Cool Britannia', *The Economist*, 12 March 1998.

12. David Sharrock, '700 Mourn Teenager Killed in Race Attack', *Guardian*, 19 June 1993.

13. Mark Redhead, 'The Justice Game', *Guardian*, 15 February 1999.

14. Comment, 'A Tragic Fight for Justice', *Daily Mail*, 14 February 1997.

15. Macpherson Report, 6.1.

16. Ibid., 6.21.

17. Ibid., 5.31.

18. Ibid., 6.45–46.

19. Nick Hopkins, 'Report Lays Bare Racism at the Met', *Guardian*, 22 February 1999; Stephen Wright, 'Racism Across the Ranks Let Lawrence Killers Walk Free', *Daily Mail*, 21 December 1998.

20. Susanna Clapp, 'Here Is Racism in All of Its Subtle Shades', *Observer*, 17 January 1999.

21. Piara S. Khabra, 'Stephen Lawrence Inquiry', HC Debate, 29 March 1999, Hansard, Vol. 328, c. 813.

22. Gerald Howarth, 'Stephen Lawrence Inquiry', HC Debate, 29 March 1999, Hansard, Vol. 328, cc. 818–19.

23. Stuart Hall, 'From Scarman to Stephen Lawrence', *History Workshop Journal*, Vol. 48, Issue 1, Autumn 1999, pp. 194, 197.

24. 'It's Time to Unload the Mango Dictators!', *The Flag*, No. 2, September 1986.

25. 'Were You Ever Asked?', *The Flag*, No. 6, February 1987.

26. Alexander McCleod, 'Neo-Nazi Politician Wins in Britain, Prompting Introspection on Racism', *Christian Science Monitor*, 21 September 1993.

27. *The Enemy in Our Midst: Exposing Racism and Fascism in Newham*, Newham Monitoring Project, 1995.

28. *Newham: The Forging of a Black Community*, Newham Monitoring Project / Campaign against Racism and Fascism, 1991.

29. *The Enemy in Our Midst*.

30. *Newham: The Forging of a Black Community*.

31. 'Facts and Fictions in the 1990s: Once Upon a Time in Docklands', Docklands Forum, April 1994, London Collection Pamphlets, Box III D25.10, Bishopsgate Archive.

32. 'Anglo-Saxon Attitudes', *Daily Telegraph*, 23 June 1996.

33. *Out of their Skin* (dir: Jay Gill), ITV, November 2018.

34. Richie Moran, 'Racism in Football: A Victim's Perspective', *Soccer & Society*, 1:1, 2000, pp. 190–200.

35. 'Kick it Again! Uniting Football Against Racism', Commission for Racial Equality, 1995, p. 3.

36. Ibid., p. 7.

37. *United Colours of Football*, Football Supporters' Association, 1995.

38. *The Enemy in Our Midst*.

39. Thomas E. Ricks, 'Empire or Not? A Quiet Debate Over U.S. Role', *Washington Post*, 21 August 2001.

40. 'Iraq: The Case for Decisive Action', *Observer*, 19 January 2003.

41. Julie Burchill, 'Why We Should Go to War', *Guardian*, 1 February 2003.

42. Tony Benn, 'Iraq', House of Commons, 17 February 1998, Hansard, Vol. 306, cc. 899–990.

43. Andrew Murray, 'Hostages of the Empire', *Guardian*, 1 July 2003.

44. Hywel Williams, 'The Danger of Liberal Imperialism', *Guardian*, 4 October 2001.

45. Lucy Ward, 'Cherie Blair Pleads for Afghan women', *Guardian*, 20 November 2001; 'Text: Laura Bush on the Oppression of Women', *Washington Post*, 17 November 2001.

46. 'Thousands Join Anti-War March', BBC News, 28 November 2001.

47. Press Release, 'Afghanistan: MPs to get letters on aid and cluster bombs', Tearfund, 26 October 2001.

48. Lee Elliot Major, 'Academics "Failing to Question" Afghanistan Attacks', Guardian, 15 October 2001; 'Students Arrested in Anti-War Protest', *Argus*, 5 November 2001.

49. 'Mark Wallinger wins Turner Prize', BBC News, 3 December 2007.

50. 'I've Never Known Anything Like It. Everyone's Saying They Will March', *Guardian*, 8 February 2003.

51. Ibid.

52. Euan Ferguson, 'One Million. And Still They Came', *Guardian*, 16 February 2003.

53. ICM Research, 'February 2003 Poll', 14–16 February 2003.

54. 'No War On Iraq', *Guardian*, 13 February 2003.

55. Runnymede Trust, 'Islamophobia: A Challenge for Us All', 1997.

56. Richard Stone et al., *Islamophobia: Issues, Challenges and Action: A Report by the Commission on British Muslims and Islamophobia'*, Trentham Books, 2004, p. 3.

57. Ibid., pp. 57, 30, 34.

58. Ibid., pp. 48–9.

59. Tony Blair, Prime Minister's News Conference, 17 October 2006, www.c-span.org/video/?194899-1/prime-minister-news-conference

60. 'Full Text of Gordon Brown Speech', *Guardian*, 27 February 2007.

61. Benedict Brogan, 'It's Time to Celebrate the Empire, Says Brown', *Daily Mail*, 15 January 2005.

62. Vikram Dodd, 'Government Anti-Terrorism Strategy "Spies" on Innocent', *Guardian*, 16 October 2009.

63. Melvyn Bragg, *In Our Time*, BBC Radio 4, 22 February 2007.

64. Moira Stuart, *In Search of Wilberforce*, BBC2, 16 March 2007.

65. 1807–2007 Abolition 200, Bristol City Council, 2007, Black Cultural Archives.

66. Jonathan Petre, 'Church Offers Apology for Its Role in Slavery', *Daily Telegraph*, 9 February 2006.

67. Hugh Muir, 'Livingstone Weeps as He Apologises for Slavery', *Guardian*, 24 March 2007.

68. Paul Coslett, 'Liverpool's Slavery Apology', BBC Merseyside, 15 February 2007.

69. 'Britain Will Not Apologise for Slavery: PM's office', *Irish Times*, 3 September 2001; Patrick Wintour, 'Blair Fights Shy of Full Apology for Slave Trade', *Guardian*, 27 November 2006; 'Blair Says "Sorry" for Slavery', Reuters, 25 March 2007.

70. Melanie Phillips, 'Yes, Slavery Was Evil. But this Orgy of Breast-Beating Is Utterly Absurd', *Daily Mail*, 26 March 2007.

71. Eric Williams, *British Historians and the West Indies*, PNM Publishing, 1964, p. 233.

72. Muir, 'Livingstone Weeps as He Apologises for Slavery'; Dominic Sandbrook, 'Stop Saying Sorry for Our History: For Too Long Our Leaders Have Been Crippled by a Post-Imperial Cringe', *Daily Mail*, 2 August 2010.

73. Jessica Shepherd, 'After Howls of Protest, Sun Sets on the British Empire', *Guardian*, 12 February 2009.

74. Ian Cobain, 'Revealed: The Bonfire at the End of Empire', *Guardian*, 29 November 2013.

75. David Anderson, 'Guilty Secrets: Deceit, Denial, and the Discovery of Kenya's "Migrated Archive"', *History Workshop Journal* 80, 1, 2015, p. 143.

76. Anthony Cary, 'The Migrated Archives: What Went Wrong and What Lessons Should We Draw?', 24 February 2011, p. 2, www.fco.gov.uk/resources/en/pdf/migrated-archives

77. Ibid., p. 12.

78. Anderson, pp. 153, 148.

79. Jonathan Freeland, 'Danny Boyle: Champion of the People', *Guardian*, 9 March 2013.

80. Stephen Glover, 'Yes, a Brilliant Show and Danny Boyle's a Genius. But Why Have So Many been Taken In by his Marxist Propaganda?', *Daily Mail*, 2 August 2012.

81. Winston Churchill, *Army Council and General Dyer*, HC Debate, Hansard, 8 July 1920, Vol. 131, c. 1725.

82. Press briefing given by Prime Minister David Cameron in Amritsar, Prime Minister's Office, 10 Downing Street, 21 February 2013.

83. 'Koh-i-Noor Diamond "Staying Put" in UK, Says Cameron', BBC News, 29 July 2010.

84. Sara C. Nelson, 'Koh-i-Noor Diamond Will Not Be Returned to India, David Cameron Insists', *Huffington Post*, 21 February 2003.

85. 'Gem to Stay Put', *Sun*, 21 February 2013.

86. Michael Gove, 'History Teaching', HC Debate, 15 November 2010, Hansard, Vol. 518, c. 634.

87. Hannah Furness, 'Don't Sign up to Gove's Insulting Curriculum, Schama Pleads', *Daily Telegraph*, 31 May 2013.

88. Richard Evans, 'Michael Gove's History Wars', *Guardian*, 13 July 2013.

89. *Life in the United Kingdom: A Journey to Citizenship*, Home Office, 2007.

90. Ibid., 2013, 2017.

91. 'Historians Call for a Review of Home Office Citizenship and Settlement Test', *Historical Journal*, 21 July 2020.

92. Daniel Hannan, 'Britain is an Island of Contentment in an EU Driven by Brussels to Populist Revolt', *Daily Telegraph*, 9 September 2018.

93. 'Commonwealth Community Leaders Back British Exit from EU', BBC News website, 17 February 2016.

94. 'The Guardian View on the EU Referendum: Keep Connected and Inclusive, Not Angry and Isolated', *Guardian*, 20 June 2016.

95. Simon Schama, 'Let Us Spurn Brexit and Remain a Beacon of Tolerance', *Financial Times*, 17 June 2016.

Conclusion: Where We're Going, We Don't Need Rhodes

1. Stephen Cottrell, Archbishop of York, 'How Queen Elizabeth II Became a Constant Anchor in Our Lives', *Yorkshire Post*, 19 September 2022.

2. 'Her Majesty the Queen: A Personal Tribute by Former BBC Royal Correspondent, Wesley Kerr OBE', *Tatler*, 8 September 2022; 'Queen's Life and Service Hailed a "Rare Jewel" at St Paul's Cathedral', *Express and Star*, 9 September 2022; English Heritage, ' "I declare before you all that my whole life whether it be long or short shall be devoted to your service." So spoke Her Majesty The Queen in 1947. She was a woman of her word, and she will be greatly missed. Our deepest condolences to the Royal Family', Twitter, 8 September 2022.

3. Simon Schama, 'Elizabeth II: An Appreciation', *Financial Times*, 9 September 2022.

4. Hannah Furness, 'Atrocity of Slavery Stains Our History, Prince Charles Tells Barbados as It Ends Royal Rule', *Daily Telegraph*, 30 November 2021.

5. Robert Hardman, 'Scuffles as the Queen Starts Jamaica Visit', *Daily Telegraph*, 2 March 1994.

6. 'Party planner behind Prince William's 21st birthday celebrations reveals the Queen "loved" the elephant head ice vodka luge on display at the "out of Africa" themed bash at Windsor Castle', Mail Online, 13 September 2018.

7. P. R. H. Wright to Denis Greenhill, 24 August 1966, and Denis Greenhill, 24 August 1966, in D. Snoxell, 'Explusion from Chagos: Regaining Paradise', *Journal of Imperial and Commonwealth History*, 361, 2008, pp. 121–2.

8. Subject: HMG Floats Proposal for Marine Reserve Covering the Chagos Archipelago (British Indian Ocean Territory), Ref: 08 London 2667, 15 May 2009, 07:00, Wikileaks.

9. Owen Bowcott and Bruno Rinvolucri, 'Exiled Chagos Islanders Return without British Supervision for the First Time', *Guardian*, 8 February 2022.

10. Owen Bowcott and Sarah Marsh, 'UK Threatens To Deport Grandchildren of Evicted Chagossians', *Guardian*, 2 October 2018.

11. Amelia Gentleman, 'Without Paulette Wilson, Windrush Might Have Remained Hidden', *Guardian*, 24 July 2020.

12. Robert Wright, 'May Says Sorry to Caribbean Leaders over Windrush Scandal', *Financial Times*, 17 April 2018.

13. Amelia Gentleman, 'Windrush: Home Office Has Compensated Just 5% of Victims in Four Years', *Guardian*, 24 November 2021.

14. Amelia Gentleman, 'Windrush Scandal Caused by "30 Years of Racist Immigration Laws" – Report', *Observer*, 29 May 2022.

15. Amelia Gentleman, 'Home Office Tried To "Sanitise" Staff Education Module on Colonialism', *Guardian*, 10 June 2022.

16. H. J. Wilkins, *Edward Colston 1636–1721: A Chronological Account of His Life and Work together with an Account of the Colston Societies and Memorials in Bristol*, Arrowsmith, 1920.

17. Carole Drake, quoted in 'Trophies of Empire', The Bluecoat Archive, www.thebluecoat.org.uk/library/event/trophies-of-empire

18. 'Massive's Attack on Slave Trader', *Sunday Mirror*, 23 August 1998.

19. Emma Wilkins, 'Graffiti Attack Revives Bristol Slavery Row', *The Times*, 29 January 1998.

20. Tristan Cork, 'Theft or Vandalism of Second Colston Statue Plaque "May Be Justified" – Tory Councillor', *Bristol Post*, 23 July 2018.

21. 'Edward Colston: Plaque to Bristol Slave Trader Axed over Wording', BBC News, 25 March 2019.

22. Jasper King, 'Edward Colston Statue: Mayor Gives Update on Statue's Future', *Bristol Post*, 8 June 2020; Rory Sullivan, 'Black Lives Matter Protestors in Bristol Pull Down and Throw Statue of 17th Century Slave Trader into River', *Independent*, 7 June 2020.

23. Press Release, 'Policy Exchange launches new history project', Policy Exchange, 28 June 2020.

24. Matt Dathan and Fiona Hamilton, 'Edward Colston Statue: Judge Told Jury To Ignore Rhetoric about Trial's High Profile', *The Times*, 6 January 2022.

25. YouGov survey, 17–18 January 2016.

26. Oriel College, Press Release, 'Decisions made by the college following the completion of the Independent Commission into Cecil Rhodes and related issues', 20 May 2021, www.oriel.ox.ac.uk/news/decisions-made-by-the-college-following-the-completion-of-the-independent-commission-into-cecil-rhodes-and-related-issues/

27. Home Office, Policy paper, 'Criminal damage to memorials: Police, Crime, Sentencing and Courts Act 2022 factsheet', August 2022.

28. British Museum, 'Collecting and Empire: Follow the Trail', 2021.

29. Oliver Dowden, Re: HM Government Position on Contested Heritage, DDCMS, INT2020/19838/DC, 22 September 2020.

30. Christopher Hope, 'Exclusive: Universities Face Fines as Part of "Twin Assault" on Cancel Culture', *Sunday Telegraph*, 14 February 2021.

31. YouGov survey, 17–18 January 2016.

32. Larry Achiampong, *Sanko-time* and *What I Hear I Keep*, 2020, the-line.org/artist/larry-achiampong/

Index

Index

penguin.co.uk/vintage